PUBLICATIONS
OF THE
ARMY RECORDS SOCIETY
VOL. 15

THE LETTERS OF LIEUTENANT-COLONEL CHARLES à COURT REPINGTON CMG MILITARY CORRESPONDENT OF *THE TIMES* 1903–1918

The Army Records Society was founded in 1984 in order to publish original records describing the development, organisation, administration and activities of the British Army from early times.

Any person wishing to become a member of the Society is requested to apply to the Hon. Secretary, c/o the National Army Museum, Royal Hospital Road, London, SW3 4HT. The annual subscription entitles the member to receive a copy of each volume issued by the Society in that year, and to purchase back volumes at reduced prices. Current subscription details, whether for individuals living in the British Isles, for individuals living overseas, or for institutions, will be furnished on request.

The Council of the Army Records Society wish it to be clearly understood that they are not answerable for opinions or observations that may appear in the Society's publications. For these the responsibility rests entirely with the Editors of the several works.

Charles à Court Repington by Philip de Laszlo. Reproduced from one of two extant copies, which belongs to the author. Location of the original is unknown.

THE LETTERS OF LIEUTENANT-COLONEL CHARLES à COURT REPINGTON CMG MILITARY CORRESPONDENT OF *THE TIMES* 1903–1918

Selected and Edited by
A.J.A. MORRIS

Published by
SUTTON PUBLISHING LIMITED
for the
ARMY RECORDS SOCIETY
1999

First published in the United Kingdom in 1999 by
Sutton Publishing Limited · Phoenix Mill · Thrupp · Stroud ·
Gloucestershire · GL5 2BU

British Library Cataloguing in Publication Data
A catalogue record for this book is available from the British Library

ISBN 0 7509 2295 8

Typeset in Ehrhardt.
Typesetting and origination by
Sutton Publishing Limited
Printed in Great Britain by
MPG Books, Bodmin, Cornwall.

In proud and affectionate memory of my father, his three brothers, my father-in-law and my maternal grandfather, who all fought as volunteers in the Great War, 1914–1918.

. . . Why were we there from the Aisne to Mametz,
Well – there's a dilemma . . .
For we never talked of glory,
. . . we never talked of Fame . . .

It is very difficult to believe
You need never again
Put in for week-end leave,
Or get vouchers for the 1.10 train
From Cardiff to London . . .
. . . so much has the Hun done
In the way of achievements.

Ford Madox Ford – 'One Day's List'

Contents

Preface

Repington was a prolific letter writer. A few of the extant letters were typed at his dictation by Mary Repington; most are handwritten. His writing, like his style, was bold and distinctive. Thus his letters are both easy to identify and to read.

Two groups of papers are designated as Repington's. One forms part of the magnificent Times Archive. In this collection there are letters written by Repington filed under the names of the addressees, and others in general files – for example 'Management'. In the H.A. Gwynne Papers at the Bodleian Library, Oxford, there is a sub-set covering the years 1917–21 entirely concerned with Repington and his work for the *Morning Post*. A large cache of letters, written by Repington to Mary in the years 1918 to 1922, has recently been given to the National Army Museum, Chelsea. These letters, as yet, remain uncatalogued.

There is scarcely a collection of significant military or political papers for the years covered by this book, that does not contain letters written by Repington and/or references to him and to his work. Many, though not all these collections, are represented in this book.

Letters have been arranged chronologically, and, so far as possible, they have been grouped in relation to particular issues or problems or events. Those letters written before the Great War that have been reproduced amount approximately to a quarter of the extant correspondence for that period. There are many fewer letters for the war years, of which about a half have been reproduced. These may be supplemented, however, by materials contained in the published war diaries. References in the end notes are designed to highlight these connections together with correspondence to and from Repington not reproduced in the document section.

As well as writing for *The Times*, Repington frequently contributed articles, often lengthy, to other journals, like the *National Review*, *Blackwood's Magazine*, *Nineteenth Century and After*, and the *Journal of the Royal United Services Institute*. He was founding editor of the *Army Review* and, at different times, for short periods, stood in for J.L. Garvin as editor of the *Observer*.

His prodigious energy served a considerable talent. He wrote with speed, clarity and apparent ease. Writing so much, inevitably there was repetition, designed as well as accidental. Articles written as 'Military Correspondent of *The Times*', were re-cycled almost immediately, to the benefit of his reputation as well as his purse, in what he deprecatingly referred to as his 'scissors and paste' books. These were: *The War in the Far East* (1905), *Imperial Strategy* (1906), *The Foundations of Reform* (1908), and *Essays and Criticisms* (1911). After he had left *The Times* and was working for his last newspaper, the *Daily Telegraph*, he published *Policy and Arms* (1924), the least well noticed of his military writings. Collectively these books provide the most convenient clue to the broad outline of Repington's thinking upon military and related problems. Unfortunately, much of that work he published while serving in Military Intelligence is no longer available, lost somewhere between various Service libraries and the Public Record Office. Whether the loss was accidental or designed is now impossible to determine with certainty. Immediately after leaving Printing House Square and while he was employed working for Lady Bathurst's *Morning Post*, Repington published his reminiscences. First, a volume covering the pre-war years, *Vestigia* (1919); next, the two volumes of his war diaries, *The First World War, 1914–1918* (1920), which proved sensational in every sense of that word; and finally, *After the War: a Diary* (1922). Among much else, these volumes print copies of letters that otherwise no longer exist.

This book is part of a larger project begun several years ago. The intention is to discover and record all Repington's extant correspondence, which is scattered over at least three continents, and to write his biography. I acknowledge, with gratitude, a grant from the British Academy to help defray part of the costs incurred in the preparation of this book.

For granting copyright permission for Repington's private letters and for the enthusiasm and interest that from the beginning she has shown in this work, I happily acknowledge a very particular debt of gratitude to Mrs Laetitia Stapleton. Also I must thank News International plc., for permission to print those letters Repington wrote specifically for his work with *The Times*, and of which they possess the copyright.

Repington's letter to Knollys from the Royal Archives, appears by gracious permission of Her Majesty the Queen. My thanks are due to archives, libraries and institutions, the staffs that serve them and certain individuals who have helped me in the discovery of letters and have answered my requests for information. Particular thanks are due to Sir Hector Munro for his allowing me to borrow the original typescript of

General Sir Spencer Ewart's *Autobiography* – a treasure house of information. Also Sir Ian Hogg who, once more, made access and use of the H.A. Gwynne papers so easy. For access to various collections in their keeping I thank: the Warden and Fellows of Nuffield College (the Mottistone papers); Mrs A.J. Maxse and the West Sussex Record Office, Chichester (the L.J.Maxse papers); the Bodleian Library, Oxford (the papers of H.A. Gwynne, Milner, Dawson, J.S. Sandars, Lewis Harcourt and H.H. Asquith); the British Library (the papers of Henry Campbell-Bannerman, General Hutton, H.O. Arnold-Forster, Raymond Marker, George Clarke, Northcliffe, J.A. Spender, Balfour and Sir Charles Dilke); the Public Record Office, Kew (the papers of Sir Edward Grey, Sir John Ardagh, Kitchener and Midleton, and papers in the War Office, Foreign Office and Home Office files); the Northern Ireland Public Record Office, Belfast (the papers of Lady Londonderry and Carson); the Churchill Archives Centre, Cambridge (the papers of Esher and W.S.Churchill); the House of Lords Record Office (the papers of J.St. Loe Strachey, R.D. Blumenfeld, Bonar Law and Lloyd George); News International plc. (*The Times* Archive); the Harry Ransom Humanities Research Center, the University of Texas at Austin (the papers of J.L. Garvin); the Rare Book and Special Collections Library, University of Illinois (the papers of H.G.Wells); the National Army Museum, Chelsea (the papers of Sir Gerald Ellison and Lord Roberts); the Liddell Hart Centre for Military Archives, King's College, London University (the papers of J.E. Edmonds, Sir William Robertson and Sir Ian and Lady Hamilton); the Naval Library, the Ministry of Defence (the papers of Lord Tweedmouth); the Imperial War Museum (the diary of Henry Wilson); the National Library of Scotland, Edinburgh (the papers of R.B. Haldane and his family); the County Record Offices of Worcester and Warwickshire; the University Library, Birmingham; the Codrington Library, All Souls, Oxford; Whitehall Library, Ministry of Defence; the Staff College Library, Camberley; the Library of the Royal Military Academy, Sandhurst; the Scottish Record Office, Edinburgh.

I wish to thank those who responded to my requests for help to understand certain specific and detailed problems: Keith Jeffery, for much useful information on the relationship between Repington and Henry Wilson; Linda Fritzinger, for her knowledge of Valentine Chirol and for the copy of an important letter that I would otherwise have missed; David French and John Ferris for information on Army Intelligence; Chris Heather for 'discovering' the long lost War Office file on Repington's resignation from the Army; David Bishop and Anthony

Morris for beavering away on my behalf at the National Newspaper Library, Colindale; Peter Boyden for answering without complaint endless questions about Roberts; M.M. Chapman who provided detailed notes on military figures and military arcana of which I was woefully ignorant. Also Eleanor Vallis, Natalie Adams, Katherine Bligh, Helen Langley, Ethel Helman, Sheila de Bellaigue, Marion Harding, Kate O'Brien, John Wood, Tim Padfield, Roger Strong, Eamon Dyas, Tony Heathcote, P.E. Bendall, Nigel Steel and Peter Simkins, all of whom showed such kindness and consideration that made the research so much more rewarding than it otherwise would have been.

Of friends and fellow members of BCMH and the Army Records Society who have encouraged me in this task and shared their knowledge of military subjects, I am particularly indebted to Keith Grieves, a most generous and knowledgeable guide to source materials that he had himself used in his researches and writing. Also, Celia Lee who saved me many hours of work by giving me a transcript of entries from Lady Hamilton's diary. I must also thank John Lee, Brian Bond, Ian Beckett, Robert O'Neill, Roger Stearn, Garry Sheffield, Alistair Irwin, and last though far from least, David Farr, whose unflagging enthusiasm and recondite knowledge of everyone and everything to do with the Great War was an inspiration.

The patient and good humoured way in which members of the York Branch of the Western Front Association and of the postgraduate seminar in military history at the University of London Institute of Historical Research, listened to and then questioned early versions of part of the introductory essay, helped to improve its content; a process further enhanced by my three brave readers, Jan Morris, John Grigg and Michael Howard, who saved me from stylistic solecisms and mistakes of fact for which I am most grateful. Responsibility for any faults that remain is entirely mine.

An exceedingly long list of helpers for so small a book; yet the greatest debt remains unacknowledged. That is owed, first, to Fiona who, admittedly with a little help from Clive, Eleanor, Jonathan and Carys, expertly prepared the final text from my rough and ready typescript; and to Cis who, as always, by her help and encouragement at every stage, has made this book a far less onerous task than it otherwise would have been, and ensured that it has been finished this side of the millennium.

A.J.A.Morris
The Old Rectory
Hopton Castle
March 1999

Abbreviations

AC	Army Council
ADC	Aide-de-camp
AG., Adj.Gen.	Adjutant-General
AR	*Army Review*
ASC	Army Service Corps
CB	Commander Order of the Bath
C-in-C	Commander-in-Chief
C of D	Committee of Defence
CID	Committee of Imperial Defence
CO	Commanding Officer
C of S	Chief of Staff
C of GS	Chief of General Staff
CIGS	Chief of Imperial General Staff
Col	Colonel
DAAG	Deputy Assistant Adjutant-General
DGO	Director General Ordnance
DMI	Director Military Intelligence
DSO	Distinguished Service Order
DT	*Daily Telegraph*
EF	Expeditionary Force
FM	Field Marshal
FO	Foreign Office
Gen	General
GGS	German Great General Staff
GHQ	General Headquarters
GOC	General Officer Commanding
GQG	Le Grand Quartier Général: French General Staff
GS	General Staff
H of C	House of Commons
HE	High Explosive
H of L	House of Lords
HM	His Majesty
HO	Home Office

HQ	Headquarters
HRH	His Royal Highness
ID	Intelligence Department
IG	Inspector General
LCA	London Counties Association
L of C	Line of Communication
Lt.Col	Lieutenant-Colonel
Lt.Gen	Lieutenant-General
MA	Military Attaché
MM	Military Member
MP	Member of Parliament
MP	*Morning Post*
MS	Military Secretary
N and M	Naval and Military Club
NDA	National Defence Association
NID	Naval Intelligence Department
NSL	National Service League
NW	North West (Frontier of India)
PHS	Printing House Square
PM	Prime Minister
PO	Post Office
PRO	Public Record Office
QMG	Quartermaster-General
RA	Royal Artillery
RFA	Royal Field Artillery
RE	Royal Engineers
SA	South Africa
SC	Staff College
SR	Special Reserve
S of S	Secretary of State
TF	Territorial Force
UVF	Ulster Volunteer Force
WG	*Westminster Gazette*
WO	War Office

Introduction

Who steals my purse steals trash;
But he that steals from me my good name
Robs me of that which . . . makes me poor indeed.

Shakespeare – '*Othello*'

I

'Who is Repington?' the First Sea Lord inquired rhetorically of the Secretary of State for War. 'A man who has been kicked out of the Army and turned out of all his clubs.' H.O. Arnold-Forster recorded Fisher's jibe in his diary with evident satisfaction.[1] If Repington were of such little consequence as Fisher claimed, why were the Admiral and the Minister so frequently exercised by what the military correspondent wrote? What credence are we to give to the opinions, frequently expressed in the diaries and letters of some of Repington's contemporaries, that he was an unmitigated villain, a bounder, a cad, a damned pimp, a lying brute?[2] Calculated insults are never the best guide to anyone's character. Many of these defamatory statements were coined as a salve to mend their self-esteem by those whom Repington had sorely wounded in public debate. Much more damaging to Repington's reputation have been the calculated public lies. Lloyd George could neither forgive nor forget Repington's censures. To punish the effrontery of one of the very few journalists that as Prime Minister he had been unable to square or squash, he portrayed Repington as a man who betrayed his country in time of war.[3] Less self-serving authors have also injured Repington's character. Particularly memorable is Paul Guinn's lapidary dismissal of the Colonel as the 'Playboy of the Western Front'.[4] Sadly, and in part undeservedly, Repington's unfortunate fate has been to be remembered as a rather unpleasant, too clever by half, intriguing, unpatriotic scoundrel. This caricature is the consequence of repeated deliberate falsehoods and carelessly reiterated mistakes.

Repington was a proud man. A well developed sense of humour and a willingness to admit frailties of character in private, do not excuse him from, on occasion, sounding opinionated and arrogant in public discourse upon military matters. Hauteur is sometimes all too apparent in the impatient expression of his absolute certainty that he is right and what others might think to the contrary is of no consequence. He did not suffer fools gladly. As to his fine conceit of himself, we, in our more democratic age, are uncomfortable in the company of someone seized, as was Repington, with the unquestioning social self-confidence of a mid-Victorian. Birth destined that Repington should enjoy a favoured place in an hierarchical society. He earned the disfavour of many of his peers because when it suited him he could be amazingly insensitive to the accepted social proprieties, careless of Society's pretences and hypocrisies.

He loved gossip, but savoured it as a gourmet not a gourmand. Unfortunately he was sometimes unable to resist the temptation to retell with advantage, tales of social, political and amorous intrigue that had come his way. Thus he became the author of a persistent and mischievous myth that has clung to his character. It was widely supposed that Repington was an inveterate and talented intriguer. Esher, the most accomplished behind-the-scenes political manipulator of his generation, frequently complained that the trouble with soldiers was they treated politics not as a jousting tourney but as war. In this, as in much else, Repington was a typical soldier. There was no bolder lance in open confrontation, but, as his sometime editor, H.A. 'Taffy' Gwynne complained, Repington was 'far too nervy and unbalanced' for the secret stratagems of the political game.[5] The choleric, impetuous Repington lacked the sensibility to be a successful conspirator.

In Society, Repington cut a conspicuous figure, both before and after he left the Army, that hinted at the *beau sabreur*. Slim, elegant, whatever Admiral Fisher claimed to the contrary, there was more of the legendary Gronow about Repington than the fictional Dalgetty.[6] A connoisseur of horses, pictures and pretty, fashionable women, he loved them all well, though not always wisely. His careless passion for beauty, generous nature and disdain for petty bourgeois notions of any connection between financial competence and respectability, all combined with disastrous consequences for his fortune. Repington worked prodigiously hard, but expenses invariably exceeded income. The undoubted blemishes of his character and rackety private life notwithstanding, as the military correspondent of *The Times*, before and during the Great War, Repington was a figure of consequence both in the national press and in determining the fortunes of the British Army. For this, if no other reason, his career merits unprejudiced examination.

II

Charles à Court[7] was born 29 January 1858. He took pride and pleasure in a family pedigree that stretched back to the Conquest and embraced ancestors who had rendered distinguished service to church and state.[8] By descent and marriage the family acquired land, wealth and a degree of influence. His father, Henry Wyndham à Court Repington, served in Parliament as had his father before him. Repington wrote that his father was a man of boundless gentleness and generosity. He was devoted to him as he was to his mother, Emily (*neé* Currie), the daughter of a wealthy banker. By his own account, he enjoyed an idyllic childhood. The indulgence shown by fond parents for a much-loved, attractive, only son, might well explain that degree of wilfulness sometimes apparent in Repington's adult character.

His education was conventional for someone of his social class – private tuition, a preparatory school, then five years, 1871 to 1875, at Eton College. Determined from an early age upon a military career, he was sent to a crammer at Freiburg. There, in the course of a year he, 'forgot a good deal and learnt very little'. At Sandhurst, which he entered in 1877, he continued to enjoy himself hugely. The day after his twentieth birthday, he was commissioned a sub-lieutenant in the Rifle Brigade.[9] He had demonstrated no particular gift, no brilliance, or anything that might have distinguished him from a hundred similarly privileged young men. Of large spirit, if small stature[10], his head stuffed with the usual romantic notions of winning instant glory and renown, he began his active service in India with the fourth battalion. There was just sufficient time for him to play an undistinguished part in the Second Afghan War. His first campaign ended with him invalided home, betrayed by his health.

Not until late 1879 was Repington sufficiently recovered to resume his regimental duties. He joined the third battalion at Richmond Barracks, Dublin. Ceremonial guard duties were interspersed with a rich and agreeable social and sporting life. But life in Ireland was not all entertainment and indulgence. During the harsh winter of 1881–2, he witnessed violent agrarian discontent. Temporarily stationed at Oughterard, Repington defused a potentially disastrous confrontation between his troops and rioters by a cool display of brazen effrontery ending with him ambushing the rebel leader. 'All quite illegal', he later happily admitted to Raymond Marker, 'but we inspired such a funk that . . . all outrages ceased.'[11] There was never any doubt about Repington's physical courage.

While stationed in Ireland, Repington began an arduous programme of study. In his own words, 'gradually and by degrees . . . professionalism was grafted upon a somewhat unfruitful and reluctant stem.' These studies, combined with visits abroad, inspired the writing of a monograph about the Italian Army published in 1884.[12] His enterprise did not go unnoticed. He continued his military studies with even greater energy and purpose encouraged by his book's *succès d'estime*. Repington wanted to get into the Staff College because it offered 'the best road to success when the royal road of active service was temporarily closed . . . for want of wars'. He entered Camberley in February 1887.[13] The knowledge he acquired and perhaps, more importantly, the friendships he made at Camberley, proved invaluable in his later career as a military correspondent. His fellow students counted him the most brilliant of their company.[14]

Repington resumed his regimental duties with service in Burma, but had scarcely arrived there before being obliged to return to England. To his delight he had been selected to serve in Intelligence. Given formal responsibility for an impossibly huge area of the globe, the almost exclusive focus of his attention became France. He familiarised himself with the French defences, attended their military manoeuvres and gained a thorough knowledge of the topography of those regions that later were to earn notoriety as the battlefields of the Great War.[15] The work he published during the five years he served in Intelligence is a measure not only of his knowledge, but also his enthusiasm and professional zeal. Two exhaustive articles, on Russian artillery and infantry tactics, appeared in the *Journal* of the Royal United Services Institute. He prepared a new edition of George Wiseley's, *Handbook of the French Army*, and made detailed notes for *Progress in the French Army*. This last clearly reveals how Repington's later, almost obsessive concern with the problem of invasion, was first inspired by his studies of French military, naval, harbour and railway installations. His 1896 article, 'Pensons y Toujours', afforded a wider, more general currency to his thoughts on this subject. And, as interesting, there is the first hint that perhaps by his writing he might alter the climate of military thought. His *magnum opus* was a study of the *Military Resources of France*. This was the first of a series initiated by Sir Edward Chapman, Sir Henry Brackenbury's successor as Chief of

Army Intelligence. It was livelier, more detailed and covered a much wider range of subjects than had any previous departmental publication.

Repington spent five years at Queen Anne's Gate before returning to his regiment, first at Aldershot, then Dublin. There was time to relax and indulge, among other things, his love of racing. But if occasion allowed, he made sure to impress his seniors with his competence, dash and high spirits. Recommended by the War Office as Milner's military secretary, he instead sailed to Egypt in August 1897 for service as DAAG on Sir Francis Grenfell's staff, one of two British officers who did not belong to the Egyptian Army.[16] It was a measure of the Commander-in-Chief's good opinion of Repington's qualities and military judgement, that Wolseley asked him to provide a regular estimate of the Egyptian Army.[17] Subsequently, Repington served upon Kitchener's staff in the Atbara campaign and at Omdurman. He was twice mentioned in despatches. Swiftly upon the heels of the fall of Khartoum came the Fashoda crisis.[18] Repington hurried back to England where he was engaged in secret service work.[19]

In November 1898, Repington was appointed to be the first British military attaché to Brussels and The Hague. Temperament, knowledge, inclination, and not unimportantly, means,[20] ideally suited Major (brevet Lieutenant-Colonel) Repington for his new posting. He was almost overwhelmed by demands for reports upon his hosts' military plans and forces.[21] All his duties, formal and informal, Repington carried out to the entire and enthusiastic satisfaction of his various chiefs.[22]

When an international peace conference assembled at The Hague in the summer of 1899, Repington was attached to the British delegation. This experience profoundly coloured his attitude towards the pre-war disarmament campaigns of the Radical Liberals.[23] In the interminable stuffiness of endless committees, amidst the ceaseless whirl of socialising, Repington could not have had a better opportunity to familiarise himself with the most influential naval, military and diplomatic representatives of the Powers. Everything he then saw and heard encouraged in him the belief that Germany could not be trusted to keep her word.[24] Had this needed confirming for him, Colonel Gross von Schwarzhoff, the German military commissioner, cheerfully dismissed the whole proceedings: '*Mon cher, c'est une blague.*'[25]

Repington returned to England in September 1899, and within two weeks had sailed for South Africa as one of the two DAAGs[26] on Sir Redvers Buller's Headquarters' Staff. Repington anticipated the worst and was not disappointed. Bluff, hard work and inspiration were insufficient to compensate for the hopeless miscalculations made as a consequence of having no proper General Staff. Repington saw lively action at Spion Kop, Vaal Krantz and Pieter's Hill. Shortly afterwards he went down with enteric fever, followed by jaundice and colitis. He was invalided home requiring a long period of recuperation, and then was fit only for light duties. He received two further mentions in despatches for his, 'thoroughly good service as Commandant of Headquarters until invalided', and in September 1901, was gazetted a Companion of the Order of St Michael and St George.

He returned to his old posting at Brussels and The Hague where circumstances were not easy. The British were extraordinarily unpopular, for sentiment at every level of Dutch and Belgian society favoured the Boers. Repington was involved in the peace negotiations, but before these were concluded his Army career had ended. The *London Gazette*, 14 January 1902, gave peremptory notice that, as from the next day, Lieutenant-Colonel Charles à Court, presently on half pay, would retire. Repington's military career and private life had collided disastrously.[27]

III

On 11 February 1882, a few weeks after his twenty-fourth birthday, Repington had married Melloney Catherine, the second daughter of the late Colonel Henry Scobell of the Abbey, Pershore. Two daughters were born of the marriage. Melloney's brother, Henry Jenner Scobell, was an officer in the Grays. Like his new brother-in-law, he was wealthy, cut a dash in fashionable society, was a fine horseman, and was fond of the ladies. He was to earn golden opinions for his moral and physical courage in the Boer War, but he was a martinet, very much a cavalry officer of the old school.[28] The two men enjoyed each other's company. Doubtless, Repington was a gay and amusing companion for his new wife. He was, however, not dutiful. Army life offered opportunities for unexplained absences from the matrimonial home that afforded a temptation there is no reason to suppose Repington resisted too strenuously. There were liaisons. How many is a matter for conjecture. Repington's reprehensible behaviour was no worse than that of many another officer.[29] The faster set in Society, following the example of Edward, Prince of Wales, winked at adultery. The social solecism was to be found out.

Repington had been married fifteen years when, late in 1897, he first met Mary Garstin. She was the wife of Sir William Edmund Garstin, a talented, ambitious and successful engineer. A chasm of age and temperament divided this unlikely couple. He was twenty years her senior; dull and matter of fact where she was mystical and emotional; he, an unbending Anglican, she, attracted by Roman Catholicism, into which church she was received in 1896. They had been married nine years and there were two children, a girl and a boy. Routine, boredom and duty were Mary's familiars in a marriage that knew little of love and nothing of passion. Repington was fascinated by Mary and began at once to lay siege to her affections. She, from the very first, was entranced by him. The affair flourished. Repington had never conducted his amours with particular discretion and it was not long before his wife learned of his latest adventure. The threat of informing his commanding officer was enough to bring Repington temporarily to heel. The affair did not end and lurched on through further forced estrangements and passionate reconciliations. It was less than a week before Repington was due to depart for war in South Africa, when his wife discovered the lovers were still meeting regularly. Cheated wife and cuckolded husband, together with Garstin's solicitors, devised a stratagem that obliged Repington to choose, once for all, between his career in the Army or life with Mary. Repington chose the Army, 'the one, true, lasting love of his life', as Mary later poignantly recalled in her memoirs.[30] To ensure that he kept his bargain, Repington was sent a document which he was required to sign before witnesses.[31] Upon his 'word of honour as a soldier and a gentleman', he promised he would never again meet or communicate with Mary. Before signing this document, he had written a letter to Georgina, Countess of Guilford, Mary's cousin, who also had been actively involved in the negotiations, stating that his undertaking would be given upon the understanding that, 'Lady Garstin will be spared all further indignities and humiliations on my account'.[32] This condition, Repington always claimed 'formed part of the transaction'. Duly signed, the parole was sent to Major Henry Wilson for safe keeping.

Henry Wilson's involvement in the enterprise requires explanation, as his actions and words were to be central to subsequent developments. Like Repington, Wilson was an officer in the Rifle Brigade. They had actually served together for a time in Intelligence. Repington had encouraged and helped Wilson considerably. At the time they would certainly have counted each other, if not friends, at least close colleagues. Wilson had much to gain from his association with his more brilliant colleague. Wilson was known to Mary as a friend of both her father, and also her cousin, Georgina.[33] Major Wilson was therefore drawn into the contretemps as a 'friend' of both parties.

Some three months after leaving England, Repington received several pathetic letters from Mary. These not only revealed how anxious she was for Repington's safety but also relayed her husband's constant, cruel taunts and bitter reproaches. Further, Mary related how Lady Guilford, pretending affection and pity for Mary's sad circumstances, constantly insulted Repington and asserted that she possessed positive evidence of his previous infidelities, providing somewhat fanciful 'proof' of the same. An angry Repington considered the condition upon which he had agreed to sign his parole had been violated by both Garstin and the Countess. He was, therefore, justified in withdrawing his parole. On 12 February 1900, in a lull between the stiff fighting at Spion Kop and Vaal Krantz, Repington summoned Wilson to his tent to inform him of his reasons for no longer considering himself bound by his promise. Wilson's only response appears to have been, 'You know this will end in the divorce court.' Repington considered he had done enough to discharge his commitment. He was after all campaigning, whereas, had he been at home, 'I should no doubt have taken more formal measures'. He wrote the next day to Mary, 'I saw Wilson last night and told him that owing to what had happened I would no longer be bound by my promise . . . '[34] Shortly afterwards, Repington was taken seriously ill and in June 1900, was invalided home.

When time and opportunity allowed, the affair was resumed. Repington had been unable to persuade his wife to divorce him; Sir William showed no such reluctance. He sued Mary for divorce citing Repington as co-respondent. The undefended suit was brought before Mr Justice Barnes on Thursday 12 December 1901. Garstin was granted a *decree nisi* with costs against Repington. As he had not been told by his solicitors until the last moment the date of the hearing, Repington, who had been at The Hague about his duties as military attaché, did not reach London until Thursday evening. He went to dine at the Naval and Military where he was much shocked to read detailed accounts of the divorce proceedings in the evening newspapers. He immediately wrote to the Military Secretary at the War Office, ' . . . had I entertained the faintest suspicion that Sir William Garstin intended to use, in order to attempt to ruin me, a promise I made to Major, now Lieutenant-Colonel Wilson, in October 1899, I should have taken the opportunity of entering a defence in order to explain how and under what circumstances I had considered, and had stated to witnesses that I considered myself as absolved from that promise.

I consider that I should have been informed of the intention to use that promise against me, and I should, in such case, have taken immediate steps to deny in the most formal and energetic manner that I considered myself bound by it, and should have put in a complete and satisfactory answer to the insinuations made against me . . .' [35] Repington had recognised immediately that the overwhelmingly important issue, so far as his future in the Army was concerned, was not his adultery but the question of his broken parole.

On receipt, Repington's letter, as 'a disciplinary question', was transferred from the Military Secretary to the Adjutant-General, Lieutenant-General Sir Thomas Kelly-Kenny. Repington's worst fears were confirmed when the Adjutant-General wrote, at the direction of the Commander-in-Chief, drawing his attention to the report of the divorce in *The Times*, 13 December, making particular reference to 'the undertaking which you do not appear to have kept', and requiring an explanation, 'before giving a decision in your case'.[36] On 19 December, Repington submitted his statement of explanation together with various additions. The next day Kelly-Kenny sent for Henry Wilson.

Wilson had been obliged to attend the divorce proceedings as a witness. The experience he described as 'novel' and 'very disagreeable'. The only other relevant observation recorded in his diary at the time was, next day there was 'much talk in club' about the proceedings, in which conversation, no doubt, Wilson played his usual lively, vociferous part.[37] Wilson must have been aware that the question whether Repington had broken his word of honour without good reason would be central to determining if Repington could stay in the Army. He must have known the import of Kelly-Kenny's invitation to recall the events of 12 February 1900. He wrote, 'So far as I can recollect, the subject of his letter to me . . . was never alluded to in any way. It certainly may have been present to his mind during our conversation but my memory is quite clear that no reference was made to it whilst talking on this subject.'[38] Thus, in the space of two sentences, Wilson damned Repington's case in the eyes of one of his chief judges, incidentally rebutting his earlier signed declaration that Repington's account of their meeting and conversation, 'substantially represent(ed) his recollection of the interview'.[39] This inconsistency was never addressed. The flabby disclaimer with which Wilson ended – 'a very hurried and interrupted interview in exceedingly busy times did not leave an accurate impression on my mind of all that was said' – was not likely to impress his interrogator half so much as the certitude of his assertion that there had been no reference made to the letter of parole.

Kelly-Kenny had clearly heard enough. His note tendering his advice to the Commander-in-Chief was brief and to the point. The civil law had dealt with the question of divorce which did not concern the Army, ' . . . however, it has come to our knowledge that Lt. Colonel à Court (Repington) has broken a solemn written promise made to a brother officer. Lt.Col. Wilson's statement and Lt.Col. à Court's explanation are in the papers. The latter is far from satisfactory, so much so that, notwithstanding his past services, I advise he be called on to retire from His Majesty's service.' Roberts concurred in this recommendation. Repington had given 'a soldier's promise which he broke, he has not behaved like a gentleman . . .' That same day the Minister for War gave his approval.[40] The obsequies for Repington's military career were as brief as they were merciless. He was informed by Kelly-Kenny of the Commander-in-Chief's decision, 'that you cannot be permitted to continue in His Majesty's Service . . . you will forthwith send in your application to retire . . .'[41]

There was no appeal against the judgement. Repington asked to be given a copy of Wilson's statement. His request was refused.[42] Thereafter Repington attached the blame for his dismissal entirely upon Henry Wilson thereby managing altogether to exculpate himself. But clearly there had been a general predisposition, even without Wilson's damning contribution, to view Repington, for all his admittedly excellent qualities as a professional soldier, as a flawed character, someone capable of breaking his word of honour. This was because of his earlier careless behaviour and reckless disregard for social proprieties and the opinion of others. Now those, neither few in number nor lacking social influence, who had previously declared how much they disliked and distrusted Repington, seemed justified. Valentine Chirol, who had been opposed to Repington being invited to help L.S. Amery with *The Times's History of the South African War*, wrote to Moberly Bell, 'It is not creditable for *The Times* to have a man of that kind going abroad saying he is employed by us when he is no longer good enough to be employed by the Army.' Repington's actions seemed to confirm that he was 'a damned liar'.[43]

IV

The abrupt conclusion of his military career temporarily shook even Repington's adamantine *amour propre*. His income had also been severely dented. There was an urgent need to find paid employment.[44] Journalism suggested itself as a likely prospect,[45] and Printing House Square, as good a place as any to begin his search. He was a long-time friend of the Walter family who owned the paper. He did not allow himself to be too obviously upset when told he could no longer help Amery. In any event, *The Times* very soon overcame its scruples.[46] He wrote to tell Moberly Bell that it was his intention 'to write a good deal on foreign, naval and military matters'. He did not doubt his writing would 'be of value'. Repington concluded his letter with stunning insouciance, 'Should you hear of any editor requiring a regular correspondent in Paris, I shall ask you to bear me in mind . . . both the Foreign Office and War Office will tell you that no one knows France better than I do.'[47] There was no reply. But an article Repington had written about Rosebery was accepted by the *Westminster Gazette*. After a conversation the next day with its editor, Repington was offered work. He eagerly accepted.

The *Westminster Gazette* was a small circulation, evening newspaper. It was never a commercial success, but its outstanding editor had made it the authoritative voice of Liberalism. J.A. Spender was the familiar and equal of the nation's political leaders. He wrote with integrity, sincerity, scrupulous fairness and moderation of expression. The arguments of opponents were invariably treated seriously. In debate, Spender, if possible, sought to be constructive. He did not eschew controversy but was a fair controversialist possessing a sense of the common good that tempered any inclination to political partisanship. As a tyro newspaper correspondent, Repington was fortunate to have as his editor and journalistic mentor such an outstanding professional exemplar. Spender had a profound influence in shaping the way that Repington presented and analysed issues.[48]

Repington never became a staff member of the *Westminster*, and made considerably fewer contributions than his distinguished predecessor as military correspondent, W.E. Cairnes. What immediately impressed Spender about Repington was his 'extraordinary knowledge and great facility as a journalist'. He encouraged Repington to concentrate upon the larger problems of military reconstruction and reform. Having scant respect for St John Brodrick's acumen or wisdom and convinced that his proposed Army reforms were impracticable, Repington needed little or no encouragement to demonstrate the hopelessness of the Minister's suggested measures. This, his first campaign for the *Westminster*, proved in many ways a paradigm for most subsequent battles. First, he never confined himself to the columns of the *Westminster* but availed himself freely of the letter pages, particularly of *The Times* and the *Spectator*. Later, when he was at Printing House Square, it was Leo Maxse's *National Review* that became the favoured resting place for comment that, for one reason or another, could not be accommodated by *The*

Times. Second, if at all possible, Repington preferred working as part of a team or alliance. Against Brodrick his fellow campaigners were Winston Churchill and a parliamentary coterie of young, Tory malcontents. By correspondence and meetings, the merits of alternative arguments were examined, speeches and tactics criticised, criticism freely exchanged and information acquired. When necessary, Repington was not averse to serving as his fellows' dogsbody, just as later he was to devil assiduously for Roberts and Haldane. In adversity, Repington was unfailingly resilient. He promised Churchill, that whatever happened he would 'keep on shooting until the enemy retires'.[49] Eventually the Minister did, in October 1903. Sadly Repington's initial high hopes for Brodrick's successor, H.O. Arnold-Forster, were very soon blighted.

Repington was as happy manufacturing ammunition for others as he was firing his own. But he did not treat lightly assertions that he took orders from anyone. His vehement denials did not stop the charge being repeated. He was accused of being Esher's creature, and most damagingly and persistently, the willing cipher, during the Great War, for the caprices and demands of the Generals. Repington always insisted that what he made of information supplied to him was a matter for his judgement and discretion. He was mindful of the duty he owed to his newspaper. On minor issues he, on occasion, deferred to editorial injunction and proprietorial whim. But he early demonstrated that he would not give second place to what he construed as the national interest, nor would he compromise his beliefs. Thus, in May 1905, when Balfour informed the Commons of the Committee of Defence findings on invasion to the plaudits and unqualified approval of *The Times*, Repington was highly critical and urged revision. He recklessly dismissed counter arguments by his editor and senior editorial colleagues as 'pails full of blather, blarney and bumcomb', earning a stern reproof from Esher and a grumbling avowal from George Sydenham Clarke that he was no better a friend of the Committee of Defence than Spenser Wilkinson. Repington ignored Clarke whom he supposed was the true author of Balfour's mistaken opinions, and repeated his criticisms with force and clarity in Maxse's *National Review*.[50] Radical politicians always sought to dismiss Repington's censures as the ill-considered mouthings of a mad militarist, but unlike so many other critics of the pacifists, he addressed their arguments with gravity, and rebutted them without resort to insolent slanders. Friend and foe alike conceded, and with good reason, that he was much the best informed of military commentators. More than that he was recognised as a significant opinion maker and shaper because he could write about complex subjects with compelling fluency and simplicity. His conclusions seemed so obviously sensible and authoritative that they brooked no possible argument. He was never less than a convincing advocate, and a damnably irritating and complacent opponent.

Although he enjoyed writing for the Liberal *Westminster Gazette*, Repington always hoped he would be offered a permanent berth at Printing House Square. The attraction of writing for *The Times* was obvious. Everyone who was anyone acknowledged that *The Times* was unrivalled among newspapers as a maker and disseminator of opinion. *The Times's* unique position among the British political élite had been confirmed more than a half century earlier under the distinguished editorship of J.T. Delane. When censured by the Foreign Secretary for publishing a secret foreign office document, Delane responded that his newspaper had behaved with perfect propriety as its primary purpose was, 'to participate in the government of the world . . . by sway of language and reason over the minds of men [and] to form aright the public opinion of this nation'.[51] The accepted wisdom that newspapers shaped public opinion, dictated the relationship between them and Parliament. In public, politicians like Arthur Balfour made a virtue of their supposed indifference to the press, but in private they courted its favours assiduously. As the franchise widened, a new constitutional convention gained ever wider acceptance: that the press – otherwise, and more grandiloquently designated, 'the fourth estate' – had an increasingly important part to play in the political process. Monopoly enhanced the attractions of the press and exaggerated its importance. Inevitably, *The Times* was quite convinced that it enjoyed a particular, privileged status. 'We are *The Times*. We mould today and shape tomorrow . . . We are where the real power lies . . . We get the ear of and influence those who have the ear of the masses.'[52]

Since the Crimean War, *The Times* had employed a military specialist upon its staff. Sir George Sydenham Clarke had filled the post with distinction in the 1880s, and continued to make contributions long after he had been succeeded by Colonel Sir Lonsdale Augustus Hale in 1890. When Hale retired in 1903, the responsibility fell to young Leo Amery. When war between Russia and Japan began, Amery's already onerous duties at Printing House Square made it impossible for him to supply the required daily articles. He suggested that Repington might help out. Repington seized his chance. His brilliant writing was an immediate and hugely popular success. In no time at all he had established a reputation as *the* outstanding military commentator. This was not simply because he wrote well. It was because from the beginning he backed the winner; he never doubted that Japan would be victorious. He was quick to point out that armed conflict between an island empire and a huge, continental enemy was a very pertinent example, a source of inspiration and instruction for the British and their empire. His articles swiftly transcended the narrow confines of the Manchurian struggle. He wrote upon a variety of subjects: amphibious warfare, invasion, ideas of national efficiency, the Samurai code of Bushido, the relevance of the theories of Clausewitz and Mahan, the supreme value of history and the urgent need to establish, under the aegis of the Committee of Defence, an historical branch to con the lessons provided and thus avoid repeating avoidable mistakes through ignorance. These articles were published as 'From Our Military Correspondent'.[53] Nevertheless, as the war drew to its end, Repington's position at *The Times* still remained uncertain. His letters on the subject went unanswered by his editor. He wrote instead to the manager, Moberly Bell, who admired his work. To his entire satisfaction, Repington was given a contract to serve as the paper's correspondent charged with the particular responsibility for military news and comment. It was a challenge that Repington relished. He responded, without exaggeration, 'There is much opening for independent criticism to-day.'[54]

V

In a paper he had written in 1900, Sir John Ardagh, then Director of Military Intelligence, had considered the part the press might play in promoting military reform.[55] He was convinced that newspapers were not fitted for this task. The instruction they condescended to provide was ignorant and partial. They were really concerned only with increasing their circulation and profit. Their readers were not interested in instruction but diversion and entertainment. Ardagh was thinking primarily of the so-called 'popular' press, newspapers like the *Daily Mail* and *Daily Express*. Except in war time, the public could not have cared less about the fortunes of the British Army. Any pride and affection they felt for the armed services of the Crown, was lavished almost exclusively upon the Navy. Similarly, in Parliament nothing emptied the chamber and press gallery of the Commons more swiftly than an Army debate. It was the considered opinion of the *Spectator's* editor, John St Loe Strachey, that when it came to military reform, most politicians were 'spineless'. To get Parliament to adopt the simplest measure, a newspaper campaign was necessary.[56] Such pessimistic assertions were correct. Military reform was a complex, technical subject that interested very few MPs except some self-designated 'experts'. The remainder, and particularly Radical Liberal MPs, made a virtue of apathy and ignorance. The humiliations suffered by British arms in South Africa dramatically demonstrated the urgent need for a change of attitude.

Unfortunately for the press, the War Office seemed unaware of any need to change its relations with Fleet Street. News briefings were conducted reluctantly, suspiciously and incompetently, generating misinformation, confusion and ill will. Some commanders in the field – Buller was a notorious example – were convinced that journalists were a damnable nuisance and an unnecessary embarrassment with their impertinent questions. They behaved as though they supposed that wars were fought solely for the benefit of the newspapers.[57] The War Office's attitude to the press was shared by every other department of government. But, as George Clarke noted, the Admiralty and War Office were 'the most stupid and impolitic of all government departments. When hard up they try to use the press. Ordinarily they keep you at a distance and wrap themselves in a cloud of silly mystery.'[58] The character of a nation's political system determines the public role of its press.[59] In Britain the official attitude was, say as little as possible, discourage thoughtful inquiry or debate, inspire respect and insist upon unquestioning conformity. The system was as inefficient as it was offensive, and positively encouraged the breach of regulations. The War Office suffered a rash of unofficial leaks of secret, sometimes inconvenient, often embarrassing information, a contagion that spread to infect the military hierarchy.[60] Like any other competent journalist, Repington took full advantage of these unofficial sources. What distinguished his enterprise was the number and status of his informants. They happily shared their secrets with the Military Correspondent of *The Times* supposing there was no better way of serving their own various purposes.

In the early days of the campaign for National Service, Lord Roberts and a journalist ally, J.L. Garvin, complained that *The Times* was 'weak and tardy' on defence policy. A national organ with an unique status, it ought to be leading opinion. Instead it 'blew hot and cold in turn'. Roberts asked the owner of *The Times* whether his newspaper had a settled defence policy. A.F. Walter angrily rejected Roberts's implied criticism.[61] Roberts had asked his question because the editor of *The*

Times allowed his naval correspondents constantly to propagate the 'Blue Water' doctrine. Every journalist knew that the first requirement of a successful campaign was editorial support. G.E. Buckle, who had been editor since 1884, conducted affairs at Printing House Square as though he was a college president. He was inclined, perhaps rather too readily, to defer to a colleague's particular expertise. Chirol admitted, this was all right if you happened to be the expert to whom Buckle deferred, 'but the system is not on that account a good one'.[62] Chirol, like Roberts and Garvin, supposed Buckle gave too much credence to the opinions of Admiral Fisher and his press gang. Buckle, however, passionately believed that the unique distinction of *The Times* was that it sought to serve national before any partisan or sectional interest.

In the anodyne recollections of his relations with Buckle that Repington published, he attributed much of his success in writing for *The Times* to the 'wise liberty' his editor had accorded him.[63] A more accurate account would have acknowledged how frequently they were at odds one with the other. But Buckle never sought to censor Repington's contradictory voice. The opinions expressed on the leader page did not always chime with those of the military correspondent in his columns. Nor did Buckle forswear Repington, despite the frequent requests he should do so from Valentine Chirol. The foreign editor's initial distaste for Repington was converted to animosity and sustained by the jealous insinuations of George Clarke.[64]

In 1912, Buckle was eventually obliged to resign. Editor and proprietor had found each other impossible to sustain a moment longer. Buckle's replacement was Geoffrey Robinson. Few then shared Clarke's apprehension that Northcliffe expected any editor he had personally appointed would do his bidding without question. Buckle had no doubts that Robinson would 'do great things' as editor.[65] To that end, Robinson was subject to as much advice from Buckle and the 'Old Guard' as from Northcliffe. But Robinson's loyalty was already pledged to his first and abiding political mentor, Milner. The ideas and the personality of the Proconsul who had shaped South Africa's destiny as its High Commissioner, exercised a profound influence upon his disciples, talented young men who shared their master's imperial vision. Robinson was not least among this coterie of dedicated Milnerites.

Repington's preference had always been, whenever possible, to work in harness with his editors. The 'pretty racket' occasioned by the Kaiser Tweedmouth episode, when Buckle and Repington had colluded in an attempt to embarrass the Liberal Government, had not redounded to the credit of *The Times*.[66] Thereafter Buckle had been most reluctant to countenance Repington campaigning in any field other than that which was strictly his field of expertise. In particular, Repington's trenchant opinions upon naval policy and strategy were no longer welcome. Repington did not take to this prohibition kindly. Robinson as editor seemed to promise an opportunity for a new, more generous attitude. The new editor appeared to welcome advice and showed a willingness to receive instruction in all aspects of defence policy.[67]

At first Repington earned golden opinions from his editor, in particular for censuring J.L. Garvin's intemperate proselytising for Unionist support of the Tariff. Repington, fondly supposing that Robinson recognised in him a benign mentor and guide to the intricacies of defence policy and politics, planned a joint campaign for compulsory service. What began in a spirit of cooperation became increasingly sour as a temporary but unfortunate change of tone overtook Repington's writing. Certainly encouraged, possibly flattered by Bonar Law's approval, Repington's tone became increasingly strident and partisan. Earlier he would have dismissed Radical influence upon the conduct of the Government's defence and foreign policies as at worst, a minor irritant. Now his contempt for them fuelled a paranoia that reduced the campaign for conscription to a sectarian diatribe. It was as though a combination of critical crises that appeared to threaten good public order and the future of the empire, disturbed his habitual cynical distrust of all politicians, and turned him into a baying Ultra Tory. This in turn inspired a furiously burgeoning outpouring of writing that did not endear him to Robinson, who had problems enough coping with increasing pressure from an unstable proprietor and unscrupulous Tory politicians. As a consequence, Repington's articles were at first delayed, then heavily cut, and finally, with increasing frequency, ignored. This was costly both for his pride and his pocket. It did not enhance his opinion of Robinson as an editor. Loyalty between editor and journalist was not entirely forfeit, but where there had been cooperation there now existed a more guarded relationship. That he might more readily circumvent the editorial blue pencil, Repington increasingly directly sought Northcliffe's approval for his schemes.

Northcliffe's personality and career embodied the revolution that overtook the British political press in the last third of the nineteenth century. When newspapers were viewed as commercial properties, where profit became the supreme consideration, the proprietor's influence grew. His, not the editor's will, determined the policies a newspaper adopted.[68]

Repington's first formal contact with Northcliffe had been in 1903, when the owner of the *Daily Mail*, the *Evening News* and thirty other journals of lesser distinction, was still plain Mr Alfred Charles Harmsworth.[69] Repington had been deputed to ask Northcliffe for funds for a new journal. His quest was unsuccessful.[70] The paths of the two men next crossed in the early spring of 1908 when Northcliffe was engaged in the secret negotiations to become owner of *The Times*. As much as anyone not directly involved, Repington enjoyed the gossip and the air of mystery and adventure that inevitably surrounded these transactions. He had not been enthusiastic about Pearson's earlier bid, but seemed not unduly concerned at the prospect of Northcliffe as proprietor. Repington would have been aware that Northcliffe's not very profound political ideas were close to his own and therefore congenial. He put men before ideas, certainly before party, was a generous patriot and imperialist, and nurtured a suspicion that Germany's intentions towards Britain and her Empire were highly questionable.[71] Once Northcliffe had successfully gained control, he looked for changes in attitude, methods and personnel at Printing House Square. He was constantly frustrated by Buckle, Bell and Chirol, the 'Old Guard'.

In response to the first notes received from Northcliffe, Repington gave the clear impression that he not only sympathised, but also had reason to understand the proprietor's dilemma. He too encountered difficulties in his work for *The Times*. Just as Disraeli when dealing with the Queen, so Repington recognised it was politic to flatter Northcliffe excessively while never failing to advertise his own many and excellent if less exalted accomplishments. Also, unlike the 'Old Guard', Repington was not averse to promoting schemes that might generate bigger profits, especially when he might reasonably hope to share in the extra largesse. He made very sure that Northcliffe was privately apprised of his contrary views on strategic issues – as in the case of the defence of the Mediterranean – where he had good reason to suppose that Northcliffe did not agree with the policy *The Times* was promoting. Most shamelessly, in his long-running disagreement with the naval correspondents, notably James Thursfield, Repington had the effrontery to suggest there should be changes of personnel. He proposed as suitable, a former Director of Naval Intelligence, Charles Ottley, 'so that naval criticism should cease to be ridiculous'.[72] For the most part, relations between proprietor and correspondent were amicable. Northcliffe was, however, unhappy about Repington editing the *Army Review*. It was bound to compromise Repington's independence as a military critic. Perhaps even more importantly for Northcliffe, it might lead, as indeed it did, to questions in Parliament. Northcliffe, who in private was frequently contemptuous of Parliament, in public was anxious that his properties should never feature as a subject of debate in either House. Repington's reply to Northcliffe's disquiet was typical. He rejected any possibility that his independence was compromised, then added that had his abilities and laborious exertions on behalf of *The Times* been better appreciated and remunerated there would have been no reason for him to have undertaken the editorship in the first place.[73] Northcliffe never seemed to mind Repington approaching him directly behind Robinson's back. If what Repington had to say did not interest him, Northcliffe simply ignored it. Their relationship prompted fewer signs of tension, impatience and irritation from either man than might reasonably have been anticipated from the collision of two such tender egos.

VI

Repington had been sanguine about the prospects for the Army's future when H.O. Arnold-Forster succeeded St John Brodrick. There was a sad and swift decline from his early estimate that the new minister was 'on the side of the angels', and therefore, 'worth backing'. Within a year Repington admitted that he had 'given up on him . . . I am sick of him and all his works . . . hopeless . . . His schemes are wholly bad . . . nothing to recommend them . . . I see nothing for it but the resignation of Arnold-Forster.'[74] Repington did not confine his criticisms to private letters, and Arnold-Forster, not by nature inclined to suffer silently, answered back in kind. The correspondence columns of *The Times* reverberated to the charges and countercharges of these two formidable protagonists. Arnold-Forster was not impressed by Repington's censures. He dismissed them as nothing more than 'a personal attack dressed up in large type and fortified by animosity, presented as a judgement on the real consideration of public needs'. In a letter to Balfour he repeated this criticism, though he expressed it more pithily. 'He is able enough . . . but his concern is for self always rather than the national interest.'[75] To Leo Maxse, Arnold-Forster addressed a more serious, substantive criticism: that Repington was 'a mere creature of Esher's'.[76] The severe drubbing the Minister suffered in Parliament and the press was enough to induce paranoia. But he was convinced he discerned a real chain of betrayal and relationships of which he was the undeserving victim. 'I gave A.J. B[alfour] my reply . . . I suppose he will now hand it to Esher, who will hand it to Acourt (Repington).'[77] Arnold-Forster had reason to suppose his hypothesis proved when, three days later, a highly critical article by Repington appeared in *The Times*. He told Maxse that the article had clearly been written at Esher's instigation and inspired by a desire for revenge.[78] The Minister was well informed upon defence issues, hard working, conscientious and well intentioned, yet he ended his term of office a failure, disliked by almost everyone. Not all his misfortunes were the consequence of press criticism. Spencer Ewart, endeavouring to be fair, had to admit that for all his virtues, Arnold-Forster was 'A strange personality. It was pathetic to see how, whilst laboriously endeavouring to be civil he usually contrived to be excessively rude.'[79] But whatever his faults of character, Arnold-Forster was no fool, and in part, his charge against Repington and Esher was well founded.

All Arnold-Forster's critics, while busily puffing their own merits, had assiduously retailed his supposed inadequacies and the faults of his proposals to the press. None had been more effective or active than Esher. Early in his career he had acquired an appreciation of and taste for journalism. Under the inspired guidance of W.T. Stead, Esher had become the master of the clandestine briefing, the leak, and the oblique and allusive reference. When he could not find a journalist to 'father' his stories which was his preferred method, he could turn a neat article himself under his own or a pseudonym. In his perception of the political process the surreptitious manipulation of the press was of paramount importance. He never doubted the power of the press to shape the opinion of readers.[80] During the vital years that Esher helped to influence British thinking on defence and military reform, he worked closely with a number of journalists; J.A. Spender, W.T. Stead, J.L. Garvin and St Loe Strachey. In his dealings with Printing House Square, Esher possessed a most useful if opinionated conduit in Sir George Clarke. Then there was Leo Amery, always anxious to help anyone he thought might further his own career. But most useful and influential of all was Repington.

A recent biographer of Esher dismisses Repington as 'nothing more than a great busybody and bore who wrote interminable letters to Regy on Army matters'.[81] This is altogether to misunderstand the relationship between the two men. They shared a passionate interest in military affairs but their chosen milieu and method of influencing political opinion and action was very different. It misjudges the value that each attached to the agreement, cooperation, ability and influence of the other. This is not to deny that both men calculated how much each gained from the alliance.

Esher made the first approach, possibly through Spender, for although freelancing for *The Times*, Repington was still the *Westminster Gazette's* military correspondent. Repington was only too pleased to comply. It brought him at once to the heart of the process of reform in which he was anxious to play a part. Repington valued Esher's good opinion of his ideas, and was not above seeking, on occasion, the Viscount's 'shrewd and sagacious' advice.[82] Despite Esher's pedantry, Repington sought to know his mind on a variety of issues before completing the final drafts of articles. But when their opinions differed, Repington invariably and unhesitatingly chose his own path. A published difference of opinion over an invasion scare in 1913 really aroused Esher's ire. Haldane advised him that it would be disastrous to refute Repington in public. He comforted Esher with the thought that, 'though the press always gets the last word . . . the silent man in authority always wins in the end.'[83] Repington was never afraid to question Esher's ideas and on occasion probed at perceived weaknesses relentlessly. The tone of the letters reflected an exchange not between client and patron but between two equals. Except in the case of Henry Wilson, Repington proffered wise, valuable and informed advice upon the capacities and suitability for promotion of candidates for high military office. His particular value to Esher was that he kept him abreast of current thinking among serving officers. Where Esher's influence stretched and his did not reach, Repington sought favours, not invariably for selfish reasons, as when he tried to help his friend Huguet out of a temporary diplomatic embarrassment. Similarly, he sought Esher's help to curb the excesses of Fisher who would never willingly admit any virtue in a scheme promoted by the Army. Sometimes Repington exaggerated Esher's influence, as when he supposed he might change the membership of the committee investigating invasion.

Esher had never been a soldier. He was interested in military history for the insights it provided into strategy and higher military thinking. He was convinced that historical knowledge was more useful than technical knowledge and practical experience. But this personal belief hardly explains, and certainly does not justify, his crucial position as the confidential adviser of the King, and as the instigator of vital changes in military thinking and organisation in Edwardian Britain. He enjoyed the powers of a Secretary of State, without being answerable to Parliament. In the circumstances, it was hardly surprising that he should be attacked in the press by those who resented such unbridled influence. A series of articles in the *World*,[84] censured him as 'the mysterious power' that unlike Prime Ministers who 'may come and go . . . goes on for ever', and linked his name with Repington's and Haldane's. This 'Cabal' was charged with undermining the defence interests of Britain by an abuse of royal influence, jobbery, and manipulation of the press. In a fit of pique, much to Haldane's justifiable annoyance, Esher defended himself in the *National Review*.[85] He did not deign to answer the charge that there was no evidence for his superior abilities other than the ascriptions of his 'many press friends from Colonel Repington to Mr Stead'. By early 1913, Repington was questioning Esher's constitutional role.[86] By then their close association was long abandoned. In later years Esher was at pains to give the impression that he had always treated Repington with caution. 'In private life the man has always been thoroughly untrustworthy . . . a journalist out for himself as well as for the country . . . Although I have known R. for years, I never said anything to him that I was not prepared to see in the Times next morning.'[87]

Repington's involvement in the extraordinary episode that initiated the secret Anglo-French military conversations need not detain us, for it is a subject that has been much written about and Repington himself provided a detailed account.[88] It is, however, notable that it was an angry article by Repington in *The Times* warning the Germans not to assume British disinterest in any Franco-German war that apparently emboldened Huguet, the French military attaché and a friend of Repington, to confide his government's anxieties to the military correspondent. The choice of Repington was clearly not accidental. No other freelance agent had easier or more familiar access to ministers, the Committee of Defence, the War Office and the Admiralty. How easily Repington slipped into a role familiar to him from his years at The Hague and Brussels! Everyone behaved splendidly, except Fisher.[89] His unwillingness to cooperate emphasised the disturbing and dangerous confusion between military and naval thinking; the kind of strategic tumult the Committee of Defence was expressly designed to eliminate.

The landslide victory of the Liberals in the January 1906 general election confirmed R.B. Haldane as Minister for War. If his plans for reform faced animosity and suspicion it was more from his own back-benchers and press than the Tories. How quickly the attitude of the majority of the Tory press changed may be judged from the letters of H.A. Gwynne, then editor of the *Standard*, to Raymond Marker. At first he claimed that he had done his 'utmost to put the Army above party politics', but in a few months the Minister's schemes were 'almost unanimously condemned as though our hostility is a party move which it is not.' Haldane had revealed himself as a 'humbug . . . a creature of circumstance, a compromiser of the worst kind', who had 'given in to the extremists . . . swept off his feet by the Little Englanders'.[90] Repington laughed to scorn such misinformed views. He had as little respect for such Tory foes of the Minister as for the 'antics' of Radical critics.[91] Haldane had no doubt that if he were to succeed in his endeavours then he needed a friendly press to explain his schemes to the electorate, for 'writing [that] is carefully read must do real good. The public needs educating.'[92] A special department at the War Office supplied the press with propaganda favourable to Haldane's schemes. This blatant exercise in public relations incensed the Radicals who stormed at 'the student of Schopenhauer' becoming 'the indiscriminate coadjutor of the *Daily Mail*'.[93] Whether the journalist's support for the minister ever transcended his function as a publicist is questionable.[94] As politicians will, Haldane claimed the exclusive authorship of the Army reforms that bear his name. Others, notably George Clarke, have questioned this claim.[95] Ellison, Haldane's principal private secretary, installed in that position by Esher with the express intention to influence his master, was closely associated with Repington.[96] As valued and well informed voices close to the Secretary of State, their arguments would necessarily have carried considerable persuasive force. But Haldane never wavered from the first in his determination of the political priorities that guided and shaped his schemes.[97]

Both in public and private, Repington frequently expressed his contempt for the capacity of most politicians and ministers, but for all this rhetorical bluster he was, almost invariably, a shrewd judge of political realities. This is nowhere better illustrated than in his campaigning with and for Haldane's reforms. Critics point to the strength and influence Repington acquired from supporting Haldane; they do not acknowledge that it was as much a source of criticism and animosity. He fought a brave, constant and cleverly judged campaign for Haldane's Territorials in the face of prejudice, tradition and vested interest, even acting as Haldane's go-between with the Tories in the House of Lords.[98] But it is on the issue of conscription that Repington best revealed what a consummate political tactician he was. He was converted to the idea of compulsion,[99] yet recognised that in the current political climate there was no possibility of it being accepted unless there was a prolonged, patient, carefully planned and orchestrated propaganda campaign. Thus he entertained higher hopes for the moderate National Defence Association, than the National Service League. One pre-war issue encapsulated all these struggles – invasion. It became the catalyst for the activities and interests of leading voluntarists, supporters of conscription, leaders and back-benchers of both major political parties and naval and military personnel. For that generation, invasion was 'nothing less than a national obsession'.[100] It is beyond doubt that this was an issue where policy makers were sensitive to public pressure, for there is a direct correlation between public scares and subsequent official inquiries.[101] 'Blue Water' theory was the agreed orthodoxy subscribed to by the leaders of the Liberal and Unionist parties. Consequently, the advocates of the 'Bolt from the Blue' were obliged to campaign largely outside Parliament, employing the press as their primary support and influence. Repington was the leading advocate for the invasionists. His persuasive and detailed writing prompted debate at Westminster, two detailed examinations by the Committee of Imperial Defence, and lengthy, contentious exchanges in the correspondence columns of *The Times*, the primary platform for informed debate of the invasion issue.[102]

At Printing House Square, 'Blue Water' thinking dominated. So long as Fisher ruled the roost, the Admiralty harboured Repington's most bitter and vengeful foe. The First Sea Lord, immensely powerful, influential, autocratic, departmentally myopic, contemptuous of the Army, viewed all Repington's ideas as a direct threat to his beloved Senior Service. He supposed, quite incorrectly, that Repington sought to destroy both him and the Navy; in Fisher's mind, the two were inseparable. Fisher believed Repington to be a Judas who had sold himself to the 'Bolt from the Blue' school for thirty pieces of War Office silver. He was profoundly wrong. For the same reasons as Repington had championed the Committee of Defence, he pleaded for inter-Service cooperation in strategic planning. When he saw it as serving the interest of both Army and Navy, Repington was happy to suggest to Roberts an accommodation with Fisher. He perceived that the independence of the Admiralty, far from serving the national interest, was positively harmful; it needed to be curbed. He rightly questioned Fisher's over-reliance upon the all big-gun battleship and revealed, in rather incongruous alliance with Admiral Lord Charles Beresford, Fisher's serious limitations as a strategist.[103]

By 1914, the Admiralty had reversed its thinking on invasion. This, however, had little to do with the arguments that 'Bolt from the Blue' advocates had pressed. And the reversal in War Office thinking from August 1911, was dictated by the overwhelming determination to despatch the maximum number of troops to the continent at the very beginning of hostilities with Germany. It was elements within the Liberal party that insisted the transformation had been effected by 'scaremongering' tactics employed by advocates like Repington. But to accuse him of being a 'scaremonger' is to ignore the way in which he orchestrated, then conducted, the invasionists' case; the assiduous collection of data, of written and oral evidence from acknowledged experts, the careful collation, rehearsal and finally presentation to the Defence Committee. On one occasion only did Repington descend to deliberate scaremongering: his ultimately unsuccessful attempt, in concert with Buckle and Leo Maxse, to embarrass the Liberal Government over the indiscreet exchange of letters between the German Kaiser and the First Lord of the Admiralty, poor Tweedmouth. That incident clearly demonstrates the limitations of so-called press 'influence'. Without the support of politicians at Westminster, the most enthusiastic, energetic and persuasive campaign was doomed to fail.[104]

It would seem reasonable to suppose that when J.E.B. Seely succeeded Haldane as Secretary of State for War in June 1912, Repington's already favoured position at the War Office would be enhanced. They had been friends for years and had campaigned together both against the Boers and St John Brodrick. But when Seely saw fit not to promote the interests of the Territorials and appeared to encourage Henry Wilson's criticisms of that force, Repington's worst suspicions were aroused. Subsequently, events in Ulster confirmed his belief that under Seely's stewardship, the War Office had sunk into confusion and inefficiency. Repington did not hesitate to inform Seely that his patriotic duty to criticise this dangerous and sad state of affairs quite outweighed any claims of private friendship.[105] Vainly Seely attempted to assuage Repington's criticisms with various schemes designed to muzzle him. Given the parlous state of his private finances, the minister's promises of rich rewards must have been difficult to resist.[106] But, as Repington told his editor, he was not impressed by these offers because Seely's intention to buy his silence was all too patent.[107] He had earlier informed Haldane that Seely simply was not up to his post and suggested the Prime Minister should be informed. Such advice might seem impertinent, conceited and a betrayal of a friend. It was, nevertheless, sound.[108] Repington's attitude towards Seely clearly demonstrates his independence, even though his inclination was always to work with the minister where possible.[109] It also shows his willingness, even to prejudice his ready access to official sources, when he believed the national interest so dictated.

Where exactly did national interest and public duty lie in the Irish question? That impossible conundrum was posed in an atmosphere hopelessly poisoned by bigotry, prejudice and passion. In his heart, Repington supported Ulster without reservation. His romantic attachment could not, however, altogether expunge the likely fatal consequences for the security of Britain and her Empire of a civil war at her back, while a truculent and ambitious Germany stood armed and menacing across the North Sea. He was equally torn in mind and heart over the possible fate of the Army in Ireland. He entirely understood and sympathised with those officers at the Curragh who said they would not take up arms against Ulster. But he knew also that contact with politics would rot the Army and that there was no way to compromise with illegality. He could not resolve this dangerous and hopeless clash of loyalties and priorities. In the circumstances, it was not surprising that Repington should prove hardly wiser in his words or deeds than other assorted pundits. What he did not lack was moral courage. Consequently, he did not hesitate to publish harsh criticism of the conduct of three friends – Churchill, French and Seely. He arraigned them as the men 'mainly responsible' for the Army's cruel dilemma.[110] The way in which Repington wrote about Ulster's preparedness to fight, his intimate involvement with Carson and Craig, his whole demeanour during the crisis, was entirely pleasing to Northcliffe. But to his editor, plagued as he was by problems and difficulties on every side at Printing House Square, the last thing Robinson required was the military correspondent too obviously 'dabbling in politics'.[111] Repington was instructed to change his focus of attention from the miasma of Ireland's hopelessly muddied politics to the confusions and perils of the Balkans. In sombre prose Repington described the swift descent that began with the murder of Franz Ferdinand at Sarajevo on 28 June 1914, and in little more than a month plunged the whole of Europe into a maelstrom of destruction, chaos, hatred and woe.

VII

Following the two indecisive general elections of 1910, Parliament had been riven by ever more vicious party political strife. When war broke out in August 1914, both front benches effectively created a coalition. Beneath the surface the poison of party antagonism boiled as violently as ever. Unable to find its fullest expression in *Hansard*, the true rage and bitterness of internecine party strife was reflected and enlarged in the columns of the national press.

The newspapers complained of an ill-informed censorship imposed by the Press Bureau, but censorship was readily side-stepped. When abused, the provisions of the badly drafted, though by 1915 draconian Defence of the Realm Acts (DORA), were easily avoided. After 1915, effectively censorship worked, upon a voluntary basis. 'Collusion, if it could be obtained, was always preferable to collision.'[112] The national press, not excluding *The Times*, insisted in exaggerated tones its patriotism and collective sense of responsibility at a time of national peril. Nevertheless, it accepted with alacrity and delight every jot and tittle of misrepresentation that came its way. It was not only profoundly corrupting, it was extremely dangerous. The public wished to know what exactly was going on. They wanted to be assured that their political and military leadership was strong and effective. They sought simple and swift solutions to problems that were grave, novel and frequently intractable. This combination proved fatally attractive to most editors and proprietors. They were deluded into supposing their function was to give the people what the people desired. Feeding upon this delusion, the press seemed to grow in power, importance and influence. When the Liberal Government fell in 1915 it was generally supposed that Asquith had surrendered to press demands. Relations between politicians and journalists dissolved into grubby alliances conducted in an atmosphere of intrigue and manoeuvre. When Lloyd George acceded to supreme political power in late 1916, the new Prime Minister's attitude to the press was simple: 'If you cannot bribe them, bash them.'

Though it might seem paradoxical, Repington, so partisan in the extreme Tory cause for the last two years of peace, with the outbreak of war put aside this prejudice and assumed instead the full armour of the paladin sworn to serve the national cause in a time of grave peril. Disqualified to serve his country and his king as he would have wished, the war enhanced his critical stature and influence as a military commentator. The outbreak of war also made more important and vital Repington's contacts at the War Office. None of this was pleasing to politicians Repington had wounded in the past, or to several high-ranking Army officers who were conscious that Repington knew more about their weaknesses than was healthy for their credit as commanders.

Douglas Haig had always been uneasy in his relations with the press. He harboured a particular distaste for Repington. He was convinced that it was 'a mistake to employ anyone who has had military training to write for a newspaper while war is going on'. If there had to be correspondents, then they should be 'Bennet Burleigh types who will write highly coloured descriptions which are of no military value, but would please 'arriet and sell the newspapers'.[113] This was Haig's old-fashioned and condescending attitude to the press. Personal factors aside, it clearly revealed why he was averse to a correspondent like Repington who generally eschewed descriptive cameos for hard-headed analyses of larger questions of tactics, equipment, strategy, and the relationship between the commander in the field and the politician at home. To Haig, Repington was a 'scoundrel' and a 'sneaking, deceitful fellow'.[114]

Repington was all too well aware of Haig's failings as a soldier, but was as conscious of his many good qualities, and gave to him that same ungrudging public loyalty he showed to all the General Staff. In time, Haig grew to appreciate the advantage of having a powerful advocate in the press. It was not, however, in his character to reciprocate with equal generosity. He would, for instance, have been amazed to have learned that on the eve of war Repington had publicly stated the need to protect military information so as not to give aid to the enemy.[115] Haig never had the wit to recognise what Repington perceived from the first. A 'kept' press which by official fiat suppresses criticism or information about failures and defeats in the field, far from inspiring confidence, inevitably creates suspicion in the public mind.[116]

Not that Repington ever supposed that the press should publish anything and everything. He always deployed the confidential information he was given judiciously, and resented urgings to the contrary from Northcliffe, knowing they were inspired by concern for profit before the national interest.[117] For someone who frequently declared his dislike of politicians in his private correspondence, he remained surprisingly attached to the notion that Westminster and not Fleet Street should be the final arbiter and guide of the nation's fortune. To Northcliffe, Repington seeking his advice as to whether or not he ought to enter the Commons, the better to prosecute the interests of the Army, would have seemed hopelessly sentimental, old fashioned and unrealistic. To the chief proprietor of *The Times*, a pulpit at Printing House Square was a far better place from which to pronounce the gospel of national salvation than the back benches of the House of Commons.[118]

Even as a seasoned correspondent, Repington never quite lost the exaggerated respect for senior commanders instilled in him as a junior officer. Respect was sometimes illumined also by affection, as with Redvers Buller, or the two royal princes, George, Duke of Cambridge, and Arthur, Duke of Connaught. But affection like respect never blinded Repington to professional incapacity. He respectfully deferred to

Roberts's unrivalled knowledge of campaigning in India. The expressions of regard in his letters to Roberts were entirely sincere. He was much moved by the octogenarian warrior's response at the beginning of the Great War.[119] But in their pre-war campaigns concerning invasion and conscription, Repington retained a clear-eyed view of Roberts's true worth, and never supposed him to be other than, 'a good figure-head, *voilà tout*'.[120] Of all his former commanders, Repington was most generous in his judgement of Kitchener. Even failure could not altogether diminish the aura of the Sirdar's glamour. Valentine Chirol's assertion that Repington promoted Kitchener and his schemes in the hope that he might be reinstated in the Army, was no more than a spiteful canard. Repington actually presumed to tell Kitchener to his face, that he would support him when he was convinced he was right, and not otherwise.[121] A conditional offer of support was not calculated to impress Kitchener. He had 'no use for people with views of their own', and assumed that others were there 'to carry out his remedies and never to disagree with him in any way'.[122]

Repington was the first journalist to urge Kitchener's appointment as Secretary of State for War.[123] Relations between the two men were then at their most amicable. On 15 August 1914, Repington published an authoritative account of Kitchener's appreciation of the war and of those measures that the Secretary of State considered necessary to be adopted for its successful prosecution.[124] This was the last time that Kitchener extended such a privilege. For the future, Repington was told, he must work through subordinates at the War House. Knowing the exact measure of the great man's failing as much as his gifts, Repington was obliged to recognise that as Kitchener did 'everything himself, it was useless to talk to anyone else'.[125] This, he judged, a greater disadvantage for Kitchener and the nation than for himself. After all, he still retained access to a retinue of willing, authoritative informants.

The war of movement in the West proved short-lived. The British Army fortified its allotted portion of the Front Line where, for the next three years, it was to be engaged in a virtually static, entrenched exchange with the enemy. August 1914's optimistic forecasts, by December seemed not only redundant but foolish. Repington's first visit to the Front, after the bold certainties of the despatches sent from his library at Maryon Hall on the heights of Hampstead, induced a sense of confusion and humility. 'This war is bigger than anybody,' he told his readers. 'No one dominates it. No one understands it. Nobody can.'[126] But then recalling his earlier injunction that, 'No disaster must affright us,'[127] he thereafter, throughout the war, never ceased to advise, criticise, cajole and lecture. The question that exercised his as everyone's mind was, what, in these unexpected and unplanned for circumstances, ought to be done? It prompted an increasingly acerbic debate that rapidly eroded the fragile alliance between the politicians and the soldiers, the 'frocks' and the 'brasshats'. To add bitterness to confusion, there were Ultra Tories who would never be convinced that a Liberal Government was either fitted for or sufficiently determined to wage war. In every doubt and hesitation they perceived proof that Asquith's administration was adulterated with pacifists and Hun lovers. This nonsense unfortunately appealed to many senior Army personnel, further widening the damaging divide.

Repington was fifty-six when the war began. That is not an age when the habits and loyalties of a lifetime are readily ignored or abandoned. It is hardly surprising that an old soldier, even one who had been obliged to resign his commission more than a decade earlier, should share the predilictions and prejudices of many of his former colleagues now serving in the highest ranks of the Army. With certain exceptions – most notably, Henry Wilson – Repington was in constant contact, by letter or meeting, with the commanders in the field and those who most directly served them. One such regular contact was 'Wully' Robertson, CIGS from 1915 until early 1918. He was the key link between the Cabinet and the British Commander-in-Chief, Haig. Repington had considerable respect for Wully's talents. He never listened, other than very carefully, to what Robertson had to say. But he was not the general's 'client', or 'puppet'. Even a world war was not enough to change an opinionated expert into a compliant acolyte. The two men continued to have differences over strategy and politics.[128] Similarly, although no one had more boundless admiration for his fighting and leadership qualities, or was more fond of 'Johnnie' French than Repington, he never hesitated to criticise the little Field Marshal when he considered he merited censure.

Repington's pre-war career demonstrated that he was not fond of the *genus* politician. Nevertheless he worked willingly with them if he thought that best served the national interest. Thus he had been both sword and shield to many of Haldane's Army reforms. For the most part he was not a slave to party loyalty and recognised there were as many 'damn fools' on one side of the Commons as the other. He preferred to judge men by the measures they promoted rather than the company they kept. But there was no denying that his natural affinity was with the 'brasshats' rather than 'frocks'. This was not simply a matter of habit or atavism. It was the direct consequence of his reading and reflection upon military history and law. He was not a particularly original or boldly exciting thinker either about tactics or weaponry. His strategic insights were shared by most of the British Army's senior personnel. He extolled the Clausewitzian imperative, preaching always the need to concentrate upon the major enemy, Germany. This implied that theatres of war other than the Western Front were diversions. He had been saying as much from January 1906. He might not have approved the strategic straitjacket that some of the staff seemed to welcome as a consequence of the Anglo-French military conversations. But, as he told Esher, the irrefutable logic of involvement 'alongside the French . . . in a land struggle on the continent (is that) . . . the heart of the war is on the Meuse and all else is mere tickling at the extremities.'[129] Thus, the quintessential element in his opposition to campaigning in Salonika or the Dardanelles was that, 'Every man and every shell to the decisive theatre is the principle upon which the war must be fought by England.'[130]

Perversity and innate antipathy undoubtedly explain part of why soldiers and politicians differed, but a major source of confusion and difference was a consequence of them meaning different things when they spoke of 'winning the war'.[131] Clearly Repington not only understood but sympathised with the difficulties the generals faced; he altogether underestimated the problems with which politicians were obliged to struggle.[132] His initial support for Lloyd George rested upon the expectation that here was a Minister who would vigorously pursue the same war aims as the general staff. It was an illusion that was bound to be replaced by disillusion. He supposed Lloyd George had the capacity finally to resolve the manpower problem. But there was not a politician alive who could achieve what Repington required, for his views on manpower were simple, reductionist and one dimensional. He refused to contemplate seriously or sympathetically the political difficulties involved. He never fully appreciated the demands made by industry and the economy for skilled manpower. It was all rather like Haig's inability to understand that the moral certitude that informed his view of strategy and fuelled his optimism and confidence as a commander, offered his troops no shelter from shot and shell. Repington had recognised immediately that a war of attrition necessarily meant a constant demand for new men. 'I doubt', he told Haig, 'whether there is a British general sufficiently fearless of public opinion to incur the losses.'[133] The observation, whether intended ironically or not, was wasted upon Haig. If Repington could perceive the political vulnerability of Haig's strategic concept, why did it not occur to him that no popularly elected political leader could accept, with that same equanimity Haig displayed superintending the shambles of Somme and Passchendaele, the horrific cost in dead and wounded? Repington did not lack imagination. It was not difficult to understand why an alternative strategy that offered the possibility of limiting, even ending the ceaseless carnage in the mud of Flanders, would appeal to a politician. Yet, Repington pledged his public support for more and more of the same under Haig's leadership, a commander that on more than one occasion he had noted was seriously flawed.[134] If there is an answer to the question why Repington acted as he did, then it is provided not by anything Repington wrote but by an admission Robertson made to Haig in September 1917. He said he would stick by the policy of waging war by attrition, 'because I see nothing better, and because my instinct prompts me to stick to it [rather] than to any convincing argument by which I can support it . . . It is not an easy business to see through the problem . . . '[135] Here was the humourless reality behind Bruce Bairnsfather's cartoon character, 'Old Bill', up to his waist in mud and slime, constantly under enemy bombardment, advising a fellow sufferer with Attic wit and faultless logic, 'If you knows a better 'ole . . . !'

In the war Repington fought, the balance of loyalty and comprehension that he struck between 'frocks' and 'brasshats', his appreciation of the workings of the political process at Westminster and in Whitehall, his understanding of the force of public opinion, all these may be judged from the part he chose to play in the extraordinary events of the late spring of 1915, now familiarly known as the Shell Scandal.[136] On several visits to the Front, Repington had noted there was insufficient and inappropriate ammunition, nor were there enough guns and mortars of the right calibre. The British Army was all too well aware of the shortages; the British public knew nothing. Repington knew that it was Kitchener's habit to keep unpleasant facts to himself. He drew the not unreasonable conclusion that the Minister had not told his Cabinet colleagues about the want of shells and suitable guns. He made three attempts to see Kitchener so that he might question him, but failed. When he wrote about the subject for *The Times*, his articles were either censored or spiked.

Repington knew that an Allied offensive was planned for 9 May. He travelled to British HQ, where he was ensconced, not as a war correspondent, for Kitchener had forbidden them, but as the friend of the Commander-in-Chief. Later he wrote that he had hoped to discover that in the months since his previous visits to the Front, the question of ammunition and guns would have been resolved. It had not. Even before the planned major offensive, British troops in the Ypres sector suffered heavy casualties. Repington was convinced this was because of 'the little return we could make on the German guns'. When the planned assault was made, the gains proved insignificant compared with the cost in dead and wounded. What particularly stoked the fires of Repington's indignation was being obliged to see the second battalion of his old regiment receive a severe mauling. Those riflemen who did return attributed their ghastly losses, 'solely to the failure of our guns because there was not enough ammunition'. At the same time he was told by French that instructions had been received to release one fifth of the reserve ammunition to be shipped to the Dardanelles. Repington vowed that his readers should learn the truth of the matter and in a telegraphic message to his editor quoted chapter and verse for his and the Army's discontent.[137]

The next day's message that Repington sent to Printing House Square somehow circumvented the Press Bureau.[138] The military censor, to Repington's fury, had removed much that he had written about the sufferings of the Rifle Brigade. But, what was left was much more significant. It included the all important sentence, 'The want of an unlimited supply of high explosive shells was a fatal bar to our success.' His dramatically headlined account of the action appeared in *The Times*, 14 May 1915. What made the story potentially so damaging for the government was that earlier, Asquith had stated publicly that the Army had sufficient ammunition. The Prime Minister's assurance now appeared to have been deliberately designed to deceive. And as Asquith's assurance had been given with Kitchener's guarantee, effectively, both men were implicated in the deception.

Repington hurried back to London. Like J.A.Spender, he realised that his report had 'put the Government neatly between the devil and the deep sea'.[139] He busied himself, meeting and talking with influential politicians of both parties. First he met Bonar Law, Curzon, Carson and other Tory worthies. He recognised that the issue had gone beyond agitation in the columns of the press. The end game, if played properly at Westminster, might destroy Kitchener and Asquith. The two men's political fortunes were bound together. Asquith's credibility as the nation's wartime leader was sustained by the basilisk-like presence of Kitchener in the Cabinet. From conclave with the Tories, Repington next hurried to a secret meeting at Lord Riddell's house with Lloyd

George.[140] The next day, Repington sent the little Welshman a letter apprising him of the documents it was critical that he should demand, and also of Bonar Law's exact intentions.[141] Two more days elapsed before the Liberal administration collapsed and was replaced by a coalition. Politically, both Kitchener and Asquith had been fatally wounded. But, in the best tradition of cartoon heroes, at the last moment they had leapt free, Asquith retaining the Premiership and Kitchener awarded the Garter.

In the account he later published of these events, Repington made no attempt to disguise an almost child-like delight and certainty that his efforts had been, 'largely responsible for blowing away the Government'. Was this large claim true? The events have been examined many times in minute detail. Historians, as they will, have reached a variety of conclusions. None has attached quite so much importance to Repington's role as he allowed himself.[142] What may be said with certainty, however, is that the part he played was vital and much exceeded that of a glorified messenger boy for French's discontent. It is a mistake to suppose that because on this, as on other occasions, he accepted, even recruited the aid of others, he was not his own man. There can be no better illustration of Repington's intransigent independent spirit than the way he reproached Northcliffe for his exaggerated campaign of vilification against Kitchener in the *Daily Mail*. He correctly pointed out it would only redound to Kitchener's advantage. No member of the Harmsworth clan ever took lightly the criticism of an employee. At their meeting, 'Repington . . . was timorous of criticism . . . desirous of currying favour at all times with the heads of the Army . . . resented being overborne by Northcliffe . . . a spiteful and vindictive man. Afraid to hit out straight but not above petty scandal, innuendo and indeed, misstatement.'[143] Northcliffe's biographers quote with relish this memorandum of the meeting written by Leicester, the youngest Harmsworth sprig, a not particularly talented, melancholic, undistinguished, Liberal MP, always keen to curry his eldest brother's favour. The note is nothing but an unimaginative rehash of very stale victuals and offers no insight into Repington's motivation. Princelings of the Harmsworth dynasty were more sensitive to supposed acts of *lèse majesté* than the 'Chief'. With so much else to occupy him Northcliffe soon forgot the incident. So long as this too-clever-by-half Colonel that he employed could shake the political firmament with a story, that served his purpose admirably. It would be soon enough to discard Repington when what he wrote no longer enhanced Northcliffe's influence or boosted the sales and profits of his newspaper.

To cross swords with the owner of his newspaper was far more perilous than to criticise a politician. Yet it was not at Printing House Square, but Westminster, where Repington's influence was enormously enhanced. John Dillon, the Irish leader, described him as, 'the twenty-third member of the cabinet'.[144] It was not intended as a compliment, but Repington would have been less than human had he not succumbed, if only momentarily, to sensations of *hubris*. The temptation to engage once more in a campaign for conscription proved to be irresistible. Asquith remained loyal to the old Liberal prejudice against the idea of a nation in arms. 'So long as we stand together', he reminded Kitchener, 'we will carry the whole country with us. Otherwise, the deluge!'[145] The unintended prophetic vision of Kitchener's imminent watery fate was unfortunate. For that matter, there was little time left for Asquith at 10 Downing Street. He was replaced by David Lloyd George as Prime Minister on 7 December 1916.

Once, Repington had been extravagant in his praise of Lloyd George. He had expected that the little minister would achieve much by his demonic energy and will.[146] But, as Lloyd George drew ever closer to the top of the greasy pole of supreme political power, so Repington's public affirmations of faith faded. In his writing, Repington seemed incapable of restraining an impatient, hectoring tone. If he aspired to influence Lloyd George, it was hardly politic to be so obviously abrasive in his comments, denouncing politicians as 'ignorant amateurs', hopelessly incapable of understanding strategy, guilty of 'cowardice' for failing to grapple manfully with the supply of trained soldiers for the front line. Throughout the autumn of 1916, in the columns of *The Times*, Repington poured out an unremitting torrent of insult, that some would have called calumny, which fell hard upon Lloyd George. In the course of a good humoured private exchange, Lloyd George's tone suddenly harshened, and he warned Repington that he did not intend to bow his knee before the military Moloch and do the bidding of the generals. If his was to be the responsibility, his the blame, then he intended to have his own way.[147] Thus Lloyd George delineated the fault line that was to become an unbridgeable abyss between himself and Repington. 'How do you propose to win the war?', Lloyd George demanded of Repington. 'What do you mean by winning the war?', Repington countered. Lloyd George responded with a legitimate answer for a politician, 'To thrust the Germans out of France and Belgium.' It was not designed to satisfy a soldier. Repington wanted the Germans 'annihilated'. And to make war successfully, he reminded Lloyd George, was not merely a matter of resources, but of resource. 'Who has the strongest will-power? In the language of the prize ring we must keep on punching.'

The rupture between the two was inevitable. Repington, however, did not make the mistake of most soldiers. He never underestimated Lloyd George.[148] A man whose strategic perceptions had determined his 'realistic' view of why it was in Britain's interest to make war on Germany in August 1914,[149] and who had demonstrated an informed interest in strategical options when French had been Commander-in-Chief, was unlikely to accept the advice of Haig and Robertson without demur. And so it was that, after Lloyd George made the political judgement that the cost of carrying on without change was too high, he pursued ideas he had long held. That, for example, it might be possible to get Austria to sue for peace separately. To free resources for other campaigns, he argued that the Allies were overinsured with men and materials on the Western Front. He sought bold new initiatives, such as the blow at the Turkish Empire in the Holy Land. Like the lawyer he was by professional training, he mastered his brief, turning what might have seemed disadvantageous, for example, the Russian collapse, into evidence to strengthen his own case. He recognised that his rise to supreme office had been helped considerably by press support. When it came to Fleet Street, Lloyd George certainly understood the value of big battalions. By a judicious deployment of patronage; minor ministries created here, high sounding offices there, vanities indulged everywhere; he recruited the magnates of the press and their properties to his side. Among the compliant proprietors were numbered Riddell and Beaverbrook, Astor and Northcliffe. The editor of *The Times* was not least among influential journalists and editors who nailed their collective colours to Lloyd George's mast. Throughout 1917, the war within a war continued. Only after Rapallo, and the agreement that a Supreme War Council would be convened, did Lloyd George finally outmanoeuvre the generals. One token of that triumph was the appointment of Henry Wilson, Repington's sworn enemy, as the permanent British military representative. By this time Repington, who saw himself at Printing House Square as, 'left alone to fight the case of the Army',[150] was alienated from all the editorial staff, particularly Steed.[151]

For more than a year Repington's position in *The Times* had grown by degrees, increasingly and more obviously isolated and vulnerable. When Northcliffe abandoned the cause of the General Staff, Repington had not perceived this as necessarily personally damaging. But it certainly emboldened the deputy editor of *The Times*, G.S. Freeman, to be more cavalier and uncaring towards Repington.

He showed no reluctance to read the military correspondent a sharp lesson, that in the hierarchy at Printing House Square, just as in the columns of *The Times*, the editor's or acting editor's opinions and predilections counted far more than those of any correspondent.[152] Robinson seemed to believe that he was treating Repington fairly and appropriately. He wrote to explain to the recently appointed manager, Howard Corbett,[153] that since the beginning of the war he had scrapped a 'very large number of Repington's articles'. This was intended to enhance the military correspondent's reputation. 'Though brilliant he is a very uneven writer and some of his articles would have brought him into contempt.'[154]

Robinson's claim was not entirely spurious. But Repington's articles were more often delayed, mangled or ignored because it was presumed they would cause offence to the editor's highly placed political friends. Repington observed, each passing week brought further confirmation that Robinson simply 'was not big enough'[155] for his job. If this assessment was inspired, understandably enough, in part by pique at the way in which he was being treated, it was nevertheless, accurate and fair. Geoffrey Dawson (as Robinson had now become and is more familiarly known), had a difficult task. He had to cope with Northcliffe's inconsistent incursions. Pushed hither and thither by his proprietor's sometimes irrational demands, Dawson gained little comfort from those he so assiduously dined, lunched and conversed with in the hope they would offer him sound advice. In the face of this confusion and contradiction, the one constant thread that guided him through the maze of war-time politics was his abiding love, loyalty and admiration for Milner. As Repington was not an acolyte of the *religio Milneriana*,[156] his blasphemous scepticism as to Milner's worth had to be laundered or exorcised.

Isolation did not breed doubt in Repington's mind, it served instead to confirm his certainty that he was right and those who disagreed were wrong. Lloyd George and his ministerial minions, to the plaudits of his Fleet Street claque, were interfering in military matters about which they knew next to nothing. They were not only jeopardising the chances of winning the war, they were putting the future of Britain and her Empire at hazard merely to satisfy their vanity. The editor of *The Times* had no business 'coddling' such a purblind administration. *The Times* was no longer independent. It was not acting as the nation's watchdog. It was nothing more nor less than Lloyd George's poodle. Repington found himself thinking the unthinkable: that he should sever his connections with Printing House Square.

A decision was not easily made. No newspaper offered the same prestige, influence, *cachet* as *The Times*. The anonymity of the title 'military correspondent' had long been forfeit to his brilliant writing and, though he would not have admitted it, a flatteringly reassuring notoriety. To leave would probably, almost certainly, prejudice even further his already disastrous finances. For at least four weeks Repington agonised over what might be done for the best. On 18 December, he wrote to Corbett to find out what period of notice he would be required to serve if it came to a parting of the ways[157] He was informed that certain legal ramifications arising from his debt arrangements might well preclude a swift departure. Meanwhile, he sought out potential future employers who would not gag his voice. His conversations with various military friends and contacts, including Haig, Paget, and Frederick Maurice, the DMO, induced in him a growing sense of urgency and panic. On 11 January, Repington received a note from Dawson. The editor was back at work after illness and had begun by publishing the first article of Repington's he laid his hands upon. The assurance that it had been published 'intact'[158] did not mollify Repington. His response was long, irritable in tone and cross-grained in character.[159] . Replying two days later, Dawson adopted a tone of sweet reasonableness, as though he were dealing with a rather obtuse, recalcitrant child. 'You do not suggest an alternative policy . . . what, as a matter of fact is your plan? . . . This is not a simple question to be solved by catchwords . . . I am quite clear how critically serious the situation is . . . It would have been infinitely more serious if *The Times* had lent itself to the kind of raging, tearing quarrel between the Cabinet and the General Staff which you have frequently tried to foment . . .'[160] Though the letter ended on a note of hoped for reconciliation, nothing would have placated Repington's fierce mood. More conversations with friends and a couple of 'pathetically silly leaders' in *The Times* fortified his sense of righteousness. He would have stormed into Dawson's room, but he was kept waiting – a long time. That did not improve his humour. In his diary, Dawson wrote, 'The final breach . . . Repington has been trying to pick a quarrel on patriotic grounds! He came to see me and began to bluster about this, so I told him not to violate his conscience by remaining another day.'[161] As was his invariable habit, Dawson, at a later date, wrote up his brief diary entry. In this extended account he insisted that he had not been convinced that Repington's rancour had anything to do with a patriotic concern for his (Dawson's) failings as an editor. Rather 'His real reason was, I think, partly financial (though we have treated him very well), and partly my refusal to publish all the articles that he wrote or even the whole of every article . . . He appeared within a couple of days in a whole syndicate of papers here and in America, showing that his final quarrel had long been pre-arranged.'[162] Later that month, Dawson wrote to Haig. A 'mutual friend had suggested he ought to know the truth about Repington's resignation'. In the circumstances 'truth' was a strange word to use. The letter was excessively long and detailed, yet it reduced Repington's supposed reason for leaving *The Times* to an overwhelming concern for his pocket. The letter's tone was snide and calculating.[163] Unfortunately for Repington's reputation, the official *History of The Times* based its account of these events on Dawson's later recollections. The better to damn Repington, for good measure, it added by implication, the long exhausted and false rumour that Repington's articles required censoring because he was inclined to provide information that was of value to the enemy.[164] Repington's association with Dawson ended with a petty recriminatory exchange occasioned by Dawson's unwillingness to publish Repington's letter of resignation.[165] This altercation was to no one's credit and provided a sad finale to a partnership begun so amicably less than six years earlier. Dawson remained editor another thirteen months. He resigned in February 1919, unable any longer to tolerate Northcliffe. Buckle supposed that Dawson's editorship during the war had been a 'magnificent performance'.[166] The compliment was not deserved. Dawson had allowed *The Times* to become a government organ, no longer independent but the uncritical, servile, public chorus to the deeds of Lloyd George and Alfred Milner.[167] The general perception of Repington's resignation was that he had been the first of the many victims of Northcliffe's megalomania.[168] Repington blamed Dawson. But the editor had been merely the agent. The true instigator of Repington's fall was Milner.

Milner had always taken a professional interest in the press from the time that, as a young man, he had worked with W.T. Stead on the *Pall Mall Gazette*. All his political life he valued easy access to a compliant press. When he had become a member of Lloyd George's small, inner Cabinet, he at first championed the General Staff's strategic views. Then, by degrees, in 1917 he came to believe that the soldiers were deluded to suppose that the war would be won on the Western Front.

His Damascene conversion was conveniently recorded for posterity by Hankey after, 'a jolly little walk and talk' in late September, along the banks of the river Dwyfor.[169] There could have been no better place than the Prime Minister's spiritual home, for a conversion of such great significance. It assured eventual success for Lloyd George's strategic views. Derby, the man Milner was to replace as Minister for War, was disconcerted by Milner's changed attitude. The way in which 'he continually sneered at the soldiers as if they were all damned fools,' Derby confided to Esher, was 'intolerable'. Derby also noted a new and significant alliance: Milner and Henry Wilson. It was a combination that Derby did not trust.[170] It was certainly not calculated to win Repington's approval. The most politically astute general in constant conclave with the strongest member of Lloyd George's Cabinet meant that Repington's censures were unlikely to go unnoticed. The day after Repington's final stormy meeting with Dawson, the editor reported to Milner. The Secretary of State, in his turn, informed the Prime Minister that 'Geoffrey Dawson has got rid of Repington. [He] has been, as you know, very mischievous . . . [and] . . . lately been disposed to run the extreme military view . . . that the whole mischief lies in a *fainéant* Government which won't take the necessary steps to provide sufficient 'cannon fodder'. Repington will no doubt now, be up to some devilry in other quarters.'[171]

Milner clearly knew the nature of his man. Repington had not been idle since his eviction from Printing House Square. He had been sounding out opinion. It had been suggested to him that it was about time he repeated his 'indiscretion about the shells . . . The War Office had failed to move the Government from its folly . . . The only chance of averting defeat was for me and some honest editor to speak out.'[172] Repington was no longer downcast. He was his old, incorrigible self.

VIII

Departure from *The Times* was as much a watershed in Repington's life as had been his resignation from the Army. In 1918, as in 1902, there was a tragic strand in the sudden change in his fortunes. Once more he had been betrayed as much by serious flaws in his own character, as by the perfidy of compliant former colleagues and friends. Repington's voice ceased only temporarily. When it clamoured from the columns of the *Morning Post*, it had changed. It was raucous, intemperate, partisan and its primary intent seemed to be to stir up trouble.

His first article in the *Morning Post*, was published without reference to the censor. 'We wondered whether one or both of us would be put in prison.'[173] Clearly the association with Gwynne had induced a kind of hysteria where martyrdom was an accepted political tactic. Gwynne was an experienced, able journalist. His great failing was a never to be assuaged interest in shaping national politics rather than editing his newspaper. Squinting at the world from the aggressively right wing *Morning Post* afforded a very particular, political perspective. Gwynne's views were further refracted by days spent in endless cabals and cliques with frustrated politicians. He had come to suppose that the governance of war-time Britain had been surrendered 'into the hands of a Junta of Press magnates with a bit of a scoundrel on the top'.[174] He was everlastingly seeking someone to take the helm from Lloyd George. For a time he was even prepared, encouraged by Margot, to contemplate the possibility of Asquith's return to Number 10. Repington was arraigned as being an active and enthusiastic plotter in these intrigues, and found guilty by association. It had been sufficient for him to be seen attending a social engagement with his long-time friends, the McKennas, for Robert Sanders, ex-Tory whip and chairman of his party, to adduce 'Asquith and Repington were playing the same game.'[175] All that consumed Repington's interest and passion in early 1918 was the vigorous promotion of the generals and the denigration of the Cabinet.

Gwynne appreciated the value of his new colleague. 'He is the best military writer in Europe,' he insisted to Lady Bathurst. His 'ability as a writer on military matters is simply invaluable to the *M[orning] P[ost]*.' And while the *Post*'s owner continued to fret about the new military correspondent's suitability, the editor kept bestowing accolades to his genius. He admitted that he did not like Repington personally, and thought 'his vanity did show itself rather nakedly'. To lose Repington, however, would be 'a terrible blow . . . a very heavy blow to the paper'.[176] The *Morning Post*'s proprietor remained uncertain of Repington's discretion in the face of assertions by Lloyd George and his ministers that, as in the past, the military correspondent irresponsibly published information helpful to the enemy. Finally she wrote to Haig. He reassured her unequivocally that there was no substance in the claim. 'Colonel Repington has rendered a very great service not only to the Army but to our country.'[177] Repington continued his verbal bombardment upon the 'absurd arrangements' the government favoured, that put at hazard the fortunes of the British Army and the prospects of victory. 'If they want to shut my mouth', he told Maurice, 'they will have to lock me up. I propose to continue my criticisms without allowing myself to be deterred by political persecution . . . Robertson has suffered in a good cause and has done his duty, as I have tried to do mine.'[178] Martyrdom was clearly desired. The government, after hesitation and several false starts, in the face of conflicting legal advice, charged Repington and his editor with a technical breach of the Defence of the Realm Acts. At Bow Street Magistrates' Court they were duly charged, found guilty and fined one hundred pounds each plus costs. Their appearance at the court – Repington in uniform – drew larger crowds than the notorious wife murderer, Dr Crippin.[179]

The success of the German offensive of late March 1918, and the subsequent calamitous retreat of the British Fifth Army under Gough, appeared sufficient justification for Repington's frequently declared apprehension about insufficient forces and reserves on the Western Front and similarly, for his constant criticism of the government's handling of the manpower problem and its 'vendetta' with the General Staff. Repington's verbal barrage reached its apogee shortly after Milner replaced Derby as Secretary for War. In an article on the *Morning Post*'s leader page, 26 April 1918, Repington tore into Milner, 'Next only to the Prime Minister it is to Lord Milner that we owe the cutting down of our infantry . . . the want of drafts, and the defeats and losses of the past month . . . The infatuation and ignorance of the War Cabinet and its contempt of the best military advice are the sole and only causes of the present crisis on the Western Front . . . It is certainly astonishing that one so fully responsible as Lord Milner . . . should be placed in charge of the Army which, by these decisions, has been brought into deadly peril.' Lloyd George was a sufficiently dangerous opponent: taking on Milner was a disastrous miscalculation.

On 12 May, in the *Observer*, at Astor's behest but at Milner's instigation, J.L. Garvin 'exposed' Repington. In the space of two pages of misrepresentation and deliberate lies, Garvin 'thoroughly and ruthlessly' destroyed Repington's reputation. In A.M. Gollin's precise and accurate assessment, it was 'the perfect Establishment "Job"'.[180] Repington continued to fulminate against Lloyd George. He was involved in the Maurice affair,[181] but only as a bit player, and in any event, his sting was drawn by the censor. The Maurice Debate in May, intended as a mine to explode under Lloyd George, fizzled out as little more than a damp squib. Though his writing in the *Morning Post* did not suggest any change in his intransigent mood, his private letters reveal that his domestic circumstances and growing financial plight impinged more and more upon his thoughts.[182] There were frequent trips to Europe to monitor the war's progress, and after November 1918, to investigate the peace proposals. He was punctilious in producing his copy for Gwynne, but there was not the old enthusiasm. He was engaged in various schemes that might bring in some much needed cash. His first volume of memoirs, *Vestigia*, covering the pre-war years, was published, in 1919. In 1920 he published, in two volumes, his diary of the war. In the previous months, this had been the project which had absorbed much of his attention, his time and his hopes. Its appearance created a sensation. Its value as an historical record and military commentary was immediately recognised. But it attracted sharp criticism and caused much offence in certain sections of society. It did not bring the hoped for relief from financial chaos.

After Garvin's inspired attack, Repington never again touched or irritated the raw nerve of government. He was a spent force. In late April 1920 he made a half-hearted effort to examine the possibility of returning to Printing House Square. Dawson had gone: he wrote to Northcliffe with just a hint of the old fire, bombast and optimism, 'I have observed with regret the articles that have appeared in The Times on military and strategic matters, and do not like to see the result of my many years of work on the paper thrown away . . . I found out L.G. before you did and in my two volumes of experiences . . . you will find the whole of L.G.'s sins traced out and severely dealt with . . . I feel that you and I have the same views and the same objects . . . If you do not want me to come back I propose to approach the many papers[183] which asked me to come to them when I left you . . . This letter is merely to give you my general views and to ask for yours.' There had been a strange echo of the letters Repington had written to Moberly Bell when he had first sought a post at Printing House Square, 'When I see our defence affairs in order, and L.G. in the street, my idea is to take post in Paris as correspondent, and as I know all the leading French statesmen, politicians, soldiers etc., and have gained their confidence, I believe that I could make for the paper a bigger position than Blowitz ever made for The Times of old.' Brave words, ancient sentiments, but to no avail. A dismissive reply from Northcliffe slammed the door in Repington's face.[184]

Viscount Burnham, owner of the *Daily Telegraph*, proved a better friend, offering Repington the post of military correspondent which was accepted with alacrity. There would be no clashes with this proprietor for he was in tune with editorial policy. Repington could not be the *Telegraph*'s Paris correspondent.[185] Instead, Burnham offered him as his immediate task a roving commission in the diplomatic field. Old enemies, like old friends, watched and waited to see what Repington might make of his new appointment.[186] He spent most of the year travelling through Europe meeting and talking with those who had inherited the new world created out of the havoc of the old. Then to the New World across the Atlantic, to attend the Washington conference on naval arms limitation. His impressions he gathered, in *After the War: a diary*, published in 1922. It was clearly designed as a follow up to his war-time diaries, but it did not enjoy their acclaim. In the preface he had written that his mission was to help his readers 'judge the future direction of foreign policy . . . now that all was changed'. He added that it was 'useless to content oneself with archaic notions'. But the *leitmotif* that runs through the diary is a regret for the old days and old ways, gone beyond recall. Watching the company dancing at the Ritz he recalls Vienna in 1815 after Napoleon's fall. Now another new chapter of history was beginning, 'undignified, indecent and vulgar . . . The war seems to have killed off everyone except the vulgarians.' Visiting Vienna provoked the inevitable sad thought, 'The old glory has departed. There is neither fashion, taste nor elegance. It is the end of a period.'[187] America was 'interesting', but it was also infernally stuffy and consumed by an impossible, unending rush.

Repington's last substantial military writing, *Policy and Arms*, a collection of essays about old quarrels and stale issues, with a few inspired glimpses of the future,[188] was published in 1924. It attracted little notice and no critical acclaim.

While in America, Repington wrote to Burnham that he had 'lost the taste for a hectic social life'.[189] His Hampstead home had long been sold to keep the duns at bay. The conditions of his daily life and comfort were much changed for the worse but he did not grumble. He was in part sustained by the eternally optimistic belief that one day soon he would produce a book that would solve all his financial worries.[190] He abandoned his flat in London and joined Mary and their daughter Laetitia in their villa at Hove. The years of frenetic activity and socialising had finally caught up with him. A serious heart condition was diagnosed. It proved a better friend than might have been supposed. He dreaded the slow, inevitable decline into somnolent senility, but avoided that fate, dying of a cerebral haemorrhage on 25 May 1925. On his desk, where he had been working, that day's *Telegraph* contained a long, perceptive and generous appreciation he had written about his old friend and comrade in arms, Field Marshal Lord French.

IX

Posterity has not dealt kindly with Repington's reputation. He was fond of noting how the great were humbled by the defects of their qualities. This was as true of him. He had great faults as well as great virtues. But this is neither a sufficient nor a necessary reason to underestimate his contribution as a writer on military affairs. All truths are partial and selective. The epitaph inscribed upon his tomb emphasises those qualities in the man and his work that make Charles à Court Repington's memory worthy of our respect.

THE MOST BRILLIANT MILITARY WRITER OF HIS DAY
HIS PEN WAS ENTIRELY DEVOTED TO THE SERVICE OF
ENGLAND AND THE ARMY THAT HE LOVED

Correspondence

I
Repington to Winston Churchill

3, Victoria Road,
Kensington,

[Holograph]

5 December 1903

Many thanks for your letter. I am very glad you and your friends[1] are going to keep in close grip of the Army question.

Your suggestion that we should show how much of your programme has been accepted and how much still awaits acceptance is an excellent one. Would that not enter very well into your next speech?

I am just off on a visit, so have not time to offer you many suggestions for your Whitby speech. I think Arnold Forster is on the side of the angels and hope we may all be able to back him up. No one wants to carp, but when one had such a hopeless creature as Brodrick in office it was folly to keep silence.

I think we ought to engarland Arthur Balfour with the freshest and finest roses. Though he talks a good deal of nonsense about the war, he is absolutely sound on the future and I consider that we owe him an immense debt of real gratitude for taking the lead in defence questions. It was certain that his intelligence would quickly show him the follies of the old W.O. gang once he had time to look into the question.

Where I think our policy is at fault is in India. We are practically transferring the 'Home Defence' rubbish to India and an effort is being made to induce Balfour to consent to a considerable increase in India with a view, solely so far as I can judge, to a huge deployment on the North West frontier. It is not in our interest to attack Russia there if war comes upon us. I am opposed to the Curzonian Raid on Thibet, because once in that country I see no reason why we should halt until we touch the Russian posts seven hundred miles to the North West.[2]

Is our military capital sufficient for the policy of adventure in India? I think not and I shall be surprised if Arnold Forster has not to admit a practical failure of the schemes of the past three years.

I also think you ought to demand that the Government withdraws Bob's idiotic Army Orders about the Volunteer camps. It is certain that this withdrawal will follow the report of the Commission now sitting and many Volunteer C.O.'s are only getting men not to retire by something like a definite promise that the obnoxious rules will be withdrawn.[3] The poor recruiting and the constant wastage in the Volunteers play the game of the conscription gang: we can at least arrest the drain on the Volunteers. I know that you are not opposed to conscription in principal. Nor am I, but it is clear that it is not suitable for foreign service and not required for home defence. Therefore, why should we cry for it?

I am engaged upon writing the History of the War for the "Times" and am doing the advance to Komatipoort and the entire history of the guerilla war under K. It is a precious tough job and takes up most of my time. If you meet any folk who have useful information do ask them to communicate with me.

My best wishes to Beckett. Your free-food friends have a very hard job before you and my belief is that Joe will beat you. You can't compete with wholesale bribery even though the payments are made with post dated stumers.[4]

Churchill Archive, Cambridge, W.S. Churchill Papers, CHAR 2/3, 128–9

2
Repington to Lord Esher

Private

29, Victoria Road,
Kensington,
W.

[Holograph]

4 February 1904

I beg to enclose a letter I sent to Spender yesterday. In consequence of our meeting to-day I have asked that it should be withdrawn, but possibly your committee may care to glance at it.

With regard to your request that I should send you my views as to the present staff of the I.D., I have carefully gone through the list of officers now there and am appalled at the change since my day. Out of 32 officers now in the division there are only 12 whom I should retain were I in charge of the branch. I give their names in the order I place their merits.[5]

Mobilization

Colonel P. Lake CB
Major A.G. Dallas

Intelligence

Colonel W. Robertson DSO
Lt. Col. I. Haldane DSO
Major E. Hills (for mapping)
Captain Holman DSO (for Russia)
Lt. Col. Callwell RA (a very able theorist)
Major A. Lyndon Bell E. Kents
Lt. Col. F.J. Davis G.Guards
Captain R.S.G. Gorton RA
Captain H.C. Lowther DSO S. Guards
Lt. Col. G. Milne DSO RA

Also, an attached officer Major the Hon. H. Yarde Buller RA who is under-studying for Paris but after Teck's appointment to Vienna, we shall not get trained men for their billets unless you put your foot down. How the rest of their crowd now at Winchester House were jobbed in, I can't think. I suggest you call for Major Turner's Staff College Report and then enquire who appointed him to the I.D. I don't know him.

This is only a personal estimate which you will of course only take for what it is worth, but it is quite impartial and given without fear or favour. I believe Lake's scheme was the basis of Mr Brodrick's Home Defence muddle of 1901, but I am told that Lake's branch had only worked out the scheme as an academic exercise and were astounded when it was swallowed whole: that point you would learn from Lake: he is a good man. I confess that before I went into this matter for you I was not aware how many fifth rate men had crept in. Now that you have destroyed that sink of iniquity, the Military Secretary's office, I feel sure we shall go ahead.

There are several real good men in the D.G.O.'s branch, Sir H. Brackenbury would give you their names.

P.S. On reading this over I should add that I do not know what Yarde Buller may be like on paper but he was under my observation in the Sudan and South Africa and did right well. Trotter is good for boundary commissions. Black, of the Indian Army, is a good man, but he has just left the I.D.

Churchill Archive, Cambridge, Esher Papers, ESHR 10/24

3
Repington to Esher

<u>Private</u>

29, Victoria Road,
Kensington,
W.

[Holograph]

9 February 1904

You may care to have my opinion on the new Army Council, as I know all the members intimately and have served with one and all in peace and war.[6]

Individually, the selections are admirable. Collectively the council is weak and will, in my humble judgement be dominated by Douglas who is by far the strongest character of the four.

I do not notice that any one of the four military members except Murray has ever had any experience of great problems of national defence, or has a mind trained to the consideration of such problems, or has ever, at any time, been in touch with naval thought.

No doubt, if Clarke becomes Permanent Secretary, the Council, will be as wax in his hands, to mould as he pleases, subject to Arnold-Forster's inspirations, but I should not anticipate much valuable initiative from the Council in these matters. You will never get Douglas beyond the regulations: they are his Bible, and his God, Lyttleton, good man as he is, knows practically nothing of great problems of Imperial defence and less than that about the problems which confront foreign strategists and military administrators, which we have, after all, to consider in our own arrangements. Murray's opinion on these points is the best worth having among the military members, but he is very cautious and reserved and it will have to be dragged out of him.

I do not think these men are capable of making that break with the past that the new ideas require. They are all too disciplined and too formed. I consider it a great mistake that Kitchener is not included. He is the only man we have, save Clarke, who is quite in the first rank, and he alone, on the Army Council, would have had the pluck, knowledge and authority to work out the details of the great principles your epoch making committee had laid down. I have sent a note to the papers on the Council with all desire of supporting you and Arnold-Forster. This is a P.S. to it and is only for you and your committee for what it is worth.

I may add that, so far as I can discover, all my friends who ragged Brodrick so severely last session are heartily with you and Mr. Arnold Forster.

Churchill Archive, Cambridge, Esher Papers, ESHR 10/24

4
Repington to Raymond Marker

<u>Private</u>

3, High Beach,
Felixstowe.

[Holograph]

25 August 1904

I am quite with you on all points. As to the Chief of Staff I spoke out most strongly on this point when examined by the Esher Committee and told them they would wreck the whole affair if they did not put K. in. Their point was that he did not want to come; to that I could say nothing as I have never bothered K. with letters. I told the Committee that I considered that there was a cabal against K. among the old military women in London and that it would be a disgrace if anyone but K. became Chief of Staff. I also wrote in the press recommending K. the Duke and Clarke for the three chief places; they took the two minor appointments and not the other. Also they were so foolish as to make the Duke practically C in C and to make the whole reform appear a gross job to oust Bobs and put in the Duke; also they pay the Duke more than the C of S which is absurd. No, I can't see where K is to come in at home – that is just where the absurdity of making Lyttelton C of S comes in. All he knows, K has taught him (cricket excluded). We must talk over the question of India.

I shall be back after September 15. My own idea is that I, or someone else, should go to India, ostensibly for manoeuvres, and write a series of articles to the Times setting out the present situation from K's point of view if he would help. It would be useless otherwise. I don't fancy we shall do much good until the Mil. Dept. is knocked on the head.

British Library, Kitchener-Marker Papers, Add. MSS., 52277B., ff. 4–6

5
Repington to Esher

29, Victoria Road,
Kensington,
W.

[Holograph]

18 September 1904

Many thanks for your kind letters. It is a very great satisfaction to have won the approval of such a good judge. I felt nearly certain that you would support the idea of an historical section, for I told Ellison some time ago that I intended to raise the question and found that he was quite in sympathy. I recognise, of course, that your Commission had so many more urgent questions to deal with that you could not waste time in elaborating every detail. I raised the point officially four years ago. Ld. Roberts supported it, but some idiot at the W.O. buried it.

I certainly did not touch the question with any personal views relating to my own interests. I should hesitate to part with my newly-found independence and nothing would induce me ever again to become a subordinate of the W.O. My idea is that the historical section must be imperial or nothing and should be under the Defence Committee. Amery is, I believe with you: he seems to think that there should be two branches, but I have not had an opportunity of discussing it with him. I have naturally based my proposals on military grounds, but I daresay you will see that my dream is to create rather Imperial history: something to bring before the eyes of all our people at home and abroad the inter-dependence of the different parts of the Empire based on the teachings of history. To do this you must get hold of the best men in all classes and in all parts of the Empire and pay them, not at fixed rates, but at their actual value.[7]

You ask whether I get information from the Intelligence Branch. Did anyone ever get anything from it except a permanent official or a Royal Commission? It does not exist for the Army or the public and is merely a vast storehouse of undigested information. But I will tell you a story. I was asked to write a monthly critique of the war for the Army Journal.[8] I accepted, more as a duty than a pleasure, and certainly not for profit, since the pay offered was one quarter of the amount I should have received from a magazine. I made it a condition that I should be allowed to see the reports of our officers with the two armies undertaking to restrict the use of information to the columns of the Army Journal. This was granted by a letter of Aug. 15. A month later I received letter enclosed dated Sept. 15. and I at once replied that under the circumstances, I declined to write on the war for the Journal. I did not give my reasons, but you will understand that I do not propose to waste my time for an office that does not know its own mind for a month together, and that 'withholds' the best information at its disposal out of sheer, stupid secretiveness. We pay a sound sum for our officers with the armies and my hope was that I might be of some use in drawing conclusions based on the best evidence available. Not at all, replied the W.O., confine yourself to what Tom, Dick or Harry say in the Daily Mail and don't expect to see what Nicholson and Ian Hamilton think about it all. You have, in short, reformed the W.O. but not all its members, the germs of stupidity have as fast hold on Pall Mall as the bugs in a barrack in Upper Burma. It is also comical to find that du Boulay was offered his new appointment and accepted it without knowing that he was to be the Editor of the Army Journal. He told me this himself. Surely you do not send out for a blacksmith from Collander and then ask him to re-set her ladyship's diamonds!

You are right about the Westminster article: it was poor stuff indeed, but Spender was away and I was too busy to attend to the manoeuvres. As to the manoeuvres, you know my views. K. of K. should have been Chief of Staff, with his own men under him.

N.G. is a sound officer and fine judge of cricket: his department of staff duties is very weak.

Many thanks for your criticism upon the 'National' map: if I write again for Maxse I will make that good: I was away at the sea and the map was prepared before the article was written.[9]

There is very much I would like to discuss with you about A-F's plans: the principles are admirable but the details hopelessly bad. It is a compromise between the old and the new, in fact, new wine in old bottles. I hope you may inspire Amery to take up his pen again: it is a thousand pities that he is tied down to the history just now. Our Haliburtons and Knoxs are left in possession of the field.[10]

Churchill Archive, Cambridge, Esher Papers, ESHR, 10/24

6
Repington to Sir Henry Campbell-Bannerman

29, Victoria Road,
Kensington,
W.

[Holograph]

11 October 1904

If you are likely to be in London soon I should greatly value a few minutes conversation on Army matters, as owing to your absence at the end of the session, I am not well acquainted with your views upon Arnold Forster's plans, or even with your reading of the nature of the understanding given not to proceed with certain of them until Parliament was consulted – a point upon which opinion appears to be divided.

Now that my "Times" work on the Eastern War may become less pressing before long, I hope to resume the "Westminster" work upon Army matters, and I do not want to run any hare that the party will not want to chase when in power.

British Library, Campbell-Bannerman Papers, Add. MSS., 41237, ff. 295–6

7
Repington to Raymond Marker

Private

29, Victoria Road,
Kensington,
W.

[Holograph]

8 November 1904

I have been asked by Spender to write some articles on the Army in the 'Westminster' with a view of crystalizing Liberal opinion upon certain points. I have hitherto avoided Arnold Forster's schemes as I was in sympathy with his principles and hoped he might change the pernicious system by which he proposed to put them into practice. But he seems to be set upon his errors so I fear the time has come to give him a dusting.

Now I propose to refer to the Indian questions, not at length but incidentally. Do you know that K has been – as I am told – in touch with the heads of the Liberal party and that they know, or think they know, that he would chuck soldiering to become S. of S. for War in a Liberal Administration? The idea is that he might confine himself to his work and take no part in any political debates and care no dot whether the Church were disestablished or anything else. Do you think K. would take this line and would he go on half-pay or what?

I do not find any objection to the idea in principle, but I am not sure how it will be viewed by the Radical wing when the news gets about. Would the gain of such a capable administrator compensate for the loss of K. as C. in C. in a great war? If the Government were over thrown would K. have gained or lost?

The home dovecots seem greatly fluttered by K's Army Order of which they were in abject ignorance. Do you suppose he has effected a coup d'état in the Council and is it the whole scheme he desired that has been accepted? I should be glad to hear any news you have on these points. There remains of course The Mil. Member question. So far as I can gather all except the old Indian warriors are with K. on this point.

I also find that what the papers would call 'influential court aides' are opposed to K. as S. of S. but that would be disposed of if K. went on half pay or left the Army as some declare he intends to do.

British Library, Kitchener-Marker Papers, Add. MSS., 52277B., ff. 12–13

8
Repington to Esher

Private

29, Victoria Road,
Kensington,
W.

[Holograph]

13 December 1904

Will you lunch with me at the Carlton Friday or Saturday 1.30? I should like to have another talk. I hear rumours that H.M. has sent for K. to come home. Is there anything in it?

I am sending you the conclusions of my W[estminster] G[azette] articles. They will be revised and published before Parliament meets and if you can suggest anything (over and above a muzzle for Lyttelton) I shall be grateful.

I am also sending you the articles on the defence of India which I have written in the Times, and a reprint of my 'Soul of a Nation' which may interest Lady Esher.

Churchill Archive, Cambridge, Esher Papers, ESHR 10/25

9
Repington to C.F. Moberly Bell

Private

29 Victoria Road,
Kensington, W.

[Typed with holograph signature]

18 December 1904

I want to discuss the future with you, but do not be alarmed, as I shall only deal with that infinitely small area of it comprised in my work for you.

I take it that my work anent the war is nearly concluded and that, relatively speaking, the amount of material you will require on this subject in the future will be inconsiderable.

Do you and Mr Buckle wish me to continue to write for you, and if so, are you prepared to give me some sphere of influence or hinterland to exploit? You see, it is this way. I have a horror of plucking and dressing other people's pigeons and am the last person in the world to desire to intrude upon other people's domains. There are an infinity of questions connected with Imperial Defence that I should like to deal with from time to time, but the proper study of these matters, collection and sifting of information, and correspondence with the big people, mean much work, and I am not at present clear whether you have any desire for me to undertake the task, or whether, in consequence, it is worth my while to worry about it. For instance I was aware some days ago that the question of the guns had been settled behind Arnold Forster's back[11] during his absence in the north and without the knowledge of the Army Council but I have no mandate to deal with this question. I find no difficulty in obtaining information from all the best sources, but at present have only scratched the surface and don't know whether it is worth my while to dig. Now digging is a laborious affair and takes time and organization. If I do not have some claim pegged out by you I have two alternatives. One is to work for other private people, or for Government. I have had various offers to write for the press nearly all of which I have refused, and I have had certain suggestions made to me from high quarters to take up work under the Government and have replied provisionally that £10,000 a year and a Dukedom would not at present tempt me to sacrifice my independence of official control.

The second alternative is to revert to the soil and to manage personally the Warwickshire estate to which I recently succeeded, instead of entrusting the business to an estate and a mining agent, both excellent people, but perhaps costing me something by the withdrawal of my continuous supervision.

My own preference would be to continue to work for you, to be allowed to take up matters connected with the Army, Imperial

Defence, and the many subsidiary questions dependent upon those subjects, and to write for you, not to order, but when the spirit moves me, since I am incapable of doing my best work under any other conditions and I am no good at all for night work at the office. I should like to make a semi-permanent engagement with you, upon a financial basis of the sum I have earned by my pen during the current year, or any other we may mutually agree upon, subject to a month's notice of withdrawal from the contract on either side, which is, I believe, your custom. This would entail, of course, work for you alone, and would enable me to refuse other offers with a clear conscience. I should, in such case, have to come to an arrangement with Spender, since I wrote for him before I wrote for you and I could not throw him over until he had found the right man to take my place. It is irksome for me to serve two masters and leads to waste of effort: it is also, I think, journalistically inconvenient. I do not care two straws about politics but I could never undertake to support any scheme of army reform or any measure of Imperial Defence unless I was convinced of its soundness.

I wrote to Buckle some days ago asking if he wished to see me before I left town for Christmas, but as he has not replied perhaps you will show him this letter and let me know so that I may plan out my time for next year.

Please allow me to add that I am deeply sensible of the kind approval and support which you, Mr Buckle and Mr Arthur Walter have given me during the past year and that whether we go on together or whether we do not, I shall look back with great pleasure to the very kind appreciation you have shown for my endeavours to serve you.

The Times Archive, Moberly Bell Papers

10
Repington to General E.T.H. Hutton

Paschoe,
Bow,
North Devon,

[Holograph]

26 December 1904

I have read your letter with interest and also ran through your pamphlet during my journey to the West.

I fancy we are pretty closely in agreement and that the example of what Australia has done under the Commonwealth Government will form a very good argument in the promotion of somewhat similar plans for this country.

I do not at all agree with you as to your best course of action now, though I have no warrant to refer to it.

The Arnold Forster scheme is as dead as Queen Anne so I do not see how you can help to build just now, nor do I think that you will find much pleasure in serving under the Army Council in view of its present management. Ask General French how he likes it! I take it that there will be nothing done now till after the General Election and that then the building will be done in Parliament. There is not one single member in the H. of C. thoroughly acquainted with the Army, its duties or its needs. It is not criticism that is required: we can get tons of that: it is guidance, advice and direction: the utilization of all the talent and energy of the younger members in the right direction. At present, and for want of anyone in the House capable of affording guidance, these young bloods – some very capable men – are inclined to run riot and once committed to silly fads of their own will not easily be turned from them. They would hunt down any fox under a master who would lay them in the right line, but there is no one to do it save Colomb who grows old. Believe me that our Army of the future will be made or marred in Parliament and that is why I hope you will reconsider your views before the General Election is upon us. You are one of the very few soldiers who both knows his business and can express his views in a speech.

British Library, Hutton Papers, Add MSS., 50098, ff. 64–5

11
Repington to Esher

29, Victoria Road,
Kensington,
W.

[Holograph]

2 April 1905

Very many thanks for the papers which reached me tonight on my
return from the country. They appear to me, from a first glance,
rather jejune. I hoped they would say where we want to go and
why we want to go there. The question is not considered from a
sufficiently lofty stand-point – at least, so I gather from a hasty
glance through; but I will study the papers carefully and return
them to you shortly.[12]

I am glad you liked the 'Times' article.[13] I have almost given up
A.F. He is a shifty customer. I expect that K. is right in the main,
but thought it advisable to get all I could from the other side
before moving in the matter and fancy that the Government at
home will have to decide the point after the receipt of the next
mail. We seem to have been on rather dangerous ground with the
Amir.

Churchill Archive, Cambridge, Esher Papers, ESHR 10/25

12
Repington to Raymond Marker

Private

29, Victoria Road,
Kensington,
W.

[Holograph]

17 April 1905

All I knew from my excellent Editor was that "A Soldier" was a
man of whom I entertained a high opinion. His name was little to
me and the only thing I was concerned with was his argument.

But, having said that, let me also congratulate the S. of S. at having two such loyal and intelligent assistants as Shute[14] and you, and let me also add that I felt that you were probably the "Soldier".

I am glad to hear that you did not imply that I wrote the W[estminster] G[azette] article. That was the appearance and I took the opportunity of stating that this was not so as there had been several things in the W.G. which I did not approve, notably a back-handed attack on old Buller who was once my chief. I rather enjoy a spar, especially with such a courteous disputant as you are, but I was too busy last week to carry on the game and I fear that the only thing which is of serious interest to the public is the intention of the S. of S. I wrote to him a month or two ago and told him quite plainly my views on the home-service army. I am afraid that they were distasteful as he did not reply. I certainly feel sure that you are perfectly honest in believing in your Chief's scheme. Can you give me the name of an experienced soldier at the War Office who is in favour of it? I fear that nothing can make it good, also I do not much care for your expression 'dead army': it seems to commit us to a division of the Regular Army, which has no charms for me at all.

I regret that I should have used the word inspired in respect of your first letter if this was not the case, but I considered from what my Editor said that the expression was justified. No, you may not hint that my articles are inspired from any source. I can only tell you what I have told Lord Kitchener; namely that I will support anything when I am convinced that it is sound, and not otherwise, and what I will not do for K. I am not likely to do for anyone else. I take orders from no man and though what I write may have merit or may have none it represents at all events my sincere conviction, independent of all personal, political or other bias. So long as *The Times* allows me to write with absolute independence I shall say precisely what I think: when I am asked to support some scheme in which I do not believe I shall stop writing in *The Times*. I confess that it is vexatious to me to have to oppose Arnold-Forster. He is much nearer to my ideal than any Minister with whom we have been blessed in our day and if he would only have frankly abandoned his home service scheme and based the second line army exclusively on a Militia footing I would have gone on backing him.

I am always at your disposal for a talk, but I shall be away from Thursday to Tuesday 25 April at Felixstowe. Why not come down on Easter Sunday to the Felix Hotel and have a long walk with me on a breezy shore after lunch? If this does not suit, invite yourself to dine here any night that suits you and we will have a good talk.

British Library, Kitchener-Marker Papers, Add. MSS., 52277B., ff. 17–20

13
Repington to James Thursfield

29, Victoria Road,
Kensington,
W.

[Holograph]

1 May 1905

My recollection is that Captain Robinson recalled Captain Bacon's paper to me some two months ago and that I had a talk with Bacon himself on the subject at the Admiralty a day or two before I wrote the article of which you are kind enough to approve. I have had many talks with Spender and he may also have discussed this matter, but, if so, it has escaped my memory. Is it not likely that you drew Robinson's attention to Bacon's paper and that your idea came through him to me? I have for many years past endeavoured to understand the naval point of view in all large questions of strategy and I need scarcely say that I have found your articles and papers of the greatest service in every way. Early in 1903, before I had the pleasure of meeting you, I acknowledged the debt we all owe you in a paper in Blackwood called "National Strategy" where I endeavoured to upset the Brodrickian home defence party. Alas! many of the voluminous notes I had amassed as naval matters were stolen from me by agents of the French police while I was on a mission at the time of the Fashoda affair. It is for this reason alone that I am not able to quote frequently from your past writings and

I can only hope that they will now be of service to the French Naval Intelligence Department!

I have a strong feeling that Bacon's ideas are sound on the point I ventured to discuss. At the same time I have letters from Admirals of repute which, while not distinctly throwing over Bacon, declare that the torpedo has been such a failure during the war that the tactics proposed are not likely to be effective. Nous verrons! Something of the sort will, I think, be attempted though I confess I would not have referred so plainly to the subject had I thought that Rozhenstvensky was about to spend a month in harbour. It is an extraordinarily interesting moment. I think, confident as we may be in our friends, that we must all feel anxious until matters are decided.[15]

The Times Archive, Thursfield Papers, AC96/27

14

Repington to Esher

Private

East Mascalls,
Lindfield,
Sussex.

[Holograph]

18 July 1905

I am in entire agreement with your letter of the 13th and I shall work on your lines. At this moment I am preparing my war articles for publication so I am not producing much. But I am about to attack A-F over his silly experiment of turning eight good into eight bad battalions: it is useless to compromise in order to save A-F's face. I am sick of him and all his works. It is true that he has endeavoured to secure the adhesion of certain so-called leading soldiers to his latest fad. He does this by the disingenuous means of sending them an outline sketch of proposals and of carefully concealing all the real facts from their knowledge. I was with one of them in London yesterday and warned him to some effect. I do not think the man should be allowed to seek advice and supporters outside his recognised colleagues and military advisers: he will throw the whole Army with cliques and parties if this goes on.

I make it a rule never to embroil myself with personal questions, but I confess I feel rabid at the news that Wilson is to succeed Rawly at the Staff College. Wilson is an arch-intriguer and a second-rate place-hunter: if this imposter is to train our future General Staff it will never be trained. I know that Colonel H. Lawson would like the billet and is a first class man in peace and war, in office or in the field. Yet Wilson will beat him, because he has boomed his fool of a General, old Hutchinson, in the press, and has made friends of every Mammon and every unrighteousness. I shall take no steps of course, but it is very disheartening.

The old Times is so Curzon ridden that it is talking rot about the Indian question. I never read more futile nonsense than the Indian press this mail. Not one argument but pails full of blather, blarney and bumcombe. It is poor fun to shoot dead game, but should I not have another cut at them?

I suppose you will be off North soon. I shall keep on pegging away from time to time. If old Roberts had not in his speech flatly contradicted his Rifle Club letter, it might have had more effect. If our so-called leaders would take a strong line and stick to it, something might result, but to hunt with the hare and the hounds and practice the cult of the jumping cat is confusing.

Churchill Archive, Cambridge, Esher Papers, ESHR 10/25

15
Repington to Winston Churchill

Private

East Mascalls,
Lindfield,
Sussex.

[Holograph]

26 July 1905

Thanks for your letter. I see that Rasch asked a question in the House on Monday on the subject of the Indian drafts for the Infantry during 1906–1907. The reply, according to my information which is good, is disingenuous and probably incorrect, but before suggesting a fresh question I will take advice so that you may not be misled by the Government comedians.

The Times is of course a Unionist paper. I do not suppose that the hostility of a political opponent troubles you greatly. So far as I am concerned I do not write to order or support any cause unless I am convinced that it is advisable and sound. I am entirely independent of all persons and parties, and intend to hold to this position with all the tenacity of which I am capable.

Churchill Archive, Cambridge, W.S. Churchill Papers, CHAR 2/23/12

16
Repington to Esher

East Mascalls,
Lindfield,
Sussex.

[Holograph]

21 August 1905

In reading the rules of the new Council of Imperial Defence in Russia, to which I have alluded in this morning's Times, I am struck by the provision that the said Council has not only to lay down the general lines upon which the Ministries of War and Marine are to proceed, but is also authorised to exercise a general control over the measures taken by these Ministries to carry the purpose of the Council into effect.

I cannot help thinking that such a provision would be of very material assistance to us in our troubles, could it in any manner harmonise with our tyrannical constitution. I am very glad that Curzon has resigned. He never meant to carry out the policy of this government and therefore there was no reason why he should remain.[16] I am going to stay with French for the manoeuvres. Are you likely to turn up? I hope so. I am ruminating over the Roberts propaganda and it does not fill me with any special enthusiasm.[17] I wonder how it strikes you.

Churchill Archive, Cambridge, Esher Papers, ESHR 10/25

17
Repington to Moberly Bell

Red Lion Hotel,
Henley-on-Thames.

[Holograph]

25 September 1905

Do you mind paying me the £40 motor car hire at the end of the month? I have long since settled with the owner. Maxwell,[18] Daily Mail, who gets £2000 a year from Harmsworth, tells me that he has paid £7 a day for a motor up to now, but that H. has now fitted him up with a 60 h.p. Mercedes car which he was using to-day. Lawson (D.T.) as you will see from my list this morning, has a similar car and it does not please me to be out-classed.

You will see from the price Maxwell has paid for hire that I should have had to pay £91 for the 13 days trip so I hope you realize that I looked after your interests in my hire.

Still, I was fairly beat to-day as the little car I have can't negotiate the hills – one must have power, and therefore I shall be glad to hear definitely whether you have finally decided the best you can do for me. I want to get about next year and am on the free list pretty well in all the commands now and should like to take advantage of it.

We had a horrible day to-day and I got soaked to the skin. This little man French is a flyer, not only a fighting man but a real trainer, and all his people swear by him.

How goes the book? I shall be ready to bear a hand after the 29th if I can be of any use. I am here till morning 28th.

I want to ask you whether you think it is advisable or reverse for me to reply to people like Hale, Fitzgerald and Company? My inclination is to refuse to reply and to go my own way, but is this courteous or advisable? What I feel is that as I hope to have a cock shy at a good many more greater images, and as the faithful may howl I could spend all my time in fisticuffs and that seems a waste of time. What do you say?

The Times Archive, Moberly Bell Papers

18
Repington to Raymond Marker
<u>Private and Confidential</u>

29, Victoria Road,
Kensington,
London, W.

[Holograph]

15 December 1905

Many thanks for your interesting letter of November 23. I am sure that you must be ever so much more at home in the saddle than upon the office stool of Pall Mall and I confess that I envy you. I have just written a letter to Birdwood upon the "controversy" subject which he will no doubt show you. You are quite right, I am sure, in considering that for Curzon and his supporters the matter has become a personal question and I fancy that he makes a mistake in taking that line and will do himself no good by it. I hope you will be able to let me know early what is being done with regard to the Secretary to the Army Department, and secondly with respect to military finance. These are the only matters which were kept somewhat indefinite at the late settlement and I should be glad to know your ideas. Also, I think that a weak point in Lord K's armour is the question of what will be done in case the C-in-C takes the field in a great war. Is it not best to say that if the C-in-C took the field he would probably be asked to resign as C-in-C in India? You see he would not decide until he was told the name of the new man, or at least he need not, and he would not take the field until sure that the new man was <u>his</u> man and would support him in every way.

Well, we have got your old man out of office and Haldane reigns in his stead. Ellison taking your old place. Do you know Haldane? He is reputed to be a good man and to have the best brain of all the new Ministers. I have met him. He is not attractive to the eye: he looks like the prize picture of the Gazette! But he is agreeable and looks a strong man. I fancy he will be difficult to humbug and jockey and he is leaning on the right people. I met him last Sunday: he had not got very far by then: all he fancied was that the deficiency in the drafts was due to Lord K's demands in case of war, so you will see that there will be a period of spoon-feeding before we get on very fast. Nevertheless I think that he will assimilate knowledge quickly. He is independent and has given up £15000 a year to take office: this is all to the good and I wish the Army Council were all in the same financial position! There will be changes at the W.O. Plumer will go I fancy and Nick will take his place. Hutchinson will get the sack and Douglas Haig replace him: Stopford is rather shaky and the General Staff side will be strengthened. These things are only in the air at present but you will know more by the time this reaches you. Plumer, of course, backed your old man and will not, I suppose, be included in the new patent as he can hardly wish to support a different policy. The idea is that Generals who dislike Nick may get accustomed to him as Q.M.G. and that later he may take N.G's place. If they don't then Wolfe-Murray is available. He is rather obstructive, but is in a military sense the best educated man we seem to be able to find. What do you say? Cannot India produce a model C. of the G.S. for us?

I have been indulging in a good wrangle with George Clarke and his merry men over the railway question in Central Asia, and have written to Birdwood about it already. We have got to this point that the question of how many troops we have to provide and the time within which they must be ready, depends upon our estimate of what the Russian Railways can accomplish. Here I am at variance with George Clarke and he, I consider, underestimates what the railways can do. When Russia means business he will see to his railways, make his rails heavier and add sidings and rolling stock and trained personnel. It will take him a much shorter time to do this than it will take us to make corresponding increases in our military organisation. The latter should therefore, in my view, allow for the improved traffic Russia can provide. I calculate that Russia can run 18 trains a day over the line to Kushk, and over its eventual extension, with ease, provided she takes note of her experiences in Manchuria. Over the [?] line she can do more. I cannot get this admitted, but I believe it is a moderate estimate. Then our wise men talk of trains of 100 to 300 tons while there are now running in America trains of 3000 tons with 180 ton engines. I do not say that Russia in Central Asia can do as much, but I am sure she can do much more than people here anticipate. They tabulate for only 160,000 Russians South of Herat at the extension railhead. This is so wrong that it makes me despair. I shall try to get the whole data reviewed by Girouard: at present he has not even been consulted, I suppose because he is the only man who knows.[19] I am entirely convinced that until you in India or we here approach the subject in a scientific manner and take into account all the modern conditions we are nothing better than a set of imbeciles: we shall never get one standard for organisation, or at least never get it right. Unless you can fix up this matter before Haldane begins to speak in the House and commits himself and his party to a policy, I shall consider that you and the W.O. between you are responsible for the results which will follow, and I shall not hesitate to say so. What you have to recognise is that Khilkoff raised the through traffic to Mukden from 6 trains to 17, concurrently with the despatch of troops and building of the Baikalaing railway. If you know foreign ways you know that 30 trains a day each way on a single line are expected, and that this can be realised with sidings 5 miles – 8 kilomètres apart. It was made the law in Germany so far back as 1878 that sidings should be made in all single lines at not over 5 miles interval, each to hold a train of 120 axles. If you compare 1854 with 1877, and then 1877 with 1905 you can judge how much more Russia may be able to do in the next campaign by profiting from experience. I need not tell you what vastly different results are obtained by giving a bias to argument or calculations. I took all things I could discover into account and let the problem work itself out. It gave me 500,000 Russians on the Helmund or near it in nine months and nothing expected from the country. That is why I backed Lord R. in his original speech on his campaign. Since then he has told us how we are to get the men and nobody has the foggiest idea what he is driving at. The fact is that he is swayed by different influences and stands on a different leg in each speech. I hope to see this Government reform the Militia and Volunteers and leave the Regular Army alone, but if Lord R. wastes energy in getting the British Public to train children to arms we shall end by doing nothing at all.

Wishing you all a happy new year.

British Library, Kitchener-Marker Papers, Add. MSS., 52277B, ff. 25–8

19
Repington to Sir Edward Grey
Private and Confidential

29, Victoria Road,
Kensington,
W.

[Holograph]

29 December 1905

I had a confidential talk with the French military attaché last night, lasting for some five hours, and though I need not trouble you with the military details of this conversation, concerning which you are doubtless much better informed by official agencies, there was one point raised which I feel that I should bring to your notice.[20]

Major Huguet confessed that his Embassy felt anxious upon the question of the attitude of the new Government in England. His people, he said, had nothing to complain of since the speeches of Sir Henry C-B, as well as yours, had produced an excellent effect. It was not a question of sympathies but rather of acts, and of what the British Government were prepared to do in a situation which presented dangerous aspects.

But, I said, surely M. Cambon has had conversations with Lord Lansdowne which have made the situation perfectly clear? Yes, he replied, that is true, but these conversations occurred some time ago, and up to the time M. Cambon went away on leave, they had not been supplemented by any declaration on the part of Sir Edward Grey.

Then why, I asked, does not M. Geoffray go to the Foreign Office and clear the air?

M. Geoffray, he said, did not like to move in such a grave matter when the Ambassador was away, or without positive instructions from his Government. But if, next Wednesday, Sir Edward Grey would broach the subject, Major Huguet was sure that M.Geoffray would be much relieved and his Government would be the same. M.Cambon, he added would not be back in London until January 12 and meanwhile things were looking rather black, and the Conference was to begin on the 16th. There is another matter, he continued. M.Cambon cannot speak a word of English: he has tried hard to learn, but says he is too old. Sir Edward Grey is believed not to be so perfect in French as Lord Lansdowne and M.Cambon feels he will have a difficulty in seizing all the nuances of a conversation on such a delicate matter.

I said that I had no knowledge of your acquaintance with French but my impression was quite the reverse of the opinion which seemed to be held at Albert Gate. I ventured to add that so far as I could judge public opinion in England would be solid on the side of France if she was the victim of unprovoked attack. Yes, we feel that, he said, but it may be a question of prompt action and immediate decisions, and I should realise how extremely important it was for his Government to possess formal assurances upon which they could count.

I said that if I could be of any service in this matter Major Huguet could rely upon my discretion, and that it seemed to me that, whatever the policy of the new Government might be, we should none of us be able to forgive ourselves if the niceties of etiquette and the formalism of official reserve prevented a frank exchange of ideas at the earliest possible date.

I hinted that I was inclined to let you know the general purport of this part of our conversation, and to this he raised no objection.

P.S. I should add that Major Huguet told me that the German Emperor had found things in the French Yellow Book with which he had not previously been made acquainted.

Public Record Office, Sir Edward Grey Papers, F.O.800/110

20
Repington to Raymond Marker
<u>Private and Confidential</u>

29 Victoria Road,
Kensington,
London,
W.

[Holograph]

2 January 1906

Best congratulations to you and Birdwood upon your new appointment. I was so glad to see them. In Birdwood's case he seemed to think he would be left at Simla, so I write to you as I see you are in with the Chief, and you can pass this on to Birdwood if he is with you.

Just at this moment things are looking rather dicky on the Franco-German frontier and you may see that I have dealt with this matter in The Times.[21] No one knows what our friend William wants and the danger is that without meaning war we may drift into it owing to the d—d stupidity of German diplomacy. I am in close touch with the French Embassy and have been assisting to smooth over some difficulties that have arisen from Cambon's inability to speak English and Edward Grey's difficulty in speaking the best Parisian.

I think that things will get straight in a few days, but Grey is away electioneering and he omitted the formality of telling Cambon before he left that the new Government meant to hold by Lansdowne's assurances, and the Froggies were rather nervous on the point. The French are in a fighting humour now and will be rather stiff at the Conference if the Germans are nasty. The latter want Mogador and there is a proposal that we should bag an adjacent harbour, but I hope we shall not and shall keep our hands clean and not play the Cyprus and Wai-hai-wei game over again.[22] We are at half-cock at sea and ready to start at 2 hours notice. Jack Fisher tells me he means to act on his own initiative at the first sign of danger. He is bringing home a lot more ships and is going to form a new Western Fleet with headquarters at Berehaven.

This will make William rather sick, but this is appallingly secret, so do not breathe a word of it until the movement takes place. The French anticipate a German attack through Belgium. The French reserves are already trooping to barracks to ask for orders. All the talk in Germany is of war. I hope that if we join in you will be kind enough to settle German East Africa promptly. This must be your pigeon and what a chance for Lord K. to connect his conquests in N. and S. Africa. Fisher has told Grey that we ought not only to join in a war but to provoke one, in order to clear up the German question thoroughly. I do not much believe in war, but Bill might risk it if he could think that we should stand out, but I fancy he knows we should not and could not for it would be fatal for us to see France crushed. She will take some crushing, though Gleichen appears to be sending home from Berlin some extravagant forecasts of what Bill and Co. propose to do and has evidently been got at by the Berliners.[23] East Africa and Kiao-chau should spare you the trouble of holding manoeuvres in 1906 if there is war.

Here is a problem for you. Which is best, to allow the 16,000 Germans in S.W. Africa to remain there and risk their offering to arm the Boers who will ride down the Orange River to join them, or to clear them out? Will not a German garrison on the flank of a self-governed South Africa act as an incentive to the latter to remain under the Union Jack? Were not our colonists loyal in N. America until the French were kicked out? I wish you would ask Lord K. to suggest the answer to this problem.

I had a talk with Smith-Dorrien to-day and hope to meet him again before he sails and post him on all the latest developments here. I have met both John Morley and Lord and Lady Curzon since writing last and have had it out with both J.M. and Lord C. Morley will do nothing rashly and there will be no more washing of linen in public. I have put the situation, as it existed in the days of the M.M. as clearly as I could before him, and both Esher and I thoroughly 'readied' him for his last talk with C. before the latter departed from the Riviera and Sicily. The argument that seemed to impress Morley most was my suggestion that the C.-in-C. with the M.M. beside him on the Council was as if he, Morley, were duplicated by a second S. of S. for India at the

Cabinet meetings. He did not relish such a position. My idea is that he will hope to take up the story from the compromise that Lords K. and C. accepted and endeavour to make it work: neither C. nor K. can object to this I suppose unless experience shows that further change is desirable. Of course, other influences might sway Morley, but I hope and believe that he will be guided by reason. Also the India Office is still fairly solid for K. and Esher's son has gone to Morley as Secretary so he will be well looked after.[24] J.M. is not at all pleased at getting the India Office: he says it is like the Roman custom and that Ministers simply draw lots for places. His ideas of the frontier questions are vague to the point of obscurity. He has asked me to come and see him and to bring a map, and if Lord K. had sent me all his ideas on these matters I might now have been of use. As it is, I can only develop my own ideas – unless I can steal a certain Memo. dated July 19 last from some office safe! Morley says that the N.W. Frontier question is like the Apocalypse – it either finds a man mad or leaves him mad. He declared that, 'If anyone in India provokes a war he should smart for it.' On the whole, I found nothing in his ideas to which exception could be taken, and we are all safer in the hands of a man of ability than in those of an ass. I fancy that C-B's dictum that 'facts are facts' will be attended to and that things will not be re-opened unless a case is clearly made out. At the same time I do not conceal from you that Lord K's position could with difficulty withstand any difference with Lord Minto. The feeling that the soldier has beaten the civilian is the dominant one, and it will be exploited, regardless of facts and logic, by Lord K's enemies.[25]

I had a dreadful wrangle with Curzon who is as bitter as ever. I fancy he has not met anyone for sometime who disagrees with him so fundamentally, or who cares so little for his knowing the fact. We thrashed out all the old points, but I need not go into this as you know all the arguments on both sides. But there are one or two questions upon which I must consult you. The first is that of the amount of weight to be attached to the opinions of the officers in high command in India. These are in my possession and I hesitate to publish them until we have to bring up our reserves.

Now Lord C. distinctly states that these opinions are valueless because those who gave them are under Lord K's orders. This was also Lord Robert's argument at Lord Lovat's dinner, of which I think I wrote to you. Now of course I strenuously denied this and declared our officers were not such wretched creatures: that their future, in most cases, was quite independent of Lord K's approval and wrath, and that in any case the suggestion was absurd. To this Lord C. replied that he had been informed by some of those who had written to impress their approval of Lord K's proposal that they had done so more or less under compulsion. I had, indeed, heard from other sources that Gen. Gaselee[26] had done this, so I said, 'Perhaps in one case.' No, said Curzon, in more than one case: several of those who wrote and approved have told me confidentially that they disapproved.

Now this is true or false and I suggest that Lord K. asks all the officers who signed and wrote, whether they have taken the steps Lord C. said they took. My idea is that this should be done very confidentially and that if the replies are satisfactory you should send them to me, or to the India Office, or let Lord K's special emissary bring them home to use in the middle of the debate, if debate we have. But anyway, this is a very disgraceful charge, and I am sure you will agree that something must be done, even if no use is made of the papers at present.

Then we had another wrangle over the artillery question and of course I put forward the arguments of Birdwood's cable. C. laughed this to scorn, and talked of 4 batteries of the Hyderabad contingent that K. wished to re-arm and add to the native army, and of 9 others that Lord K. wished to add to them. I said I knew nothing of this. Exactly said C. because you are not accurately informed.

Then we had another dispute about the Imperial Service troops and Lord C. declared that Lord K. wished to bring them under himself. I said that all my information showed that this was a fable and Lord C. could not produce any proofs of his statement. Then I asked his Ex.-Ex whether he had not himself opened the question of the Princes making larger contributions in men or money and whether he had not taken a fall over this affair. He said he had written 60 letters to the Princes with his own hand and that the replies were highly favourable except three which were slightly critical. I smiled at this and he got rather cross and asked why I raised the point. I said, because it seems to me that as Lord K. is being saddled with the charge of causing trouble with the native states it will be necessary for me to see the saddle on the right horse. I asked him why he had not proceeded with his plans after receiving all these favourable answers, and he was unable to explain the reason, merely saying that he did not complete his plans.

I will not weary you with further points and need only say that Esher joined us towards the close of the conversation that then became more amicable and returned to old Eton days when Curzon and I were schoolfellows. He finally undertook to show me all the papers and correspondence on points of fact that I desired to elucidate, on his return. He is off to the Riviera, and then Sicily, and I am told he is to undergo a special treatment for his neuritis on his return. Much may happen before then. You will see that his Lordly idea of representing the City without a contest has fallen flat. He expected the City dignitaries to emulate the burgesses of Calais and come to him in their shirts with ropes round their necks. Perhaps some paltry constituency may do this, but I doubt that any man can take part in English politics and refuse to accept the normal conditions of strife. What can voters make of a Unionist, Free Trade, Imperialist, anti-Unionist, Government Member? It is a d—d rickety platform.

As to other matters, I have had a long talk with Haldane and you may have seen an article I wrote on the New Government and the Army afterwards. I wish I could learn Lord K's views of the article. I do not mean to father the ideas upon Haldane, but still he wrote to me approving of it, and I should be glad to have your criticisms. The only point in my talk with Haldane when I found much difference of opinion was on the question of officers, upon which H. is rather inclined to branch off upon the Sagittarius tack. Lord K. used to have similar ideas in Sudan days. Does he have them still? I am extremely suspicious of them and believe they will wreck the first man who ventilates them.

You will see that Nick is installed once more as Q.M.G. and you will wonder what he has to do in that galley. The truth is that he has made so many enemies among our big generals that he is put in as Q.M.G. on trial to see if they will get used to him. He promises to be good and at present butter will not melt in his mouth. When the C.-K. controversy was started at a dinner party the other day at which I was present Nick refused to express any opinion. He is becoming quite wise!

You will be amazed that little Plumer has been ousted – my idea is that your late chief's schemes were imbecile. Give me this for the sake of argument and then you must admit that if Plumer did not know they were imbecile he was unfit to hold his position; if he knew and still supported them he was equally unfit. I do not think that loyalty to a chief is so important as loyalty to the Army and country. I do not think that Plumer was bound to go on backing A-F when he was obviously in error. I know we are divided on this question. Anyway the short service experiment has closed and I am thankful. I have been reading of your big review with the greatest interest. It seems to have been a splendid affair and I envy you having seen it. I shall no doubt hear more about it from Rawly. What the devil were you doing in a 'busby' (vide Pioneer)! Did you rob a rifleman or a hussar, or did you don a bearskin to keep your head warm? I was amused to read of the maidan planted with cress; I suppose that Lord C has sown so much mustard that there was none left.

I forget whether I told you of my meetings with Lord Roberts and Milner. I never intended to take one step to meet Roberts, nor have I done so, but when he and Milner both wrote asking me to help to arrive at a compromise between the Voluntary and Compulsory schools I did not think it right to stand out just because I have my own opinions about certain activities of Lord Roberts. I sat next to the latter at dinner and had the pleasure of totally disagreeing with him on a number of points. He does not take opposition very cheerfully, but when we came to argue round the table after dinner he was fearfully weak and expressed disorderly ideas. We talked till the small hours and again the next day. Finally, Milner, by my suggestion, drafted a compromise to bring us all onto one platform. I cordially approved of it and we are all to meet again at the National Service League tomorrow to discuss it further. My idea is that the compulsionists must help us to improve what we have got and that the voluntary school must go as far as to bring in compulsory 'physical drill and use of the rifle' for lads over 12. We cannot go further yet as there is an ocean of prejudice against anything you call 'military', and the great thing just now is to back Haldane in regenerating the second line army.

This is a long screed, but at all events it will tell you all I know of the situation. I am trying to do you out of your new guns as they may be wanted in Belgium. I do not think Lord K. would object, in view of the paralysis of Russia and the very delicate situation here in Europe.

British Library, Kitchener-Marker Papers, Add. MSS., 52277B., ff. 29–34

21
Repington to Esher

<u>Private</u>

War Office.

[Holograph]

14 January 1906

Clarke has had a thoroughly unsatisfactory talk with Sir John Fisher who is apparently unable or unwilling to suggest the general lines upon which the French Navy should be prepared to act: he is not prepared to devise a code of private signals so that co-operation in an emergency may be effective; he is opposed to the employment of our troops alongside the French and is apparently not anxious to protect the Channel Ferry although prepared to convoy a landing force to the Baltic which is a much more risky undertaking.[27]

Now as to the employment of our troops on the continent alongside the French, I think we are most of us opposed to participation in a land struggle on the continent if we can avoid it. But circumstances alter cases, and the circumstances at present are that the highest French authorities tell us that it is not the <u>amount</u> of our military support that they regard, but the <u>principle</u> of joint-cooperation and the moral effect to be produced by the appearance of British troops. Can we allow our desires or prejudices to stand in the way of giving them the satisfaction they require? I think we shall be eternally condemned by history if we do, and I beg that you will explain this matter to Sir John and obtain his support for the principle upon which our potential allies set so much store. The thing is not possible within the short limits of time the situation demands and the French lay down, unless Sir John will guarantee us the ferry. Unless we show a disposition to share in the real struggle at the decisive point, good bye to all ideas of a French Alliance!

It is not for me to say whether Sir John is right or wrong to refuse to give any general direction of the task he would assign to the French Navy in the case of war. They have agreed to accept Sir John's plan but he has not one to offer. The French Navy practically shows its readiness to follow the Admiralty lead, and there is no lead given. I thought that we had a St. Vincent at Whitehall but apparently I was mistaken.[28]

However that may be I must give some sort of answer to the very handsome offer of the French to accept our plan of naval action, and I must say something about the code. May I say that Sir John realizes their position, is quite content with their present disposition, will look after the Germans himself and will propose a plan for joint co-operation when the affair comes to a head? May I also say that he will cause to be prepared a private code of signals by day and night to prevent the accidents the French anticipate and will communicate it as soon as circumstances appear to require it? This will not engage Sir John's responsibility very much and may satisfy the French. It will not be all that I hoped, but that is Sir John's affair, I am told he does not anticipate war and therefore is not inclined to make any advance. So was Grenville in 1870 who said there was not a cloud in the sky just before that war began.[29] I think our business is to hope for the best and prepare for the worst. I do not expect war but is that any excuse for failure to prepare?

Unless the ferry is guaranteed all the ideas we have discussed fall to the ground and we should do the honest thing to tell the French that we cannot meet their views. Considering the conversations that have taken place, not of course of my initiation, and the cordial manner in which our questions have been answered, I do not consider that anything short of a Government decision should make us now draw back. Sir John's decision as to naval action may be final, but it is not final as to the nature and amount of our military co-operation unless he distinctly refuses to guarantee the ferry. He certainly asked me to tell the French to line up their submarines and torpedo craft towards the Narrows and they say that they are doing so, but he also told me that even if they did not, he would cover the Channel. Why then cannot the ferry be covered? And if he cannot cover this, how can he cover the movement of a huge unwieldy fleet of transport into the Baltic?

In any case, my dear Lord Esher, please see Sir John and explain the situation to him and let us be able to give the French some definite idea of the general lines of our co-operation, provided that the Government are forced to side with the French. Either this, or let me say plainly that owing to unforeseen objections on the part of the Admiralty we cannot promise anything at all, even if the Government joins with the French.

You see, it is useless for us to tell H. that we shall begin to arrive on a certain day and be ready to entrain so many days later if Sir John is not prepared to cover the crossing. I understand that Ottley saw no difficulty in this. I should also have thought that the bait of the transports in the Channel would make the Germans try a torpedo raid and give our cruisers and destroyers a rare opening.

As for the Baltic operation, that is a side-show, and will in my deliberate opinion, affect in no way the course of the war or its decision. I do not think it ought to be proceeded with, so far as land forces are concerned, until the German naval menace is effectually dispelled. The heart of the war is on the Meuse and all else is mere tickling the extremities.

Churchill Archive, Cambridge, Esher Papers, ESHR 10/26

22
Repington to Esher

29, Victoria Road,
Kensington,
W.

[Holograph]

18 January 1906

I am delighted to hear that you had a satisfactory interview with Sir J.F. These sailors hold us in the hollow of their hand and we cannot go on unless they carry us. I forgot to tell you that H's colleague, the naval attaché, should be the medium for any communications, whether official or unofficial on the naval points we have discussed. Such, at least is H's proposal and it seems to me reasonable enough.

Do not forget that there is not the slightest link between Army and Navy in France, and that the two services are even further apart than they are here. There is no C of D, and it has been only thanks to H's resolution and Rouvier's decided action that we have got upon one paper the joint views of the two departments over the water.[30]

I notice at Metz, Brest and many other places there is much evidence of highly strung nerves. My solution of the police question in Morocco is to have no police. Révoil did a smart thing in jumping up at the Conference and proclaiming the "triple principe de la souveraineté du Sultan, l'intégrité de ses états et la porte ouverte en matière commerciale".[31] This ought to knock out Mogador and will leave Morocco in such condition that France will hereafter be able to deal with it.

Churchill Archive, Cambridge, Esher Papers, ESHR 10/26

23
Repington to Esher

<u>Private</u>

29, Victoria Road,
Kensington,
W.

[Holograph]

18 January 1906

Clarke tells me that Grierson is upset that I should have had any dealings with H. I do not know who told him. I have not spoken to a soul on the subject except to you, Clarke and H. Do tell Grierson how impracticable it was after Grey's ruling that these conversations should have been initiated officially.

I am not sure whether I told you that H. informed me yesterday that, as Grierson had opened relations with him, the natural inference was that he was authorized to do so by Mr Haldane and the Government. I presume that H will say this in his report to his own Government, and as I do not know what Mr Haldane has written to Grierson I am not in a position to tell H. whether the inference he draws is correct or the reverse.

In my opinion it would have been better that Grierson should not have come on the scene until after your talk with C-B, unless of course the S. of S. has the Prime Minister's sanction for official exchange of views.[32] I am sure that you and Clarke will agree.

Churchill Archive, Cambridge, Esher Papers, ESHR 10/26

24
Repington to Raymond Marker
Private and Confidential

29, Victoria Road,
Kensington,
London,
W.

[Holograph]

26 January 1906

I am writing to Birdwood by this mail to thank him for all his trouble in writing to me and saying how very pleased I shall be to hear from you occasionally when there is anything worth the telling.

Just now the best way in which I can help Lord K. is by spoon-feeding John Morley, so yesterday I gave him a lunch and asked Ian Hamilton, Smith-Dorrien, Buckle, George Clarke and Esher. I put Ian and S-D. on each side of Morley with instructions to ply him hard. As Ian has probably cabled and will certainly write I need not repeat all he told J.M. while Dorrien will soon be with you and will tell you all about it. He is to go and see J.M. at the India Office next week so that one way and another there will be no possible excuse for J.M. not to be thoroughly posted. He was in great form and we had a most agreeable party. I cannot say what precisely he means to do, neither have I tried to find out, but my decided impression is that so long as there are no ructions on your side all will be well. Only it is not the right note just now to talk of Lord K's resignation and so on. Morley is to be convinced by reasoning but will not be moved by anything else. Very fortunately Ian had a letter from Lord K. in his pocket that said the nicest things about Morley: it went away in J.M's pocket – and I fancy you are smiling!

The weakest part of our case is the situation that will arise when Lord K's time comes to an end. Can his successor run the show? Is he to be mainly a Carnot[33] at headquarters or a field leader or inspector? Can he do both jobs properly? Can he afford to leave the Government of India without his advice and assistance, and can any subordinate act for him once he is away! Some of us incline to think that the C. in C. in the future must be more of the Chesney[34] stamp and less of the Roberts, and that the delegation of powers of inspection of troops will be easier than that of advisory functions to the Government of India. We hardly think a C. in C. can conduct a campaign against Russia and remain C. in C. in India.

But Morley's idea seems to be to abide by the compromise and to allow India to settle itself down without jolts from outside. I cannot think that any new and acute crisis can arise, and feel sure that tact and diplomacy will make things all right. Anyway J.M. has proved open to argument and ready to hear everything that can be said, and if he goes wrong and brings down a storm upon himself it will be his own fault. I do not think he will. He is too clever and too moderate. He has been nigh on 20 years in Opposition and that sobers. I confess I am optimistic and only hope that the worst of the trouble is at an end and that little more time may be wasted in their dreadful wranglings. Thank goodness, Lord C. is out of sight and out of mind, and it is important to have matters quite settled before he returns.

I am very glad that the Tories are out. They have dissipated a fine inheritance and must find a real leader and agree upon a united policy before they will have a look in again. I hope much from Haldane. He is the best S. of S. we have ever had at the W.O. so far as brain and ability are concerned. The rest is on the knees of the gods and everything promises well.

C-B returns tomorrow and goes to Windsor when a very important question will be decided. So far as it can be without a full sitting of the Cabinet, namely whether the Government will take up the threads of unofficial conversations between us and France and establish definite bases for mutual cooperation in case of war. H.M. knows all that has passed and strongly approves. It has been a d–d delicate business, complicated by tendencies on the part of Jacky Fisher to be cantankerous. He has some frousy ideas of a campaign of his own in the Baltic and use of all our Army in a secondary not to say tertiary operation there. You might just as well try to kill a tiger by tickling his tail. This war will be decided on the Meuse or thereabouts and my idea is that nothing else counts save weight in the decisive quarter. John French was a little unsound too at first, but he has come round, as everyone must who is not a brazen idiot. I will tell you more of this when matters are straighter: the French have been superb. In the end we shall have to consider whether we should not do well to make a firm Treaty of Alliance with them. Ask Lord K. what he thinks. Nothing can be done till Algeciras is over, as any talk of this just now will only irritate the German animal. Meanwhile our fleets are at single anchor and ready to act at two hours notice: the French nearly ditto, but as yet unable to mass in the Channel owing to uncertainty concerning Italy, and fear of irritation if they send round their Mediterranean fleet. This is the curse of their geographical position from a naval point of view. It don't much matter for we can do the job ourselves. Our sailors have some wild-cat schemes which may lose us our fleet without profit: happily we are on the 4 Power standard and can bear it without vital injury. My idea is that our sailors have thought out nothing: have the very vaguest idea of strategy on a large scale and that they will learn something to their cost before the war is very old. Moreover I doubt Jacky's capacity for assuming responsibility. I fear his masterfulness is a good deal on the surface. Just now I am preparing the devil's own bomb to throw at Bill if he repeats in his press certain statements he is making in private conversation. Cambon, the French Ambassador, is helping me. When this bomb is thrown – it may never be – there will be Hades.

The old W.O. croons along: quite a happy family and all on the best terms now: Haldane has done the right thing all round and even Edward Ward is propitiated and made to help. Most of these gentry are simply children under Haldane's genial smile! It will be interesting to see how it all pans out.

The meetings with Roberts and Milner and Co. have bored me so that I have ceased to attend them. No grasp of the general situation and hours of futile talk: it was a waste of time to have shared in them. What is the use of big people taking up other peoples' time unless they know what they want and how to get it? Nothing has resulted save a mere dribble-drabble of desultory conversation. Meanwhile a little party is to collect at Munro-Ferguson's house the first week of the session to keep an independent though friendly watch on the proceedings in Army matters, mostly M.P.s and a few outsiders like myself. It will not be quite as breezy a party as Ernest Beckett's old crowd – Winston, Hugh Cecil, Tommy Bowles, Edgar Vincent, Jack Seely, Dickson-Poynder, Ewart Gordon and others with whom I acted during the Sessions of 1903–1904, but I intend to make it a strong and independent group with power of detachment from Government if any gaffes are made by Ministers here or in India. We shall see. I hope we may be only part of the applauding chorus, but that will depend upon the front bench. All Army and N.S. Leagues are played out. The only thing that counts is Parliament and the Press and there are materials to hand for a big combine in both if C-B and Co. go astray.

P.S. By the way, I don't know if Rawly is back. He has not been near me anyway, so I did not ask him to meet Morley. Rawly wrote me a letter from Calcutta that made me laugh. It was in the good old official secrets style, telling me that it was not good for my health to know certain things. Now my dear chap, this is all futility. I have seen every secret paper that I have wanted to see, and have half a dozen different ways of securing them in the future – or more. I do not publish things that are not suitable for publication, but unless you can write freely and tell me what you really think and want I can't promise to back you. How can I without knowledge? I see, for instance, a paper that professes to give your views but are they your views? I ask certain questions and am told that the Russians must not have the replies: am I then a Russian agent? Heaven forbid! If you want me to base my line upon Curzon's and Morley's and other people's information, then say so and I will do it, but my idea was to support Lord K. and it can't be done unless you can write to me quite freely. Simply say that a thing must not appear and it will not, but don't let us have this hocus of official secrets when none exist.

By the way I don't usually concern myself about individuals but there is a chap at the W.O. – Robertson, head of the foreign sections at the I.D. whom Lord K. should annexe. I have only met him lately. He has no friends and rose from the ranks, but he is an A1 man or I am no judge. If he had [?] of interest I would not mention his name to you. He ought to be head of your I.B.: his time is up in October and he is too good a man to be lost to the Army.

British Library, Kitchener-Marker Papers, Add. MSS., 52277B., ff. 35–9

25
Repington to Leo Maxse

Private

29, Victoria Road,
Kensington,
W.

[Holograph]

17 February 1906

I hope you will succeed with HH.[35] It is true that K. resented the Strachey article because it was full of inaccuracies and Curzonisms. A Strachey was Lord C's major domo and no doubt all the materials reached the brothers from this source which is polluted.

I regret your attitude towards certain members of the Defence Committee. Individuals pass but principles remain, and in my humble opinion the principles upon which the Defence Committee rests are unassailable and you will be doing a great disservice if you allow your forceful pen to be placed at the disposal of the Spenser Wilkinson folk who care more to 'savage' individuals than to support principles.

I do not agree about Clarke. I think he is trying to do a great work and deserves hearty support. If you care to tell me any instances of the cases in which his activity has been mischievous I should like to examine them. We have to deal with the stupid jealousy of the departments and with a lot of hide-bound reactionaries to whom anything in the way of progress is anathaema.

As for individuals, they count little. I ask you not to lower yourself to these trivialities and to hold fast to the great principles which have been established by history and cannot be much changed by the personal experiences, likes and dislikes of 20th. century pigmies. If you take the other course you exchange the search-light for the miserable tallow-dip of personal experience which will serve you not at all save to show you the road is damnably dark.

I ask you to support the principles of the Defence Committee because I believe that it is an indispensable part of the machinery of government and a powerful means of suppressing idiots and for co-ordinating the work of the various departments. I am sure you must feel that decisions in which men like Grey, Haldane and Sir J. French join are not likely to go very wrong. You can do so much to help or to mar the work and I beg you to be a helper.

West Sussex Record Office, Chichester, L.J. Maxse Papers, 455, f. 264

26
Repington to Leo Maxse

Private

29, Victoria Road,
Kensington,
W.

[Holograph]

27 February 1906

If I have done you an injustice in associating you with Spenser Wilkinson's criticisms, please accept my apologies.

But I still think you are unfair to Clarke. I do not agree with him on several points, and as you recall, I have not hesitated to oppose him when I have thought it necessary. Doubtless he inspired AB's defence speech, but you yourself might inspire me and I should still write d—d bad Episodes of the Month. One cannot make A. entirely responsible for the lucubrations of B, even though the inspiration came from A. I daresay Clarke feels now that there is a considerable difference between irresponsible advocacy and authoritarian statement. We all have to learn the difference by experience.

As to the question of German coaling stations, I don't fancy Clarke has any illusions on the subject of what the German objective may be in naval policy. The Germans have told us again and again. But the real point is whether a coaling station, i.e. a defended naval station abroad, is an advantage to the weaker naval power or the reverse.[36] If it is not used by warships in time of war you will grant that it is a useless encumbrance and that the money spent on its works and garrisons are moneys lost. If it is used by warships, then the weaker naval power chooses dissemination in place of concentration and enables an enemy to act unitedly against a separated foe. Commercially the Germans are now cutting us out by establishing coaling depots in neutral territories, and the naval coaling station will not much affect this one way or the other. Do you consider Kiao-Chou a source of strength or weakness to Germany? I look upon it as a most useful lightning conductor for us, and if the Germans can't get out of it you may be sure that the Chinamen will one day kick them out. All German colonies are hostages to fortune so long as the enemy has a bigger and better navy. I think the existence of the German colonial possessions and maritime trade makes for peace, since our William will not face certain loss for uncertain gain. True, as you say, these possessions are used as a lever to increase the German Navy, but I am not clear that this increase would not come just the same whether German colonies existed or whether they did not.

My feelings towards the Defence Committee are impersonal. I want to see it become in course of time the nucleus of a great Imperial staff, with representatives on it from India and all our great colonies. I do not think that the individual opinions of the present members are matters of supreme importance for once you have a body capable of collecting and of knowing the best opinions of our authorities all over the world you cannot fail to establish sound and settled doctrines. The eccentric will always drop out when met by the weight of considered opinion from all sides. There is no body save the Defence Committee to collect and co-ordinate opinions and I consider that it is the duty of all of us to support the institution with all the power at our command. If you identify the institution with its first secretary and then attack him you do bad work for the cause. If a Prime Minister gets up and talks nonsense, then prove him in the wrong and my firm belief is that the error will not be repeated. Do you expect weighty and considered views from a P.M. who has taken to the study of strategy late in life and has only a half-fledged institution to guide him? It will be an affair of many years to sort out all our ideas and get them in order.

The new and so called General Staff is very jealous of the C of D. I do not think we ought to pander to this jealousy for an Army Staff can never deal with opinions of all departments and possessions as can a central body like the C. of D. I look upon the latter as embodying a sound idea and as promising the first practical step in the direction of real Imperial confederation. Take it away – as you may by criticism in these flabby days – and you are back in the old and disastrous system of government in compartments. Your war will be Neville Lyttleton's war – and we shall have to add a paragraph to the Litany!

West Sussex Record Office, Chichester, L.J. Maxse Papers, 455, ff. 272–3

27
Repington to Leo Maxse

29, Victoria Road,
Kensington,
W.

[Holograph]

1 March 1906

Yes, we are both too busy to waste more time in argufying, especially when we do not differ upon essentials. Of course, if you think that this government will not maintain a bigger and a better navy than Germany, then we are in very serious danger. But I am inclined to doubt this. If it is true, and the consequence follows that we are beat at sea, then I take it that all our coaling stations pass to Germany and they have little need of others.

I am not at all for giving Germany anything. Far from it, but as a purely academical question I can see no advantage in coaling stations abroad to the inferior navy.

West Sussex Record Office, Chichester, L.J. Maxse Papers, 455, f. 275

28
Repington to Esher

Private

29, Victoria Road,
Kensington,
W.

[Holograph]

4 May 1906

I enclose herewith a proof of the article on England and Turkey which you asked to see. Publication is withheld so that there may be no risk of increasing Turkish resistance to our diplomatic representations. Similarly I do not like to point out the military action we may have to take because we cannot afford to warn the Turks beforehand. These are the reasons why I refrain from comment at this juncture and I expect you are in agreement with me.

Show the article if you like to Clarke, French, Sir E. Grey and Mr Haldane, but do not show it to any weak men.

I am strongly convinced of the necessity for allowing Sir E. Grey line to play his fish.[37] We must avoid a rupture and above all a local collision, at all costs.

I have carefully considered your very kind suggestion that I should serve on your committee to consider and advise upon Mr Haldane's proposals for the Territorial Army.[38] I think it would be better for me to stand out, in order that I may maintain a perfectly free hand in the subsequent discussion. I am in favour of the proposals and of the War Minister's general policy, but I do not approve of the proposed reduction of Guards and artillery which are forced upon Mr Haldane by circumstances and appear to me arbitrary and without reason in view of the general military situation. I do not think anyone will blame the War Minister for the reductions. The Government in its corporate capacity, and the Prime Minister in particular, will be saddled with the full responsibility for any after effects which may result.

Churchill Archive, Cambridge, Esher Papers, ESHR 10/26

29
Repington to Raymond Marker

Private and Confidential

29, Victoria Road,
Kensington,
London, W.

[Holograph]

25 May 1906

An attack of lumbago has laid me by the heels this week and I have not much news to send. I was to have dined with John Morley but have to postpone it till Tuesday now. He tells me he has had Lord K's answer, and wants to discuss with me the chapters of my new book which relate to the defence of India, so it ought to be interesting.

I don't think I told you that Chirol brought back from India a little tale of a cock and a bull to the effect that Lord K's staff had been abusing me and saying that I had been squared and expected personal advantage from supporting Lord K. and Haldane, in fact that I desired to be in Government harness again. A very pretty little tale, and my only reply has been that I was afraid Chirol had taken so little trouble to ascertain the views of Lord K's staff on any subject that I hardly thought he could have ascertained it in such an unimportant matter as my affairs. However, if you hear tell of such tales on the part of ex-members of the Military Department you can say that I prize my liberty too much to give it up and that £10,000 a year and a peerage would not again make me the slave of the d—d fool class that misgoverns this benighted country. No doubt Curzon and his minions want my blood, and yours and Lord K's and a few others, but there are still some graven images to be overthrown and when that is done then I shall have said all I want to say. I am not surprised that the class of gentry we have been dealing with can allow no good motives for anybody's action. They judge others by themselves.

Chirol I have not seen since his return and I have steadily avoided him: we have had some frigid correspondence. I don't know whether past Secretaries of State for War think I have played my cards well to ingratiate myself with them. I fancy that Brodrick and A-F. want my scalp just as much as Lord C. As for Haldane, he very kindly asked me to join Esher's new committee, popularly known as the Duma, but my anxiety for office led me to ask permission to stand out, as I do not want to be implicated in any governmental proceedings as I may have to belabour this Ministry before long if they allow their tail to waggle them.

Dealing with Roberts and Co. lately proved to me that there was only one way of dealing with such a team as the Duma, namely to ask them definite questions and ask for definite replies, yea or nay, by a certain tick of the clock. Otherwise discussion went on for all time and to no purpose. This hint was taken, but they would not have my suggested hour-glass with the sand running out. From what I have seen of the agenda papers it is all going fairly well, but I shall keep an open mind till we have the whole plan and proposed action.

I am very angry that Gorringe[39] is preferred to Girouard for Lawson's[40] billet. I call it a d—d shame: they are all as jealous of Girouard as old cats.

Pritchard R.E.[41] has been working out the supply of a Russian army in Afghanistan and he gives the same results as I do – 500,000 Russki's on the Helmund at Giriskk and well fed within 18 months. As his estimate is a technical study taking it up point by point and in great detail it is valuable confirmation of my estimate.

Buckle has not sent me back a copy of my reply to Winston's note so I must keep that for next mail. I have a lot of articles on the way about various matters which you will see in due course. I expect Lord K. will have heard from Sir John French by the last mail. I am going to Tidworth to take stock next week. Forgive a dull letter.

British Library, Kitchener-Marker Papers, Add. MSS., ff. 52–3

30
Repington to James Thursfield

29, Victoria Road,
Kensington,
W.

[Holograph]

26 May 1906

I am obliged for your letter. Neither personally nor on behalf of the "Times" am I committed to support anyone or anything in relation to military policy. It is not human not to have preferences but my endeavour is to remain entirely independent and to back nothing unless I am convinced it is sound. It was for this reason that I thought it best – this is confidential – to refuse to serve on the committee now sitting. So I shall be very pleased to meet Sir Charles Dilke[42] again and hope you will tell him that I am quite at his disposal and should be very glad to know his views.

The Times Archive, Thursfield Papers, AC96/27

31
Repington to Raymond Marker
Private and Confidential

29, Victoria Road,
Kensington,W.
London.

[Holograph]

5 July 1906

Thanks for yours of June 14. You are aware that I did not attach the slightest value to the Chirolian suggestion that Lord K's staff had been saying that I was in their pocket. But I am interested to hear that Chirol saw no one of the C. in C's personal staff except you.

Chirol and I are absolutely at daggers drawn and I have told Buckle that I entirely refuse to make any advances to his Foreign Editor and that if the interests of The Times suffer on that account he must lay the blame where it is due. I may add that

Amery is quite sound on the whole question and that he is of great service to the cause.

I am sending you Pritchard's calculations herewith as Lord K. wishes to see them. I could not ask P. for permission as I think he would have had to refuse, so I will stand the racket, but please guard P's interest and let me have the paper back by return. George Clarke does not approve the findings of the paper and declares that Chancellor[43] knows more about railways than Pritchard. Chancellor is a very keen intelligent chap, but I cannot pick many holes in Pritchard's estimates and I think we ought to legislate for the most dangerous situation that can arise. In connection with this, will you kindly ascertain for me, through the Finance Branch if they are amenable. What is the estimated income of India and also the capital, i.e wealth capitalized in £ sterling? Your d—d super calculations make me dizzy, and are quite obscure to the B[ritish] P[ublic].

My idea roughly is that India is more highly charged for defence than England and infinitely more than the Empire as a whole. Do not hocus the figures, but leave me to deal with them. Giffen gives India's capital at 600 millions, so far as my memory serves, but I cannot find the reference. Anyway he shows that India's contribution to defence is far higher in proportion to taxable capacity than that of the rest of the Empire (Economic Inquiries II, p. 375), and if this be so then there seems no way to increase the Army except by shortening up service and increasing the Reserves. You will also have seen the Tsar's order of May last decreasing service with the colours to 3 years, which means, under Russian conditions, an equivalent of 18 months in any Western Army. You will, in fact, have only to deal with the Militia and the question is whether you prefer to get larger numbers and slightly reduced efficiency, or keep your Alexander's Army and count heads as little or nothing. Let me know what you think.

You will see that I have opened the ball, concerning the reductions that you speak of, in The Times of today, and have expressed my almost unqualified disapproval of them. I have also, as you will see, the damaging support of Brodrick, and the Editor faces me with a fairly useful leader. It was only at the personal request of the S. of S. that I omitted the exact figures of the line infantry reductions. The Cabinet began to consider Haldane's schemes yesterday and when they continue the process to-day they will know what they have to face. I sent Haldane a proof of my article and discussed it with him for a long time yesterday in his private room at the House of Commons rather expecting to be committed to the Tower. He was however very agreeable, and though he would be the last to admit it, I do not think he is injured or amazed by a severe attack upon the policy of reductions. I think on the contrary that it will be helpful, for these reductions are merely dragged from him by force majeure and we must beat the big drum now and begin to commandeer all the guerilleros who will fight.

Your Maxse has sent me a very good paper on the loss of the 3/Coldstream, but he only ends by urging that the Irish Guards should be preferably reduced and this argument is of no use to me as I am opposed to all reductions. It is not practical politics to wipe the Irish Guards off just after they have been formed.[44]

You will see that I have gone into the whole matter and there will no doubt be many opportunities for returning to it. I do not suppose that we shall win but we must keep our wicket up as best we may and establish a funk if we can. I think the financial stroke is the best we can make on this infernally tricky wicket.

There are ructions concerning the Militia. Their spokesmen say they won't play unless an understanding is given that the Militia go abroad in units. Now, as I have shown when dealing with the Cardwell system, this is not a promise that can be given for the Militia must serve several ends, and, no one can say which will be most important. Moreover, Haldane's idea is to reduce the Militia to one battalion per territorial regiment, and then, still less. Can you guarantee that a Militia battalion will go abroad as a unit, for then the depot plus a wretched provisional battalion, will have to feed 2 Regular (perhaps) and 1 Militia Battalion in the field? Haldane has been advised to stand up to the Duke of Bedford to-day and to refuse to concur with the Militia terms and I think he will do so. If they prove cantankerous they will be told that they can be spared and that the field army can be maintained by an increase of the paid Army Reserve from resources of the Territorial Army. In short, if the Militia will not play, they will be merged with the Territorial Army or will disappear, as they please; we shall save a couple of millions and less than half that sum will give us the lien on 100,000 extra Reservists who will probably undertake liability for service in war time by the offer of 6d a day. They will be old Volunteers and so far as I can see we shall get plenty of them to take on; some people think at £5 a year. The Manchester Vol. Brig. Bearu Co. were asked to find 250 men for this liability at 6d a day: they are 100's strong and found the numbers at once: they were then told that the question was postponed! Anyway, it is an indication.

The naval manoeuvres have made the dinghy school look increasingly foolish, as May with 4 battleships swept the Channel and landed at Scarborough unfought. The next few days will see everybody trying to show that things are not what they seem. I am going to produce Moltke's views on this interesting subject after Parliament breaks up. We have been too much spoon-fed by the schoolmen and it is time for a little counter-irritant. Buckle thinks it will lead to the devil of a rumpus. The point is to destroy the effect of the Balfour pronouncement of last year respecting invasion, and Moltke gives me all I require for this purpose as you will see.[45]

The 'National Defence Association'[46] waxes stronger: we have some hundreds of the best names in the country and we shall put out a programme with the names before long, and in the Autumn expand in the provinces. We are giving Haldane a dinner this month and are inviting guests. I think I shall ask John Burns and Francis of Teck. We are nothing if not catholic. We put old Bobs in the chair at Committee meetings and a more useless person for the job no one could find. Sammy Scott has found a trade in handling Bobs. We give Sammy a programme of procedure and sit him by Bobs with a lot of cigarettes. He then keeps the old man's nose down. If this were not done we should talk for hours into space. The real work is done by a smaller body and we have annexed Jackson the Navy League[47] man who is as crisp, business-like and practical as you can wish.

I went down to Eton on Monday and lunched with the Head.[48] He has promised compulsory gymnastics and Swedish drill and has given me some ideas for an article on the Public Schools and the Army. Not too many ideas, but some. He wants a qualifying exam and nominations by Head Masters and Heads of Houses for commissions. The naval plan in fact, and I believe the best. I have just had uncarted upon me the first Vol. of the Official History of the S.A. War by old Maurice and Co. and do not relish doing a review of it so I am trying to unload it upon Amery.[49]

The work I want to tackle is a series of articles on the next Peace Conference. Ministers are drifting into a course of folly on this question and I am going to make myself unpleasant to Stead, Avebury, sentimentalists and co. After that, and the necessary comments on Haldane's speech and any other affair that comes up, I hope to get away for the cream of the drill season to see French, Ian, Methuen and Co. at work, and also to run over to France for the manoeuvres in the north.

Nothing doing in Russian Entente business. Tsar's are at a discount and we are sitting on the fence to see whose throat is cut first – Nicholas's or the Duma's. We shall fall on neck of t'other.

British Library, Kitchener-Marker Papers, Add. MSS., 52277B., ff. 72–7

32
Repington to Thursfield

29, Victoria Road,
Kensington,
W.

[Holograph]

22 July 1906

I regret very much that you are displeased with my article in The Times of the 20th, as I value your opinion greatly, but I think it would have been more fair to me had you waited to read the whole argument and to consider the measures I shall suggest in my fourth and concluding article for approaching your objective by a different road.[50]

The Vivian motion may be, as you say, common ground for all parties, but that does not prove that the ground is solid.[51] The proof, you say, is in the social and economic condition of the country at this moment. I admit that, but what is this condition? Increasingly and amazingly prosperous as I showed in my article of July 5 giving figures which neither have been, nor I think, can be refuted.

You say that the proper measure of security should be the extent of the forces which, on a reasonable estimate of probabilities, may be arrayed against us. I accept that, but when you assume, tho' only for the sake of argument, that our defences are not in excess of this measure, and that any reduction on one side of the equation may safely be accompanied by corresponding reduction on the other – then I think you are on very shaky ground. If we had attained to the measure of security you premise then a parallel all round reduction would be sensible, if it could be arranged, which is unlikely. But as we have not attained to that measure with our land forces, a reduction is inadmissable.

My idea is that we are now on a one fourth Power Standard for the Army. If sea and land power were convertible terms, we need not worry. But they are not, and I therefore think that we should increase our military armaments for our land forces. The Navy hold to their programme. The Army is the sport of political Tom-fools, who reduce it by 42,000 men and compel me to declare, in all good faith and conscience, that the Empire cannot be successfully defended in the event of serious attack upon a land frontier. I will not follow you into the very abstruse and contentious question of what might or might not be done with the moneys cut off the service estimates. You admit in your letter that everything necessary for security is priceless, and my contention is that we have not sufficient land power to guarantee our security. I do not believe that our excessive and partly accidental margin of sea power is an unmixed blessing. It beguiles us into a building programme below the Two Power Standard[52] and if this process continues our superiority in course of time will be mainly numerical, and it will consist of out of date ships. I would like to see the Two Power Standard steadfastly maintained in the building programme so that we may always be sure of superiority in the best modern ships.

I hold to my statement that disarmament would mean the greatest economic crisis that can be imagined. But please remark that I mean disarmament and not limitation or slight reduction of armaments. Have you ever considered the figures of the population which lives on armaments? It is immense and has its roots in every class and every trade. Decree disarmament and you throw a vast labouring population into the streets. How can this be anything but a crisis? It would be worse than the worst strike ever known, and there would be no end to the strike.

Tomorrow I hope to deal with the question of the Laws and Practices of Naval Warfare and I hope you will favour me with your views as nothing is more helpful to the beginner than the frank opinion of the master.

The Times Archive, Thursfield Papers, AC96/27

33
Repington to Thursfield

29, Victoria Road,
Kensington,
W.

[Holograph]

27 July 1906

I am just starting for Warwickshire to look after my somewhat neglected property and have not the time to answer your letter as fully as I should wish to do. But I really must protest against the accusation that I have been a scoffer at humanitarian priciples. What I scoff at is the argument of those who live in a world of their own imagination, their insular fancy, and not in the world of to-day as history will know it, and as most foreign nations know it to be. I enclose for you to read an extract from to-day's Bulletin de l'Etranger of le Temps, on the subject of C-B's speech,[53] and I can only add that the opinion of le Temps represents what I believe to be the truth, and also a truth which our sentimentalists ignore. It is because I have been so much abroad that I have considered it indispensable to reflect these views, unpopular though they may be, and not to leave people in ignorance of the hard, unpleasant and stern brutal facts of the real situation. I want to arrive at the same ends as the humanitarians but I want to get there by an easy route, and not by a mountain pass which is almost impracticable. I consider that the Alps must be turned and not crossed, and that compulsory arbitration is the true road which leads to our common end. It is all very well for us to say that we must have a predominant Navy. I think we must, but if I were a German I would say precisely the same thing, and then, as I think Giffen once asked, if both must be predominant who is to predominate? I regard all attacks, direct attacks, on armaments, as quite unpractical and very dangerous, and I want to head off the pack from this false scent and make a case for the track of compulsory arbitration. I have considered all this question for long and feel positive that this is the only practical course to pursue. I feel sure that history will justify this opinion. You may scoff at my idea and talk of the Greek Kalends, but concurrent limitation of armaments falls to the ground when you approach the practical difficulties of the step. If you have any practical proposal, I beg you will produce it. Your suggestion that we should form a League of Peace[54] and compel Germany to disarm is merely another way of saying we should form a sanctimonious coalition and make war on Germany. How can she disarm? If the coalition is disarmed Germany will laugh at it. If armed, she will resist to the death, and you mobilise all Europe and return to the bloody days of the Sainte Alliance. I would vote for compulsory arbitration on all questions if I get the chance. At the stage of Empire which we have reached it would be an ideal solution for us, but it would not be for the young and rising nations who have aspirations, and I am not sanguine that our ends will be reached in our lifetime or that of our children's children.

I can assure you that I use no hyperbole in talking of you as a master and of myself as a beginner. I have read your papers for years: I have recognised your ideas and turns of phrase in anonymous writing. All this time – for twenty three years – I have been quartering this world and acting as the submissive tool of a usually incompetent government. Now I am trying to puzzle things out for myself, and it is only three years since I began. How can I be anything better than amateur?

I believe that England is today – as I told John Morley the other day – like a Quaker who has succeeded to the rich succession of a burglar parent, and wishes to hold both to Quaker opinions and to the paternal swag.

The Times Archive, Thursfield Papers, AC96/27

34
Repington to Moberly Bell

<u>Strictly Private</u>

29, Victoria Road,
Kensington,
W.

[Holograph]

29 July 1906

The serpentine dove is getting a headache. The dovelike part notices that you are out of pocket:-

Rembrandt Co. £96.5.8 (85.15.0 in March).
Adverts . . . £223.16.0 (177.18.0 in March)
Fisher . . . £150.0.0
Total £470.1.8

But the serpentine part wants to know why £470.1.8 from the £600 produced . . . . should not leave a balance of £129.18.4 to divide, or, with October promise, a total of £890.18.0. The same s.p. also wants to know what it has left out of its serpentine calculation?

You ask me to say what I am to get by taking a hypothetical arrangement and regarding a result which did not follow. I don't think that would be fair to you, for if Murray and I divide balance there is none for the Times and the £223 spent on advertising in the Times would have to be refunded.

The question is rather the practical one of a fair division of spoil amounting to £890.18.0. or such other figure as you may show me I should take in preference.

Considering:–

1. That The Times has already made £223 by advertisement of book and that I have made nuppence.

2. That I have worked for 2½ years without a days holiday, and for d—d long hours.

3. That I give up one of the best country houses in the Midlands which I can have for nothing and lease a house for 300 guineas a year and spend £1000 on decorations for the pleasure of doing your work and entertaining guests for your benefit.

4. That I have made your military correspondence the best and most authoritative in the U.K. as I said I would and cause you to be regarded as a Delphic oracle in my branch of your business.

5. That I shall probably improve when I can get into the new house and spend a few hundreds upon my library.

6. That my expenditure for the first quarter of this year was £1769, representing, were it continued, an outlay of £7000 a year, a large part of which is incidental to my work for you.

7. That I lose money on agricultural property by being an absentee landlord, and my colliery has only raised 1000 tons a week from my own land when it ought to have raised 2,000 if I had been on the ground.

8. And lastly, that you will not easily find such another idiot to do or leave undone all these things:- (Therefore) my firm and unalterable conviction is that I should have for my share of the swag just as much as ever I can get!

The Times Archive, Moberly Bell Papers

35
Repington to Esher

Private

29, Victoria Road,
Kensington,
W.

[Holograph]

19 August 1906

There are a few matters which I omitted from my last letter and upon which I want your opinion. I am thinking of writing an article later on to suggest that the Inspector General of the Forces should have a seat on the Army Council in order that the link should be closer between the Army and the W.O. I have mooted the matter to Haldane who admits the need for a closer union and tonight I am dining with Conkey Maxwell to talk round the subject. I rather fancy that your idea is that Lord K. will get a two year extension and that French would succeed H.R.H. as I.G. I daresay you may also think of Haig as our future C. of G.S.[55] No doubt, French and Haig would work closely together and in this case there would be no absolute need to put the I.G. on the A.C. But this is legislating for a special case and I think we ought to let the I.G. have a seat on the A.C. so that when any important matter is under inquiry he may be present to explain the views of the Army. I hardly ever see a member of the A.C. among the troops, and as you know, the Military Members are not fond of horses.

There is no doubt that we do not get good value out of the Inspectorate and that we should do so. I spoke to the Duke on the matter and he told me how A-F had endeavoured to make him alter his report because it did not please the late S. of S. I never heard of such impudence![56]

What are your views, as to persons and also principles? What is your idea of H.R.H.'s future usefulness. I do not quite see where he comes in the shuffling of the pack if J.M. will not send him to India.

Now there is soon a vacancy at the Staff College and I am sorry to say that H. Wilson may be jobbed in there by N.G. I am personally an enemy of this intriguing imposter Wilson, and my views are prejudiced, but on Friday last some S.C. officers came up to me and asked me to try and prevent this job. They say that they know Wilson and despise him and detest his character.[57]

There are at least three good men, any of them would do: Colin Mackenzie the Seaforth man: Robertson from the DMO's branch, and Lawson, now in Ireland. I do not know Mackenzie, but poor Henderson had a tremendously high opinion of him and I am convinced that his appointment would be hailed with delight. Either of the other two would be infinitely better than this low class schemer whose sole aptitude is for worshipping rising suns – an aptitude expressed by those who know him in more vulgar language. It is difficult to over estimate the influence for good or evil of the commandant at the S.C. and I hope that you may be able to do something to get a first rate man put there when Rawlinson leaves this Autumn.

Some of the army class masters in the Public schools are getting up a protest against the staff duties department. It will probably appear in September. How Haldane can keep old Hutch and Wilson to bedevil things in that branch I can't imagine.

Churchill Archive, Cambridge, Esher Papers, ESHR 10/26

36
Repington to Esher

Private

> 29, Victoria Road,
> Kensington,
> W.

[Holograph]

> 24 August 1906

I quite agree that the selection for the G.S. List should be vested in the Selection Board and should not, at present, be handed over to the C. of G.S.[58]

You seem to think that I fear the consequences of our acts. That is not so. What I fear is that the tendency of the A.C. is to assume that there is a General Staff science and that ability to command troops in the field and administrative experience are of less value than what you call the G.S. mind. The only G.S. officer who will ever be of any permanent service to this country will be one who is equally capable and equally experienced in all the business of an Army, for the work of the General Staff in the field presumes and demands all this previously acquired knowledge, and so does the act of generalship. My opinion is that the AO is narrow and inadequate and that it will neither serve your needs nor content the Army.

You do well to make the reservation that 99 men out of 100 have some notion of administration <u>provided</u> they are given responsibility, but how will your new G.S. officer obtain these notions if he never has administrative responsibility? He will be an amateur and will impose tasks upon troops and services which they cannot carry out. The true G.S. type of mind is based upon this previously acquired knowledge and is not, as you seem to think, irrespective of and apart from it. I agree that a well trained G.S. is a prime necessity but my complaint is that you are not going the right way to get it. However, I am not going to oppose the A.C. and we will see how it works and judge by results. I supposed that you would condemn all idea of placing the I.G. on the A.C. It is a matter of indifference to me how and by what means the Army is brought into closer talk with the W.O. so long as the thing is done.

Yes, you kept distinct command, administration and inspection and I think you did not supply the trait d'union[59] and I have yet to find it. The Inspectorate officers all tell me that they are less and less in touch with the W.O. instead, as they should be, more and more, and further that their proposals are only occasionally carried out. The public pay a round sum for the Inspectorate and they are not in my opinion getting their money's worth. You say the Duke's reports are excellent. I have not a doubt on the subject, but of what service is talk if not followed by action? You also say that it is not the business of the W.O. to move about among the troops. Certainly not if they are in close touch with the Inspectorate, but if they do not care a twopenny damn about the Duke's reports then their divorce from the troops must have deplorable consequences. I suppose that the only way to harmonise our respective views is to demand that the I.G's reports shall be published. I find no objection to this course on the side of the Inspectorate and I think on the whole it will be the best course to adopt, though I doubt we should get the thing done without a fight.

You say you are thinking of principles rather than persons. But it is men that make success as much as if not more than systems. Your own valuable work for the Army is a case in point. I am sure that no one of the probable successors to the Duke will be content with the present situation. I should like to see an expansion of the I.G's sphere of usefulness. I would like him to have a larger staff of senior men who need not be highly paid. I should want to see the Inspectorate extend to India and the self-governing Colonies and I consider that the links binding the Empire together would thereby be strengthened. A self-governing Colony would like to get an unbiased opinion of their forces from our best general. What they hate is a Curly, and Ivor Herbert, or a Dundonald who mixes himself up in their local politics. These Colonies would naturally pay the travelling expenses of the I.G. or his nominee, as the Cape and Natal did for the Duke so far as railway travel was concerned. It is true that at home some faces are suffering from a plethora of inspections, notably the Yeomanry. That is because each Inspector, as a rule, wants to earmark a day for himself, whereas all that is required with forces trained for a few days or weeks only, is that he should be on the ground and should not make himself conspicuous. I also think that the D. of M.T. should be constantly in touch with the I.G. and should often be present at operations. To sit in the W.O. and spin manuals is folly without acquaintance with things being done. I observe a variety of training methods and different commands and I read a good many memos and circulars which show a variety of ways of looking at tactical problems. This may be all very well in some instances but when I remember the record of some generals still in high commands I doubt whether we are wise to allow everybody to give his personal impress to training.

The I.G. should coordinate training because he is the only man who understands, or should understand, the general effect of all being done in the several commands. He must act at once to do this, and should have some well-defined means of advising the A.C. and C. of G.S. and Co. As things are, you know that old N.G's idea of happiness is to have no questions asked, and that he rates men according to their capacity for leaving him alone. I love old N.G. but that does not blind me to the fact that he and many of his officers are the laughing stock of the Army and a fraud upon the public. I hope we may meet at Sir John's manoeuvres. I go to France 30th, and motor from Dieppe to Compiègne. Why not still join me at Dieppe or Newhaven morning of the 30th?

I hope you will not miss an article on "Moltke and Over-sea Invasion" [60] which the Times will publish soon. I expect I may be pelted after its appearance.

Churchill Archive, Cambridge, Esher Papers, ESHR 10/26

37
Repington to Esher

<u>Private</u>

29, Victoria Road,
Kensington,
W.

[Holograph]

5 October 1906

I hope to support the S. of S. in every way in my power, but that is no reason why you and I should treat one another as if we were a public meeting.

Mr Haldane has reduced the Army to propitiate a section of his party who are not worth propitiating; he has irritated the officers of the Army and has now manipulated the soldiers' pay by Royal Warrant. He has instituted a new system of training for Militia which can only appeal to wastrels, and has threatened the existence of half the Militia Force. He would, by your advice, impose upon the Volunteers an administration which they utterly distrust, and he has vexed the soul of the improvisation school by saying he will not give another shilling to the second line elements of whatever kind.

The difference between you and Mr Haldane is that you ride straight and at the price of an occasional heavy fall will always be in at the death. Haldane rides for a line of gaps; his seat will be safer but the worry will take place in his absence. You, as Minister would secure strong friendships and equally strong hatreds. Mr H. is a Laodacian neither hot nor cold and striving to please everybody will end by pleasing nobody. I am quite aware that if persuasion failed <u>you</u> would try force. I will believe that Mr H. will do so when I see it and not before.

The non-nebulous scheme you present in three paragraphs is very pretty, but where is the G.S. mobilisation scheme showing what force we require? Is it the same force as at present? Then why change anything? Is it more? Then how can it be done for the same money? What are the Associations but post offices for the cheques sent from the W.O. to the units? The scheme remains absolutely nebulous because it is only a generality and because you and others refuse to admit that soldiers should tackle the problem <u>as a whole</u> and present a working plan with full details of numbers, command, administration, finance etc. When Douglas Haig has settled something which the S. of S. dares to produce to the public, then we shall get on.

I am a strong supporter of the C. of D. in the abstract but when I am asked to give concrete expression of my fidelity to my ideal, then I can only think of faith, hope and charity. The C. of D. for all I know may have worked wonders. I hope so. The only concrete expression of their views was Arthur Balfour's speech of May 1905 which left much to be desired. When the C. of D. have produced "the bases upon which the military organisation of the Empire should rest", I will affirm that they have fulfilled their mission. This hole and corner business is useless in modern democracy. You must come out into the open, explain your policy, give details, lash people who disagree with you and carry policy out with a strong hand. I am sick to death of political alternativement!

Let Mr. Haldane, in the name of all that is practical, make an end of generalities and come to the point. What are our political commitments in India, Egypt, the Low Countries and so forth? What are our needs to fulfil the military needs of the defence of these interests? So many troops, guns, stores etc. in such a time. How are we to obtain these forces from home, India and the Colonies? How many troops from the Regular and Second Line forces? These things we want to have plainly stated so that everyone may see where we are going and why we are going there. When you have your standard you must work up to it, and you may then allow voluntary effort to work beyond the standard as much as it will without serious cost to the public. The standard already laid down for the Regulars or rather for the Senior Regular Expeditionary Force, is something for War Office purposes. In relation to strategic necessities it is a purely arbitrary and conventional figure meaning <u>nothing</u>.

I am writing this to irritate you as much as possible. I am not going to write in the Times like this; but everyone who gives serious consideration to these matters will arrive at the conclusions I have expressed unless you come to the business and make an end of generalities.

Mr. Haldane, I know, has the great gift of conquering all who approach him. His implacable serenity is a better shield than triple brass. He comes, he smiles, he conquers – but when he passes on, people compare impressions and agree they have been fooled. I confess I am one of Mr. Haldane's victims and am going to support him all the same simply because he has the big idea which every other Minister of War has lacked. But unless he will get the soldiers or somebody to work out the details of a working measure, he will follow the course of Dizzy's Protection and be not only dead but damned.[61] You may talk of the political majority but of which elements is it composed? You know as well as I do that it is about as safe an anchorage as the Goodwin sands. If we are to do any good we must have a policy upon which the Centre Party of both sides of the House will vote solid. Who cares for Keir Hardie and Co?[62] They will never go in harness so let their men loose. No one in the old days cared a fig for the extremists. Now the tendency is to bow to every breeze. I want Mr H. to succeed, but he cannot unless he takes a firm line and announces a clear policy. I read nothing in the press but criticism of the S. of S. scarcely a note of approval. His friends scarcely dare put pens to paper, because the saint they may vow themselves to may not prove to be <u>his</u> saint, and then they will be in the cart. Can't you get some lymph from a good, pigheaded priest from the propaganda College in Rome and innoculate the S. of S. with a single idea and purpose?

Churchill Archive, Cambridge, Esher Papers, ESHR 10/27

38
Repington to Thursfield

29, Victoria Road,
Kensington,
W.

[Holograph]

27 October 1906

Can you tell me who originated the term 'Blue Water School',[63] and where I may find a clear announcement of the principles of this school, if such exists? There appear to be so many shades of blue that a definition is to be desired.

The Times Archive, Thursfield Papers, AC96/27

39
Repington to Esher

<u>Private</u>

29, Victoria Road,
Kensington,
W.

[Holograph]

22 November 1906

You missed a real treat by not coming to our (NDA) dinner at the Ritz – not on account of the dinner itself, not on account of my paper, but because Mr Balfour took the opportunity to speak for nearly three quarters of an hour after I sat down and to give us certainly the best speech on Imperial Defence that he has ever delivered. You thought that Mr Balfour would never let pass the things I wrote in my paper. It is true that I altered the text and added a few things as I went along, but there was no substantial difference, yet A.B. supported me nearly throughout and declared that he agreed with every positive proposition that I advanced, I told Mr Balfour that it was a misfortune that his speech could not be published all over England the next day, but we had barred reporters and except for a few rough notes which some of us jotted down, I fear that the record of the speech – except those parts which were burnt into our memories – will not be preserved.

All the Admirals spoke – Custance, Noel and Bridge, but none of them ventured to tell us why we limit raids to 10,000 men, nor why two such raids can never occur, nor yet how many raids make one invasion. In fact they criticised very little while Noel frankly said he did not belong to the Blue Water School and he said many things that the public ought to know.

I am going to publish the revised version of my paper in the Times and I fear that it will give George Clarke and Thursfield fits and bring a whole flotilla of Navalists down on me. The more the merrier. Until we have put an end to all the damned nonsense that is written about sea power we shall never get our national Army.

When will you be up in town again?

Churchill Archive, Cambridge, Esher Papers, ESHR 10/27

40
Repington to Lord Roberts

29, Victoria Road,
Kensington,
W.

[Holograph]

28 November 1906

I am very much obliged to you for calling my attention to Mr Ellis Barker's book,[64] and I have passed on your powerful recommendation to the Editor of the Times. I read the XIX Century article by the same hand and was greatly impressed by it. I was glad that you mentioned it the other evening. I hope that the book will now be very thoroughly well reviewed. We are greatly in need of a strong civilian pen to back us up, as there is a curious idea in the country that great soldiers like your lordship have some occult reasons for desiring to see their country strong and respected. The more frock-coats and mutton-chop whiskers we can whip up the better. Mr Long has proposed that we should get someone to read a reply to my Blue Water paper, and I have asked Buckle whether his Naval correspondent will come up to the scratch. We must give him a very bad time if he does!

National Army Museum, Chelsea, Roberts Papers, R62/10

41
Repington to Lord Knollys

Private

29, Victoria Road,
Kensington,
W.

[Holograph]

15 December 1906

In September last I was informed by the Foreign Office that His Majesty had been graciously pleased to grant me his private permission to accept and wear any decoration that might be conferred upon me by the French Government. I have now received the decoration of Officier de la Légion d'Honneur, and it is suggested to me by the Foreign Office that I should be in order to express my thanks to His Majesty through you. May I therefore enlist your kind services for the purpose of expressing to His Majesty my dutiful thanks for the permission so graciously accorded to me to accept and wear the cross of this honourable order. I prize it not only on account of its historical interest and the many memories of the past which it conjures up, but also because it marks the interest taken by a friendly government in the labours of a work-a-day artisan of the entente to add a stone to the building of which His Gracious Majesty has been at once the architect and the master-builder.

Tiresome though family history often is, I should like to add that I think I can now finally and decently inter a family feud with France which has lasted for over six centuries. The Repingtons have only moved house once since the Conquest and that move was owing to the capture by the French of the Repington who fought at Poitiers. The heavy ransom exacted for his release compelled the family to sell their Lincolnshire property and to move to Amington near Tamworth where they have remained ever since. It has been handed down as a family duty to cry quits with the French, and the Repingtons have always followed the King in the old wars. Roger Repington was in your Lordships position and accompanied the Empress Maud to Germany: Sir Richard Repington was killed before the King in the 12th century: his son fought through all the French Wars of his day: Adam Repington was standard-bearer to Richard II, while to come down to later days, my grandfather, General à Court Repington captured a French colour with his own hands, and his brother took a French ship full of troops with a boat's crew of nine men.

We have got something back, and I hoped, when the crises of 1893 and 1898 arose that I might have added something more.

But since times have changed and His Majesty has been so happily inspired as to set the example of forgetting and forgiving, all that remains for me to do is to follow his gracious lead and to bury the hatchet.

Royal Archives, Windsor, RA w50/114

42
Repington to General E.T.H. Hutton

29, Victoria Road,
Kensington,
W.

[Holograph]

13 March 1907

Very many thanks for your letter of March 8 and for your encouraging and kind remarks about my articles.

I think that the Territorial Army Bill will lay the foundations of a National Army and that we should all support this constructive part of the government programme. I do not think the numbers are sufficient, but, given the formation proposed we can hereafter add to the numbers as we please, and it does not matter whether by voluntary service, quotas, or conscription. It gives us a large Militia force in second line, as you will doubtless see, and not be misled by the Balfours and Arnold-Forsters who try to queer the pitch for political ends.

No one has yet raised the question of the Ballot.[65] I understand your desire to retain some form of compulsion in an emergency but not to use this weapon in peace. Is this your view? I think it would be satisfied if the Ballot Act were re-cast and modernised and we shall all have to go for this but I am inclined to believe Haldane has the same idea at the back of his head. In any case there is a vast field opened up for future progress on the right lines, and no one can misdirect our efforts very much in the future once we have a big territorial scheme planted out in the counties.

We ought all to go for larger numbers, and we can only get them by forcing the government to consider the strategical needs of the Empire and to admit them. The C. of D. is now at work on this business and ultimately the truth and the facts will emerge and action must follow.

To make the National Army liable to serve where it is required abroad is a very difficult business. We must get the Associations this year: the Territorial Army gradually formed and completed in 1908 and 1909, and then we can see how we stand and begin to talk of liability for over-sea work. It will be a most difficult liability to <u>impose</u>, though it may be voluntarily undertaken, and I think will be. We cannot get all we want at once and must proceed by stages, gradually giving the public education and such food as their weak digestion can stand as they mature.

I hope that you will be very much benefited by your holiday, and will not forget the great opening that awaits you in Parliament.

British Library, E.T.H. Hutton Papers, Add. MSS., 50098, ff. 114–15

43
Repington to Raymond Marker

Brighton

[Holograph]

14 April 1907

Thanks for your letter. I will try and get hold of your letter to The Times and write again on the subject you have taken up.

I suppose I ought to be highly flattered at the good opinion of Wyndham, Dilke and others but to tell you the truth it is a little embarrassing and I would rather do without it.

All the criticism in the House has been piffle. The opponents of the S. of S. draw their arguments from the arsenal of compulsion. What is the good of this unless they are prepared to speak and vote for compulsion? Are they? No, not one of them; therefore it is all futility.

There were three courses open to the opposition. They might find serious defects in the scheme which might be made good: they might present a better alternative scheme on the voluntary basis: or they might go over frankly to compulsion.

They have done none of these things, and not one practical proposal has come out of two day's debate. The Tories have been more stupid than I could have imagined possible. The plan will go through and will be a success and the only thing we will owe to the opposition will be some delays and misconception. They are a dead party in a Military sense unless they go over to compulsion. Then they can bring in a better scheme – and not before.

Any d—d fool, even a front bench Tory, can make a scheme with compulsion.

Don't waste your brains attacking me. Try to help.

British Library, Kitchener-Marker Papers, Add. MSS., 52277B., ff. 133–4

44
Repington to R.B. Haldane

<u>Private</u>

29, Victoria Road,
Kensington,
W.

[Holograph]

17 April 1907

You asked me the other day my opinion of the chances of your Bill in the Lords and I have since been reconnoitring in that direction.

Lord Lansdowne has asked me to go and talk the matter over with him. I have fixed Friday morning in the hope that I may be able to see you at any hour that suits in the course of tomorrow Thursday and learn from you the latest developments. I am quite at your service and if I can do anything to smooth matters over I shall be glad as I think that divergence of parties on a question of this kind is a national misfortune.

I have given Lord Lansdowne my views upon the attitude of the opposition in the plainest terms. I find him disposed to be friendly. He admits that your scheme has some very good points and disclaims all desire to make party capital out of its imperfections: he allows also that the uncompromising attitude of the Militia has to some extent forced your hand.

But he says that he is not behind the scenes and does not know whether an attempt was made to find a way out of the impasse. "Is it" he asks "conceivable that a way might be found even now?" He greatly regrets the "abolition" of the Militia because he is not, as at present advised, convinced by the ingenious attempts which are being made to show that the Force, or a substantial part of it, will after all survive and be found still

118

recognisable by its friends, and retaining its old traditions, within the new Territorial Army.

The above, I think, represents the line of attack which will be adopted and it remains to be seen whether you can offer Lord Lansdowne any solace or compromise which will make matters more easy. I have not seen Ellison, except for a moment or two, since the debate began, and I am not posted in any developments should such have taken place. I have had some correspondence with Dilke on the financial aspect of your scheme and have made my position quite clear to him. He tells me to-day that you are disposed to give more money, and I shall be glad to know whether there is anything in this.

However, this is secondary: the main point is to know whether I can do anything to assist you and Lord Lansdowne in finding common ground upon which both parties can stand and join hands.

P.S. Will you kindly consider my talk with Lord Lansdowne as confidential and ask Ellison to do the same. This is Lord L's wish.

National Army Museum, Chelsea, Ellison Papers, 8704–35–173

45
Repington to Haldane

<u>Private</u>

29, Victoria Road,
Kensington,
W.

[Holograph]

19 April 1907

I saw Lord Lansdowne this morning and had an hour's good talk with him. I find him very sympathetic and reasonable, and – to cut a long story short – he has no intention of wrecking your Bill. We discussed the whole of your scheme and I do not find that his Lordship has any other remedy to suggest for our troubles. He is disposed to agree with my view of the debate so far as it has gone, but he will be guided a good deal by Mr Balfour's speech and by yours next Tuesday. I think he is disposed also to desire that the Militia should go over bag and baggage to the special contingent, but though I have a sneaking fondness for this solution I pointed out its inferiority to that at which you have arrived. Lord Lansdowne is also inclined to think that too much has been made of the drafting question. I therefore explained to him the condition our battalions might be in a fortnight after a declaration of war and after a single battle in Western Europe. His Lordship favours his old plan of the three years term running concurrently with the longer service in order to swell the reserve. I said I thought you might get your equipoise in the artillery by this method, but that the men would probably have to be extra and that your 37,000 recruits would have to be increased as there was at present little or no margin after supplying the drafts.

I expatiated upon the advantages of the true Militia system which I consider you are introducing. Lord Lansdowne wished me to thank you for your suggestion that his Lordship should see any member of the Army Council. He seems to be pleased with the concessions you are prepared to give to the Territorial Army. He tells me that he is not working on the Army question with any other statesman or politician and that he has no knowledge of the Duke of Bedford's attitude beyond what he gathers from the Duke's speeches. I told Lord L. that I considered the issue of the Duke's circular to C.O's a breach of discipline and against the letter and spirit of the King's Regulations.

I need not trouble you with a summary of the conversation on the subject of compulsion, but I think Lord Lansdowne favours the view that until our military liabilities have been fairly estimated by the D[efence] C[ommittee] and the General Staff, and voluntary effort has proved itself to be inadequate to bring us up to standard, no change of principle is likely to occur. My own view, as you know, is that the Government after full inquiry should lay down the basis of the organisation of our forces on a scale to give us reasonable security in all contingencies that can be foreseen. This standard must be the largest number required in the shortest time to meet the greatest danger. We get from that the numbers in the first place, and in the second place we get the <u>time</u>, i.e. the amount of training necessary before war comes. I have not been fortunate enough to obtain your adhesion to this point of view at present, but I hope that when the General Staff emerges from its chrysalis condition it will be more lucky. Meanwhile I commend enclosed extract from Moltke's writings which exactly expresses the point of view I hold. Will you show it to Mr Balfour?

National Library of Scotland, Edinburgh, Haldane Papers, Ms.5907, ff. 144–5

46
Repington to Esher

Private

29, Victoria Road,
Kensington,
W.

[Holograph]

30, September 1907

Please consider the following extract of a letter which I have received from a high military authority as strictly private and for your information alone.

"Whilst French is beyond all question the man in the Army I would soonest serve under in war, there is no use at all in blinking the fact that he is out and away the worst member of the existing Selection Board. It is not that he consciously wishes to do jobs but that he seems to have considerably less insight into character than even Lyttleton or the Duke and is therefore willing and eager to put any incompetent acquaintance of his own into the most vitally important posts. Nevertheless, if he insists, as he certainly often will, upon his war responsibility, I at any rate do not think I shall be able to see my way to say him nay . . . Please don't imagine that I am discontented about the I.G's new position. What I dislike is the sham of the Selection Board being continued. Far better give French the M.S. and let him make the appointment. The big responsibility and the fear of hostile criticism would then be a great steadier. Now he will make the nominations but the responsibility to the public will be borne by the Selection Board – not a healthy state of affairs."

These remarks carry weight for me, because I have heard so many growls about Sir John's proceedings in the matter of appointments, and as I wish for his success I desire that this tendency of Army opinion should be checked by a cessation of its cause.

You and I know perfectly well that Sir John cares little about A or B, but he does care if he thinks he sees a good man, to push him on regardless of opposition, precedents, and the custom of the Army. This is all very well, but if it results in hostility to Sir John personally, he will not be able to carry out the good work which he could otherwise do. I do not know anything else likely to wreck his future usefulness, and I leave it to you to consider the matter and to exercise your diplomacy for the general good.

I want to talk with you about the Defence Committee Inquiry in Home Defence when you are in town and free. I think that Nick should be on it for many reasons. I also hope that all the practical men of the Navy who can speak on the subject of the North Sea, distribution of fleets, present condition of fleets, intelligence etc., will be called. I regard this of the utmost importance and so I am sure will you.

Churchill Archive, Cambridge, Esher Papers, ESHR 5/23

47
Repington to Esher

Private

29, Victoria Road,
Kensington,
W.

[Holograph]

7 October 1907

Your letter of October 1. was very interesting and I think you make out a very good case, prima facie, against my military friend.

But to state the case fairly it must be shown that the 14 first-rate men you name are Sir John's nominations, and that others of less merit are not his. I shall ask my military friend to state a case. All I really care for in this matter is that Sir John, in his new position, shall not give any cause to the enemy to blaspheme, that he shall be absolutely impartial and judicial and not mislead by private friendship. I have seen so many people lose the good opinion of the Army by descending to a few jobs, or at all events, errors of judgement, in support of their friends, not to desire very keenly that Sir John's bark shall not be wrecked on the same rock. I should not like to approach him on this subject, so I leave the matter to your attention.

I am very pleased that you approve of the two articles on the manoeuvres: there is a third, rather more dull, and I am not sure whether I shall publish it.

I am glad to hear that Sir John is backing Rawlinson for Murray's place. No, I should not call that a job, because he is the best man I can think of and has all the qualifications for the post. I am inclined to think, however, that there is an idea at H.Q. that what is called the Aldershot ring must be broken up, and the importance of Aldershot as compared with other commands be diminished. I am all against rings, and the worst is that at the W.O. itself since for many years past officers have gone from one post there to another, and I think the system might be made an end of.

I have just finished a report of my secret mission in 1898–9 and shall take it to Ottley and ask him to print it for the use of the Committee on Home Defence, or whatever it is to be called. I want you to see that this is done for I think I have shown not only what can be expected from a secret service, but also, which is more important, what can not be expected from it.

I hear of the composition of this Committee and it seems to be alright if I am well advised, especially the presence of Nick, French and Esher, and the absence of heads of W.O. and Admiralty and of N.G. and Fisher. That will give much more liberty and freedom, though I scarcely dare to expect it will be arranged until I hear the fact confirmed from the highest source.[66]

Now I want to know whether you can tell me whether any of us who sent the notes to Balfour are to be examined: when, and on what points? The subject is a very big one, and I think you ought to warn the witnesses a good long time in advance so that they may get their bearings. I presume there is no idea of keeping off the sailors, and that chiefs of all squadrons at home, and their staff officers and subordinate admirals, will be examined. The same respecting those misnamed 'coast defence commanders'. I do not think that any other inquiry by the C. of D. promises better than this, or is more important.

I have written to the S. of S. to suggest that he should decide at once whether the Volunteers are to be allowed to remain on, as they please, under the old terms, or whether a drastic change is to take place when the Associations are formed. I sent him a copy of some regimental orders of a Volunteer Corps in which the C.O. assured his men that they would do as they darned well pleased, and this is the general impression which seems to prevail, and it is, I think, justified by some remarks made by the S. of S. during the debates though I have not looked them up and only write from memory.[67] Obviously it is best to prevent the perpetuation of a duplex system, and it is the old wrangle whether we are to say "shall" or "may". If the S. of S. is not committed, the "shall" is best on the whole, but Volunteers think he is committed, and the view is that the whole lot will come in fairly soon if they are not squeezed and commanded at the outset. All I say is that if the drastic course is to be taken it should be taken at once and explained in a circular, for orders like those I have sent to Mr Haldane will certainly cause an outcry if he decided to harden his heart. I daresay he will send you on my enclosure if you ask for it. I did not keep a copy.

If I was to hear that I was to be examined by the committee I should take a run over to certain foreign watering places which shall be nameless, and bring back the latest news, to complete the 'Notes'.

I did not write to you at Balmoral because I felt rebellious on the subject of Bully Oliphant, and H.M's praise of the Home Fleet, which is contrary to all I hear from sailors, and to the little atom of personal investigation which I sent to you a month or two ago.[68] I think Oliphant is one of the most charming companions one can desire, especially if one is a card player, but as for supervising and controlling a big idea like the Territorial and Reserve Forces Act, well, what do you think? I do not know who advises H.M. in these matters, or indeed whether anyone does, but I repeat that I feel rebellious, and so did not write to Balmoral, having no desire to date my next letter from the Tower. Shall I throw a bomb, or shall I write and explain that an officer who has been passed over four times for promotion is obviously the right man for the Crown to impose upon the A.C. for a very important command?

Have you heard the story of the white ammunition columns for India? It is a jewel, and exposes the perfect uselesness of N.G. and Edward Ward. May[69] writes and commits the War Office to substitution of whites for blacks in these columns. India growls and objects and finally gives way. Then W.O. discover that it means 900 more artillery at home and an increase in home estimates of £45,000, and finds that N.G. and Ward initialled and passed the proposal without consulting the departments concerned. To throw over May and Co. will make the W.O. look foolish, so it appears they do not know what to be at. My solution is to write, 'Dear Lord K, when we said white, we did not mean pure white, only chocolatey white, i.e. Eurasian. Please arrange.' But I don't know if this will wash!

P.S. I see in the papers that Lucas[70] has arranged County Associations for two Northern counties, and a joint committee. I hope that you are keeping your eye on what is being done as I don't much like these implications.

Churchill Archive, Cambridge, Esher Papers, ESHR 5/23

48
Repington to Leo Maxse

29, Victoria Road,
Kensington,
W.

[Holograph]

15 October 1907

I saw your kind references to my article on German naval policy in your October number and am much obliged to you for them. I am now taking on the Blue Water men in 'The Times' to keep my hand in and intend to make myself unpleasant. They carry many guns but I shall try to knock them out all the same, even if I have to fight a score of them alone.

I am sending you herewith an article on "Invasion and Home Defence" which expounds fully my views on all this question. Will you look at it and tell me whether you can find room for it in your November number?[71]

I ask because we are so full up I doubt that I can publish it in "The Times" before the Defence Committee Inquiry into this question comes on next month.

It will be better to say nothing about the Inquiry which Roberts, Lovat, Sammy Scott and I have wrung from the Government and a very hostile Admiralty. It will begin about 20 November. Do not run down Arthur Balfour on this question. We four have made great efforts to convert him this year and he has written an admirable letter to the Defence Committee forwarding our views and will, I think, come over to us. This is all very confidential for your personal information, and the less said about it the better.

P.S. If you use the article you might entitle it as by the M[ilitary] C[orrespondent] of The Times, as it is continuation and explanation of my views in the paper.

West Sussex Record Office, Chichester, L.J. Maxse Papers, 457, f. 587

49
Repington to Lord Roberts

<u>Private</u>

29, Victoria Road,
Kensington,
W.

Holograph

22 October 1907

I have been awaiting your return home to thank you very much for your kind letter of a few weeks ago on the subject of the manoeuvres. It was of great value to me to know your views, and you may perhaps have seen that I said something more on the subject of the marked enemy and of the distinction between direction and command in a further article on the operations.

But the chief matter concerning which I desire to write to you is the question of the Inquiry into Home Defence. You are no doubt aware that the Prime Minister has given some sort of promise that such inquiry shall be held, and Mr Haldane has given me an assurance to the same effect, mentioning December or January as the probable date. I hear however that efforts are being made to burke inquiry, and I hope, sir, you will do your utmost to impress upon everyone the extreme importance of the inquiry being held. Since Lovat sailed we have continued our investigations and I hope that we may soon complete them. Scott and I propose to run over to Germany, possibly next week, and it would be a very good thing if we could meet you in town before we went.

I have been engaged in a controversy with some of the navalists in the Times, and I hope I have proved conclusively that both in the past and the present the scale of a ton per man has been the rule; in the past as regards important expeditions, and in the present as regards infantry. You will find my concluding letter in to-day's Times, and I shall have an article on "invasion" in next month's National Review.

I have also had some confidential talk with Lord Charles Beresford and also with Sturdee his Chief of Staff, and I am most anxious that these and other practical men shall be examined, for they seem to be far from satisfied that they can defend these shores with existing arrangements, or rather the want of them. I fear that Sir John Fisher fears that awkward questions may arise and is opposed to inquiry. The first cabinet is on Nov. 5. and it will then, I suppose, be decided. Perhaps it would be best, sir, that you should communicate with Mr Balfour and learn his views. Hoping that you have enjoyed your trip abroad.

National Army Museum, Chelsea, Roberts Papers, R62/12

50
Repington to Esher

29, Victoria Road,
Kensington,
W.

[Holograph]

31 October 1907

Mr Haldane has given me an assurance that the inquiry will be held and before this happens I want very much to show you the results of my investigations. When you have a couple of hours to spare I will bring maps and papers and go through the whole story with you, if it would not bore you to excess, because I want you to understand my case before the witnesses come before you. If you could get Sir John French too, it would be most useful to me.

I am prepared to show that I can bring over 150,000 Germans, with 200 field guns and howitzers, 60 machine guns, 500 rounds per gun and rifle, and some 7,000 horses on 200,000 tons of shipping. I want to explain my point of view concerning:-

(1) The general strategy of the North Sea with regard to this problem.

(2) The German organisation so far as it is affected by the expedition proposed.

(3) The selection of German units and their concentration at ports by rail.

(4) Situation at the German ports and facilities for embarkation and rapid despatch: ships and tonnage.

(5) Probable points of landing, with the reasons for selecting them.

There is much more. I do not care whether you accept my point of view or not so long as you are prepared to see the weak points in the other side before the witnesses come before you, as you did in the N.W. Frontier case, to the very great benefit of the inquiry.

Churchill Archive, Cambridge, Esher Papers, ESHR 5/23

51
Repington to Lord Roberts
Private and Confidential

29, Victoria Road,
Kensington,
W.

[Holograph]

20, November, 1907

Please see and kindly return the enclosed letter from Colonel Stackpole.[72] We must certainly bring him forward even though I cannot get out of him the pith of his evidence so I do not know what he will say. I think I made it perfectly clear what we required, namely, greatest rapidity with which all arms can be embarked with good arrangements, but I rather gather that he is a little huffy about his treatment, and will only speak when called upon by the Committee.

I enclose a short draft statement about Major Huguet's communication to me. It is so important that I am inclined to think you, sir, might use it as a proof of the utter foolery of neglecting the enemy's point of view – the course usually followed by our people and the Navy in particular.

If you care that I should run through my evidence with you before you appear on the 27th I shall be entirely at your disposal any day and hour. The general purport of my evidence will be to show step by step how your hypothesis works out as a problem for the German staff. I take every point in succession. The defences in the Forth are, I find, as follows:–

On Inch Keith	3 – 9.2" guns
	4 – 6" "
at Kingham/	1 – 9.2" gun
Kinghorn	2 – 6" guns

Inch Keith fort is from 6 to 11 miles from the landing places East of Leith in the Forth, and 13 miles from Largo Bay on the north shore. Kinghorn is the same distance from Largo Bay, and 2½ miles further from the landing places east of Leith. Both forts should be 'cut out' at the first surprise by night, or dealt with by a few old type armour clad ships. This ought to be a simple affair, and even if it is not the landing could go on well out of range. You will of course, sir, regard all this as confidential.

<u>Secret</u>

<u>Draft</u>

The French Military attaché has recently informed Colonel Repington that, at the time when Mr Balfour spoke in 1905, France not only had a plan of invasion ready, but that everyone concerned in the plan was confident that it would prove successful. Major Huguet told Colonel Repington that the plan was based on surprise, and that such surprise could be counted upon owing to our state of mind upon the issue in question: that all the material required for a rapid disembarkation had been secretly accumulated at the French Channel ports: that the intention was to land one Sunday at dawn on the open beach on the South coast, and that the subsequent fate of the Transports was a matter of no moment. I mention this very important admission because it shows that unless we are able to place ourselves in an enemy's position and to study the problem from his point of view, we should do much better not to study the question at all, and thus avoid comforting conclusions which may prove to be devoid of all value, and, in short, full of danger.

National Army Museum, Chelsea, Roberts Papers, R62/25

52
Repington to Lord Roberts
Private and Confidential

29, Victoria Road,
Kensington,
W.

[Holograph]

20 November 1907

I am sorry to bombard you with letters in this way but I have had a talk with one or two members of the future Committee in order to feel their pulse, and beg to offer the following suggestions which might be incorporated in your opening statement in some way if you approved.

(1)   It will be well to lay a little more stress upon the fact that our hypothesis is merely an example and that many others will naturally occur to the Committee, such as the employment of part of our Fleet elsewhere: the sudden occurrence of some critical incident: the accession of one or more other Powers to a German League against us, and so forth.

(2)   We must say, and lay great stress on the fact, that no matter how strong our Navy the main deterrent to invasion is a numerous and efficient army, and the main temptation to invasion, the reverse state of affairs; that this fact is particularly true of great military states in which soldiers have the predominant influence, and that consequently, even if the Navy were double as strong relatively to other Powers, as it is, the necessity of maintaining a strong and efficient field army at home would still be an essential condition of peace and security, as well as of public confidence.

National Army Museum, Chelsea, Roberts Papers, R62/25

53
Repington to Lord Roberts

Private

29, Victoria Road,
Kensington,
W.

[Holograph]

24 November 1907

Lord Charles Beresford called here yesterday evening and we had a talk. He advises us to omit the suggestion about laying mines in the Straits of Dover as he thinks it is possible we might be upset on some technical objection owing to strength of tides. Perhaps therefore it would be well to act on this advice and to eliminate reference to mining the Straits, and the Channels between the banks off the Norfolk coast. The reference to mining up Sheerness should however remain in, as Lord Charles thinks this can and will be done, but we had better only state that in general terms and not refer to mining <u>channels</u> in the Thames Estuary. I should say that one could invent a mine to act in a tideway when anchored, but until we have thrashed this out with some technical expert we shall do best not to give an opening by alluding to it.

I asked Lord Charles whether if the German High Sea Fleet appeared in the Straits last night, they could hold it for 48 hours. <u>He thought they could,</u> and he said the question has never been examined from that point of view. This is rather an important admission.

On considering the Dogger Bank case, I expect that if we alluded to it the answer will be that the whole object of the redistribution of the fleet was to prevent its recurrence.

Lord Charles says that if he is asked whether a German invasion could take place at present his answer will be in the affirmative.

P.S. On thinking over Sir G. Clarke's memo on our notes, I think it would be best that we should draw up a reply, and hand it in to the Committee in January when we have all considered it and signed it, Lovat included. We had better say nothing about this in the interval, because if we ask permission to do this, the Committee may refuse; whereas they cannot refuse to accept a paper from us which actually reaches them. If your Lordship agrees I will set to work on a draft when you can spare me the paper. George Clarke would never have <u>dared</u> publish such a paper because it would have been torn to shreds.

National Army Museum, Chelsea, Roberts Papers, R62/26

54
Repington to Lord Roberts

Private

29, Victoria Road,
Kensington,
W.

[Holograph]

29 November 1907

I got through the remainder of my evidence yesterday in an hour or so, and the Committee then deliberated for an hour. I have waited to write to you until I could learn what had been said and done. I believe that they are much impressed with the manner in which the whole case has been presented and that we have done a good day's work in placing all the facts before them.

But, after I left, Sir John Fisher, I understand, took the floor and was very rude and violent, endeavouring to bluff and bully the Chairman who seems to me a trifle weak. Of course, with a man like John Morley such a performance on Sir John Fisher's part would have been promptly suppressed, and it seems to me a great admission of weakness. We shall have to stand no nonsense from him when we are cross-examined.

Two questions were decided, and in both cases against Fisher. He wished to postpone matters as long as possible, but the Committee decided to meet again on December 12. Fisher also wished that the W.O. and Admiralty should draw up a joint statement in reply to us, but this was negated, and each department is to draw up its own statement. That is practically the whole result of the deliberation so far as I can learn, but I believe Fisher hopes to palm off some statement of his own as a complete answer to us and to evade the calling of witnesses. In this case, what was the use of a Committee? The Prime Minister would have asked for Fisher's views without assembling a committee and I think this must become obvious before the next meeting, when I hope the soldiers will have had time to determine upon a firm line.

Fisher also tries to make out that we try to dictate to the Committee what witnesses they should call. This of course is a mere trick. When Asquith asked me if I wished to call any other witness I said that you had handed in a list of names which we suggested to the Committee but that we left it to them, and had presented our case, so far as we can be said to have a case of our own. Asquith is too much inclined to make us the protagonists in this affair and I think we must explain to him that we do not consider that such a view will conduce to the public interest, our view being that the Committee should prosecute their inquiries through responsible authorities.

One real difficulty is this. Both with regard to W.O. and Admiralty, if the Committee dare to learn the truth, both Lyttelton and Fisher are not unlikely to have to appear in the white sheets of penitents, and as fellows in misfortune they may combine against us. Much hinges on Nicholson and French. If they are bold and strong we may have a full inquiry, but I am by no means certain what the result of the next meeting will be.

In any case, Sir, we have done our best, and I think that when your statement reaches the various members of the Cabinet they can scarcely fail to understand the real situation of affairs.

National Army Museum, Chelsea, Roberts Papers, R62/27

55
Repington to Lord Roberts

29, Victoria Road,
Kensington,
W.

[Holograph]

12 December 1907

I must write to congratulate you again upon the splendid stand you made to-day against Lord Tweedmouth's vicious and deplorable attack – for I can call it nothing else. You certainly kept your temper in a wonderful manner, and I only regret that Tweedmouth did not examine me as I meant to have a cut at him. Anything more <u>ludicrous</u> than a person like Tweedmouth setting himself up as a superior authority to you on matters of war can scarcely be conceived, and everyone is impressed with the deplorable character of his undignified attitude towards you. I hope he will be ashamed of himself when he sees the evidence.

Many thanks for your valuable assistance during my cross-examination. The way you countered Fisher was splendid, and your remark that he would not know where the convoy was knocked the bottom out of his argument that he would evade the German Fleet in the Straits. As if he could! when we know that the German High Sea Fleet is a 16 knot fleet, and our Channel Fleet only 14½ knots!

There are one or two points in your replies to Lord Esher about which I should like to talk to you. I think he <u>wanted</u> you to say that when you were C. in C. plans were made against invasion, but that after Balfour's speech no one took any more trouble.

Also I suggest, sir, that you should carefully review and revise your answer about the number of troops required to meet 150,000 Germans. I think it would be well to draw up a statement and send it to Asquith, saying – as I think was the case – that you did not understand the question. I did not understand it myself but I see it now. What Esher wants to get at is a <u>standard</u> for the home army in the absence of the regulars. Now I must say that taking the Volunteers and Yeomen as they stand, and with the training and organisation they are to receive in future, I do not think that one could make anything of a fight with less than 4 to 1. When we began the Walcheren Expedition Napoleon sent orders to his second line troops that they were not to attack unless 4 to 1 and or with a superior and more numerous artillery and I think that until training periods are increased we might take the same figure. This gives 600,000 Territorials for the active army in Great Britain (second line); then there are the fortress troops 150,000 or so, and then the reinforcement for Ireland, perhaps 50,000. So that, with the Regulars out of the country, we ought to have <u>800,000 Territorials available</u>, at least.

If your Lordship does not amend your reply on this point, and if you leave standing the figure of 2 to 1 without further explanation, the sailors will say "What more then do you want, for Mr Haldane promises 300,000 men, and these in the Militia and surplus Regulars besides." I also think, sir, that we ought to make clear to the Committee that the military value of the Volunteer Corps varies from 100 to zero, and that the above figures include good, bad and indifferent.

The great point – and I am sure, sir, that you will agree with me – is to get the future standard for the national army in second line, and I think that the purport of Esher's question escaped us both. It is <u>most</u> important to make this right, and perhaps sir you will decide what is best to be done to put the matter right.

I think we held our own right well, and scored a good many new points besides, and I must once more congratulate your Lordship upon the splendid manner in which you handled the whole case. It will always remain with me as a deeply interesting example of the great public work you are doing, and of the wonderful energy and ever-fresh mind you bring to bear upon the most serious problem of national defence.

P.S. I think that considering the manner in which papers are kept from us, we had both better get the proofs of our cross-examination typewritten so that we may have copies, both for ourselves, Lovat and Scott.

National Army Museum, Chelsea, Roberts Papers, R62/32

56
Repington to Lord Roberts

29, Victoria Road,
Kensington,
W.

[Holograph]

2 January 1908

Scott is critical of the memo and as I am a believer in his judgement I am rather disposed to abandon the idea of reading it if you approve. There is trouble at the Admiralty about the Estimates which are 32 millions and the Cabinet is kicking. Now is not this a good opportunity for us to settle the matter out of court? What do you say to a compromise with Sir J.F. and his merry men, on the basis that if they support our views for a strong Territorial Army and withdraw their pretensions to play the part of the Army and Navy, we will support them on their increased estimates? I feel that we both have the same objects in view, and that the more we wrangle the more we shall both suffer. If you are not averse to such a compromise I will feel my way to an understanding, but we shall have to make quite sure that our position is resolutely maintained. Perhaps sir you will write me your ideas on this subject. I shall go down to Scott's on Saturday afternoon till Monday – Westbury Manor, Brackley.

P.S. If you will send me a wire here to say you approve a compromise on lines proposed I may be able to open negotiations on Saturday. There is no time to lose.

National Army Museum, Chelsea, Roberts Papers, R62/35

57
Repington to Esher

29, Victoria Road,
Kensington,
W.

[Holograph]

4 January 1908

I had just written you a long letter containing some further information about 'Times' affairs when I received a letter from Arthur Walter begging me to keep the whole affair secret until an announcement was made. So I will only say that all goes well and that one important matter will be different from what you expected.

I want you to meet Walter, as, at a pinch, he can and does control the policy of the paper, little as a rule though he interferes with Buckle. Will you lunch Savoy 1:30 Monday Jan. 13? Or fix your own day that week.

Walter is impressed with your idea of a Times Defence Committee, as am I. I think it may come off though Buckle rather shies. I would like you to draw up a paper embodying heads of a policy and we might talk it over one day next week, but you are a busy man and I may be making too great a claim upon your time.

If we have the meeting I think Walter would like you to come to it, in fact, he suggested it.

I have been reflecting upon our last conversation. It seems to me that the Roberts and Fisher parties ought to arrive at a compromise because they have the same ends in view and only different means of attaining those ends. A prolongation of differences will only allow the politicians who care for none of these things, to play off one against the other. I approached Lord Roberts but found him averse to any action in this sense. But I think you might find a way and I want you to consider it. Any compromise must of course accept the view that Mr H's general policy is to hold good and that a large national army in second line is indispensible. Until the Fisher folk acknowledge this, we must fight, and if they suffer in the contest tant pis pour eux![73] I need not tell you that one word from the King to Fisher and Roberts that an agreement is desirable in the public interest would settle the matter at once. I do not know any other authority that the two fighting cocks would accept.

Churchill Archive, Cambridge, Esher Papers, ESHR 5/25

58
Repington to Lord Roberts

29, Victoria Road,
Kensington,
W.

[Holograph]

29 January 1908

I shall be lunching at the Carlton Restaurant with Spender (Westminster Gazette) at 1.15 to-day, so I cannot accept your kind invitation. But I will call at the Senior directly Spender leaves, on the chance of catching you. Should you have finished lunch earlier and care to come over, you will find us in the upper restaurant.

I did not take away any very clear impressions from the last meeting, as the proceedings were so fragmentary and discursive. We went there to disprove Balfour's facts and figures and were mainly occupied in a discussion of naval strategy and tactics, which really had nothing to do with the point.

All I feel sure of is that Slade did not attempt to traverse any of our statements of fact, and in fact seemed to me to give away the whole case about ships and tonnage. As Ewart admits the military facilities for concentration and embarking, we seem to me to have established our case in all except the question of naval risk, which is and must always remain a matter of opinion.

I am extremely dissatisfied with Slade's statement about Huguet's admissions. I have not the shadow of a doubt that Huguet is correct and that Slade has made enquiries from the French naval folk who have misinformed him. I propose to address a letter to Mr Asquith on this subject.

If this meeting closes the inquiry as far as we are concerned I think we might address a short memorandum on the whole case to Mr Asquith – so soon as we have seen and revised the proofs of yesterday's proceedings.

National Army Museum, Chelsea, Roberts Papers, R62/37

59
Repington to Lord Roberts

29, Victoria Road,
Kensington,
W.

[Holograph]

15 February 1908

In reply to your letter I have some confidential, and some published information. The first shows that the total reductions in strengths on Nov. 1 last, as compared with October 1905, are 20,356 all ranks on British Establishments (including Colonial and Indian troops on these establishments), 22,230 including Indian establishments. In the above, officers strengths were 7,846 on British establishments end of 1905, and 7,576 in Nov. 1907. Including India, total strengths of Regular officers was 10,775 end of 1905, and 10,641 in Nov. 1907. Strengths of other ranks were 183,945 British Establishments and 76,715 Indian total 260,660 end of 1905; and 163,859 British, and 74,705 Indian, Total 238,564 in Nov. 1907.

The following is published information – reply by Mr Haldane to a question by Mr Pike Pease in the H. of C. some days ago. The dates compared are Oct.1905 and Jan. 1. 1908.

The total are for infantry of the line only and I think are strengths.

	Officers	NCO's and Men	Total
1905	4,423	146,532	150,955
1908	4,321	131,512	135,833

Same dates the Militia stood at:–

	Officers	NCO's and Men	Total	Reserve
1905	2,395	85,814	88,209	7,657
1908	2,143	83,672	85,815	2,321

I hope that this information will be what you require: Army Reserve is excluded.

You will see that I have a cut at the policy of 'raid and scuttle' on the frontier this morning, and that my good editor opposes me in order to confuse opinion, or at all events with that effect. I may have to answer the leader by saying that if India is disturbed it is not a good time for starting raid and scuttle at all: secondly that I fully accept the policy of dealing gradually with the whole Afridi, Orakzai, and Mahsud Wazari areas: lastly that the Amir has no more reason than we have to delight in the existence of marauders on his frontier.

He may be cross at not having been consulted about the Anglo-Russia agreement, but that is a different matter.

National Army Museum, Chelsea, Roberts Papers, R62/44

60
Repington to Mrs Mary Haldane

29, Victoria Road,
Kensington,
W.

[Holograph]

27 February 1908

Your kind messages, and those of your daughter, have given me great pleasure, and I only wish that all the politicians and critics would adopt the view of your son's policy which I hold and endeavour to make others accept. Unfortunately it is still difficult for some Unionists to admit that any Liberal can do anything good or useful, while the tribe of Laodiceans[74] is particularly numerous and more harmful than open foes. I have to pander to these gentry by criticising details of your son's policy, because, if I were to fail to do so when fair matter for criticism arises, I should be dubbed a partisan and the effect of my general support of his policy as a whole would be lost. I am convinced in my own mind that your son is the best Minister for War that we have had in our time, and I only hope that the tail of his party will never compel him to vary by a hairsbreadth from the policy of his memorandum.

I am so very sorry to hear that you are among the influenza victims and I hope most sincerely that you will be able to throw off the effects of the attack and be soon restored to your normal health. Will you please tell your daughter that I have still to thank her for a very kind letter written earlier in the year, and that I trust I may be able to do so in person when she comes south.

Your son has been most plucky, too plucky I think, during his illness, and he attended the Militia Club dinner when he ought to have been in bed, but I hope and think that he is fast recovering now.

National Library of Scotland, Edinburgh, Haldane Papers, Ms.6080, ff. 5–6

61
Repington to Sir Charles Dilke

29, Victoria Road,
Kensington,
W.

[Holograph]

10 March 1908

No increase that has been made in our Regulars in India since the Mutiny has brought up the strength of these troops to a higher figure than that recommended by the Peel Commission in 1860. The fact that increases have been made from time to time must be taken in conjunction with the decreases below the standard and is inseparable from them, as surely you must agree.

No indeed, I did not for a moment think or suggest that you asked that money should be taken from the Regulars for the Territorials. I heard your speech and you made no suggestion of the kind.

It was made by MacCrae[75] whom I take to be a good and useful man. This part of his speech did not appear in "The Times" report so I did not like to mention his name, but I heard him say it, and have no doubt it will appear in the proof of the official report of the debate.

It is a hard enough job to make the average Regular do anything but laugh at the Territorials, but naturally, if enthusiasts propose to starve the Regulars to make the T.A. better, then there will be a reaction, and the T.A. will prove a failure. I believe the Haldane plan is the best we can obtain for the country at present, but it must be regarded as a whole. I do not much mind the enthusiasm of your Dukes and Marquises for the T.A. just now because the work cannot be fairly begun without the prevalence of this enthusiasm. I would not do anything to suppress it, especially as I think that when the novelty has worn off the Associations will be less strongly manned than they are now.

You and I, of course, take different views about the necessity for retaining the so-called Cardwell system.[76] I am an opportunist in this matter, and if Parliament always consisted of reasonable beings I would gladly see the whole question reconsidered. But, as things are, the only result would be a general weakening of our military strength. Therefore I will not look at it until we have the Special Reserve and the T.A. in being, and efficient. I wish you would raise, in Committee, the question of mobilisation to which I have referred. Nicholson is capable of putting it right when he takes up the reins, but a good racket from you in the House would do a lot of good.

My Imperial bomb[77] has caused a panic among all the office holders of your party, and has brought maledictions, to which I am quite indifferent, upon me. Our diplomacy is at a disadvantage if Ministers are to be approached and influenced by seductive monarchs, and I was determined to put a stop to a thoroughly unconstitutional practice. Is the House of Commons dead to its tradition that it should not support me?

British Library, Charles Dilke Papers, Add. MSS., 43920, ff. 52–3

62
Repington to Leo Maxse

29, Victoria Road,
Kensington,
W.

[Holograph]

11 March 1908

You are quite right about the jealousy of "The Times". It has been rather a revelation to me, showing as it does that a number of papers care more for their own than for national interests. I do not expect to see any adequate treatment of the Episode until I read the National of next month. I have given you a pretty effective weapon to use at meetings for you can say that a servant of the public was unable to disclose his communications to a foreign potentate.

I certainly claim Asquith's statement on naval policy yesterday to be a direct result of my action. They have had the devil of a scare and have been terrified lest I should print both letter and reply. I think you wrong Haldane. Anyway, he has stuck up for me in the Cabinet, and as to his communications with Germany I know nothing except that he is more likely to profit by them than William if they have taken place. I do not think that I should be likely to <u>pactiser</u> with anyone who was promoting German interests, and I frankly confess that I trust Haldane and like him, as do all the soldiers who work with him.

There has been a great outcry for my blood among the Tapers and Tadpoles who have been shivering for their shekels. They only provoke my derision, and have no power to do me harm. They can square or silence the rabble who are seeking for office and rewards, but you and I they cannot square unless they convince us, and that is why they will always hate us like the devil. What a blessed thing is independence!

I hope you will slate that plaster of Paris platitudinarian, Rosebery, who asks the British public to act according to its fears of 4 million Germans. I have never read a more lamentable effusion!

It is a great pity you have not a daily paper under your hand these days. As for the Opposition, I presented them with an unequalled chance and they all remained tame as tom-cats. What can you do with such a crowd?[78]

West Sussex Record Office, Chichester, L.J. Maxse Papers, 458, ff. 663–4

63
Repington to J.L. Garvin

29, Victoria Road,
Kensington,
W.

[Holograph]

15 March 1908

I am obliged to you for sending me the "Observer", but naturally I have read it ever since you became Editor, and I congratulate you upon the proof you have given of how one man can transform a paper in one day. Whether we like it or not, and whether we agree with you or not, we have to read you, and you have made the British Sabbath almost bearable.

I am sorry to see that you condemn the Territorial Army a fortnight before its mother is taken with the pains of child-birth, because I fear that this may discount your views upon the subject of a more truly national army hereafter. There are already serious signs of financial stringency, and if your cry and Lord Roberts's is taken up, I fear we will not get our artillery material distributed over the country.[79]

I think it wiser to wait a bit before starting a serious campaign for compulsory training perhaps six months or a year, so that voluntary effort may have a fair field. Après, nous verrons.[80] We shall be in a much stronger position if we have the whole organisation laid out, and money spent upon it than if we have to start from scratch. A little patience, that is required, and then we ought to bring about a dozen press people who count together, and all start together. Please weigh this.

Humanities Center, University of Texas, J.L. Garvin Papers

64
Repington to Leo Maxse

29, Victoria Road,
Kensington,
W.

[Holograph]

18 March 1908

You will have seen your correspondence in The Times today.
I cannot move any more in this matter which is closed as far as we
are concerned. We have incurred much abuse and resentment for
doing a national service, and if public and parliament like to close
their eyes to the whole matter, that is their affair. I think that if any
action by the public, which you and others represent, can compel
the government to disgorge, it will be a great advantage. How can
letters exchanged between a foreign Monarch and a British
Minister concerning naval policy be 'Private and Personal'? It is a
rank absurdity: even the Germans admit as much. I think we
ought to have the letter, Tweedmouth's in any case. Parliament has
not done its duty, it has simply evaded it. I do not believe that the
great parliamentarians of the past would have permitted this
evasion of public duty. Parliament seems now to consist of office-
holders, office-seekers and lackeys.

West Sussex Record Office, Chichester, L.J. Maxse Papers, 458, f. 668

65
Repington to General Sir E.T.H. Hutton

Maryon Hall,
Frognal Lane,
Hampstead

[Holograph]

30 May 1908

Many thanks for the copy of your correspondence with the N.S.
League.

Your doubts, and mine, and those of other people, concerning
the real aims of this League are due to want of definition of their

plan, and they will never do any good until they put their cards down. I be hanged if I know what they want for they talked some time ago of 3 to 4 months initial training, and now Bobs crabs the Territorial artillery and says that even if they have 6 months training they will not be trained. All this is as confused as it is confusing, and I think we do best to go on backing Haldane who is <u>doing</u> something while others are only talking.

I can't think why Bobs has suddenly taken his new line, unless it is to attract attention. The only possible thing he can do is to prevent the creation of any artillery for the second line and how one is to create a National Army without artillery I do not know.[81] Happily he cannot effect this object for Haldane has a backbone and will go straight on regardless of all the old boys and professors who beat your "dead donkeys of pedantic professionalism". At the same time, my dear General, we must not in one breath boast our voluntary service and say we are in favour of compulsory military training.

My view is that we must give the Haldane plan a fair trial, and then say how many men we really need (a million I think) and show that only compulsory training can give it. If Bobs had taken his stand on want of numbers – he would have been on much firmer ground. Don't you agree?

British Library, E.T.H. Hutton Papers, Add. MSS., 50098, ff. 172–3

66
Repington to Miss Elizabeth Haldane

Maryon Hall,
Frognal Lane,
Hampstead.

[Holograph]

26 June 1908

It is good news that your scheme has been passed up to the Army Council and I am much obliged to you for promising to let me know later how the work goes on.[82]

I do not wonder that you are somewhat disturbed that your brother should be looking tired. War Ministers and military writers have had one misfortune in common during past years, namely that many of them have killed themselves by over-work at the office or the desk. My own Uncle, Sidney Herbert; Henderson and Cairns among the writers, have been among the victims. People do not understand the immense scope of defence questions, and the innumerable difficulties in the way of progress, until they take a hand in the work.

I think it is for you and your Mother to look after the Minister while he is looking after us, and to get him up to the north as soon as you can and for as long as you can. It is more important that he should keep fit and reserve himself for great occasions than that he should elect to 'payer de sa personne'[83] on every occasion and all over the country. He has set the machinery to work, and it will begin to grind out good results very soon.

I was vexed to see the paragraph in yesterday's Times, but in a way it has done good as it has led to the Birmingham announcement which is a good slap in the face for the Winston-Lloyd George intriguers, and I am delighted to see it. I am meditating another whack at them.[84]

National Library of Scotland, Edinburgh, Haldane Papers, Ms. 6020, ff. 202–3

67
Repington to Lord Northcliffe

Private

Maryon Hall,
Frognal Lane,
Hampstead.

[Holograph]

7 July 1908

Your messages were duly delivered to me and my idea is that we should meet in order that you should learn at first hand some of the difficulties I encounter in my work for "The Times", and thus be in a position to help me.

I shall be leaving Town in a fortnight and shall not be back until the close of the training at Salisbury Plain.

British Library, Northcliffe Papers, Add. MSS., 62253, f. 1

68
Repington to Sir G.F. Ellison

Maryon Hall,
Frognal Lane,
Hampstead.

[Holograph]

19 November 1908

I reciprocate your kind regrets that we see less of each other than before. I find that it is less inviting to leave these heights than it was to leave Kensington and I am not so often at the W.O. as before.[85] But I will look in and have a talk with pleasure.

You are very good to suggest that I have been of some slight assistance. We all know how much <u>you</u> have done and the immense help you were to the S. of S. – in fact I am convinced that without you things would not have taken the present course. It is a pleasure to think that you and I were in agreement throughout to support the best War Minister of modern times. I am firmly convinced that the next government will adhere to the lines laid down and that the only advance, on a great scale, likely to occur in our day, is the substitution of compulsory for voluntary training for the second line. I agree with you that our modern military regeneration is only beginning. It is a pleasure to hear of all the good work being done at the W.O. in almost every direction, but a modern army system is a plant of slow growth and festina lente[86] is a good maxim.

I have spent all the afternoon of to-day endeavouring to impress on the L.C.A. Recruiting Ctte. the need for local recruiting committees in the London Boroughs, and generally the necessity for the decentralization of recruiting work and organisation of local effort in London. I hope I have launched them on the right course and that they will get forward now: hitherto they have been muddling.

Much exercised at our Bob's motion on Monday and am wondering how I shall be able to hunt with the Robertian hounds and ride with the Haldanian hare![87]

National Army Museum, Chelsea, Ellison Papers, E8704–35–691

149

69
Repington to Esher

Private

Maryon Hall,
Frognal Lane,
Hampstead.

[Holograph]

20 January 1909

H[uguet] had unfortunately reported the conversation[88] to the French chargé d'affaires, but I hope after the explanation I was able to give, that no report will go to Paris. Cambon was to have returned yesternight. It took a great deal to disabuse H's mind of the impression it had received, but I think I succeeded, and have even a slight hope that it may be kept from Cambon. In any case, as I have told Haldane, I have a formal assurance that if any report gets to Paris I am to be informed, and I shall then warn Haldane and also you. You see Cambon has already given Clemenceau a formal assurance that he can count on us, and there is a risk that he may now go to Grey and ask for something more definite than Grey can possibly give. I therefore exerted myself to the utmost to prevent this. The odds are in favour of nothing happening, but after Cambon's clumsy entrée en matière[89] over the naval business I have a less exalted opinion of his diplomacy than before.

If you can be civil in some way to H[uguet] and the chargé d'affaires it may help to smooth matters down. He thinks he must be brûlé[90] for repeating the conversation to me. I have told him that you are above such littleness and that none of us can afford to do anything to render the entente less cordial.

Churchill Archive, Cambridge, Esher Papers, ESHR 5/29

70
Repington to Lord Roberts

Maryon Hall,
Frognal Lane,
Hampstead.

[Holograph]

26 March 1909

Your kind letter of the 18th has just reached me. I am glad that you liked my article which you mention.

You will have seen that your cause of national training has received an unexpected fillip by the revelations made by government speakers on the Naval Estimates.[91] The talk of naval supremacy has suddenly vanished and we are told that German constructive powers equal ours and that in 1912 we shall have 16 or 20 Dreadnoughts to the German 17. There has been a pretty hullabaloo, and I have driven the lesson home as well I could, and am now engaged in combats with the extreme navalists who are attacking me with their customary venom and inaccuracy. I hope you have seen the letters by Rosebery and Frederic Harrison in The Times. I feel sure that you will raise a debate on this question again soon, with Milner, and Curzon to support you, and I am sure that you will find much better support in the Lords than before. It was all very well for the navalists to talk when they boasted a supreme navy, but now they admit that the navy may not be supreme and still oppose national training!

We miss you sadly, but I am sure that you will make up for lost time on your return, and I trust that you have greatly benefited by your change and rest.[92]

National Army Museum, Chelsea, Roberts Papers, R62/60

71
Repington to Lord Roberts

Maryon Hall,
Frognal Lane,
Hampstead.

[Holograph]

14 April 1909

Yes, certainly, the home battalions are unfit for service till mobilized: I think we are all in agreement upon that point. I think that one of the great advantages of the N.S. League plan is the fact that it will allow us to maintain intact the Regular Army. Of other schemes, requiring longer compulsory training – say one or two years – I am very shy, because their cost will inevitably impose a large reduction of the Regulars at home. Do speak to Nicholson on this point, as I do not find his ideas quite so fixed as I should like, though please do not mention that I said so. With regard to your main point I have had various reports from Associations and Territorials and good talks with the W.O. people. I have asked the latter when they are going to tell us what numbers and what training the T.F. requires. Until we get an authoritative statement from the Gen-Staff on this point, we cannot get on. The G.S. say that they cannot answer till the autumn, because the numbers required will depend on the amount of training received and its results, and this latter cannot be judged till after this year's camps.

I do not know, sir, whether you are aware that the minimum drills are now very greatly exceeded in the great majority of corps. I hear of 3 and even 6 drills a week, but am unable to generalize without further particulars. I hope very much that you may be able to come to the Plain this Summer and see all arms of the T.F. at work and give us your opinion upon the results.

I quite agree that we must try to hurry up National Training, but when Kincaid-Smith stands on this platform and the Tories run a man against him it is enough to make one despair. I hope you will castigate this miserable party move.[93]

My view is that we may have to fight with the organisation we possess, for what it is worth,. We cannot go on having ultimatums and revolutions once a week without trouble in the end, and Germany is now in such a strong position by land and sea, Russia is weak, and France so divided, that we may find ourselves isolated at any moment. We ought to be prepared for this, but we are not. We have not an army strong enough to make our alliance worth having, and the T.F. is not numerically strong or well trained enough to release the Navy from coast guard business in the absence of the Regulars. We tell Australasia she must depend upon the Navy, well knowing that we cannot send a battlefleet to the Pacific.

All these, sir, are grave dangers against which you have warned the country continually, but we have few politicians worth their keep, and from neither party can I hope for support, still less action.

I should like very much to discuss the position with you one of these days. My paper has joined the Navy monomaniacs and can think of nothing but Dreadnoughts.

This is not a very hopeful letter, but I agree with you that the outlook does not justify hopefulness.

National Army Museum, Chelsea, Roberts Papers, R62/61

72
Repington to Esher

Maryon Hall,
Frognal Lane,
Hampstead.

[Holograph]

15 April 1909

I quite agree about affiliating the Frontiersmen to the T.F. though in principle I am opposed to the creation of more or less military bodies outside the recognised organisations, and by taking in the Legion of Frontiersmen one rather encourages similar extravagances. I will see Driscoll one day and will keep the papers for a few days if I may.[94]

I would like to have a talk with you one day about my conversation with the C.G.S. yesterday. I am to see him again on the 20th and could meet you anywhere in the morning of that day or at lunch as my appointment is for 3 pm.

Churchill Archive, Cambridge, Esher Papers, ESHR 5/30

73
Repington to Sir Edward Grey

Private and Confidential

Maryon Hall,
Frognal Lane,
Hampstead.

[Holograph]

10 May 1909

Owing to the difficulty of obtaining accurate information about the condition of the Russian Army from our people, I have recently made inquiries through the French General Staff who are more accurately informed.

I propose shortly to publish an article to explain the reasons why the Russians bent before the German menace to throw 600,000 men upon the Vistula. I need not trouble you with these reasons for doubtless you know them, but there are one or two points which I may bring to your notice as I may not find it expedient to publish them.

The Russians can place 2 Army Corps and the great bulk of their cavalry on the frontier between the 6th and 8th days of mobilization. The remainder of their Army of operations, amounting in all to 1,200,000 men will be ready by the 20th day of mobilization, and will be in a position to cross the frontier by the 30th day: 800,000 will be directed against Germany and 400,000 against Austria. The new Minister of War in Russia is bent upon improving this situation, and is of firmer character than his predecessor General Rediger who had no confidence in himself, Russia or in France, and whose pessimism was entertained by German influences in Petersburgh. I need not point out to you the immense military and financial resources of which Russia disposes beyond saying that they, and other indications, appear to show that nothing but the weakness of character of Russian Ministers allowed Russia to be stampeded by the German bluff.[95]

Should there be any other information on this subject which you may desire I will apply for it.

Public Record Office, Sir Edward Grey Papers, F.O.800/110

74
Repington to Leo Maxse

Maryon Hall,
Frognal Lane,
Hampstead.

[Holograph]

15 May 1909

My instinct tells me that the Humber report is a sham but I know nothing, having been laid up with a cold. I cannot believe that the Germans would be such consummate asses as to give themselves away by such a silly move. I will make inquiries and let you know if I hear anything worth telling you.

I believe that our naval secret service is bad. I think they have money but no brains. I had a smart passage of arms with Jacky, and Slade late D.N.I. upon this subject during the invasion inquiry when I had the satisfaction of telling them before five Cabinet Ministers that I did not trust their information. It has since come out how precious little they knew last year of what the Germans were doing. I wish you would recommend that the sub-committee of the C[ommittee] of D[efence] should overhaul our secret service system in the Navy. Jacky is all bounce, and Slade was as vain as a peacock and a silly old fathead to boot. Our naval officers and men are good and some ships are good, but in all big matters such as strategy, war plans, and secret service there is not a naval Power in the world to be compared with us for ignorance and presumption.[96]

It may interest you to know confidentially that I have been making inquiries through the General Staff of the French Army about the late German ultimatum, the reason for the Russian surrender, and the state of the Russian Army. I have sent an article to Buckle conveying the result of the French investigation and of mine, but as it may be a trifle too hot for Buckle's digestion I am going to send it on to you if it comes back.

The game for us to play is to hearten up the Russians into confidence in themselves and in the French, and to preach that the 3 Powers must stand together and all go in together when any one is attacked no matter what the cause or pretext of the attack on any one.[97]

You are doing harm by crabbing our military power. I have never attempted to influence you because I know it is useless and you would only misconstrue my remarks, but I repeat that you are doing harm and injuring unwittingly a great cause which you have at heart.

Some day when we meet I will tell you what has been done and then you will see as clearly as I do the importance of altering your tone.

I am sure you do not mind me writing so plainly.

West Sussex Record Office, Chichester, L.J. Maxse Papers, 459, ff. 180–1

75
Repington to Leo Maxse

Maryon Hall,
Frognal Lane,
Hampstead.

[Holograph]

18 May 1909

I have made inquiries about the Humber affair and find that neither the head of the German section of Ewart's branch, nor the young men of the C.I.D.[98] have any information on the subject. This is only negative evidence of course and I agree that the German is <u>capable de tout</u>, but I recommend you not to touch the subject unless you get positive proofs.

No indeed, I do not consider you intolerant. Very far from it. I know that we agree upon essentials and that differences upon points of detail are inevitable. No one deplores the reductions of the Regulars more than I do but when the voters return a party vowed to reduction in the cost of the Army what can a War Minister do but reduce? I don't think Haldane would have occupied any position at all had he stood out. He would have got the sack and that is all. He has had some terrible times with his party and it has only been by means of the most capable diplomacy, assisted by German aggression, that he has managed to save his party from ruining the army. It is not much use to expect that when a party has gained office it will not follow its own policy, good or bad. Haldane has saved all that could be saved, and much more than I dared to hope, while he has done everything possible to make up for the original crime.

I do not think that we can get a much bigger Regular Army, because 38,000 recruits a year can only produce a certain result and no more. The frog may blow himself out till he is tired but he is still a frog. The expansion must be on other lines and Haldane has made the old Militia into an oversea force and has organised a very tolerable second line Army behind. We have over 320,000 men in these islands, less recruits and sick, to draw upon for the campaign in Lorraine, Regulars, Reserve, and Special Reserve, and we have the 264,000 Territorials behind them. We have taken 74,000 recruits for the T.F. in the last 4 months, and the force is very popular among all classes and especially among the Tory peers and squires who are working on the Associations. I firmly believe that we can do no more than we have done so long as voluntary service is the law. Change that and any fool can make an Army. Certainly I want it changed, but meanwhile we may be at grips any day and any hour so I think we must make the best of what we have.

Why take your views of the T.F. at second hand? Why not come down this year and judge for yourself? If you are willing I will arrange for you to have a good look at all sorts of troops this Summer and to meet all the people who know and can enlighten you. London is full of old fogies and asses who do not know what is being done and talk of what they do not know. I am going off with the Yeomanry at the end of this week and hope to be with troops pretty well till the end of September. I should like you to see (1) Yeomanry May 24 to 28 any day: (2) Lancashire Territorial Divisions show parade July 5 to 7, Liverpool. (3) London Territorial Divisions Salisbury Plain first fortnight August (4) Regular cavalry Sept.14 to 16 Oxfordshire (5) Army manoeuvres (Berks, Wilts, Ox, and Glouc.) Sept. 20 to 22.

If you care to come I will arrange days. All that I want is that you should judge for yourself.

West Sussex Record Office, Chichester, L.J. Maxse Papers, 459, ff. 177–9

76
Repington to Leo Maxse

Private and Confidential

Maryon Hall,
Frognal Lane,
Hampstead.

[Holograph]

19 May 1909

I send you a few reflections on your last letter. I quite agree that we should endeavour to place a large army alongside the French and I have no doubt myself that we can put 150,000 men on the Meuse in a fortnight and that no Frenchman who knows the facts doubts the moral and material advantage of such support. I think we might increase this figure perhaps to 200,000 as we have over 300,000 men in these islands liable to overseas service, and in a few weeks time we might bring another division from the Mediterranean and 3 or 4 from India to make up your 250,000 – a figure with which I quite agree as it is the average strength of a modern army and both France and Germany will have 6 or 7 such armies in first line.

But I do not think that we can even hope to produce the modern style of armed-nation-army in France, because we must keep up the special type of Regulars which we require for our foreign service, and we cannot have, in addition to that, a conscript army, without Army Estimates of 50 to 60 millions.

I am all for the N.S. League plan which would soon supply a million Territorials, but please remember that the type of Army you will get that way will be at best only a slightly superior Army to the Territorials in point of quality and training, and will not be suitable for the particular war which you and I have in mind, namely the massenschlacht 14 days after declaration of war.

But if we can work up to 250,000 Regulars at or nearly at the first go off, and work hard with the Territorials – whether they are raised on the voluntary or compulsory basis after war has broken out – I think that we might well have a large and very fairly efficient force in the 2nd line which would weigh in the balance after the combatants were a bit exhausted. I am anxious in any case that given voluntary enlistment, we can do no better than we are doing. Admit compulsion and any fool can make an Army. I am convinced that the time for compulsion has come and that the N.S. League plan is the right one, but please do not credit that it will help us on the Meuse at the first go off. As to Clemenceau, it is true that we only talk of sending 4 divisions at first. We have got into a cleft stick over this because the evidence which we gave before the Invasion Inquiry frightened the Government into retaining 2 divisions at home. That was not our object I need scarcely say. But I tell the Frenchmen, and I hope you will tell them, not to fuss about this, because the naval situation will be cleared up before the mobilisation is completed. If we get licked at sea, no troops will go to France. If we win the whole lot can go and in my opinion certainly will go. That is why I give the figure at 150,000. It is actually 167,000 all told. There are a few medical and A.S.C. people still to find, but I can assure you that we have a net surplus of 40,000 Regulars after mobilising the 6 Divisions and the cavalry and I have told Haldane a dozen times that we can and should guarantee the whole lot to France. When we have the whole of the infantry and guns it is absurd to keep back 2 Divisions because a few of their auxiliary services are not quite complete, and especially as, in my opinion, these services are provided on an absurdly extravagant scale.

I think it is almost time that people who crab what is being done should tell us how we could do better with the laws we have. Not one single shadow of an alternative plan has been proposed. Read the last two days debates in the Lords, there is not a symptom of suggestion, it is all crab and by men who have failed in office. I am convinced that if Balfour returns to office he will continue on Haldane's lines because every other possible alternative has been tried and has failed, or else has been examined and rejected. There only remains the N.S. League plan, and this, as I have already said, while giving us the numerous second line of our needs, does not help us or France on the Meuse in the first decisive fights. I shall be curious to see how the Roberts, Middletons and company take it when Balfour comes in and changes nothing. I don't think he will ever restore the lost Regular battalions and I fear he will not go for compulsion. It appears to me that the Tory leaders fear compulsion because they fear to arm the people and prefer the better class T.F. (better I mean than a conscript army) because the T.F. is a conservative force and will not paint the town red if there are riots or troubles. This is my idea though not a word has been said about it.

I have turned it over scores of times and cannot see any way to improve matters very materially so long as we have voluntary service, nor to add weight on the Meuse in time if we have compulsion on N.S.L. lines.

West Sussex Record Office, Chichester, L.J. Maxse Papers, 459, ff. 188–92

77
Repington to Esher

Mildenhall Rectory,
Marlborough.

[Holograph]

15 September 1909

Thanks for your letter. I'm here till Friday when I go to the Crown Hotel, Farringdon, Berks, where Sir John will be. The Times will have two people with the Armies during the Army manoeuvres so I shall probably not write till they are over unless Sir John wants something said.

Here I am staying with A[rthur] P[aget] for his interdivisional 3rd and 4th divisions which have begun well.

You have correctly judged my views about the cavalry. I think that Allenby is a good man, strong, self-reliant and firm in character as well as leading, a very fine type. I asked Sir John whether he would have any objection to the appointment of an inspector of cavalry and he seemed to be in favour of it.

I was very well satisfied with the cavalry division and am sure it is on the right track. You will see what I have said in 3 articles on the subject and I hope that the views will be supported editorially when the last article appears – I hope today. I went at Lloyd

George about it when he was down at Lambourne. Very little is needed to make the division first rate.

But perhaps you have heard that the 1st brigade and Smith-Dorrien have had a difference.[99] The cavalry are a bit incensed about it, but I believe Dorrien to have been in the right, even if his temper was a little irascible when he spoke to his people. I had a talk with him about it: he had not heard before of the feeling which his criticisms had aroused. You will now appreciate some allusions to this affair at the end of my third and last cavalry article. I catch an occasional and fleeting glance of Maurice and shall no doubt see more of him and his chief at Farringdon.[100]

We have had most detestable weather this Summer and I am in rags. However, it has been a great experience to have spent four months on end with every class of troops and keeps one in touch. I wonder when you come South. Hoping that you and all your party are well. I am.

P.S. Excuse this scrawl written at dawn with a bad pen.

Churchill Archive, Cambridge, Esher Papers, ESHR 5/31

78
Repington to Esher

Maryon Hall,
Frognal Lane,
Hampstead.

[Holograph]

27 October 1909

It is always a great encouragement to me to have your good opinion upon work of mine, for, as I am sure you know, I value your opinion very highly.

I certainly hope that my proposals concerning the S[pecial] R[eserve] will not be viewed askance by the S. of S. and Nick as they are only a development of the theme which I touched upon at the W.O. conclave some months ago when you were present. They are of course more in line with Murray's ideas than those of Ellison, and the S. of S. is hardly prepared to go as far as I should wish in the direction of brigading and rendering potentially mobile the 74 S.R. battalions, though he is willing to do this for the 27 extra Reserve battalions in principle.

What I have tried to do is attract the Militia people towards the new policy and to make them see that all their ambitions can be realised within the cadre of the policy. If happily I could be successful we should cut the ground from under the feet of certain Tories who are playing up the old Militia prejudices by more or less committing themselves to a reversal of the S.R. policy, a reversal which would be, to my mind, fatal to the Army though it would please the squires. I regard it as of more importance to rope in the Militia than to make sure that official people are ready to go so far as I wish them to go. They will be bound to do so in time by force of circumstances and meanwhile I want to preserve the new policy intact. I have had a lot of correspondence with people like Lord Salisbury, and sent a proof to Sir C. Douglas before publishing, after telling Haldane that I am doing so.

Respecting officers, my view is that if we wish to preserve the type of officer who has made the Army and helped to make the Empire we must break with the public schools and establish Military Osbornes where education on modern lines will be thorough and cheap for those willing to engage to serve as officers for a certain term of years. I have just written two articles on "The Staff under Napoleon" which will, I hope, interest you when space admits of their publication, and I am contemplating other articles concerning which I want to talk to you.[101]

I dined with Sir John last night and we had a great talk upon every conceivable subject. I hope very much that the rest will have done you good and that you are feeling quite fit again.

Churchill Archive, Cambridge, Esher Papers, ESHR 5/32

79
Repington to Miss Elizabeth Haldane

Maryon Hall,
Frognal Lane,
Hampstead.

[Holograph]

29 December 1909

I am so much obliged for your two letters and am relieved to hear that your brother was better last night.[102] His illness is a great anxiety to all his friends and we shall not be happy until he is completely restored to health.

Please tell your mother how much I sympathise with her.

I will certainly come if you have need of someone to tell the electors what your brother has done for the Army during his administration but I hope with you that he will have no need of any support but that which his name and fame give to him. I make no doubt that he will get a smashing majority if your North Britons have not suddenly become demented. With Mrs Repington's kindest regards.

National Library of Scotland, Edinburgh, Haldane Papers, Ms. 6021, f. 160

80
Repington to Leo Maxse

Maryon Hall,
Frognal Lane,
Hampstead.

[Holograph]

12 May 1910

It will do no harm to delay the Austro-Italian article till July I think. If you send me a proof later on I will bring it up to date. I rather gather that you are not set upon the K. article for June. I am inclined to agree unless some decision respecting his next appointment happens in the next 10 days. K. wants India and Morley won't have him. I expect that the King backs K. as he is a firm friend. I suppose that they will put in some dummy – there are none but dummies available in Morley's party – and then a few years hence they will have a racket and K. will be sent out to restore order. The Viceroy's Council has not one strong man on it so the ground is being well prepared for Rebellion.

I don't think that K. can possibly serve a Radical Government as Secretary for War. It is all very well to suggest an attitude of detachment for him. But he must attend Cabinet Councils and share in the collective responsibility for its acts. I think you will understand that the situation will be impossible for him. If a Tory government came in it might be different, but we are not at that point yet.

I believe that K. is very fit and well, and ready to take off his coat again for any big job and not to care a hang whether it is popular or not so long as it is sound. But he is not going to hang about and be used and advertised as an adviser and see his ideas executed by people whom he cannot control. I think that before we write anything we must make up our minds what we want K. to be, and all combine in pressing it. It is no good writing into the blue. However, I shall see him directly a decision is made and will then write again.

West Sussex Record Office, Chichester, L.J. Maxse Papers, 461, ff. 631–2

81
Repington to J.L. Garvin

Maryon Hall,
Frognal Lane,
Hampstead.

[Holograph]

24 May 1910

I am much concerned to think that I have caused you any inconvenience and beg to express my regret.

I understood that I should only write when I had something to say worth saying. I found that I had nothing to say on the subject of the Crown and the Army that I had not said already in The

Times. Knowing that you always have more copy than you need, it never occurred to me for a moment that the absence of my article would cause you any editorial vexation. I do not lack platforms, nor you contributors. I want to write for you because I am convinced that if we work together and both hammer at the same nails we can drive them in. It is your driving power that I admire and wish to supplement so that people may have to dance to our tune.

We are neither of us indispensible to the other, but I think we should be silly to fall out at this stage when the big battle for military efficiency has still to be fought against considerable odds.

Humanities Center, University of Texas, J.L. Garvin Papers

82
Repington to Lord Northcliffe

Private

Maryon Hall,
Frognal Lane,
Hampstead.

[Holograph]

26 May 1910

I have asked Blackwood[103] to send you copies of his magazine for June and July as I am dealing with questions of submarines and airships and know your interest in these subjects which I am not permitted to discuss in The Times.[104]

I am hoping to get H.G. Wells, who is a neighbour of mine here, to come round this Summer and see Territorials with me. But I wish to be sure that you know my position. Not only has my pay from The Times been reduced, but no money whatever for the expenses of my usual Summer tour with the troops is now allowed to me. I do not want to re-open the question with the Board but only to be sure that you know the facts. It is a grief to me that I shall not be able to spend the 5 months May to September in touring round and in seeing everything and in keeping in touch with military thought, as heretofore. I keep a couple of horses and a man but cannot run to a car without which these days one can see little. Wells is no rider and I shall be a bit ashamed that when every representative of the most insignificant paper is provided with a car, Wells and I will have to go on foot. If you are satisfied there is nothing more to be said.

British Library, Northcliffe Papers, Add. MSS., 62253, f. 6

83
Repington to St Loe Strachey

Marine Hotel,
Elie,
Fifeshire.

[Holograph]

7 July 1910

Thanks for your letter. I have now read the article with much interest and approval. I am sure that the line which you are taking is the right one. It is much more important, in peace, to think what we can do for the Veterans, than of what they should do for us.[105] The position of the Veteran must be made honourable and attractive, or else, after the first blush of the affair, interest in it will wane. The Veteran seems to me to have fulfilled his duty when he registers and consents to turn up and fight at need. But there is a lot to be done by the government and the public before the position of the Veteran will become sufficiently attractive to insure the continuing success of the movement, and this is where our real worth lies at present. I am not very keen about giving rifles to the Veterans, nor am I sure that the place of the Veteran is within existing cadres. These are the only points which I think you might leave open for the moment.

I am inclined to think that we may spoil the fine point of young and dashing troops by an infusion of Veterans. I want the Veterans to take over eventually all the garrisons of G.B. in time of war, and thus to set free several divisions of Territorials which are now allotted to these duties.

Don't forget that our S.A. experiences were not entirely favourable to Section D. of the Army Reserve. There is much to be said on both sides of this question but I hope that you will not commit yourself too deeply until you have thought it all well out.

As to central control, please note that many Scottish Associations have decided to make their own rules for the Territorial Reserve. I expect that they will take the same course about the Veteran Reserve, and so may Wales, the North, the Midlands etc., and then we shall repeat all the errors of the organisers of the Kaiser Vereine and have the very devil of a trouble in getting a common system brought into force.

I shall read your National article with the utmost interest.

House of Lords Record Office, J. St Loe Strachey Papers, S/17/1/1

84
Repington to Lord Northcliffe

War Office,
Whitehall,
S.W.

[Holograph]

29 June 1911

I am sending you by to-day's post a copy of the first number of the Army Review, hoping that you will help to make the new venture widely known and that you will make any suggestions for improvement that your experience may dictate.[106]

I think on the whole that it is an advantage to The Times that its military correspondent should edit the Review but I keep an open mind on this subject, and shall be able to judge better after a year's experience. I hope that you will be content with my first editorial effort. I have no assistant, not even a clerk.

The leading idea is that the General Staff is now capable of teaching and that the time has come when we should endeavour to establish principles and doctrines so that we may have continuity in policy, tactics and administration while keeping clearly before us all reforms which new developments impose. We obtain for the Review authoritative expressions of opinion on military subjects from leading men in the Army and I think that this should prove of much benefit not only to the Army but to the public.

A short and fragmentary conversation with you in a damp field on a cold day at Guildford has left in my mind a desire for a little further talk so that I may become better aware of your opinions and ideas.

British Library, Northcliffe Papers, Add. MSS., 62253, ff. 7–8

85
Repington to Northcliffe

Maryon Hall,
Frognal Lane,
Hampstead.

[Typed]

9 July 1911

It is news to me that you did not know about my editing "The Army Review" until the arrangement was concluded.

My main object was to retrieve the £500 a year by which my pay and expenses were reduced some two years ago. I found that I could not do The Times work properly at the reduced rate owing chiefly to the heavy cost of my Summer campaigns, so I had to obtain the sinews of war from some other source. I wrote to you about it at the time, but you were away, and I had no reply.[107]

I find some advantage from The Times point of view in having a room at the War Office, while some of the generals in the Commands also approve as my semi–official position gives them an excuse for granting me special facilities.[108] But in principle I agree with you. I should prefer to concentrate exclusively upon Times work and have always recommended that I should do so. It is simply a question of money. I am not set upon continuing the Editorship. I have started the Review, and established a standard.

Inside a year the thing will run by itself, but I don't know anybody else who could do the spade work at the beginning. The Army is a very conservative institution and is slow to accept new ideas.

I shall only ask that if you desire me to abandon the editorship you give me as much notice as possible for I do not wish to place Lord Haldane in a difficulty.

British Library, Northcliffe Papers, Add. MSS., 62253, f. 10

86
Repington to Geoffrey Robinson

Maryon Hall,
Frognal Lane,
Hampstead.

[Holograph]

20 July 1911

I have been away in the West and have written to Buckle to say that before we take the naval action which The Times recommends – and of which I heartily approve – it would be well to look after ourselves nearer home. This German act of brigandage has been carefully planned and I am not clear that deeds will not continue to precede words.[109] I have been looking at our Home Fleet at Portland by day and night and see that not only are no precautions whatsoever taken, but that hundreds of men are leaving Weymouth on furlough for all parts of the country. My view is that a period of diplomatic tension has begun and that owing to German action already taken, and owing also to the new men who inspire German action, we must expect acts of vigour if German ambitions cannot be satisfied by a French (or a British) surrender. With our military system we have no right to run these risks.

P.S. I wrote an article on this subject a fortnight ago, but to no purpose, as it was not printed.

The Times Archive, Robinson Papers

87
Memorandum by Repington to G.E. Buckle

Secret
Suggestions for the organisation of war news in case of war with Germany.

[Holograph]

26 July 1911

The Times obviously must excel in the abundance and accuracy of its war news in the event of war with Germany. But competition will be keen, and we shall only beat our rivals and at the same time keep within reasonable bounds of expenditure by methodical organization based on complete recognition of modern conditions and by the abandonment of archaic systems which have had their day.

The question may be considered under three heads: (a) service of news within the United Kingdom: (b) service of news from abroad, and finally (c) headquarter organization.

(a) <u>Service in the U.K.</u>

At the outset of the war the interest will be mainly maritime. Operations of land forces, other than raiding parties and colonial expeditions, will not come into play unless we have allies or unless a preliminary naval success by Germany justifies her in risking invasion. There will, in any case, be about a fortnight during which the interest will be mainly confined to events at sea, and during this period we must affirm our superiority over all our contemporaries in a decisive fashion. Full reports of all movements of hostile fleets, ships of war, and merchant vessels, and accurate deductions from these reports, will be the supreme interest at the opening of a war. How far we can or should report movements of our own war vessels will depend upon laws and regulations which will be passed in the moment of first panic. There is a draft Bill in existence and it is drastic, but we must in any case know what our ships are about in order to comment with knowledge. We must have several copies of all the latest standard works (e.g. Brassey, Jane, Bethoncourt and the Taschenbuch) giving complete descriptions and silhouettes of warships, and of lists of merchant ships. We must have a good reasoned report from Lloyds every day and give it a good place and large print. We must keep touch with all the markets, not only Mark Lane [?], but the markets for cotton and copper where I expect we shall suffer from short supplies. We must naturally be in close touch with the Admiralty, and we must also organize a service of trustworthy agents round our shores.

Coastal Agents

The number of these latter agents must depend upon the amount of money which The Times is prepared to spend, but as the main duty of these men will be to report facts and not to paint word pictures, their services should not be very costly. We must have men at Scapa Flow, Cromarty, Aberdeen, Dundee, The Forth, Newcastle, Middlesborough, Flamborough Head, Grimsby, Yarmouth, Harwich, Sheerness, the North Foreland, and Dover. The coastline should be divided into sectors and be distributed between these agents so that no part may be left unwatched. Each agent must have a press pass, and a copy of Jane's Fighting Ships or some similar publication. The coastline agents should be authorised to hire motor cycles or motor cars for patrolling the coast and must be in touch with the Coastguard and Yeomanry patrols. They should send their reports in every few hours by telephone, telegraph, despatch rider, or railway express. They must not hesitate to use motor cycle messengers when telegraphs are closed. I think that these agents should preferably be chosen from ex-employees of the merchant service, or retired naval men, but they must be fairly young and enterprising.

If many German ships either break out of, or are found outside, the North Sea when war begins we may have to extend this service to Newhaven, Portsmouth, Weymouth, Plymouth, Falmouth, The Scilly Isles, Swansea, Milford Haven, Birkenhead, Barrow, the Clyde, Bantry Bay, Cork, Belfast, Lough Swilly, and Blacksod Bay. Total 14 coastal agents at the outset and a possible increase to 30. These agents, of whom we should have a list ready, could also visit the local defence forces. They should be in close touch with the shipping companies at their centres. Each man should have a code which will enable him to keep us informed if war news is stopped and cypher forbidden – as we must anticipate will be the case. To explain this matter I may remark that when I was in charge of secret service in old days at a time of strained relations, my man at Toulon would be 'Mother is ill, come at once.' This read in the code, 'Reserve Squadron of the Mediterranean has mobilized and is putting to sea.' It was allowed to pass over the French wires, and the news of my agents was usually 24 hours in advance of that from other sources. The preparation of these codes takes a lot of time. The coastal agents should visit as many incoming ships and fishing boats as possible and offer good pay for good news. It would of course be excellent if we could send reporters with fleets and flotillas but I expect that this will not be allowed.

The coastal agents should have a fixed salary with bonuses for getting good news in first. Detailed instructions should be drawn up for them, but it must be stated that much is left to their initiative and imagination.

Wireless

I have considered whether we can use wireless but I am dubious about it. Of course it would be splendid to have a receiving station on PHS and stations at the Orkneys, the Forth, Hull, Harwich, and Dover. We might even ask the Marconi company for estimates and time taken to erect, cost of working etc. but I expect that the Government would lay their hands on our stations. I have seen a good many private wireless stations while travelling about the country. These are licensed by the P.O. and could be traced by inquiry. Some probably belong to Germans. There is one hidden away in the hills some 15 miles north of Portland. It is worth studying whether we could not lease some of these while allowed to work them, but I am not confident that we can make much use of the service in war, so far as the U.K. is concerned.

(b) Service Abroad

Our regular agents at foreign capitals will of course continue and extend their excellent service. They should be given one or two extra hands to read and precis all the war news in the local press. During the last war I found an immense amount of information in the foreign press which never came to us over the wires. It is most important that this work should be thoroughly done in case of war with Germany, and instructions should be issued to this effect.

I think that we should also surround Germany with a network of correspondents, preferably at Brussels, Rotterdam, Amsterdam, Copenhagen, Friedrichshafen (Jutland), Christiansand, Bergen, Libau, Warsaw, Prague, Zurich and Nancy. Some of these men might be foreigners, and in any case they must be able to read the press of the country in which they are posted. Their duties would be to report all events of interest, to read all the local papers, to keep their eyes and ears open, and to be most particular about their facts. They should occasionally send people to travel through Germany and return. Much can be learnt in this way and such messengers are seldom interfered with. All these men would be under a 'director of personal services' who might also supervise the coastal agents. My experience is that agents will work better for a man whom they know and trust than for a Board or corporation.

The agents at Amsterdam and Copenhagen I would entrust with a spy service: the first at the North Sea ports of Germany; the second at the Baltic ports. The spies should be placed at Emden, Wilhelmshaven, Bremerhaven, Cuxhaven, Hamburg, Brunsbuttel, Kiel, Stralsund and Danzig. Heligoland is useless as the reports would easily get out. These spies should know nothing of The Times and should only know their paymasters at Amsterdam and Copenhagen. They should be engaged, as I engaged mine, by advertisements for commercial travellers in the D[aily] T]elegraph]. They should have a stock of goods with them and ply a trade. They should take no notes, use no maps, and only write business letters. They should each have a code drawn up in a commercial form, numbers being multiplied or divided by some agreed figure. Thus if the Wilhelmshaven man wrote to Amsterdam 'I require 5 Paris hats of the first quality' it might mean '10 destroyers of the 1st flotilla have put to sea.' After the first few days commercial telegrams to Holland might very likely get through. These men should be warned of the risk they run and must be well paid. They should be carefully coached and should be in position before the war begins if possible as new arrivals will be closely watched. The service at Kiel and Wilhelmshaven will be particularly dangerous. I expect that most of our cables will be cut the day war breaks out. In this event wireless will be a resource and we should have a map showing all wireless stations abroad and their range. Our overseas correspondents must be instructed to use this machinery as best they can when cables are cut. They must engage men who are going to Europe on neutral ships to send code messages about any German ships they meet, giving tonnage, exact latitude and longitude, speed and course of the ships observed. We ought to have a succession of agents sent out from the Baltic in neutral ships during the first days of a war.

(c) <u>Headquarters Organisation</u>

London is the nerve centre of the world. We shall receive countless messages about the war, our own and those of the press agencies. I think that The Times will have to issue special "Times War News" sheets, say at noon, 5 and 9pm, or at uncertain hours according to the news received. These should be prefaced by a short comment. The sheets might sell at 1d a piece, and be telephoned to select provincial towns for reproduction, say to Birmingham, Manchester, Edinburgh, Liverpool, Glasgow, Hull, Dublin, Belfast, Cardiff and Devonport. A service of quick delivery in neighbouring towns should be organized at each one of these places. With a complete service of information such as I have ventured to suggest, these sheets should beat all competitors out of the market and do a large business with advertisements.

We should have a room at P.H.S. where maps can be pinned out on large tables: a large scale map of the U.K. on which we could show troops; a chart of "Ocean routes and distances" on which should be marked positions of German cruisers and commerce destroyers; and a chart of the North Sea on which we could mark positions of vital fleets.

We shall have to issue charts and maps constantly to illustrate operations. Before war begins we should get ready blocks of North Sea charts to cover the whole area of this sea and we should be prepared to print maps and charts of any other likely theatre of operations. The Times maps in war could scarcely be worse and we must improve greatly in the next war. The work should be confined to an expert cartographer who must be warned in advance by the naval and military correspondents of what is needed.

I regard the Archibald Forbes business as almost played out.[110] No Army or Navy means to have its secrets given away and its official news forestalled if it can help it. What has become immensely more important is good professional criticism of events from day to day. This can only be carried out properly by men acquainted with the armies and navies concerned, and able to draw approximately correct inferences from a mass of contradictory and often wilfully misleading evidence. Few men are capable of doing this work because few have the necessary knowledge and experience. I believe M. de Blowitz[111] once said that news was nothing and that comment on the news was everything. I daresay that some people think that any clever fellow can separate wheat from chaff in news, but this is not the case. News which says nothing to the majority of people gives the expert a key to the whole situation. Therefore my advice is to keep the best men in London and not to waste money on expensive campaigning outfits. What did our news service in Manchuria cost, and what did it bring in?

The items of war news must be arranged and classified by half a dozen smart clerks. Files should be kept by them divided into naval and military, each with sub-heads for different theatres of war.

If the Germans cut our Channel cables they will be quickly repaired, but in the interval we may have to hire a fast packet, and our agents abroad must send their reports to the French port of embarkation of the packet. Havre–Southampton or Dieppe–Newhaven might serve the purpose. The Calais–Dover line will be too exposed.

These are only a few ideas to be cut about and amended by the Times staff until the best system can be evolved.

P.S. The cost of all the new agents etc. proposed I reckon at between £2000 and £3000 a month inclusive of telegrams.

The Times Archive, G.E. Buckle Papers

88
Repington to Geoffrey Robinson

Maryon Hall,
Hampstead,

[Holograph]

13 August 1911

I have written to Buckle several times during the last month to warn him of the dangers which we are running by the absence of all serious naval and military precautions in the face of German pretensions. Please note that everything in Germany that can float and fight is now at sea and that in a few days there will [be] over a million men in arms in the land forces. The Franco-German negotiations appear to have failed. If they fail, Germany must settle accounts with us, as Asquith clearly said, and this will be difficult. To avoid this settlement it is on the cards that Germany will now send an ultimatum to Paris and our labour troubles are an additional incentive to this course.[112] I am not allowed to say anything about our naval dispositions but I consider them perfectly damnable.[113] You ought to get ready a map showing where all our divisions and flotillas are from day to day, and get Grigg[114] to have news from Berlin of the strength and dispositions of the German fleet from day to day. The Foreign Office will not move till too late unless it is pushed, and with a First Lord who dreads a depreciation of stocks I hope for nothing from admiralty initiative.

The Times Archive, Robinson Papers

89
Repington to Robinson

Maryon Hall,
Frognal Lane
Hampstead.

[Holograph]

16 November 1911

You <u>are</u> disappointing. Such a nice party and the very pick of our best officers and all for you and you cannot come!

I want to consult you on another matter. By the week after next I intend to know all that is to be known about the new naval schemes. Keep this to yourself.

Now what am I to do about it?[115] I think of telling Buckle and of suggesting that I should write anonymously about the scheme, presuming that I approve of it. I have a complete scheme for an Admiralty Staff in my drawer and have some reason to suppose that something very like it is in the wind. There was a great risk a few days ago that Sir A.Wilson would go at once as Winston was in such a d—d hurry. I have implored them not to be so silly, for this would put the whole Navy in opposition, and as Wilson goes by age in March five months are not too long for Winston to get his bearings. We might cut Winston's political throat if Wilson went now, but imperilled national security is too high a price to pay for that pleasure. Let me know what you think.

The Times Archive, Robinson Papers

90
Note by Repington for G.E. Buckle

<u>Confidential</u>

War Office,
Whitehall,
S.W.

[Holograph]

28 November 1911

Note for Editor

Announcement to be made tonight that a new Board of Admiralty constituted – Bridgeman 1st Sea Lord; Prince Louis of Battenberg 2nd Sea Lord; Packenham 3rd; 4th remains unchanged. Present 2nd in command Home Fleet takes command. Jellicoe becomes 2nd in command.

These changes necessary because present 1st and 2nd Sea Lords time is taken up in March and January next, and as at this period, policy, estimates, etc., all have to be passed in review, it is desirable that the new First Lord should have under him a body which can give continuity to the work to be undertaken. King's approval obtained. It may be hoped, and indeed expected, that these changes are not unconnected with the creation of a War Staff which has long been desirable.

Bridgeman has proved himself an exceedingly able commander of a great fleet and will be a fitting representative of the conservative side of the Navy, while Prince Louis is a representative of the most modern and progressive side, while Packenham was present at Tsushima and brings the latest experience of sea service with him.

The Times Archive, G.E. Buckle Papers

91
Repington to Robinson

Maryon Hall,
Hampstead.

[Holograph]

30 November 1911

I send you the papers on the Naval Staff as promised. You will see Ottley's marginal remarks on the first. He writes to me that he agrees in the main.

The question is – What are we to do? I cannot publish these papers as they stand for a variety of reasons, but of course I could work them up into two good articles or perhaps three. I should not care to entrust them to anyone else to use as he would probably make a mess of them and miss all the points. I showed them to Thursfield when he was writing on the subject but he did not comprehend them, having no knowledge of the subject. I might write them frankly as a soldier's view and explain that the ideas were probably inapplicable to a Navy in some ways and merely a soldier's vague ideas – with other deprecating remarks – but add that we soldiers have found ourselves in a situation not unlike that in which the Navy stands to-day, and then show the way out, by the light of our experience. The thing might be done without wounding naval feeling. Or I might write anonymously in an authoritative tone, rather de haut en bas, or I might turn on von D. und B. to make the points and insert them with a knife.

What do you think? There is a fair chance that Winston may go wrong unless the thing is put clearly to the public, and unless the latter can tackle him if he makes mistakes.

In any case, where you and I are agreed, I had better send the papers to Buckle and make a proposal. Let me hear from you as the thing should be done soon.

The Times Archive, Robinson Papers

92
Repington to Buckle

<u>Private</u>

Maryon Hall,
Hampstead.

[Holograph]

7 January 1912

I am too well aware that you have no confidence in me as a naval critic and that it is your habit to regard war as something that can be divided into naval and military compartments, whereas it is all one, and so is the strategy of war by land and sea. I am not greatly depressed by your letter for everything that I have written on naval matters has been translated by sailors into foreign naval periodicals in which I seek in vain for any similar tribute to your 'naval' experts.

You are quite wrong to suppose that I desire either service to boss the other. My idea always has been and is that both services should be directed by <u>instructed</u> statesmanship, and the first step to secure this result was to instruct statesmen, an object which is gradually being attained by the Defence Committee. My next object was to bring the admiralty to the heel of statesmanship, and this has been secured by the Invasion and Beresford Inquiries and by the late crisis which opened the eyes of the Cabinet to the fact that the Navy desired, not to follow policy about, but to direct it. All this will now be changed, but the result is not due, as it should have been, to The Times, but to the pulling of strings behind the scenes.

We are agreed, I fancy, about the Naval War Staff, but I am not sure whether you realize all the difficulties which have beset the War Office owing to the rotten wood in the head of the Navy. Our trouble has been that the N.I.D. has no executive authority and that until a naval warstaff was formed there was nothing to speak with the General Staff on equal terms, and no progress was possible in the preparation of combined operations, colonial and coast defence, military transport and escort, and a score of other important matters.

In discussing the new plans with Churchill and Haldane some weeks ago I found that there was still a tendency to dethrone the Defence Committee from its proper place, and further that Churchill did not intend to place the head of the War Staff directly under the First Sea Lord. I pointed out these faults and we argued them at length. You will see from enclosed letter from Haldane – which please keep to yourself and return tonight – that the right course has at last been taken. But when the scheme is published this week, please ask yourself whether the war course, which requires reorganization from top to bottom in system of entry, instruction etc., has been placed on a proper footing. I fear not, and though I have tried at the last moment to get the necessary changes made, I am not sure whether they will appear in the manifesto. It is only by a long and strenuous course of training in staff duties that staff officers can be formed and you must not think that because we have the name we have the thing. I shall not reply to Thursfield at present in view of the forthcoming announcement, but Clemenceau, Cambon, and every other French statesman will tell you that the only help of real service to them is the military force which we can place in line in 14 days. Thursfield's article has fortunately not been noticed yet in France, but if it is it will do serious harm. The whole argument, which bristles with controversial points, is designed to lead up to Thursfield's Radical view that no military force should be sent to the continent. This means the end of the Entente and you must not make any mistake on the subject. I do not want to fight Germany with allies. I want us to fight her alone. But if an act of aggression is committed against France, it is vitally important for us to stand by her. It is not a military advantage to us, but a vital necessity of our existence. So for Heaven's sake do not publish any more advice not to prepare for this act in advance, for it can only make England distrusted abroad and The Times ridiculous at home.

I have told you that the two last First Sea Lords agreed that the despatch of troops to France could proceed safely. With our great superiority at sea over Germany, and with French aid, what risk can there be, 600 miles from the nearest German base, and with the Straits of Dover and all our Navy intervening between the German ships and our transports? The passage only takes 2–4 hours, is carried out by day, and wireless gives ample warning of attack. If the German Navy attempts to interfere, there is our Navy's chance for which it longs.

It has not been my fault that The Times has fallen from its high state in naval matters and follows rather than leads. We should long ago have had meetings to thrash out these problems and have taken a strong and united line. Whereas, I regret to say that the views of The Times on naval matters have no consideration and do not deserve it.

The Times Archive, G.E. Buckle Papers

93
Repington to Buckle

Confidential

Maryon Hall,
Hampstead.

[Typed Copy]

8 February 1912

I was asked this morning by various authorities of The Times and Daily Mail to find out about Lord Haldane's Mission.[116]

You doubtless know that he is now in Berlin with his brother and that the story is put about that his visit is connected with University matters. This is for the public intelligence that Grey seems to rate rather low.

The truth seems to be that the tension between us and Germany has become serious and that something has to be done (1) to see whether any arrangement of an amicable character was open to us and (2) to satisfy the Radical tail that all possible had been done to come to such an arrangement, so that, if it failed, the party might stomach the natural consequences, namely increased estimates – or at all events not decreased naval estimates as promised by McKenna.

The Buxtonian idea of a special mission was considered and rejected, because, had it failed it might have meant war, and it probably would have failed. The Haldane mission is an alternative, and so long as the official character of his mission is kept out of sight it is thought that his failure, of which there is of course a strong probability, might at least do no harm. The Kaiser was of course consulted and is to see Haldane. He will probably be away 10 days. I do not think that he will give any point away. His views have greatly changed and have hardened towards Germany of late, and I know that he desires and intends to meet the German increase with a reply which will satisfy the most combative of us.

Winston is similarly inclined, and so are the rest of the inner circle of the Cabinet (Asquith, Grey, and Lloyd George), but of course they have to humour their followers, and I suppose that this mission is as good a way of setting about the matter as can be suggested.

All the above has been told me in confidence, and I send it to you in confidence. It would of course be very unwise to repeat it in print, as it would upset the whole apple cart. I suggest that you might play the game as Grey has arranged it, dilate on the interest in University questions which Lord Haldane is known to feel, mention his brother's journey, and then go on to say that of course Haldane is <u>persona grata</u> with the Kaiser and many of his Ministers; that he has many influential friends in Berlin, and that it would afford no surprise were his presence in Berlin to result in conversations of a friendly private character, calculated perhaps – with goodwill which on one side will not be wanting – to facilitate the opening of a period of less strained relations etc. etc. But it would be best to underline the unofficial and private character of the journey, so that failure and retreat may subsequently be covered.

Personally I do not anticipate any result from the mission except possibly some increased reasonableness among the Radical Left whom Haldane will purr to sleep when he returns.

Perhaps you will take steps to send on this letter to Lord Northcliffe for his confidential information, as one of my messages this morning was sent by his direction.

The Times Archive, G.E. Buckle Papers

94
Repington to Robinson

Maryon Hall,
Hampstead.

[Holograph]

28 February 1912

Many thanks. I am mending and have been out. The attacks on me, or rather on the W.O. on my account, are good value and a fine advert for the Army Review. The circulation is becoming so great that I am at my wits end to supply the maps to meet the demands of the Stationery Office.[117]

Seely made me scream. I have never changed my room since I took over the Editing, but to read Seely I must have wandered round the W.O. looking for a desk. I suggest a short serial for The Times on April 1 entitled 'From Lift to Lavatory' or how I edited the Army Review.

Yes, of course I will do the article for May 24. What say you to 2–3 columns? I suppose there is little more to be done than to take a glance round and state as concisely and clearly as possible the general trend of policy and preparation in the various Dominions. You might ask your Colonial Branch to send me cuttings on Dominion Defence questions, and especially the best reports you have of the S.A. Debates. I am publishing in the A.R. the last reports for Australasia and the Memorandum on the S.A. Defence Bill and this can form a basis for your article.

The Times Archive, Robinson Papers

95
Repington to Robinson

War Office,
Whitehall,
S.W.

[Holograph]

16 May 1912

Seely had a talk with me to-day and touched on Press in War Time, saying that Northcliffe had raised the question. I suggested our old policy, i.e. a small committee first and a private discussion, to be followed by a larger committee when the terms were as good as settled. I also said that I thought we could do more with the Press by kindness than by cruelty, and I advised Seely to get a report upon the working of the very successful censorship of war news in Italy, and to submit this to the committee.

Are these still more or less your ideas? I have not talked to you on the subject for some months. I suggested you or Nicholson, Burnham or his nominee, and a man from the Press Association for the Press members of the small committee.

Let me know your present views.

The Times Archive, Robinson Papers

96
Repington to Sir Edward Grey

<u>Confidential</u>

Maryon Hall,
Hampstead.

[Holograph]

20 June 1912

The Marquis Imperiali, who is an old friend of mine, and Djevad Bey of the Turkish Embassy, have visited me here and I have discussed with both sides from time to time the incidents of the war in order to enable myself to comment on the war with a little knowledge.[118]

During the last few days, as both parties have shown a desire for an arrangement, I have been endeavouring to bring them together and have made better progress than I would have hoped, so think it worthwhile to let you know the point to which I have arrived.

After various exchanges of ideas which came to nothing, I suggested to Djevad Bey a peace on the basis of the <u>fait accompli</u>. To this he agreed, leaving the question of a neutral zone between the forces in North Africa for subsequent consideration.

Somewhat to my surprise the Marquis Imperiali, whom I saw this afternoon, consented to an armistice on the basis of <u>ati possidetis</u>,[119] which amounts to the same thing. This seems to me hopeful, and the main outstanding difficulty is the question of the Turkish garrison which Imperiali asks to be withdrawn though I pointed out that this seemed to me outside the principle which he had agreed. I expect to see Djevad to-day to discuss some 'transaction' on the garrison question. It may be that he will consent to gradual withdrawal, or conversion into gendarmerie or we may hit on some better plan. Of course the negotiations are purely private and commit nobody. Also tho' the two Governments may be cantankerous, but so far as the two Embassies here are concerned there seems to me now very little between them that cannot be settled.

I have not the least wish to figure in this affair in any way, but it seems easier to bring the belligerents together by a private talk of this kind than by mobilizing <u>diplomacy de carrière</u>.[120] I have not told Imperiali that I am dealing with the Turkish Embassy, nor the latter that I am talking to Imperiali, but I give both sides the credit of understanding this.

I have informed the Times people about this affair and have asked them to say nothing about it. Very probably it will all come to nothing, but at all events it may be worthwhile to let you know how things stand.

You will of course see that the course proposed turns the difficulty of the Annexation Decree to some extent and saves amour propre on both sides so far as can be done. The armistice will probably peter out into a permanent peace as things get quieter, but there seems to me no need for hurry in this matter.

I should naturally value your advice if you care to give it to me.

Public Record Office, Sir Edward Grey Papers, F.O.800/110

97
Repington to Reginald Nicholson

Maryon Hall,
Frognal Lane,
Hampstead.

[Holograph]

21 July 1912

I think that the time has come when I resign the Editorship of The Army Review. The Review is now firmly established and has a large circulation so that one of my principal objects has been obtained. I am not entirely in sympathy with Colonel Seely whose goings-on cause me some anxiety, and I do not think that my presence at the War Office is compatible with the attitude of opposition which I may be compelled to assume towards him at any moment. I also find myself hostile to the Trans-Persian railway project in common with all our best soldiers, and I am dubious whether the new Mediterranean policy will be one to content The Times. I have also to take into account that some influential people desire that I should resign the Editorship, and further that the work is increasingly onerous and prevents me from doing some important work for The Times and from studying foreign literature and preparing for military eventualities.

You are aware that the expense incurred by me in doing Times work was one of my chief reasons for accepting Lord Haldane's offer. The question is whether your Board can see its way to make up to me in some degree for the loss of £500 a year which my resignation of the Editorship will entail. I need not go into the details of my expenses again, but I daresay that you recall that they amount to approximately £500 a year in travelling, hotel charges, horses and car hire. If the Board can add £300 a year to my salary I should be content to lose the other £200 a year in order to concentrate entirely upon Times work and I think on the whole that it would now be better in all interests that I should do so. I shall not take any action until I hear from you.

The Times Archive, Nicholson Papers

98
Repington to Reginald Nicholson

Maryon Hall,
Hampstead.

[Holograph]

1 August 1912

The Admiralty are coming into line with The Army Review in the January number and Sir John French is very anxious that I should remain on till the issue of the January number in order to help them over the difficulties of amalgamation. They cannot at present think of anyone to replace me, and perhaps on the whole it would be to the advantage of The Times that I should see the matter through and leave them on January 1 next. I shall then be able to give the review the form and character which I originally intended it to take; and I hope that the publication will serve to help Army and Navy together and to give the public sound advice and good information. I am not making any secret of the fact that I have asked to be relieved.

The Times Archive, Nicholson Papers

99
Repington to Robinson

Private

Maryon Hall,
Hampstead.

[Holograph]

7 August 1912

I should tell you about my lunch with Seely yesterday. He absolutely refused to accept my resignation and I absolutely refused to withdraw it. He based his demand upon the fact that in his first interview with Marschall,[122] the latter (after first telling Seely that he had been a captain of irregulars 10 years ago and was now War Minister, and shrugging his shoulders contemptuously) had at once opened out about me and after various compliments had complained that I had attacked the German Army and went on about it nohow. Seely appears to have stood up to him by his own account and now says that my going will be truckling to the Germans. I don't really think that this is Seely's motive for begging me to stay. I got out of him that he thought I was going to attack him, and his real fear, to my mind, is that the dog may get off the chain and bite him.

I told him that he had not played the game by me: that Haldane had always told me everything and had consulted me before taking any step, whereas he, Seely, had not even answered my letter and that I had no intention of serving at the W.O. when a policy might be sprung upon us of which I knew nothing. He was apologetic and promised amendment, saying he had 600 letters still unanswered and that he was worked to death. I was not so unkind as to remind him that he only came to the W.O. three days a week for a couple of hours. I told him that I thought he would be wiser in his own interest to tell me things that were happening before they occurred, because in 9 cases out of 10 I usually supported the official view when I had all the evidence before me, and that it did him no harm when I occasionally differed from his official advisers.

He then opened up a new project, namely that he should have the exclusive use of my services and talked of some scheme for placing me in charge of the Education of the Army and connecting it in some way with the Defence Committee. He practically asked what I wanted. I said that I was a free lance and preferred the life to official harness, that if he made a definite proposal in writing I would of course consider it, but that I was too expensive a luxury for . . . [word indecipherable] as I should not look at anything under £2000 a year and probably not even then. However, he said that he meant to make me an offer, and I can only say that if it is worth £4000 a year I shall not take it. He tried to coax me by reminding me how I had been the military adviser to the Tory Cave in Brodrick's day and now, now that two members of the Cave were First Lord and War Minister, they wanted me back in my old position. I was not much impressed. It will be amusing to see the offer, but I told him that I was more use where I am and was overdone by the Editorial business and wanted to give it up. He begged me in any case, if I insisted on going in January, not to make an announcement of the fact and to go quickly without beat of drum. He wanted to say, if attacked, that I was keeping the job on 'for the present'. I agreed to his using those words and no more and gave him clearly to understand that I should not go on after January 1 next. We then agreed that we were completely reconciled and parted good friends again.

This is a d—d long story, but you may make more out of it than I can!

I am off to Wales in the morning. George Wyndham wants me to go to Clouds week beginning September 9. I rather want to accept as the house party promises well, but I shall only see the 3rd Division and miss the interdivisional of 1st and 2nd Divisions. What do you say? I can't do both as they are same dates.

The Times Archive, Robinson Papers

100
Repington to Robinson

Maryon Hall,
Hampstead.

[Holograph]

5 November 1912

I thought that you might not care to publish that little article of mine at present, but I wished you to know my views.

I am inclined to think that we are over-doing our pro-Balkanist policy. If we press it, we may get up against Austria and her allies, and in my view there is nothing in the Balkans worth fighting for so far as we are concerned. Whether one little state or blackmailing Power gets more or less does not concern us at all, and I deprecate very much any policy which may require either a retreat on our part or use of force. On the other hand appetites are so whetted that I begin to tremble for the existence of Turkey as an independent Power, and my view is that we have an unequalled opportunity for binding Turkey in our interest by a firm conciliatory policy. Turkey must always be the shirt next our skin, and we store up immense military difficulties in the future for ourselves unless we take long views and realize the situation after the war. This is only my view for what it is worth. I have no personal preferences except for our future security.

The Times Archive, Robinson Papers

101
Repington to Robinson

Maryon Hall,
Hampstead.

[Holograph]

8 November 1912

The article on 'Policy and Power' was inspired by the attitude and language of Ministers to their intimates after the Cabinet of the day before yesterday. I anticipate that they will go too far and I do not like the position and thought a counter-blast very desirable. My idea is that Grey may wish to re-establish his Radical position by bending to Radical sympathisers while Winston openly tells his friends that now is our time and that 5 years hence we shall be much weaker at sea. We stand a very good chance of being licked if we go to war, and while it is my business to tell you my views, it is yours to use your discretion and judgement whether it is opportune to state them.

I don't think that I am at all opposed to your pro-Balkan policy as I consider that a solid Balkan confederation would be a good thing for us, but I regret your total abandonment of the Turk who might, I think, by sympathy and kindly advice be brought more into touch with us again after the settlement. I consider that he is the shirt next our skin in the Near East and that we should identify him with our interests and not kick him when he is down.

I am lunching with one of the Ministers to-day and will ring you up if there is anything worth repeating.

The Times Archive, Repington Papers

102
Repington to Lord Haldane

<u>Confidential</u>

Maryon Hall,
Hampstead.

[Holograph]

27 November 1912

You asked me to let you know how things went at the W.O. and I must tell you that they are going badly in certain respects. Charles Harris[123] and I are fully in accord on this point. The general efficiency of the office has fallen about 50% since it lost you, Lord Nicholson and Murray. I like your successor personally and get on with him, but he does nothing and carries no guns. As Harris says, it is useless to look behind a screen when there is nothing there. Seely's jealousy of you leads him to accept placidly criticisms of your work, and to this alone can I attribute the headway which he has allowed to be given to the movement against the T.F. This is being engineered by Wilson who now has Sir John in his pocket. Wilson has gone so far as to abuse Bethune[124] for heartening up the T.F. in the provinces and even Sir John has taken him to task about it. Bethune comes to me and asks what he is to do. I tell him that he is doing an honest piece of work, and ought to go on, but he is anxious and dispirited at his treatment.

You know my opinion of Wilson. His famous appreciation of the situation in the Balkans, hopelessly wrong, has given you his measure, but I must say that he is a serious danger now that his constant intrigues threaten the existence of the T.F. There are things that might be done. Wilson ought to go and be replaced by Robertson who would give you the ballast now wholly lacking. Then I think you should get the Prime Minister to get the King to announce that he will hold two or three reviews of the T.F. this year, and H.M. should further distinguish in a special gazette the Regular and Territorial officers who have done specially good work by the force. Cowans would give you a list. I personally think that an Army Order should be published warning officers deprecating our armed forces in the press in very firm Wellingtonian terms. In no other country is the license permitted that we allow, vide the "Daily Mail" and "Standard". It is all part of a game to destroy the voluntary system, and it is more than high time to put a stop to it. Whether the ultimate object of the game is in itself desirable or not I feel sure that great harm is being done to discipline, numbers and efficiency by the present campaign which has a purely destructive tendency for you know well what years must elapse before we could substitute any other military system even if we desired to do so. It would be useless for you to talk to Seely, but the situation is so serious that I think you should ask the Prime Minister to intervene with a firm hand and put matters to rights.

P.S. I am only free on Friday night this week and shall be away for the weekend.

National Library of Scotland, Edinburgh, Haldane Papers, Ms. 5909, ff. 272–3

103
Notes for Geoffrey Robinson on a speech by Lord Roberts
<u>Private</u>

[Holograph]

27 November 1912

<u>Editor</u>

(1) When the T.F. were created we were limited by two conditions, voluntary service and a 28 millions Budget. I have yet to learn that we could have done anything more on those conditions. If either one of these conditions is altered for the better we can make a better army, but not a soul has ever suggested that we can do this so long as the above conditions remain unaltered.

(2) These conditions were laid down by the Government and not by soldiers. The War Office is capable of raising and training any Army that the country requires. If the country desires an Army 500,000 or 1,000,000 strong we can raise it quite easily but we cannot make silk purses out of sows' ears. It is for the Government to say what Army is required and then for the War Office to act, as it will successfully.

(3) Lord Roberts himself allowed the best opportunity of our day to pass by. He was omnipotent in military affairs for 3 years and did nothing. He left the Volunteers without organizations, guns, engineers, medical and transport and supply services as well as very badly trained. The T.F. is now well organized and has these services while it is at least twice as well trained and has a fine spirit. In the points named by the F.M., namely discipline, equipment and energy there is no comparison, while in numbers we are practically the same.

(4) The soldiers who created the T.F. looked steadily to the eventual arrival of compulsion. It was for this reason that the force was distributed on the basis of population. A turn of the compulsion screw, whether county quotas which I have always advocated, or any other form of it, would make up the present deficiency in a moment and could produce any numbers required.

(5) But scarcely any trained soldiers support the N.S. League plan of 6 months preliminary training and refresher courses of a fortnight afterwards. Many N.S. Leaguers do not support it – vide Amery's writings. It is now felt that we must go the whole hog when we move: have 2 years compulsory service and create a large army equal in training and efficiency to the armies of the continent. In what numbers? No one knows because the Government has not spoken. It is felt that while the N.S. League plan may give us large numbers and more efficiency (though some doubt the latter) it will only add to our defensive power and not to our offensive strength. They would rather see another 8 or 10 millions, if the money is available, thrown into the Navy than into a Home Defence Army, and I suspect that the F.M. would vote at once for a 2 years Army rather than for his plan if he were given the option.

(6) I agree that the numbers of the T.F. are inadequate and have always said that, on the present plan, 600,000 men are needed. The argument has often been given. You merely – assuming the Expeditionary Force to be abroad – add up your local garrisons, and the garrison of Ireland in war, deduct recruits and sick and arrange for 3 to 1 against 70,000 invaders and you get your figure. If we are to keep one Regular Army as we know it I am still for this

plan and for county quotas, but if our policy is to be able to place 500,000 men or more in Europe and elsewhere then all this plan falls to the ground and a totally different conception is opened up.

(7) The 2 years Army scheme will allow us to defend the country and to intervene effectually in Europe. Short of unendurable cost it entails however, the disappearance of our Regulars at home: the change of the Army abroad into a colonial long service force fed by drafts from depots at home, the loss of the instrument supplied by our present Expeditionary Force which is capable of going anywhere and for any length of time; and finally if the Radicals bring in the scheme as they alone I think can do, it entails the complete democratization of the Army to gild the pill of compulsion for the electorate.

(8) The introduction of this scheme entails a long period of transition and weakness at home and abroad. No one has ever yet proved to my satisfaction that we can keep up our foreign garrisons, and supply drafts, and still less reliefs, under this system, and no sane Minister will accept this scheme until he has this assurance. A colonial Army must go down in efficiency. It was the unpopularity of spending all service abroad that compelled Cardwell to introduce his reforms, and I am clear that the 2 years place will greatly lower the vitality of our foreign garrisons, make it difficult to supply, relieve and reinforce them, and thus sacrifice the daily needs of the Empire for the pleasure of being able to place 500,000 or more men in Europe when needed. You have to balance profit and loss and glance over the whole field of Empire before you make your decision, and you have also to pay regard to the social upheaval entailed by taking the youth of the country away from its work for 2 years of the best of its life.

(9) I could, of course, suggest a middle course. We could raise the Expeditionary Force to 200,000 with our present system. We could fill up the T.F. by county quotas and insist on some "preliminary training and musketry and a fortnight for all each year". It is not our usual practice to revolutionize but to evolve, and we cannot ignore the fact that our naval expenditure must rise to dizzy heights and that there is only a certain amount of money to spend. I am dead against 'crabbing' any force we have until we know what better we

have to put in its place. Frankly I have never seen any project for reform which would bear an hour's investigation. Criticism is easy; constructive Army reform is quite another matter.

(10) We must define responsibilities. It is for the Government to say what numbers we need and for what purposes. It is for the War Office to create this Army.

The Times Archive, Robinson Papers

104
Repington to Robinson

Maryon Hall,
Hampstead.

[Holograph]

11 December 1912

I am entirely in agreement with your main argument of yesterday and admire the rigour and brilliancy of the leader. But as you will, I am sure, always wish me to tell you all I think in letters only intended for your eyes, I must say that I think you made a bad mistake in describing the T.F. as a sham.[126] That phrase will be, I fear, the only part of the article which will be repeated. It is not true. It is a feather-headed observation worthy of Garvin and Co. but unworthy of The Times. It will handicap you badly whether the Unionists come in or whether we are called on to send an army abroad. It is not much good for me to continue to inspect and take an interest in a Force which my Editor calls a sham, following the fatheads who know nothing of the Force and of all the good work and good will put into it during the past five years. I have no taste for the destructive line in military criticism. The only interest I have in them is constructive, but all the critics of the T.F. are alike: they cannot build: they cannot add one brick. This tone will lead to a steady depletion of the Force by natural discouragement, and you have nothing to suggest to put in its place except unexceptionable phrases and high principles which are beautiful in their way but butter no parsnips. From pure chaos we have built up in 5 years a good second line army, and the right course in my humble judgement, is to encourage it in every way possible, but at the same time to show, as you do in the leader, the great need for military training on grounds of social discipline, and the need for more numbers and steadily improved training. It is not in the least necessary to crab the T.F. in order to advocate this advance.

You realize of course that if you pin the label of conscription to the party you run the risk of keeping them out of office for years. This risk I personally hope you will accept, for national service is a big idea, and while we shall always be beat on the bribery tack, we are easily first in an appeal to national sentiment. It is the noblest flag to fly, and I should like to see the party committed to opposition until they carry it to victory.

You say that you are no judge of military necessities. There are no mysteries about such matters, and after all the main questions which you have to answer are political. I cannot write until you have decided certain leading principles. I put them in my last note to you. Are you satisfied that naval predominance is assured by our arrangements: are you content that your foreign policy can be sufficiently backed by an E.F. of 200,000 Regulars? On these questions all Army policy hangs and until you say 'Yes' or 'No' firmly and finally my muse is dumb. I think also that you should decide how much money we can fairly ask for Army Estimates, and to do this you should project your mind over future revenue, increase of national income, and naval needs. The little sketch of a policy which I sent you is the plan of a centre party, not content with our present position, but not yet ready to go as far as the General Staff and ask for 2 years compulsion in barracks and an army of half a million or more to fight in Europe. After my trials these last 8 years with an Editor who really detested defence questions, I do not want to start until I have a clear impression of your wishes and policy, and know that I can agree with both. I do not desire to press any particular policy upon you. You decide the policy and then I help you to suggest how a constructive military policy should match with it. That seems to me the only suitable course, but I should be glad if you would decide upon your policy soon for we cannot keep out of the fray with credit much longer.

The Times Archive, Robinson Papers

105
Repington to Robinson

Maryon Hall,
Hampstead.

[Holograph]

1 February 1913

It was such bad luck that you could not stay and talk to guests other than those who were next to you. We sat on for two hours after you left and had some very frank expressions of opinion all round. It was a cheery party, was it not?

I am much exercised that the Defence Committee is going to re-examine the invasion question. In principle I agree, but I recall that some months ago one of the lesser members of the Government confessed to me that they were terribly hampered by the last decision of the Committee about the 70,000 men invasion, because they could not get the Territorials to match the argument! My fear is that they will upset our standard just to salve their political consciences, and that they will be helped thereto by our G.S. which is lamentably weak at the W.O. and lacks men with ballast, experience, and judgement. All they care for is this war on the Meuse and they will pass any folly regarding the "impossibility" of invasion in order to get their head about the continental war. The Radicals will win all along the line for they will say that invasion is now no danger and so the deficit of the T.F. does not matter, and they will take d—d good care that our army does not go to France. Great watchfulness is necessary.

The Times Archive, Robinson Papers

106
Repington to Robinson

Maryon Hall,
Hampstead.

[Holograph]

4 February 1913

I have made a few additions as suggested, and have, with regret, taken out most of the paras. to which you demurred in Art.II, p.1. The para. immediately following the sub heading "Evolution" should however stand because it is important to get people to understand the difference between the short and long range army and the difficulties of combining two aims in the Army.

It is difficult to paraphrase 'compulsion'. The Dominions have not shied at it, nor I think need we.

With regard to the E.F. you will find the 166,000 men fully explained in my article in The Times of April 1, 1907, reproduced in Ch.XVI of my "Foundations of Reform".[127]

I hope that you may find time to glance at the Invasion papers before you set your leader writer to work. I propose to hear the debate in the Lords and to write about it, for the paper of February 12 if it suits you.

I forgot to tell you tonight that a Bill has been prepared by the Government to authorize shooting at airships if they repeat their visits to our shores.[128] I am thinking that you might point out the dangers of these visitations and demand legislation. Then they will say that you did it when the Bill is produced.

The Times Archive, Robinson Papers

107
Memorandum by Lord Esher to the Prime Minister of a conversation with Repington 14 February 1913

2 Tilney Street,
14 February 1913

About a week ago Colonel Repington called here. He rang up on the telephone and asked to see me, saying that he had something very important that he wished to discuss.

He began by remarking that he had three questions upon which he wished me to express an opinion.

He prefaced his observations by saying that the change in the Editorship of <u>The Times</u> had altered his personal position, that he was much more comfortable, that he got on extremely well with the present editor, and in short that on political as well as military subjects they had much discussion together and worked in common.

The first topic he broached was his impending articles on the state of the Army. They have since then appeared in the "Times". He foreshadowed their import and it was evident that he thought, and that Mr. Robinson, the Editor, shared his opinions, that these articles would exercise considerable influence over the debate in the House of Lords and might lead to something in the nature of a compromise on the question of compulsory service between the two Parties.[129]

The second subject upon which he desired to speak he said was of still greater importance. He had heard, by what means I cannot imagine, of the sub-Committee upon Invasion recently appointed by the Prime Minister.[130] We, he said, are very much concerned about what we hear of this committee. According to their view it originated in the General Staff who are, said Colonel Repington, entirely engrossed with the idea of fighting the Germans on the Meuse and are ready to sacrifice everything to this idea. The suggestion is that Sir John French and the General Staff desire to, what he called "get rid" of the figure 70,000 as the number of the enemy's troops that we should be prepared to meet in this country, because in the view of the General Staff if this figure is maintained the Expeditionary Force would not be allowed to leave our shores in consequence of the depleted condition and the inadequate training of the Territorials. Their object, said Colonel Repington, is to show that invasion is impossible and that therefore the need to provide against a raid of the magnitude of 70,000 men is illusory.

I told him that all this was quite new to me, that I think I know as much as anyone about the origin of the sub-committee, coupled with the fact that the Prime Minister himself is to preside over it, precluded any idea of the enquiry being conducted otherwise than with perfect fairness and any decision being influenced by considerations other than those which had guided the previous committee in 1909.

The third subject he said upon which he desired to speak was the most important of all. He asked me if I had read Mr. Bonar Law's speech in which he referred to the Royal Veto as defined in the Parliament Act and its possible exercise by the King. We, he said, meaning again the Editor of the "Times" and I suppose Lord Northcliffe and Co, are giving most earnest consideration to this question and we are in considerable doubt as to whether the King has about him men competent to advise at a constitutional crisis and we have been discussing whether public attention should be drawn to this fact and suggestions made which might lead to placing about the King persons competent by their abilities and experience to advise him. He then asked me what I thought.

I said that I had extreme difficulty in catching his meaning and that I could not for the life of me understand what it was he was suggesting or proposing. Did he mean, for example, that the Sovereign should be provided with a Board of Advisers? If that were so, I could quite imagine that a Board composed of Mr. Robinson of <u>The Times</u>, Mr. Spender of the <u>Westminster,</u> Mr. Donald of the <u>Chronicle,</u> Mr. Massingham of the <u>Nation</u>, Mr. Strachey of the <u>Spectator,</u> etc. etc., might after due discussion tender excellent advice to the King.

That, however, seemed hardly to be in question. The important thing would be to know what the two great organized political

Parties of the state would think of such a proposition, and what the great masses of the people outside both Parties would think of a Press Bureau of that character. Speaking seriously, however, I asked whether he meant to substitute by means of a Press campaign some other persons for the King's Private Secretaries, and if so, who were the men that he proposed. He mentioned, of course, the obvious people: Lord Rosebery, Lord St.Aldwyn, the Archbishop of Canterbury, and so on. I asked, "Why not Lord Kitchener? for if you want to introduce a Strafford into the situation you might as well select the most courageous man available at the present moment and one who might, if the difficulties became sufficiently great, wield a sword with some effect."

He regarded this as a jest but persisted in saying that "no one" had or could have any confidence in the King's entourage composed as it is of men of no special experience in great affairs, and this is what the Editor of the "Times" specially felt.

I asked him whether it had ever occurred to him that under a constitutional monarchy the men who were nearest the King were bound to remain obscure, and that any other system would be certain to produce strong jealousies and possibly criticism and revolt. He kept pushing me to express a personal opinion upon the point he had raised. Finally I said to him that if the Editor of the "Times" desired to know my opinion, which I can hardly believe since I have not the honour of his acquaintance, and if he has asked you to talk to me upon the subject, will you tell him this that the King is perfectly capable of exercising his own judgement if it becomes a question of giving or withholding the Royal Assent to the Home Rule Bill. If the King, however, thinks the situation so serious as to necessitate seeking advice, there are, under our institutions, only two men in England who can constitutionally and with safety to the Monarchy tender him advice. One of these men is the Prime Minister and the other is the leader of the Party in Opposition, should he feel strong enough to carry on the King's Government according to the prevalent practice of Parliament. No man can safely finesse with the British Constitution whether he be King or Minister. Still less can he do so if he is neither the one nor the other. If Mr. Robinson desires to destroy the Home Rule Bill, and I can quite undestand his desire to do so, he should concentrate the great power of the Amalgamated Press and of the Harmsworth family upon upsetting the present Government during the next twelve months. Any trick would be fair and any means legitimate within the rules of the Parliamentary game. When it comes, however, to using the King as a stalking-horse greater and Imperial considerations come into play. It appears to me inconceivable that you should desire to create indirectly a republican party and, by bringing the Monarchy into the arena of party conflict, to jeopardise, not in this case the unity of Great Britain and Ireland, but the unity of the Empire.[131]

Bodleian Library, Oxford, Asquith Papers, 24, ff. 116–21

108
Repington to Robinson

Maryon Hall,
Hampstead.

[Holograph]

25 February 1913

I congratulate you on your leader. It is a very pleasant change for me to work in close co-operation with my editor, and I am sure that by pulling together we can more than double the effect of individual effort.

I am very busy with the Invasion Memo. hoping to get clear of it before other military matters become critical.

The Times Archive, Robinson Papers

109
The George Saunders, André Tardieu Incident[132]
7/9 March 1913
Saunders to Robinson

The Times, Paris.

2, Chaussée D'Autin.

[Holograph]

9 March 1913

I enclose copies of letters which have just been exchanged between Repington and myself.

As I wrote to you, I shall be delighted to see Repington in Paris; but, I must say, I was rather astonished by his letter of the 7th. inst. He assumes (1) that there is a private quarrel between Tardieu and myself. (2) That I allow this quarrel to influence my correspondence for the paper. (3) That I am so ignorant (unwise to say the least) as not to perceive the dangerous and eventually disastrous consequences of this supposed situation.

Now, in the first place, there is no private quarrel between Tardieu and me. It is true that I entertain a very low opinion of his character and conduct in political and journalistic and financial matters; but when I meet him in private – which I do not happen to have done for some time – I treat him with the same outward courtesy with which I treat other acquaintances, some of whom are, unfortunately, tarred with the same stick. I behave towards him precisely as Lavino behaved, that is to say, I neither seek to avoid him nor do I endeavour to meet him. Long before I had full proof of what his character and conduct are, the Embassy had warned me repeatedly against him. As this is a confidential letter, I may tell you that Sir F. B[ertie] strongly suspects him of having accepted money considerations from more than one Foreign Power . . .

Repington to Saunders

Maryon Hall,
Hampstead.

[Typed copy]

7 March 1913

I hope to be at the Hotel Majestic next Wednesday evening and will call at your office the following afternoon between 4 and 5 if possible. I wish to ask you to help me to do a service to the interests of the entente. The quarrel between you and Tardieu is a journalistic handicap to both papers, but it is a serious danger to our mutual interests in a large sphere, and I write to ask whether you will come and meet Tardieu at dinner, if I can get hold of him and make peace. I have no doubt that your attitude has been perfectly justified, but I beg that you will give me your help to compose a quarrel which may otherwise lead to disastrous consequences of all kinds. The Editor knows of my wish which has his sympathy.

Saunders to Repington

Private and Confidential

The Times, Paris,
2, Chaussée D'Autin

[Typed Copy]

9 March 1913

I shall be glad to see you in Paris. As for Tardieu, I have no personal quarrel with him at all and have never exchanged any words with him. If, in the ordinary course of things, I were to meet him in a private house or at a reception I should do so in the same way as I have always done. To accept an invitation to meet him in order to "make up a quarrel" is a different thing, and, while thanking you for the good intention, I must absolutely decline. I have my own opinion of Tardieu's work and aims, and I must retain the right to hold it and express it, subject to Editorial control. If it be suggested that this well considered opinion is prejudicial to the interest of the paper or to higher interests, I must simply leave myself in the hands of the Editor.

While asking you to regard this letter as <u>private and confidential</u>, I have no objection to your showing it to the Editor and to him alone.

The Times Archive, Saunders Papers

110
Repington to Robinson
[Holograph]

2 April 1913

You fitted us out to-day with a right good supply of information re: the aerial problem. I agreed with your leader except in two points. I do not agree that the preparations of foreign countries have not reached a dangerous stage, and I make out that the money allocated to naval air work in Germany by the supplementary naval estimates of 1913 is £2,500,000 and not £1,300,000. The period covered is not 2 or 3 years but 1913–1918. We can learn from the allotment of the money that a maximum of 11 naval airships and 150 naval aeroplanes are on order, and just as the Army increase will practically be completed this year as regards new formations, so we can only take the 6 years of the naval air programme as a provisional supposition.

All this is apart from the German Army Aerial Vote, and this is why I want Mackenzie to reconsider his reports and tell us the exact facts on which alone we can form proper conclusions.

May I know the name of 'Pegasus'? An admirable article and I am sorry that your leader did not refer to it as so few people read your supplements. I should like to get the D.C. to call on Pegasus for examinations.

There seems to be a lot still to be said on all this question and particularly on the military side of it. Shall I write again? If so, I should like to write this week as next week I expect to be much occupied with private affairs including Pembroke's funeral, and I want to be fairly free.

It seems to me that we must get better engines which can develop 1000 h.p. at least for a low weight in our future dirigibles, and I think we ought to buy the best foreign models. My view also is that we must not concentrate upon any one type but must experiment with them all, and I want particularly to bring out the military requirements which do not appear to me to be understood by the Daily Mail. I should also like Mr Shepherd to make me a map showing German aircraft and aeroplane stations, and a second map showing the North Sea with circles on a radius of 750 and 250 miles respectively to show radius of action of present airships and aeroplanes: the centre of the circle can be Duisburg.

You might put the latter map in hand at once: for the other we might await Mackenzie's revised report, but I have a list of many stations already. If you deal editorially with this subject again I think you should impress on the Government the need for starting airship sheds at once, and the future need for taking into account the increase of size which the future is sure to bring about. There is no popularity to be had out of building airship docks and therefore we ought to hunt Ministers till they act.[133]

The Times Archive, Robinson Papers

III
Repington to Robinson

Private

Maryon Hall,
Hampstead.

[Holograph]

13 April 1913

In this article I have directly challenged the opinion of the General Staff quoted by Seely last Friday. I hope that you may be able to publish the article tonight. We must fight this out. Esher tells me that I was right and he was wrong about the motives which underlay the Invasion Inquiry. He says that there was a political intrigue. He cannot tell how the thing will go, but adds that we have the brains of the Committee on our side and hopes for the best.[134]

I hope that the Lords will stand no more nonsense from Haldane in this week's debate.[135] Bonar Law has become admirable. We have told him everything and he will be of great value to us. He has asked me to come and coach him before the Defence debate. I presume you have no objection?

I enclose a letter from Sammy Scott which will help my article.

I may be sending you a letter from Esher tonight.

Our revised Memo. has now gone in and we are waiting to take on the Committee. Lord Percy was here Friday and will be of use to us. A very determined and serious young man.[136]

The Times Archive, Robinson Papers

112
Repington to Robinson

Maryon Hall,
Hampstead.

[Holograph]

3 July 1913

I also am concerned about Ulster and the Army.[137] I know that many officers will <u>wish</u> to resign, and that some N.C.O's are talking of refusing to fight against Loyalists, and, if blood be spilled, I have no doubt that there will be great indignation and that a very serious feeling will be aroused.

I have no doubt that our line ought to be to deprecate in the strongest manner any inconsiderate and hasty action on the part of officers in the Army. We can sympathise with them, share their indignation, and throw the whole onus of any trouble upon the Government. But we should, I think, in a temperate but firm manner, hold up the maintenance of discipline as the first duty of the corps of officers, and even suggest that disciplinary measures will have to be taken against any who desire to retire for the purpose of aiding Ulster in resisting the law. We <u>dare not</u> admit politics to the Army, and I think that you should make a special appeal to regimental feeling and invite senior officers to set an example and to repress at the first symptom not only any rash disposition on the part of officers, but also any conversations and tendencies which might lead the younger hot heads astray. The firmest discipline that we have is that of the regiment, and if this goes, all else goes with it. We must have no compromise with illegality on the part of the Army. It might be the end of us.

The Times Archive, Repington Papers

113
Repington to Robinson

<u>Private</u>

Maryon Hall,
Hampstead.

[Holograph]

6 July 1913

We had a most unsatisfactory meeting of the Defence Committee last week.[138] We were not allowed by the P.M. to ask the C.I.G.S. questions which went to the root of the matter under investigation, and in my opinion the morning was wasted upon tittle-tattle. We are asked to come again next Tuesday to listen to the views of various generals about the T.F., but I have written to Lord Roberts to say that I do not propose to attend and that I see no object in our further attendance unless we are permitted to ask the questions which we have handed in.

So, unless Lord R. makes a special request for my attendance on Tuesday, I shall go off tomorrow on the staff tour and expect to send you my report of it on Sunday next.

The Times Archive, Robinson Papers

114
Repington to Robinson

Maryon Hall,
Hampstead.

[Holograph]

17 July 1913

I will call to see you early next week if we cannot arrange a meal together. I have written to Hooper. You must be much pressed by work. All my congratulations on the success of the Crystal Palace fund. The paper is good reading and I find myself in agreement with you on all the big questions – except divorce!

I had an opening on the Defence Committee today as the P.M. asked me what was needed to make the Army better. So I slung it in and gave them my views of what should be done on the P.M.'s assumption that compulsion was barred. They all listened very kindly and I made all my points. Had an amusing lunch with Seely afterwards and told him I had only come to plot with him the details of my next attack on the W.O. There is a good lot to tell you but it must not go on paper.

I shall be away for the weekend if you do not want me.

The Times Archive, Robinson Papers

115
Northcliffe to Repington

[Typed Copy]

20 August 1913

I find on enquiry and by analysis that the "Times" military news no longer gives that advance information by which its prestige was built up. I was reminded of that yesterday by a very distinguished soldier who asked me why the news was always known in the clubs, before it appeared in the "Times".

Is it not a fact that Major-General Robertson will become director of Military training vice Henderson? If so should we not publish it or hint at it?

I am anxious to see a little of that pride of priority instilled into the paper by John Walter[130] and Delane,[140] revived in our columns.

British Library, Northcliffe Papers, Add. MSS., 62253, f. 19

116
Repington to Northcliffe

Maryon Hall,
Hampstead.

[Holograph]

22 August 1913

I generally know about all the appointments beforehand but it has been my practice hitherto to reserve indiscretions for important occasions, because people would not speak to me as freely as they do were I to publish everything I know and hear. However, I am sending a batch of indiscretions to Freeman[141] tonight to meet your wishes. Personally I consider that the chief value of your military correspondent lies in expert criticism of home and foreign military affairs, and not in the divulgation of secrets which infuriates the authorities and especially the Crown.

Just at present I am a little out of favour at the War Office because I have had to oppose them. Before taking this line I informed Robinson that one result would be that I should not get, nor could I ask for inside information as before, but we agreed that the critical line had to be taken, and that we should make the best of the attendant disadvantages.

I only write this in order that you should have my point of view and why I have not made a feature of the 'accurate priority of information' of which you write. You must remember that I have a particularly privileged position, being the only press representative admitted to conferences and the only one who is shown secret papers on many subjects. It is a question of confidence, and I am sure that you will see that this confidence would not be reposed in me were I to announce in The Times everything I hear about new appointments.

Perhaps you will send me a line to say what you think after reading this.

British Library, Northcliffe Papers, Add. MSS., 62253, ff. 20–1

117
Repington to Robinson

Maryon Hall,
Hampstead.

[Holograph]

9 October 1913

I enclose a letter from Sir John French, from which you will see that the F.M. is exceedingly angry with me, and that though he alleges that my facts are erroneous he gives no reasons to make me change my views.[142]

I should, of course, greatly prefer his opinion to mine were I sure that when he criticized his divisional commanders he knew the facts. But I think he did not know them, and while I have altered the article and made it as mild as honest criticism permits, I am not personally disposed to withdraw it.

The decision must rest with you. I send you herewith letters from Sir D.Haig, commanding the 1st. Army: Gen. Forestier-Walker, Chief G.S. Officer of the 2nd Army; Sir W. Robertson who was with the King; and from Generals Lawson and Sir H. Rawlinson commanding 2nd and 3rd divisions. These letters form the basis of my criticism of the direction of the Exercise, and confirm opinions which I formed on the ground.

Many of the F.M.'s and great Generals present as spectators were more critical than I have been, and perhaps you will care to consult some of them. I have given due weight to Sir John's opinion, but I think that facts and the weight of opinions bear out my views, and I am not disposed to withdraw anything, even at the cost of the loss of a valued and old friendship.

The Times Archive, Robinson Papers

118
Repington to Robinson

Maryon Hall,
Hampstead.

[Holograph]

1 November 1913

You may care to see enclosed. It represents the views of the average British officer I suppose, but I have been told about that "rising within two years" for the last ten years.

I disagree with Townshend[143] about the Cawnpore case.[144] Last Tuesday – I think it was – I lunched with the Aga Khan and the Chief Justice of Bengal. They thought the Cawnpore case the worst that had happened since the Mutiny, and regretted that Hardinge had not frankly acknowledged that a mistake had been made and thrown over Meston[145] the Lieut.Governor. I forget whether you have dealt with the case, but it appears to have had the worst possible effect upon the Mahommedans of India.

As for the general situation you may care to know Sir Lawrence Jenkins'[146] views. He is for decentralization, for provincial semi-autonomy, the Central Government to remain a distant power on a mountain, more or less invisible, and only concerning itself with foreign affairs and defence: everything else to be done by the provincial governments.

I don't think the present moment opportune for raising military questions. You are right, Ireland blocks the way. But I am at your disposal if you want anything done and am watching affairs.

P.S. I came across enclosed letter from Sir P. Lake[147] the other day. I don't think you have seen it. Please return it. It is old but interesting.

The Times Archive, Robinson Papers

119
Repington to J.E.B. Seely

Maryon Hall,
Hampstead.

[Holograph]

30 December 1913

I must write you a few lines to wish you all health and good luck during the coming year, and to express my very earnest hope that you may be able to find in your work some slight consolation for the great sorrow which the past year had the misfortune to bring you.[148]

I will confess to you that I am not at all pleased that I should find myself so much out of touch with you and Sir John, and consequently so apt to drift into constant opposition to you. From my own point of view my work is on the whole facilitated by remaining completely apart from officialdom in all its aspects, and I have never felt the need for running after anybody. But in my view of the public interest The Times should, when practicable, support authority represented by the Government in all matters which relate to foreign politics and defence, and I consider that the work of your party has been considerably facilitated by our attitude towards Grey and your predecessor at the War Office. This attitude was only rendered possible to me by my close association with Lord Haldane, whom I saw nearly every week, and with whom I discussed almost every step of his measures before he adopted them. The cessation of this intercourse – as I am sure you must understand – has the natural effect of causing me to judge your work on public form alone, without knowledge of your political and other difficulties, and it is a very short step from this to opposition, to which the professional bias – as Mahan would say – and perhaps the natural spirit of combativeness inherent in us all, naturally tempted me.

I do not desire that this much easier course for me should be continued if by resuming the old relations I can facilitate much-needed reforms and make your path easier. I therefore, after meditating upon our last conversation, have written to Sir John a letter holding out a little olive branch which he can accept or reject as he pleases. I was influenced by your opinion that the difference between him and me caused you embarrassment, and I found no difficulty in overcoming the feelings which had prevented me from communicating with him since his letter to me relating to my criticism on the Army manoeuvres. I have at the same time told him that my Editor and I should not attribute any value – and we are sure that he would not – to the resumption of the old relations unless it were understood that I remain entirely free to express my own opinions, for what they are worth, on any military question, as public interest may appear to us to dictate.

I have never hesitated to criticise your predecessor when I found it necessary, and he never once objected to such criticism or allowed it to interfere with the cordiality of our relations. In such a complex business as our military policy differences of opinion must arise, and I do not believe that any advantage is gained by concealing them.

What answer, if any, Sir John will return to my letter I do not know, but I hope you will agree that I have adopted a frank and a friendly course in endeavouring, so far as I can, to enable us to pull in the same boat.

Nuffield College Library, Oxford, Mottistone Papers, MOT. 22/ff. 4–6

120
Repington to Lord Roberts

Maryon Hall,
Hampstead.

[Holograph]

3 February 1914

I am glad that you are interested in the Mediterranean article. It seems to me that this is the Achilles heel of the military position, politically and otherwise. According to present programmes, our naval position in that sea, as against Germany's allies, will steadily become worse. The 16 to 10 arrangement with Germany limits our building but does <u>not</u> limit that of Germany's allies. This arrangement is consequently all in Germany's favour. We cannot send more ships to the Mediterranean safely because we are unarmed at home, and have to give ourselves a considerable naval superiority over Germany at all times. If we had your national army we could risk a larger detachment from the North Sea, but in my opinion the knowledge of our military weakness at home will keep all our ships here in war time. I should not be surprised were the frightful cost of a Navy, regarded as a "bonne à tout faire",[149] to cause eventually our people to ask themselves whether they are on the right path. I quite agree with you about the despatch of troops from India. I merely threw out the idea as one of the courses which might be open to us, and did not at all intend to advocate it. I don't think that anything but naval superiority in the Mediterranean can save Egypt, and this superiority is not within sight with current programmes.

The last I heard about the Invasion Inquiry was that the Report was being drafted. I will make further inquiries and will let you know if I have anything worth telling.[150]

I hear the Regulars are 10,000 short and will be 18,000 short by the end of the year. You know what this means. The supine and docile attitude of the Army Council surprises me. I hope that your Lordship will raise the question as soon as the P.M. has stated the conclusions of the Invasion Inquiry.

National Army Museum, Chelsea, Roberts Papers, R62/69

121
Repington to Robinson

Maryon Hall,
Hampstead.

[Holograph]

8 February 1914

In view of the aproaching Radical attack on armaments[151] I have thought it advisable to review in this short article the past failures of disarmament and arbitration schemes, and to show the cost of defeat in war.

I was at the first Peace Conference as a technical delegate, and became convinced of the hopeless inutility of the disarmament cry. I had some hope of compulsory arbitration, but the action of the American Senate disillusioned me on this subject also.[152] To listen to our Radicals one would think that all these schemes were novelties which had never been tried, whereas they have been tried and have failed, leaving armaments alone in the field. I do not want a proof if you wish to publish enclosed article tonight.

Arthur Lee[153] writes to me that he proposes to attack the Government on its Mediterranean policy on the lines of our articles.

Have I told you that Seely will probably bring up supplementary estimates for aeronautics? Your man should be prepared to deal with them. David Henderson[154] tells me confidentially that he resisted the abandonment of dirigibles as hard as he could but was overruled. I hope you will not condone this fault, from which we are bound to suffer in our next war.

I hear that our Regular deficit at home is 10,000 and expected by the actuaries to amount to 18,000 by the end of the year.

The Times Archive, Robinson Papers

122
Repington to Robinson

Maryon Hall,
Hampstead.

[Holograph]

4 March 1914

I send you herewith a short first article on the Ulster Volunteers to accompany the map which I have arranged with Shrapnel to-day. If you publish this tonight I will let you have a second article tomorrow describing the training, spirit and mobilization of the rebels. Continuous travelling and a night in the train are not very favourable for scribbling, and if you decide to wait till next week, I may re-write the article. But I should say on the whole better publish now.[155]

The Times Archive, Robinson Papers

123
Repington to Robinson

Maryon Hall,
Hampstead.

[Holograph]

9 March 1914

I note your objections to the course which I took and will pay regard to them in the future. I realize your objections, but the urgency of the case is my excuse, and on several occasions in the past I have showed proofs in confidence to leading men, so that precedents for my article are not wanting. I have not heard from the P.M. yet, and scarcely expect a reply, as there was nothing in my missive which required one, nor was there anything which could afford him pleasure or consolation.[156] I do not suppose that the publication of the articles will be prevented because I deal solely with the military aspect of the case, and the P.M. is most unlikely to touch upon this in his speech to-day. I propose to come to the office after dinner tonight to consult you upon any changes which may be required in the first article.

Army Estimates. I propose to be at the H. of C. these next three days to hear the debates and am asking Brodribb[157] to keep me a seat. I think I might send you rough notes for a leader after Seely has spoken, and perhaps after Baird's[158] motion on Tuesday if you wish it. Then towards the end of the week a considered article on the whole debate. Let me know tonight if this suits you.

The Times Archive, Robinson Papers

124
Repington to Robinson

Navy and Military Club,
94, Piccadilly, W,

[Holograph]

13 March 1914

Will you please consider whether we are not losing ground by withholding the Volunteer articles? It seems to me that the hardening of Nationalist and Radical opinion against any further criticism, even on the time limit, is due largely to the Westminster Gazette and similar articles on the Volunteers and that a 'riposte' is needed.

You will judge. I think we ought to lay our lines on the assumption that Ulster will reject every solution except the exclusion of the whole Province, and that we ought to anticipate a General Election this Summer and fight it on the question whether Protestants are to be coerced by English rifles.

The Times Archive, Robinson Papers

125
Repington to Edith, Lady Londonderry

Maryon Hall,
Hampstead.

[Holograph]

18 March 1914

I am obliged for your letter and for your kind approval of my first article on your Volunteers. It is very kind of you to ask me to Mount Stewart.[159] I am going to Ulster for ten days or so at Easter to see what I can of the U.V.F., and I have one or two invitations already but shall be charmed to accept your hospitality. My movements will depend upon what Sir E. Carson and Sir G.O. Richardson wish me to see, and upon the plans for the Volunteer camps, a subject upon which I am not at present fully informed. If you will allow me to write to you a little later and offer myself for certain dates it will perhaps be most convenient. It sounds very ungracious, but we are living in strange times, and à la guerre comme à la guerre.[160]

Northern Ireland Public Record Office, Belfast, Londonderry Papers

126
Repington to Robinson

Mountstewart,
Newtownards,
Co. Down.

[Holograph]

9 April 1914

I duly received notice of Hone's arrival and that I was to restrict myself to the Volunteers. So I have told Hone that I shall not interfere with him, and shall probably write little until after I return to London. I quite understand that as you have sent Hone I must not dabble in politics and the rest of the subjects which are weaved into the U.V.F. question but it is pretty difficult to dissociate the Volunteers from the things around them so I think I had better leave writing alone while I am here for it is useless to write when one can only say a bit of what one thinks and knows. I am going to the various drills and affairs as they come along and shall be at Derry on the 16th for Carson's show. (Limavady). Meantime I walk on the shores of this inland lough and talk of love and lotus with old Lady L. This would make better copy than the U.V.F. but it might lose you some middle class puritan contributors. Charlie B. is here, as amusing and violent and inaccurate as usual – also Harry Lawson and Gwynne and various fair ladies. They don't seem to know much more here than we do in London.

The Times Archive, Robinson Papers

127
Repington to Robinson

Private

Mountstewart,
Newtownards,
Co. Down.

[Holograph; part transcribed in type and attached to letter.]

Night of 13–14 April 1914

The following must not appear in print in any form until Saturday morning. Carson arrived this morning. There have been two meetings of the leaders at Craigavon to-day, besides the review at Antrim Castle. It has been decided that there shall be a full council meeting on Friday next April 17, at which the whole of the evidence of the plot against Ulster shall be produced. It is expected that it will create a great sensation. There is anxiety that it may lead to local collisions but every effort will be made to prevent them – collisions, I mean, between Protestants and Nationalists. A series of mass meetings of protest will then be held, the first at Belfast probably Friday week April 24 but this date is not yet finally decided. At the meeting on the 17th it is probable that a demand will be made for a judicial inquiry, and it might be well to study precedents. They mean to make the devil's own row in the House of Commons.

Everybody here is convinced that there was a plot and that Churchill was the instigator. Things here are pretty bad: feeling very bitter, and if the King signs the Bill I don't think he will be able to show himself in Ulster again in our time. The military preparations are going on well and I will write of them when I return. There is not a shadow of improvement anywhere and a most serious view of the situation is taken by everyone with whom I have talked, and you can see it in the demeanour of the Volunteers who are working very hard and never smile or look at a girl when at work.

I don't suppose that they will get an inquiry out of the H. of C. but they may get it out of the H. of L. even though witnesses may plead privilege and not give the required evidence. But at all events it will be an attack, and it is time to attack in Parliament. I am concerned about two points. I think it will be <u>fatal</u> to the covenanters to abandon the Ulster catholic counties for the sake of compromise. There is some talk of it, but I can't think that Carson or James Craig will ever agree to it. Then there is much talk of setting up the Provisional Government directly the Home Rule Bill receives the Royal Assent. There must be bloodshed I think, and if a General Election has been promised this Summer our electorate would not understand Ulster's haste. The argument here is that the British voter will never believe in Ulster's determination until they see the Provisional Government in being, but I dissent from this view. Ulster stands on velvet and only has to keep quiet. If the Bill becomes law it cannot easily be enforced. Most assuredly the people here will fight like wild cats, and I don't know who is to fight against them. Masterly inactivity on the political side and steady progress on the military side seems to me the right policy. But these people cannot afford to let the thing drag on. It is too great a strain on all.

Meanwhile there has been much progress especially in armament, clothing and equipment.

You should tell Hone to attend the Council on Friday and have a full account of it. I shall be with Sir George Richardson that night (Maryville, Malone Road, Belfast) and on Saturday I hope to see Gleichen and then cross that night. I shall be at Glaslough tonight; at Northland House Dungannon, Co. Tyrone Wednesday and Thursday, and shall attend the Limavady parade on the latter day. It is on the cards that there may be a row in Derry that night when the Volunteers return to the town as the Nationalists will be afoot.

I should not be surprised to hear of a row anywhere and anytime. Derry seems the most dangerous point. It is wonderful that peace has been kept up to now.

The Times Archive, Robinson Papers

128
Repington to Robinson

Maryon Hall,
Hampstead.

[Holograph]

9 June 1914

I received enclosed letter from Paget[161] just as I was leaving for Ireland. Please return it. I presume that I shall see him on the 15th and shall then learn his decision: If you have any views concerning the course which he should take please communicate them to me. I have told him that I will gladly give him my views when I have the complete statement of his views before me.

He can clear himself by a Court of Inquiry or by resigning and making a statement. I can see no sufficient grounds for a Court of Inquiry, and he might not get one if he asked for it. He is in a difficult position and I should like to help him if I can, for though he made some silly speeches he pricked the bubble and had the interests of his officers at heart. It was not a soldier's job that he was given. The question is what he should do now. I will of course do my best to get you the first information of any action that he may contemplate.

The Times Archive, Robinson Papers

129
Repington to Robinson

Maryon Hall,
Hampstead.

[Holograph]

18 June 1914

(1) Your articles on the oil agreement have been brilliant, but I ought to tell you that I am in favour of the agreement which seems to me necessary. I don't think that the investment of 2 millions in the neutral zone in Persia any more compels intervention there than do our 200 millions invested in Mexico,

and the arguments in favour of the agreement seem to me to outweigh altogether the objections to it.[162] Of course, I am astonished, with you, at Sir E. Grey's levity in treating of military action in the zone of the oil, but levity distinguished much of our Persian policy, and especially the weakness shown about the Trans-Russian railway, so there is no change.

———————————————

(2) Will you send back to me a long article on Anglo-American concord – I forget the exact title – which I sent you in January, or possibly in December last? I want to look it over. I think recent events have strengthened my case.

———————————————

(3) I paid a long visit to the W.O. yesterday and arrived at the conclusion that the P.M. means to do nothing in his department and is merely playing out time. He is rarely there, does nothing, and does it extremely well. The military members think that changes, in the circumstances, are best postponed till a new man comes in, and that with a moribund government nothing can be done. Even if the P.M. gets up and makes a splash with the Invasion Report nothing can come of it without executive action, and there is no sign that the P.M. is prepared for anything of the sort. So I expect he will merely announce general principles, and that no attempt will be made to apply them until fresh blood comes in after an Election. The old 70,000 men standard is safe. This is what Bobs and I and Simon fought for, and all that we expected from this crowd, but I shall ask you to suggest later on that the whole evidence shall be reviewed by the next Government, and that the whole question of defence in its widest aspects shall be made the subject for searching inquiries. The trail of politics is over all these recent decisions.

The mass of the D[efence] C[ommittee] consists of politicians, and they are not such mugs as to draft a report which will prove inconvenient to them. So I think, if the Tories come in, we can fairly put in a claim for reconsideration of the whole matter.

The Times Archive, Repington Papers

130
Repington to General Sir Ian Hamilton

Secret

94, Piccadilly. W.

[Holograph]

27 July 1914

Yes, I heard after seeing you that we were awake, and I was glad. It is so novel. My talk with L.[163] was interesting. He assured me that his Master is entirely opposed to war and will do everything in his power to prevent it. Was there not a strong party on the G.G.Staff in favour of hitting Russia before she became too strong? Yes there was, but it will not overbear the reasonable masses of opinion. As for the Austrian Ultimatum, Germany knew nothing of the text of it. The style and tone were Count Forgách,[164] who, as you may recall, got into trouble in Belgrade some years ago over a political forgery case, was restored to favour by Berchtold,[165] and is now said to be 'everything' at Vienna. L. and I know Forgách well. He is a charming companion but vain and vindictive. He has had his chance to score off Servia and has taken it.

As to the future, L. admits that when the Austrians cross the frontier there will be a Russian ultimatum to Vienna.(Yermoloff the Russian M.A. told me he expected them in Belgrade today). Then all will depend on the phrasing of the Russian ultimatum. If it asks the Austrians not to go any further until an attempt had been made by diplomacy to settle the quarrel, then there was a chance that it might be accepted, and I shall pass this on to Yermoloff for what it is worth.

L. expatiated at length on the sin of England siding with the Slavs against the Teutons, but of course I told him that there could be no change now. He was very sarcastic about French and Russians, declaring that the latter need not be feared either now or ten years hence, that the reservists would run away into the woods when called out, and that the whole country was rotten.

And much more which I will spare you. Pass it on to W. if you like.[166]

Churchill Archive, Cambridge, W.S. Churchill Papers, CHAR 2/64/2

131
Repington to J.S. Sandars

Quarry Down,
Hythe.

[Holograph]

15 August 1914

I am away from books of reference, but my recollection is that the initial act of concentration in 1870 was completed in three weeks, and now I assume it has been completed in a fortnight. The gain in time has not been so very great, but the gain in numbers has been immense. Including both features I should judge that the Germans have assembled four times as many men as in 1870 and in seven days less time, and this only refers to the first time.

I am honoured that Mr Balfour should find my articles to the Times worth reading,[167] and I hope you will tell him how much I should like to know what he is thinking about this mighty contest. But for him, we should never have had the Defence Committee[168] and we therefore owe to him the fact that for the first time in our history we are prepared with business-like arrangements in all departments. This has been an immense benefit and has steadied the whole of our people.

No human being can foretell the result of this terrific shock impending in Belgium and on the Meuse. All hitherto, except the misfire at Liege has been according to programme prepared laboriously in long years of peace. Now we enter the region of the unknown and of improvisation and when I think of the fat old French and German generals I mourn for the Napoleonic chiefs among whom Augereau,[169] aged 38, was considered an ancient of days.

P.S: I return to town tomorrow. It is nice playing golf here within sight of the warships and the aeroplanes.

Bodleian Library, Oxford, J.S. Sandars Papers, MS. Eng. hist. c. 766, ff. 137–8

132
Repington to Lord Roberts

Maryon Hall,
Hampstead.

[Holograph]

19 October 1914

I am ashamed to have delayed my reply to your letter, but I have been kept at work day and night and have not yet been able to get down to the troops and judge of their present condition. Without knowing this at first hand I can add little to your admirable survey of the situation. The difficulty is to suggest any better constructive policy than that of Lord K. It will not be much use to criticize unless we can do so, and I am not yet clear in my mind that we can do more than we are doing.

You may be interested to hear that after my last article on invasion many correspondents wrote to ask that you should be appointed C. in C. in the British Isles. I don't quite know what you will think of this suggestion, but I have always said that the public would ask for you directly things got warm.

National Army Museum, Chelsea, Roberts Papers, R62/70

133
Repington to Lord Roberts

<u>Private</u>

Maryon Hall,
Hampstead.

[Holograph]

22 October 1914

I return to you the two memoranda.

I am much exercised about the new armies and the whole subject of home defence. I hear from battalion commanders of the new armies that though the progress is very good, it will take two months more for companies to be fit to go on to company field training, but that some have been ordered to go on at once to "war training" before the elementary work is completed.

Then, as regards home defence, I endeavoured to deal with this last night, but I see that the censor has cut me out. I am afraid that the Censorship is being used as a cloak to cover all political, naval and military mistakes, and I wish you to realize clearly that I am muzzled and that the Press is no longer free.[170] I think the general result is that the country regards all 'official' news with suspicion, and I doubt whether this is the best way to create confidence in the direction of the war.

P.S. I suppose you know that Balfour is sitting on a Sub-Committee of the D.C. on Home Defence. Are you on it?

National Army Museum, Chelsea, Roberts Papers, R62/71

134
Repington to Robinson

Maryon Hall,
Hampstead.

[Holograph]

19 January 1915

I am sorry that you did not publish my tirade against the German Army. Fortify yourself reading the French report which the Chronicle has translated and rages about to-day. Read the Russian accusations, and the D.T. leader to-day, and take heart of grace!

I send you the promised article. It will enable you to use your draft article on condemnation if you are disposed to do so. I do not disagree with your leader on the war to-day but it seems to be a trifle terre à terre[171] to keep on messing about around little trenches which do not matter two straws, and to neglect the wider aspect of affairs. If you want to imitate Belloc, give up a page to it and have a score of diagrams. Otherwise it is futile and no one is the wiser.

Arthur Paget is going round to Warsaw and the Balkan states, partly to give the new decorations. He sees the King this afternoon about it.

The Times Archive, Repington Papers

135
Repington to Robinson

<u>Confidential</u>

Army Headquarters,
France.

[Holograph]

11 May 1915

The operations now going on will be scarcely comprehensible to you without a word of warning. Please keep it strictly to yourself informing only Fraser and Steed and those who have to write War Leaders, and begging them not to refer to the points directly.

We are suffering from the results of the French flight from the first gas attack North of Ypres. This cost us about 20,000 casualties. We had to chuck in men from anywhere. It was thought that Smith-Dorrien mishandled them, and so he was sent home Friday last, and is succeeded by Plumer. Allenby has taken over from Plumer: 5th Corps and Byng now has the Cavalry Corps. I am sorry that such a hard fighting General as S.D. is gone, but I find that the majority think he had become impossible. The Germans ought to have destroyed our troops left in the Ypres Salient, but they did not understand their success against the French and we got out of the worst of one battle on the night of May 5, withdrawing from close touch all along the Salient without being observed, and with the loss of only 3 men. The Germans have given us a rough time up there since. They have plastered our men with shells and have driven us back a few hundred yards. We have taken out of the line the poor 28 Division which was utterly done and have replaced them by 2 cavalry divisions. The present line is not very strong but Plumer and Allenby think they will be alright there and to-day repulsed with heavy loss an attack at 7 am. Plumer tells me that the German infantry are not what they were and that their leading is bad. But the German guns, Maxims, wire and gas are the devil.

In the general offensive which began on Sunday last, we took a bad knock to begin with. The 4 and 1 Corps attacked N and S of Neuve Chapelle and the Bois du Biey respectively, the Indian

Corps between but only on a short front. The 4th Corps (8 Division) got in after the 40 minute bombardment, but were so raked by Maxim fire from the flanks that they were driven out. The 1st Division attacked three times, but only two regiments got a few men in at the third attempt and could not maintain themselves. The Indians never got in at all.

In the 8 division, the 2nd R.A. did best and got furthest in. They sent in 29 officers and 1090 men and came out with one company officer and 245 men. The 13th London (Kensington battalion, I think the 13th London T.F.) also did finely and suffered much, also the Irish Rifles. The failure of these two attacks cost us 10,000 casualties. I attribute the failure to want of high explosive of which we only possess 6% for our 18pdr. field guns while the French have 75%. It is impractible to level the German defences as the French do, without unlimited high explosive, and our forty minute preparation is not equal to the French four hours. There was much wire still uncut, parapets not knocked down, and most of the Maxim positions uninjured. Hence the losses and the failures. I think the two Divisions that attacked did all that men can be asked to do, but the German positions are three times stronger than they were at Neuve Chapelle, and our troops after all these losses, especially in officers, during the campaign, are not quite as good as they were, though they are better than the Germans. The latter expected us to attack when we did. We have a limited choice of places, unlike the French. But we are holding up the German 4th and 6th armies, and having relieved most of the French in the North our Allies are putting in 7 Army corps in the Arras-Lens line and are doing well and hoping to do better. They fired 270 rounds a gun from over 800 guns in the first day of their attack, and then walked in. But the Germans stuck to certain villages (Carency, St. Vaast etc.) and it is taking time to get them out. Some of the villages are almost surrounded but the Germans still hold out in them. The French have a bit of the Vimy heights which command the ground North and East, and hope to get all the high ground. Foch is commanding, and d'Antal has one of the armies under him. We have done our bit of holding the Germans on one front, and by allowing Foch to go away and attack where he was not expected. We are continuing our attacks, and hope to atone for our recent disappointment by a good success, but this front is a devil, and only heaps of high explosive can break it. If the French make a big enough hole we may go in there and so work up North.

You will hardly believe that on the first day of the offensive here, and after we had hoarded shells like gold, we were ordered to send 25,000 rounds to the Dardanelles. This has caused exasperation. We protested but it was no use. Winston was here Sunday and Monday last. It is unbelievable, and Seely has got out here with his dismounted yeomen. Do not mention Winston's visit unless you hear it from someone else, as he and I were here as private guests. I hope to be back at the end of the week

This letter is marked "passed by censor" but he will not have seen it.

The Times Archive, Repington Papers

136
Repington to David Lloyd George

Maryon Hall,
Hampstead.

[Holograph]

17 May 1915

I enclose the notes on our artillery in France. The three documents which the Cabinet should extract from Lord K. are:–

(1) A report from Sir J. French to the S. of S. for War, written some 6 to 10 weeks ago, on the whole subject of artillery ammunition.

(2) A Report, ditto, on the subject of guns, sent in 1 to 2 weeks ago.

(3) The Army Council Letter of May 14, despatched by A.G's branch, initiating a new departure in the question of reinforcements, and practically saying that no more of the New Armies would be sent to France.

Bonar Law will see the P.M. on the subject, and I feel sure that you will put things to rights.

<u>Confidential</u>[172]

Artillery

<u>Ammunition</u>.

(1) In September last, W.O. was informed that we needed 25% of high explosive with our field batteries. In December this proportion was raised to 50%. On May 9, when we began our offensive in cooperation with the French, our field batteries (18 prs.) had not more than 7%.

(2) There is no high explosive at all for the 13 prs. (horse artillery) or for the 15 prs. (field guns) of the Territorial Divisions. Shrapnel is almost useless for the attack on trenches, consequently the preparation for an attack on trenches has to be carried out by our heavy guns and howitzers, some of which are bad guns, while others are too few in number.

(3) The 4.7 in. gun, of which we have about 150 in France, is the heavy gun with the new Regular divisions (7th., 8th., 28th., 27th., etc.) and with the Territorials. It is a bad gun and no one trusts it. The 60 prs. with the 6 original Regular divisions is an excellent gun but only a few are being made though at least 200 are needed. The 4.5 in. howitzer is a good gun, but as the available guns have had to be divided amongst the new formations we have actually a smaller number of the weapons with the Army per division and per thousand men, than when we began the war. The new 15 in. howitzer is a formidable gun but we have only some 5 or 6 of them and one has been sent from France to the Dardanelles. The 9.2 in. howitzer is a good gun and we could do with more of them. The old 6 in. howitzer throwing a 100lb shell is most valuable and we ought to have a new gun of the same type as it is very mobile and can destroy the parapets.

(4) We have some 700 field guns in France but as we have practically no high explosive for them left – there are actually not more than 2000 rounds altogether in France –

all the preparatory work of artillery falls on our heavy guns which are too few in number, and in part inefficient. At Ypres and elsewhere we have lost many lives owing to the superiority of the German heavy guns. The French have not only a great number of heavy guns now, but also use the 75 mm. for preparatory work, firing high explosive of which they appear to possess an unlimited supply.

(5) It is only by concentrating all, or most, of our heavy guns on a comparatively restricted front, as at Neuve Chapelle, that we can break in; but we need to attack on a broad front for success to be achieved, while the withdrawal of guns for a special attack leaves us inferior at other points, e.g. as during the past week at Ypres.

House of Lords Record Office, D. Lloyd George Papers, D/18/6/1

137
Repington to Lloyd George

<u>Private</u>

Maryon Hall,
Hampstead.

[Holograph]

20 May 1913[173]

I send you my other note of the 17th on the question of men for France, in order that this matter may be clear to you. It is as serious as, if not more serious than, the question of high explosive. Please keep it entirely to yourself, and send back to me the originals of my two notes.

Send for me if I can be of any use to you. My main hope is in you. I should welcome you at the War Office, but I do not believe in divided responsibility. I hope that you may have extracted from Lord K. the Army Council letter (A.G. Branch) of April 14 on the subject of reinforcements, and the replies of Sir J.F. to that letter.

For Heaven's sake don't give Lord K. the command-in-chief in France. That would be too high a price to pay even for your arrival at the War Office!

Confidential[174]

The Question of Men

(1) We have roughly 600,000 men in France, 100,000 in East Mediterranean, and something like 1,500,000 or more at home. These are aggregate ration strengths. To find the number of rifles available for fighting, the figures have to be divided by 2.

(2) The offensive which began in France on May 9 was undertaken by us in the belief that the 1st New Army, of which the 9th. Division and the advance parties of the 14th. Division are already in France, would all be available in the course of the present month. In that belief the offensive began, and we took over more of the French line to set free more of their troops for use elsewhere. Now the 14th. Division at Aldershot has had its departure counter-ordered, and it is believed that no more troops of the new armies are at present destined for France.

(3) The reason, or pretext, is that the Special Reserve is so depleted by drafts that it cannot be used for Coast Defence; that the Territorial Reserve Divisions have also to find drafts; and that the new armies are needed at home to meet an invasion, on some unknown scale, which the Admiralty declare they cannot prevent in the present distribution of our fleets.

The Army is also informed that the Territorial drafts cannot be kept up until the 3rd. line Territorial formations are filled up and are trained.

(4) The Army abroad laugh at the fear of invasion; declare that Germany cannot spare the men; allege that we know and can account for the position of every German Army Corps; and that the invasion scare is of German origin and intended to chain our troops to home defence. Others believe that K's jealousy of Sir J. French is the cause of the change, and his inability to grasp the conditions of modern war; while others believe that the Dardanelles sink is the reason for the new policy which is heart-breaking to the Army in France and is likely to wreck the success of the war.

(5) What new fact can have caused the change of policy? The Army wish to know the reasoned opinion of the Admiralty with regard to invasion. The standard for defence against invasion was laid down by the Defence Committee, and unless the drain of the Dardanelles has unduly weakened our fleets at home, or submarines and mines have effected greater changes than the Defence Committee anticipated, it is not understood why the Navy should now profess themselves unable to carry out in war the duties which they contracted to do before the war began. The Army doubt whether the Navy have changed their views, but until this question is cleared up we are all working in the dark.

(6) Any failure to continue to pour troops into the principle theatre means the bankruptcy of the military policy of the Cabinet. Apart from the new invasion scare there is no new fact which might not have been anticipated. The Special Reserve is fulfilling its normal function, and it should not have been entrusted with a second duty which the provision of drafts made it incapable of fulfilling. It is the Cabinet which has sent all but two of the 14 Territorial divisions abroad and it is a confession of incompetence and want of foresight to say that they cannot maintain them in the field. Every one knew that if the Territorial Reserve divisions were to be used for home defence to replace their active formations it would not be fair to call on them for drafts, and that a 3rd. line would have to be formed to play the part allotted, in the case of the Regulars, to the Special Reserve. But this need was understood too late, and in consequence the 3rd. line is a skeleton and can as yet perform no useful function. If the Territorial Units at the first cannot be kept up then it would be better to send them home and replace them by the new armies. If this is not done, the only course open to the Army in France will be to form composite battalions of Territorials, made up of the remains of different units after various actions.

(7) We must know the new invasion standard before we can pronounce on the subject of the new armies, but to keep

800,000 men (6 armies each of 135,000) at home in order to make good the deficiencies of 300,000 Territorial Reserves appears to be unnecessary. Besides either the Territorial Reserve divisions <u>will</u> supply drafts or they will not. If they will, then there can be no question of not keeping the active divisions full. If they will not, then why retain the new armies at home, unless the new invasion standard is higher than anyone can contemplate?

(8) It is probable that if the present policy is maintained our Armies in France will have to restrict themselves to the defensive, and serious cooperation with France will be at an end, for to make war is to attack. The Cabinet seem unaware of the conditions for a successful offensive in France. We cannot ask – the French do not ask – troops fighting in the front line to remain there more than a few days, so intense is the strain caused by modern fire. We must continually replace them by troops from a reserve, and the reserve of infantry must be very large in consequence. We have to leave divisions several weeks in the fighting line – e.g. the 27th. and 29th divisions recently at Ypres – and they become dead to the world and dazed by the strain. The Germans are in like state and are just now in worse case than we are. It is the moment for a great effort, and it is at this precise moment that Sir John is told, practically that he is to expect no more reinforcements.

(9) There may be reasons, unknown to me, for the new policy of the Cabinet, but on such evidence as is available I think the direction of the policy which controls our strategy should be called in question, and Ministers made to give reasons for their actions. We have enough cloth for one coat and appear to be endeavouring to make two coats out of it. I should imagine that the Dardanelles adventure is at the bottom of the new policy, and that just as drink was dragged in to excuse the ammunition failure, so the bad direction of our armies in France is to be given as the pretext for not reinforcing our armies in the principal theatre.

(10) We have had 51,000 casualties in France since April 23. We must expect at least 20,000 more during the attack which

began so well last Saturday night. If the whole of the 1st. new army were now in France, as it might have been and in my opinion ought to have been, we and the French should have secured a great success. But with what heart can a Field Marshal call upon his troops for a mighty effort when a Cabinet behind him closes the flow of reinforcements?

House of Lords Record Office, D. Lloyd George Papers, D/18/6/2

138
Repington to Lloyd George

Maryon Hall,
Hampstead.

[Holograph]

3 July 1915

I am going to suggest greater activity in aerial warfare and large purchases of aeroplanes in the United States. As the case for this policy seems to me so strong as to carry conviction I write you a line in case you may think it is advisable to secure an option immediately upon the American factories.

I need not tell you how closely I am following your actions in your new department and how much I should like to have a talk with you when you have a moment to spare.[175]

House of Lords Record Office, D. Lloyd George Papers, D/18/6/3

139
Repington to Northcliffe

Maryon Hall,
Hampstead.

[Holograph]

14 July 1915

I see that Hilaire Belloc has been shooting at you. It is largely thanks to the wild optimism of this individual that the country has been so badly misled. If you care to set Lovat Fraser or anyone else to work at Belloc's articles in Land and Water you can demolish him for all time as a prophet. I have not the time to do it but it is worth doing as he has done much harm.[176]

British Library, Northcliffe Papers, Add. MSS., 62253, f. 39

140
Repington to Northcliffe

Maryon Hall,
Hampstead.

[Holograph]

2 September 1915

I see that the Manchester Guardian declares that there is no chance of conscription being adopted and says that the military case against it is overwhelming because the War Office has, and will for months to come, have more men than it can supply and send to the front.[177]

By this I presume it means more men than the W.O. can arm. This is true but it makes an overwhelming case against the War Office and not against conscription. A case against conscription can only be made out when proof is given that voluntary service can supply the men needed by the General Staff to secure victory. The General Staff have been consistently and deliberately prevented from telling the Cabinet how many men are needed for this purpose. The General Staff were made responsible by the Esher Committee for "military policy, strategy, war organization, and operations" and I believe that their views on these subjects have never been submitted to the Cabinet, and that the case for and against conscription can never be made out until they are.

It is perfectly shameful that men of the 4th and later new armies, men who have been in training since September 1914, should still only have 80 rifles per battalion of 1100 men. The 3rd line Territorials are in similar case, and the 2nd line Territorials have Japanese rifles. You can ascertain this for yourself by visiting Salisbury Plain or the East coast.

The Government shun all inquiry, and keep the General Staff at arm's length, because they know that if there were an inquiry, and if the views of the <u>best</u> <u>men</u> on the General Staff were given to the Cabinet the whole imposture would be exposed.

British Library, Northcliffe Papers, Add. MSS., 62253, ff. 40–1

141
Repington to Lloyd George

Maryon Hall,
Hampstead.

[Holograph]

18 September 1915

Can we have a little talk one day next week?[178]

I need not tell you how heartily I sympathise with your recent speeches and letters. You pulled us through the munitions crisis and you must now pull us through the crisis of numbers. Do you know all I wonder? I cannot help feeling that if the country can be told the truth about recruiting and our needs we should all toe the line.

Can you lunch with me any day 1.30 at the Carlton restaurant?

House of Lords Record Office, D. Lloyd George Papers, D/18/6/6

142
Repington to Andrew Bonar Law

Maryon Hall,
Frognal Lane,
Hampstead.

[Holograph]

16 November 1915

The rumours of an impending change in the command of our armies in France prompt me to give you my views on this subject.[179] I do not believe that the appointment of Sir D. Haig to the Commander-in-Chief will be to the public interest. Haig is a staff officer. He is not, and will never be a commander. I have watched his operations in peace and war, and have never observed in him any talent for command. He is incapable of conveying his views to subordinates by word of mouth, as you can judge if you get him before the War Council and examine him yourself. He is a cavalry officer, of whom we have already too many in high command and in a war which mainly concerns other arms. It is to him that we mainly owe the losses and disappointments of Neuve Chapelle, Festubert and Loos.[180] If you ask Wilcocks[181] about Haig's treatment of the Indian Corps you will learn how he treats troops under him. He is an excellent staff officer but has not the great qualities of character needed for the Command in Chief.[182]

It is true that I seek in vain for the Wellington type. Allenby comes the nearest to it, but he too is from the cavalry. Charles Monro has character, decision and intelligence but will I fear be dragged down with this Salonika adventure.

Smith-Dorrien has the character needed in the high command. Of the younger men Cavan, and next Gough, are the best. Robertson and Sir A. Murray I admire and trust greatly, but both are best in the positions which they now hold. I know of no one who excels French in the qualities of character needed in the high command.

House of Lords Record Office, Bonar Law Papers, 51/5/27

143
Repington to Andrew Bonar Law
Confidential

Maryon Hall,
Hampstead.

[Typed Copy]

24 November 1915

The dinner table is not a very good place at which to discuss strategy, and I therefore venture now to expand the ideas of which I gave a brief indication last Friday night.[183]

THE BALKANS

I am a confirmed Westerner and believe that the decision of the war is to be sought on the principal fronts. But the German Drang nach Osten[184] has to be met, and the question is where and how. I am dead against operations in the Balkan area, because the Germans now control the operations of about one million German, Austrian, Bulgarian, and Turkish troops in this area; because the attitude of Greece and Romania is to say the least uncertain; because the position of the enemy is superior; and because the country is most difficult, and unsuitable to our armies until they are completely re-equipped with transport and guns suited to this mountainous region. Worst of all, we drag into the contest Balkan forces which would conceivably remain quiescent if we did not stir them up, if we do not antagonise them now, and might come over to our side when we begin to assert a general military superiority. I do not think that Bulgars, Greeks, Serbs or Rumans will ever march very far outside their own countries under German banners, and I am not sure that we shall see so many Turks on the Dvina or the Meuse as the Germans hope. Let us leave the Balkan states alone and not attempt to coerce them, or by entering their territories compel them to take sides. I trust much to the mutual antagonism of these people, and to time and events for us to gather the fruits of it. I do not believe in the circular tour to Victory via Athens, Belgrade, Pesth, Vienna and Berlin. Study the practice of Napoleon. The shortest road to his enemy's capital was always the path that he preferred. I am not in the least impressed by the French rhapsodies which would entangle us in the Balkans. I believe that Joffre's unfortunate intervention on October 29 was due to personal and political considerations on which I need not dwell, and that his temporary falling away from principles which he has hitherto consistently held must be attributed to these considerations alone.[185]

GERMAN PLANS

I assume a liquidation of the Salonika and Dardanelles adventures and pass on to consider other measures. We must discount the presence of the Germans at Constantinople and all the racket which it will cause. We cannot stop them from going there. Their object I assume to be to break the encirclement; to impress opinion and intimidate the Balkan states; to provide themselves with men, food, copper and cotton; and to threaten and attack our position in Egypt and the East. I do not imagine that the Germans will ever employ large armies of their own in these regions, their position on the main fronts is too insecure and their supplies of men too diminished to authorise such large detachments. I suppose that the German Great General Staff must view with the deepest concern the probable recovery of Russia during the Winter, and that they will not devote more than a few Army Corps to their Asiatic adventures, and will probably draw most of them home again before next May. They will bring cadres, arms and leading to the Turks, and endeavour to vex us with their submarines, but I doubt the employment of large German forces on secondary campaigns while the decision on the main fronts is still awaited.

TURKISH FORCES

I imagine that the Turks have some 700,000 men under arms; 300,000 in the Thrace-Dardanelles area; 200,000 in Arabia, Syria, Smyrna etc; 150,000 on the Caucasus front, and 50,000 in Mesopotamia. You will know whether this is near to the truth. The Germans on reaching Asia Minor have the choice of three objectives, namely the Caucasus, the East and Egypt. The first concerns Russia mainly; the second is a long business which will take much time; the third is the most attractive of the three and is in consonance with the German principle, stolen from Napoleon, of beating the sea by the land.

DEFENCE OF EGYPT

My idea is to concentrate in Egypt and at Cyprus and Malta all the troops which we now have in the Eastern Mediterranean or in transit thither. The numbers are over 250,000, but the actual figure will depend upon the result of the liquidation at Gallipoli and Salonika. I would ask France and Italy, who have large interests East of Suez, to assemble strategic reserves, amounting in all to another 250,000 men, at any Mediterranean ports and islands convenient to them, and to earmark them for special operations. I would place the whole under Lord Kitchener,[186] if this can be arranged with our allies, and give him full civil, naval and military powers over the whole Middle Eastern theatre including Mesopotamia. I would give him transports sufficient to carry 100,000 men at least at one trip for short voyages, and place the ships at Malta, Alexandria and in the Canal. The French and Italians can find their own ships. The whole of the troops must be equipped for service in Asia Minor and Syria and you can assume lines of communication never over 100 miles in length.

My idea is not to restrict ourselves to the passive defence of Egypt until we are driven to it, but to wage an active war of attack upon the whole of the Turkish-Syrian coasts from the Dardanelles to the Sinai desert inclusive. I would attack according to circumstances, with anything from a boat's crew up to 300,000 men, and I would attack every day and night at some fresh point, and establish a warm alarm upon the whole of the Turkish coasts which gives us a front of attack of some 1200 miles, not counting Arabia. I should expect with this strategy, to chain down forces very superior to ours to the passive defence of the long coast line, the towns and the railway.

If the enemy still advanced in Egypt I would leave 150,000 men at the canal and cut in behind him with 350,000 at El Arish, Haifa, Beyrout, Alexandretta or wherever I could best influence and ruin the Turkish expedition and break up its communications. It is quite true, as you said the other night, that the Turks can concentrate force at Alexandretta, but if they are there they cannot be on the march to Egypt, and with our quick moving amphibious force we can be at one point one day and at another several hundred miles away a few days later. In these circumstances I should reckon that our 500,000 men would prove superior to double or triple the number of Turks, and if we had good commanders and proper naval equipment I feel confident that we could guarantee the successful defence of Egypt. You have only to plan the Turkish defence against this strategy to see how difficult it is.

NAVAL EQUIPMENT

By naval equipment I mean adequate transports, suitably fitted up; ample lighters and boats suitable for landing troops, preferably lighters able to move under their own power; a perfect organization for embarking troops, horses, mules, guns and stores rapidly and for disembarking them; and all the necessary arrangements for protecting transports at anchor against attack by submarines. I should not be content with less than the disembarkation of 50,000 men in one working day, and this result can only be obtained by very thorough and perfect preparation. I regard the naval equipment of the expedition as vital to its efficiency. I know that the coast presents difficulties but in war these exist to be overcome.

LORD KITCHENER

I was on Lord Kitchener's staff in the Sudan and know him well. I tell you frankly that you must control him. I hear of mad schemes for joining Nixon via Damascus, and of plunging into the centre of Asia Minor. In my view Nixon's advance beyond Kurna was a mistake and his column should be ordered to return to that point.

If you propose to control Lord Kitchener you must send him explicit instructions. You must give him a good staff, including a naval section, and representatives of the staffs of the French and Italian contingents. You must order him to work through his staff, to issue all orders in writing, and to keep copies of them, and acknowledgements of their receipt from the addressees. He hates doing these things and will not do them until you tell him that he must. You must make him and his commanders keep staff diaries and send them to you once a week, and you must direct that he shall inform you of all his projects and obtain your sanction before any important operations are begun. The General Staff in London must keep their fingers on the pulse of these affairs. I should prefer that the actual fighting should be done by anyone rather than Lord Kitchener. My idea is that Lord Kitchener should winter at the Cairo Agency and spin webs all over the Middle East. He knows all this country, including Syria, like the palm of his hand; speaks Arabic like a native; can deal with the people, and is the only great Westerner with an Eastern mind. He fully understands the French maxim "à trompeur, trompeur et demi".[187] I should suppose that he will get in touch with Djemal Pasha[188] in Syria, who shows signs of restiveness under Young Turk tyranny; will promote an Arab rising in the Yemen; stir up the Druses in Palestine; hold up in Syria the mirror of a separate principality, and in general make things warm for the Turks. He would be in his element, but, once more, you must control him and insist that he acts, in all military and naval matters, through his staffs by written words.

Pray excuse this long letter which you are welcome to show to any of your colleagues.

House of Lords Record Office, Bonar Law Papers, 51/5/44

144
Repington to Bonar Law

Maryon Hall,
Frognal Lane,
Hampstead.

[Holograph]

26 November 1915

Yes, I am well aware that for many reasons we must not lock up more transports than are absolutely necessary. It is a naval question, and I should imagine that 150,000 tons would be enough, considering the shortness of the projected voyages. This amount will not be needed until the attack upon Egypt begins to materialize, and in the initial stages I should be content with 50,000 tons which would enable us to harry the coasts with anything up to 30,000 men.

If you cannot afford the transports you will alter the whole character of the strategy which aims at meeting numbers by mobility.

Please allow me to add that my remarks about Mesopotamia were made before the news came of the Ctesiphon set-back.[189] Now you cannot go back until you have recovered the lost ground.

The General Staff asked me some time ago for my views on this campaign, and I then suggested Kurna as the limit for the advance, adding that the nearer we remained to the sea the better I should be pleased.

We may have to fight a great campaign in Mesopotamia later on, but I think that we are stupid to initiate it. My Russian friends tell me that their Caucasus strategy is defensive, and ours, surely, ought to be in line with theirs. I know what India is in these affairs; they like to fight a campaign 'on their own', with their own generals, troops, plans, and honour lists. This is one of my reasons for wishing to see the Mesopotamia strategy controlled by the War Council, through Lord K. or the general whom you may place in chief command for the Syrian campaign.

Please do not trouble to acknowledge receipt of this note.

House of Lords Record Office, Bonar Law Papers, 51/5/53

145
Repington to Robinson

19, Frognal Lane,
Hampstead.

[Typed]

22 December 1915

This job you have given me is very long and tiresome.[190] There are a great number of other subjects which I should have preferred to turn my hand to. Robertson takes over on Friday, Murray leaves for Egypt on Tuesday. He will be in the position of Commander in Chief in the Mediterranean with entire disposal of all the troops, but he will probably shape out for Maxwell a sphere of subordinate command in Egypt itself, on the Western frontier of Egypt and in the Soudan. He takes over Monro's Staff and Monro himself will probably revert to the First Army in France. Murray has done as admirably as the P.M. says and I think most of the Ministers greatly regret his departure. I ascertained yesterday by the way, when looking into a lot of matters at the W.O. (of which more anon.) that the General Staff was never consulted in the initiation of the Dardanelles enterprise, and never asked to write a paper on the subject. Callwell himself saw Winston and warned him of the dangers. I do not know whether old Wolfe Murray may have mumbled approval to Lord K. but there is certainly no General Staff memorandum in existence on the subject.

Robertson is bringing home with him Fred Maurice and Whigham, two quite good men. Kiggell, now Director of Home Defence, goes out to Haig as Chief Staff Officer in France. On the whole I consider all these recent changes as disadvantageous, removing as they do men from positions where they have done admirably to others to which they are less suited. None of these changes came before the Cabinet. I consider them intended to throw dust in the eyes of the public. It's the politicians and not the soldiers who want changing, that is my view, and it takes a very long time for all these people who have been the military mainsprings of the work in hand to accustom themselves to their new duties. The best thing about the changes, so far as I can understand it before consulting Robertson who is, I believe, still in France, is that the new C.I.G.S. will be free from the interference of the Secretary of State in all matters concerning strategy and operations, will issue orders <u>in his own name</u> direct to Commanders far and near, and will have unimpeded access to the War Council to whom he will continue to submit his papers as Murray has done since October last. The new work of Lloyd George, Derby, French, and Robertson appears to me to be a steady and intentional undermining of Lord K's position, who is sinking back, tamely I am told, and not before it was fully time, into the position of a civilian Secretary of State. All his colleagues want to get rid of him but no one can quite bell the cat. Mrs George Keppel told me two days ago that Lord K. had been offered India and had refused. Steele-Maitland however tells me that if Lord K. were sent to India, Austen Chamberlain would resign.

I made a speech two nights ago at the Hotel Cecil to the Unionist Agents from the North of England, no reporters present. I gave them my views quite freely, showing what we have suffered from the mismanagement of the P.M. and Lord K. Steele-Maitland who spoke after me abounded in the same sense. If we had said these things six months ago we should have been thrown into the street.[191] Knowledge of the real state of affairs is penetrating but I don't think it has yet got into the mass of the people, so these agents tell me, and I hear it from other sources too.

I don't think we need worry about East Africa just yet. The delay in raising the levies in South Africa until after the late elections has made it too late to undertake important operations before the rains, which, as you know, last from April to June, and make German East Africa practically impassable. There is also a great shortage of rolling stock and locomotives on the railway. I expect therefore that there will only be preliminary preparations before the rains and the evictions of the German posts on our side of the frontier. The real campaign will not begin much before July next. The Germans have fewer than 3,000 whites but they have 20,000 – the Agha Khan says 30,000 – black troops and 63 guns. They also continue to receive rifles, though from what source I do not know, perhaps blockade runners. I fancy that there is no intention of conquering the whole German Colony but only the most important districts including perhaps Dar es Salam. I think it is probable that the Germans may take the offensive this Winter as we are so behindhand. Our failure to raise native troops from the Masai and other fighting tribes during all these months deserves the strongest reprobation. What dreadful slackers we are!

Perhaps you will kindly let Lord Northcliffe see this letter.

The Times Archive, Repington Papers

146
Repington to Northcliffe

<u>Private and Confidential</u>

Maryon Hall,
Frognal Lane,
Hampstead.

[Typewritten]

12 January 1916

I have been approached privately to know whether I will stand for a division of Manchester in place of a member who will resign in my favour. I should be glad of your advice.[192] I have not yet mentioned the subject to anyone else and have merely replied that I will consider the matter.

British Library, Northcliffe Papers, Add. MSS., 62253, f. 53

147
Repington to General Sir W.R. Robertson

<u>Private</u>

Maryon Hall,
Frognal Lane,
Hampstead.

[Holograph]

3 February 1916

After our talk yesterday[193] I think it best to send you the information in my possession regarding Townshend. Please regard it as confidential and do not show it to anyone except Macdonogh.

There are four documents. "A" is a letter from Townshend to me which gives his state of mind. "B" is a set of mainly congratulatory messages. "C" is a letter from Townshend to his wife. Some private messages and remarks about Nixon are alone left out. "D" is Townshend's appreciation of the position before he fought at Ctesiphon. The letter was forwarded to Mrs Townshend by the Viceroy's (word not legible) from Simla, so

I assume that Hardinge must have seen it. Townshend appears to me to have fought well and judged well. I am all the more lost in astonishment that his advice should have been disregarded. You quite understand, I am sure, that I send you these papers relying absolutely upon your discretion to keep their contents to yourself. Kindly send them back as soon as possible.

Liddell Hart Centre, King's College, London, Robertson Papers, I/33/72a

148
Repington to G.S. Freeman (an exchange)

Maryon Hall,
Frognal Lane,
Hampstead.

[Holograph]

8 October 1916

Herewith a note on the Geddes appointment. Northcliffe knows the whole story and will, I believe, strongly support me. L.G. has obtained Haig's consent and will of course flaunt this before us, but actually L.G. forced Geddes upon Haig who was too busy with the battle to understand what was in the wind.[195] Geddes went to France August 5. L.G. went later. Haig's first official letter about it reached the W.O. on October 5.

P.S. If the censor objects to the article, write a hot leader.

Maryon Hall,
Frognal Lane,
Hampstead.

[Holograph]

9 October 1916

Proofs revised and returned herewith. I notice that the proof of the article on 'The Military Situation' is described as 'uncensored', yet parts of my manuscript are omitted. Will you kindly explain why?

Maryon Hall,
Frognal Lane,
Hampstead.

[Holograph]

11 October 1916

(1) You have not done me the favour of replying to my last letter and of telling me by whom were removed paragraphs in my article in a proof marked 'uncensored'. Omissions are also noticed by me in my article of to-day, and I only wish to know who made them and why, so that I may know where I stand.

(2) I see in the Chronicle that Mr Fell is asking a question in the Commons about the Channel Tunnel, and the Chronicle with an article evidently inspired by the Tunnel Party, has the face to assume that the Government will accept the Tunnel.[196] Now our General Staff refuse to accept any responsibility for this project until the conditions after the war, and the lessons of the war, have been fully examined, and as we have always opposed the Tunnel, tonight is the time for saying a word. I therefore enclose an article on the subject which Mr.Robinson has already seen and approved. We were holding it over until the other side moved openly, and now that they have moved and are moving, we must speak out. The present Parliament have been thinking of other things and must not be allowed to let this thing slip through from lassitude. Give us a strong leader on it if you can.

(3) As I can generally be found on the telephone I think that you might have consulted me about your article on the Volunteers. I wholly dissent from the concluding paragraphs which will be understood by all Tribunals to have been written in ignorance of the facts. I am assumed to be responsible for these things as the public does not know that every sort of person in your office is a better judge of military affairs than I am and feels himself competent to mangle my own articles and to express his own views without reference to me.

P.S. I should tell you that the Tunnel party have been writing confidential papers to the Foreign Office and trying to catch them asleep, out of fear of our opposition if they came out into the open, but fortunately the F.O. have sent the papers on to the G.S. who have taken the line above-mentioned.

'The Times'
P.H.S.
(G.S. Freeman to Repington)

[Typed Copy]

11 October 1916

Passages were omitted from your last article on the military situation because, so I was informed, later information put them out of date, and you were not here to revise them. Any omissions in to-day's article were made by the censor.

Your article on Sir Eric Geddes was not inserted since I satisfied myself that its insertion was not desirable.

I do not propose to deal with the question of the Channel Tunnel this week.

I note that you dissent from the leading article to-day, but surely if your friends insist on attributing its views to you, you have only to explain to them that the Editor, and the Editor alone, is responsible for leading articles in <u>The Times</u>. At present I am Editor.

The Times Archive, Repington Papers

149
Repington to Northcliffe

Maryon Hall,
Frognal Lane,
Hampstead.

[Typed]

13 October 1916

I read the Daily Mail leader after we had spoken on the telephone this morning and liked it very much.[197] All is now well for the moment, but when a Welsh mystic honestly conceives himself to be sent by Heaven to win the war, there is no accounting for what he may do. I wish he would surround himself with proper men but I do not like his cronies a bit.

I am very glad indeed that you are going to support the Government if they play the game by the soldiers. My idea has always been that we had to be in violent opposition until we got the munitions, compulsion, and the direction of operations by the General Staff. Having got them I was for a clear cut and the support of the Government. But the best protection of our interests is that you should join the Government and hold there a watching brief for us all.[198] They would be bound to run straight both with regard to the soldiers and the peace if they knew that you would go out on the first signs of any weakening and set the country on fire. The real danger just now is that things may happen in councils of the Government and we not know in time. A few hours are enough for the most fateful decisions to be taken. I hear that Austen is ill and may be unable to go on.[199]

British Library, Northcliffe Papers, Add. MSS., 62253, f. 95

150
Memorandum: Repington to Steed

Secret

The Times,
P.H.S.

[Typed with Holograph Corrections]

11 October 1916

The Real Situation.

(1) As I am prevented by the Censorship from giving a good deal of information of interest, and from expressing my real opinions on the War in The Times, I propose to jot my views down in this paper for the confidential information of the Editorial Staff.

The West.

(2) The offensive on the Somme has now lasted 3½ months. It has cost us some 300,000 casualties and the French 150,000. There is no reason except eventual want of men to prevent the continuance of the offensive, for our expenditure is not exceeding our income of shells, and though the autumn and winter will render operations more difficult and fragmentary it need not

entirely arrest them. But we began the offensive with a shortage of 25,000 men, and though we have sent out 250,000 drafts, and have expended nearly 4,000 of the 5,000 surplus officers accumulated in view of this offensive, we are still 75,000 men short mainly in the infantry, which should number about 640,000 rifles out of an aggregate of 1,600,000 men in France. There is a chance that the Somme offensive may be arrested from want of men. Our recruiting resources are also drawn upon for our other forces overseas, and Lord French's troops have been so drained to supply our armies in France that our home defence forces have not now much military value. I should say that the German Navy contemplates renewed activity, and that the heroics of the submarines off the U.S. coast, are partly intended to distract our attention from home waters. An old Napoleonic trick.

(3) I do not agree that "victory is assured". It is only assured if our efforts are not only continued but increased. The work of the Man-Power Board must be watched. We have between 3,000,000 and 4,000,000 men of military age employed in a civil capacity in Great Britain and at least 200,000 available in Ireland, but the same influences which for so long postponed compulsion are being brought to bear to prevent the maintenance of our armies. We need not only maintenance but growth. We have 83 divisions and another promised by Canada; the French 103; the Russians 150 excluding the Caucasus; the Belgians and Serbs 6 and 7 respectively; the Italians 50; and the Roumanians 20; total 419, but 26 of our British divisions are not available for France at present, so the real figure is 393. The Germans have 190; the Austrians 76; the Bulgarians 12; and the Turks 52, total 330, but only 7 Turkish divisions are available North of the Balkans at present. Balance credit 63 to the Allies, or 108 if we exclude the missing Turks. This superiority is counterbalanced to a large extent by the central situation of Germany, her fine railway system, and her unity of command. Our resumption of the initiative, and our failure to annihilate, correspond with the results which might fairly be expected from relative strengths and advantages. If we want better results we must deserve them. I see no reason to count "victory assured" unless we raise more divisions, do better in keeping up the strengths in the

field, and constantly increase our heavy artillery. I see no sure means of winning the war except by the wearing down of German Man-Power, and we can only wear it down by an increasing numerical superiority of our guns and men. I think that Germany can find the men to keep up her present field strengths during the year 1917 and I will not go further than that just now. I do not believe that economic pressure will defeat Germany, and I suppose that we are prepared for the abandonment by Germany of the gold standard after the war. She will then reduce the war debt by 50 to 75%

(4) The German official view is that we have lost 800,000 men in the West and the Russians 1,000,000 in the East since July and June respectively. I hope that we may knock 40% off each figure. The Germans claim that we in the West have won no strategic success and that the tactical gain by us of a little ground means nothing. The Germans on the Somme are now mostly back on a fresh line of hills where they will obtain better observations for their guns, and we have to descend a valley and ascend to the further attack on the line Miraumont–Bapaume-Sailly. It will take us some days to prepare this fresh attack. Here the artillery fight will be more equal. If we gain this line, the Germans will go back to the next which runs through Frémiscourt and Rocquigny to Guzoncourt. It is a hard and prolonged struggle which may still go on for long. Only the sum of the results in the end will count, and, while our moral gain has been great, the material profit will not be conspicuous unless, by such use of our guns as has marked the more recent phases of our attacks, we cause the enemy at least as great losses as we suffer. Then, as he is weaker than us, he will suffer proportionately more.

(5) Having felt some doubts about the Von Arnia memorandum I have made enquiries and find that only those paragraphs which tell against Germany have been quoted, while all those which tell against us have been omitted. This is alright for propaganda abroad, but I disapprove of the procedure followed, as it leads our public to false conclusions, and they are much too prone already to declare "victory assured". I think that it would have been better to have given the full text, when our people would have realised the need for greater efforts.

Russia

(6) The Russians have about 2,500,000 men in the field and their depots are full, but owing to want of artillery, especially heavy guns, and of motor lorries and aeroplanes, the value of their armies is only equal to that of 1,500,000 men in terms of British or French troops. It is most important to supply their requirements, but, in fact, the armies in France naturally receive all our attention, and Russia only gets our leavings. I hope that the Murman line will be open for traffic by January 15 but the Germans are dead set on injuring the traffic by their submarines. We must contrive to pour in heavy guns and shells so that the Russians may be kept going during the Winter and be all right by next May. I think that Hindenburg means to try and knock the Russians out. I think that he counts on their shortage of shells. I hope that he is too late, but one never knows exactly what the Russians can do or will do, and the last people to know are always the Russians themselves. I think that we can count on Italy to go ahead on the Carso and keep the Austrians busy on this side during the winter.

Romania

(7) Hindenburg's present scheme is, I think, to smash Romania, and then with Falkenhayn's and Mackensen's armies to assail the left flank of the Russian armies and to move towards Kischeneff and Galatz. There are 21 enemy divisions already in position for the stroke, of which 13 are with Falkenhayn near Kronstadt, and 7 with Mackensen. Romania has about 26 divisions, including 3 Russian and one Serb. But, directly Brussiloff stops his advance, Hindenburg will send more troops southward, and the Romanian leading is so vile, their dispositions so bad, and the quality of their army so dubious, that only the despatch of strong Russian forces to the South, and the taking over of the command by a first-rate Russian General are likely to stay the rot. The three Romanian armies on their West front are now only 11 or 12 divisions in all, and they are much scattered. Another Army of 6 divisions is similarly scattered along the Danube. The rest are in the

Dobrudcha and at Bukarest but probably a redistribution is in progress. Of Falkenhayn's 13 divisions only 4 are good German troops. These include the famous Alpine Corps under Krafft von Delmensingen, formerly Chief of the Bavarian General Staff. Mackensen has at least 2 good Bulgarian divisions with him and eventually may have 5 Turkish in all. The best talent of the German command is employed upon this Romanian campaign. The Romanians appear to have no more knowledge of strategy than infants. Our chief Franco-British military authorities advised Alexeieff as early as September 7 that he must take control and find the troops to save Romania, but the Russians despise the Romanians and the latter distrust the Russians so things are not very bright. All the same, Alexeieff has ordered down three more Army Corps, or 6 divisions to Romania, and this will help. My impression is that there will be a steady flow of troops on both sides towards the Romanian battle ground during the next few weeks.

BULGARIA, SALONIKA and EGYPT

(8) Bulgaria has 8 to 9 divisions, equal to 16 or 18 of ours, facing Sarrail, and with them are three regiments of the 101st German division. Two Bulgarian divisions face the Struma front. 1½ and the Germans are on the Doiran front, and 4 are in the Monastir region. All are covered by serious fortifications. The Bulgar wings are now drawn in, and the enemy is back in his main positions. We must not make too much of this, nor talk of victory. Sarrail has 17 divisions, 5 British, 5 French (one partly Russian) 6 Serbian, and 1 Italian. Our British troops have suffered much from malaria and dysentery and the infantry are only about 50% of their proper strength, but 23,000 drafts are on the way to them although they are badly wanted on the Somme. The Serbs have lost 25% of their total strength in the recent fighting and have no reserves. There is but little chance of any serious offensive on our part owing to the want of communications, the absence of local supplies, and the character and strength of the enemy and the country. Even if Sarrail reaches Monastir, the situation in Romania will not be altered.

We must never forget that the Germans can always reinforce the Bulgars and send troops far quicker than we can send them

(9) M.Briand now asks for two more Italian divisions, and 2 more British from Egypt. Cadorna says he can only spare a brigade, but Lloyd George is pressing for the Allies to send 8 divisions, contrary to the views of our General Staff and of the War Committee. I have been appealed to by the French.G.Q.G. and have said that I am entirely in agreement with our General Staff's views. For Joffre's paper sent to me by a messenger see Appendix. We have some interesting plans to work out in South Syria, and in any case 4 divisions in Egypt are little enough to defend the country and to serve as a reserve for Mesopotamia and India.

It is quite possible, as stumps have been drawn in Anatolia for the winter, that the Turks may come down and have another out at us in Egypt. Lloyd George's 8 divisions for Salonika can only be found by depleting our armies in France, and to my mind this would be criminal. I said in a recent article, – it was scratched out by someone but that does not make it less true – that there is a flagrant disproportion between the country round Salonika and the large force which we have sent there. The idea of a successful offensive from Salonika haunts the minds of Briand and Lloyd George. French soldiers must deal with their own politicians as best they can, but, on our side, if Lloyd George is allowed to run the strategy of the campaign, soldiers will wash their hands of their attempt to conduct this difficult war on its military side.

MESOPOTAMIA

This campaign looks up, thanks to a good new commander and more order on the L. of C.

The railway from Basra to Khamiseh on the Euphrates should be opened in a few days time, and then it will be easy to get supplies to Masariyeh. The Qurnah–Amarah railway is also getting on and it may go up to Sheikh Saad. This is a 2'6" line: the other is metre gauge. It is like India to start two gauges. When all these transport difficulties are straightened out and the rivers rise, the expedition will be able to get on and leather the Turks. But for Russia, I should prefer to see the troops withdrawn to Basra. We cannot now desert the Grand Duke. Nixon recommended these railways over a year ago and the Government of India refused them.

Strategy of the War

I am in favour of continuing the offensive in the West relentlessly throughout the winter; of devoting all out spare resources to help Russia; and of maintaining at Salonika, in Egypt, and in Mesopotamia, the strict minimum of forces required to hold the troops opposing us and no more. For this strategy we need men, guns, and shells as always. We must support the Man-Power Board and the Tribunals, and force Ireland to keep up the Irish divisions.

APPENDIX
Note from the French G.Q.G. for Colonel Repington.
(In English as received)

For the common benefit of the Coalition, it is highly desirable that the threat which obliged Roumania to withdraw in Transylvania should be removed at once.

The Russian forces alone are in such a position to be able to support in a direct way the Roumanian forces in Transylvania. This seems to be the intention of General Alexeieff who is the most interested in the fact that his left wing should be made unassailable.

The energetic offensive carried on the Western, Italian and Eastern fronts, can bring an indirect help to Roumania in preventing the enemy from assembling its available reserves for the purpose of invading that country: but the attacks from Salonika prove much more efficient in keeping on that front the German and Bulgarian forces, thus preventing them from threatening the Southern frontier of Roumania.

A continued and prolonged action is accordingly necessary to develop the success which has already been attained: this can only be achieved by reinforcements, on account of the extension of the present front.

These reinforcements must be derived from the quiet theatres of operations or from those which will become so during the winter season.

General Joffre has urgently asked General Cadorna to despatch units to Salonika if the stopping of operations in the Trentino should render any available. The British Empire has in Egypt several divisions, where it seems unlikely that the enemy should attack. On the other hand, should these forces be kept for an offensive movement, this movement, although it may bring interesting results, can be held as untimely, for it keeps forces far away from the principle theatres of operations and scatters efforts instead of concentrating them on the main objectives of this war. The same could be said about Mesopotamia.

(Handed to me Monday evening October 9. Probably identical with the note handed to the War Committee the same day.)

British Library, Northcliffe Papers, Add. MSS., 62253, ff. 84–94

151
Repington to Northcliffe

Maryon Hall,
Frognal Lane,
Hampstead.

[Holograph]

17 October 1916

I enclose a copy of a secret memo. which I sent to Steed last week. Kindly return it when read.

I spent yesterday looking into the Man-Power question and hope to send you a report on it tomorrow.

There is much to talk over with you.[200]

British Library, Northcliffe Papers, Add. MSS., 62253, f. 82

152
Repington to Northcliffe

Private

Maryon Hall,
Frognal Lane,
Hampstead.

[Typed]

19 October 1916

I think that our people will tolerate anything to win the war, and prefer that power and responsibility should be combined. However, you are the best judge of what is possible. I expect you are right as Mrs Repington agrees with you.

Thanks for your suggestions on my paper. I receive daily from a confidential source very full accounts of the political and economic situation of Germany and keep close watch on it, but I have not the scope in The Times now that I had in the Russo-Japanese war and am compelled to limit myself very closely to the military side of the business.

My paper did not deal with combing out as it was limited to the military situation, but I send you a page of my diary for last Monday showing the whole situation with regard to Man Power.[201] Robinson has a copy which I asked him to send to you. Kindly return enclosed copy when read. I should value any remarks of yours on it.

I am sending this to St. James's Place as I believe you will be up today.

British Library, Northcliffe Papers, Add. MSS., 62253, f. 97

153
Repington to Robinson

Maryon Hall,
Frognal Lane,
Hampstead.

[Holograph]

25 October 1916

I return Hird's letter. He and Love have postponed action for so long that it is too late to take action on our side until they are in the Army.[202] Then, if they will tell us where they are, and give the names and addresses of their C.O's and of the generals over them, you or I can represent their merits and help them. You realise I am sure that there must be thousands of employers who worry the authorities as we shall do.

Fix a day next week for lunch and I will tell you what I have to say. Perhaps I will send you a note on the subject as a basis for a talk.

Will you kindly return me my diary for last Monday week on all the man-power question? I have no other copy and I asked you to return it.

I shall not write in your absence next week end as Freeman makes a point of making himself unpleasant and of not consulting me about anything. I only waste my time in sending him articles to be rejected or mangled.

The Times Archive, Repington Papers

154
Repington to H.G. Wells

Maryon Hall,
Frognal Lane,
Hampstead.

[Typed]

6 March 1917

I return herewith the indictment of army methods by your two disgruntled sea-lawyers. As all the instances they give, except one, are without any indication of names, I am unable to express any useful opinion on them. But no one need suppose that in an extraordinary improvisation like our present military organization things can go on oiled wheels and mistakes not be made. Of course we have got inefficients in all ranks, among regulars and non-regulars alike. But the men of real grit and spirit realise the necessary imperfections of the improvisation, bear with them in a cheerful, good tempered spirit, and unselfishly go on to try and improve things by adding something to the common stock. I do not find this spirit in the paper which you send to me and it leaves, I confess, a very unpleasant taste behind it. The only one of the cases in which the name is given is on page 3 General Cases B1 where General Townshend's name is said to have come up at an R.F.A. Brigade Head Quarters when the military record of Townshend was apparently completely unknown, and your friends cannot even spell his name right. Anyone with superficial acquaintance with recent military history would have known that Townshend has fought with distinction on the frontier of India, in both Soudan expeditions, and in South Africa, and that he had received the thanks of the Government of India for his defence of Chitral. In Mesopotamia he won several actions against the Turks, advanced to Baghdad against his own recorded opinion, and fought the battle of Ctesiphon against a very superior force, losing half his men in a gallant attempt to carry out his orders. I think that the implied sneer of your friends is very regrettable. I should recommend them to buy a Who's Who. Now I take it that the pith of the indictment is contained on page 5.(1) (2) (3) and in the last paragraph of the paper. Naturally, intelligent men distinguished in various walks of life, who join our new armies, expect to find places equal to those which they held in their former employments. I think it is not true that the brains which have come into the army at this crisis from civil life are not being used. I think that they should be, and are being to a large extent. For example, I believe that 40% of the General Staff Officers at Army Headquarters in London are non-regulars. I am told that some 129 Staff appointments at home are held by non-regulars to 90 held by regulars: that there are 10 Brigade Commands in France held by non-regulars, and that a large number of Brigade majors and other Staff appointments at the Front are held by non-regulars and you know of course of the work being done by Granet,[203] Eric Geddes, Fay,[204] Rothermere,[205] and a lot of other men – for example A.C.Geddes, who was a Professor of Anatomy at Toronto[206] before the war and is now Brigadier General and Director of Recruiting.

Soldiering, my dear Wells, is a pretty hard profession to learn in these days, as no one knows better than you. It requires apprenticeship, and professionals are not in a hurry to confide the lives of men to those who are not fully qualified to lead. I do not know any other profession in which men with two years apprenticeship rise to the top or anywhere near it. Would you have a serious operation by a medical student of two years experience? I am sure you would not. I think that the Army is doing its best to use these brains and that nothing but merit is allowed to count. Go to the Ministry of Munitions and see what marvels have been accomplished. It is really worth your doing, it is a romance. But in a war like this it takes a long time to get the best men to the right places and much forgetfulness of one's own opinion of oneself has to be contributed to the common good.

Hoping to see you again soon.

Rare Book and Special Collections Library, University of Illinois, H.G. Wells Papers

155
Repington to Northcliffe

Maryon Hall,
Frognal Lane,
Hampstead.

[Holograph]

5 April 1917

I will write to Sassoon and fix up a visit.[207] I am going round all the E. and S. coast defences between the present date and April 25, but shall then be free. Various French people wish to see me in Paris and M.Thomas wants me to inspect some of his munition works.

I addressed the 1900 Club last night. Geddes came and supported me well.[208] I have now addressed the Unionist War Committee, the Unionist agents, and am trying to arrange with the Labour Party so as to tell them the truth about man-power.

Robertson was good yesterday.[209] I discussed the speech with him beforehand. You realize that he cannot give the figures on which the whole argument hinges, but Geddes told us last night that he has only the drafts to make good the casualties of a fortnight's hard fighting.

The only way to make the Government move is to have a secret session, and to give the Government the figures if they will not produce them. Various M.P's undertook last night to do this and the Navy League is proposing to organize local meetings of leading men to whom the facts and figures can be made known privately. I have given the figures at all the three meetings which I have addressed and were I in Parliament I am convinced that I could make the Government move. One cannot give the figures in the Press.[210]

That wretch Robin has held up for a week my explanation of the Hun retreat.

British Library, Northcliffe Papers, Add. MSS., 62253, ff. 107–8

156
Repington to General Sir W.R. Robertson

Maryon Hall,
Frognal Lane,
Hampstead.

[Holograph]

10 April 1917

Many thanks for your letter with the enclosures. Haig's success is splendid, but I am thinking of the drafts to replace casualties, and so, I am sure, are you and the A.G.[211]

I do not agree about drafting Yankees into our Army and hope that the question may not be raised.[212] It will make America suspicious of us and I don't think that you will get the men. If you did, you would be faced with difficult questions of pay, and you would have endless trouble about discipline. The Yankee would bring disturbance into our ranks and would upset our men. If you shot him for disobedience of orders, as of course you would, our enemies in America, who are many, would exploit it against us. Take my advice and keep off this lay and keep others off it. Let the Yankees and the French work together. They are old pals. I hope they will like each other on closer acquaintance, but I am not sure.

There is no reason why you should not call upon all <u>British citizens</u> of military age in the U.S. and other allied and neutral countries. I think you should. They are full of grooms, valets, jockeys, golf-course keepers, tutors etc. etc. But this is quite a different matter to your suggestion.

Liddell Hart Centre, King's College, London, Robertson Papers, 1/33/75

157
Repington to Northcliffe

<u>Private</u>

Hotel Ritz,
Place Vendôme,
Paris.

[Holograph]

27 April 1917

I have had a most interesting tour around our front and have just sent off a first article about it. I am now starting for Châlons to visit Pétain and have a talk with him, and hope subsequently to visit the G.Q.G. and the other French armies.[213]

We are doing very well and Allenby's men have killed a mighty lot of Boches since the 23rd. Our French friends have had a bad knock. They have lost 120,000 men in a week and are much depressed. We have only lost 60,000 April 9–23. It is possible that Nivelle may be dégommé but this is not yet certain. Haig came in here yesterday and heartened them up a bit. The operations are to continue according to plan for another fortnight anyhow, but before the Government meet the Chambres on May 22 they will have to take a decision about Nivelle. Pétain as C.I.G.S. in Paris is the best solution I think. Painlevé asked me for my views and I gave them on the strategical question, whereupon he said that they exactly conformed with those of Pétain, and I am going to see if this be so.

The one dominating question is that of men. Everyone on our staffs implores us to push the man-power question. We are short, and are going to be very short. My views formed in England are more than borne out by information here, and I have been told everything. We are also short of horses, and many guns promised have not come, having been given away to French, Russians, Italians and so on, to the general wrath of the Army. We are also very short of fast one-seater fighter aeroplanes. But on the whole the one pressing need is men. There have been some schemes on paper since I left London but I cannot judge of their effect at a distance. We seem to be doing badly with the submarines but I suppose the Navy is still sacrosanct and above all criticism.[214] I hope that in a few days, the 1st Army on Allenby's left will get their guns up and be able to go on, and that Gough's 5th Army on Allenby's right will then chip in. But there are more German Divisions than we have on one front, and miracles must not be expected. The Boche has 68 divisions in front of our 64, and we have no right to expect a decision until the folk at home do better.

I may be back by the end of next week. Kindly let Robinson see this letter.

British Library, Northcliffe Papers, Add. MSS., 62253, ff. 112–13

158
Repington to Lloyd George

<u>Private</u>.

Hotel Ritz,
Place Vendôme,
Paris.

[Holograph]

29 April 1917

After a visit to the British front I went to the East of France to stay with General Pétain at the suggestion of M. Painlevé who had asked me for my views on the situation and had found them the same as those of Pétain.

I am writing now because I hear that influence is being brought to bear on your side of the water to oppose the appointment of Pétain to the chief command on the ground that he holds certain views which, in fact, he does not hold. I have stayed with him and have had long and confidential talks with him and ask you not to credit the silly chatter which attributes to him a want of go and resolution.

He sees the situation clearly and is a man of strong character and determination. He will not promise the moon as others have done. In this last French offensive our friends have lost 120,000 men, equal to two thirds of the French class of a year, and are much depressed. Pétain foretold failure to the War Council and gave his reasons which were the same as I gave, for not writing about this offensive for which I had not a good word to say. His views accord with mine in every particular. He sees that we are practically on an equality with the enemy, and must wait until you in England, and the Americans, provide the superiority of force necessary for victory. He is therefore in favour of prudent offensives like that of Haig on April 9 – short-ranging attacks supported by a mass of guns. He is against trying to do much with little, and prefers to do little with much. He faces the real situation which he proposes to explain to the War Council at their first meeting if he is appointed, and he fully realizes that it is not possible to effect miracles and that he will be called Pacifist and Cunctator[215] by the boobies who refuse to regard the mechanics of the situation. He will most certainly support Haig in every way, for the arrest of this mad Rheims offensive does not at all imply quietism and want of activity. In fact yesterday morning I was in a crow's nest at the top of a firwood with Pétain to watch an attack on the Moronvilliers heights, and only the haze, which prevented the airmen from co-operating, postponed the blow.

You have only to send me a telegram and I will return to explain Pétain's views at length. Believe me that he is the best general in France. Poor Nivelle now comes to seek advice from his old chief, and it is really pitiful to see the strength of character of Pétain contrasted with the wisdom of Nivelle. I am sorry for Nivelle who is a charming creature, but really the situation is too serious to allow personal considerations to weigh in the balance.

The trouble here is that the various governments seek peace quickly and above everything else. They therefore select men who promise them the moon. I like Painlevé who is a man of sense and trustworthy. He knows that the situation here demands great prudence and patience.

Our men have fought famously, and both Allenby and Horne have done right well. It is a stupendous battlefield round the Scarpe – Salisbury Plain with the complexion of the Long Valley at Aldershot. Your shells are very good, and, thank Heaven, very plentiful. We have taken heavy toll of the enemy.

Your speech has done a rare lot of good here and is much appreciated. It has been well translated, and in full.[216]

House of Lords Record Office, D. Lloyd George Papers, F/43/4/1

159
Repington to Northcliffe

Private.

Maryon Hall,
Frognal Lane,
Hampstead.

[Typed with Holograph additions]

14 May 1917

You may like to see enclosed letter from Murray.[217] I do not think that either the public or the War Cabinet fully realise the situation which Murray is in. He has a heterogeneous force and neither old Regular nor New Army divisions with him. He has five or six divisions of Turks against him with a hundred guns in a strong position as you will judge from his letter. He has to rely on a pipe line for his water and he has all the desert behind him. The War Cabinet are disposed to crucify Generals when they do not succeed and not to worry about the causes.

I am sure that you will do justice to Murray. He is one of the Generals who keeps me accurately informed almost from week to week of what is going on and the type deserves encouragement.

I am as pleased about Salonika as you are but getting away will be a precious ticklish business. We ought to have gone in the winter when the Bulgars could not move. We shall now have to act under every disadvantage and I wish that Monro were there to do the job for us.

Kindly send Murray's letter back.

Do you know that there is a plan to send us American recruits? I don't like it and want to speak to you about it. They all should go to the French, I think. If you agree you must act quickly to stop it.

British Library, Northcliffe Papers, Add. MSS., 62253, f. 114

160
Repington to Geoffrey Dawson

Confidential

Maryon Hall,
Frognal Lane,
Hampstead.

[Holograph]

4 October[218] 1917

I enclose an article on the military situation for which I hope you may be able to give me a good place as it covers the whole ground.

I have not dealt in it with the General Staff question except in one passing remark, but I am greatly concerned about it. We are allowing this matter to go by default, and, I have little doubt that Robertson's days are numbered unless we support him, and that we shall then be responsible for the consequences which, I consider, will be most serious.

Robertson is trusted by the Army, by our commanders, by the public, and by our allies. The man who is likely to replace him is Wilson, who is distrusted by the chief men in our Army, and is brulé[219] with the French because he intrigued against Pétain and Painlevé's policy, and is in my opinion a political general of the most dangerous type. He has done nothing in the war but lose a part of the Vimy ridge on May 21, 1916. He will do anything that the politicians tell him, and as I am profoundly distrustful of his judgement I expect the worst consequences from the change. I do not know any military question that has arisen during the war in which you can more help or mar the cause than by your action now.

If Robertson goes, Derby will go too, and so probably will the Army Council, which is the result which the gang around L.G. desire, as they will then fill it with their creatures.

I shall be dining with the Scarboroughs[220] in Park Lane tonight at 8.15, and if you like I will meet you at the N and M before dinner. Will you telephone here? I shall be in by 5.

I must now alter the Palestine article to include Gaza.[221] Will you send it back to me? I enclose my Diary of the last trip to France. Please keep it safely locked up, and show it to no one else.

The Times Archive, Dawson Papers

161
Repington to Northcliffe

Maryon Hall,
Hampstead,
N.W.

[Holograph]

12 November 1917

Welcome home! You have returned to find an Allied Staff created at Paris contrary to the desires of our leading soldiers at home and abroad, and contrary to the public interest. I want to see you about it as soon as possible.[222]

British Library, Northcliffe Papers, Add. MSS. 62253, f. 119

162
Repington to Dawson

Srictly Confidential

Maryon Hall,
Frognal Lane,
Hampstead.

[Holograph]

11 January 1918

Thanks for your letter. I trust that you have not really been ill. It was indeed an agreeable surprise to see an article of mine appear in the form in which I had written it.

How much you know about the present situation I cannot say, but I will tell you how things stand according to my information, and you will judge how serious they are.

Our armies are 130,000 men in deficit, including 114,000 infantry in France. The Army Council have asked for 616,000 men, and the War Cabinet have only been able to offer them 100,000 general service men, and the boys of 18 of the yearly class. The Army Council have sent in a strong paper reviewing the position, and unless the decision is changed I regard the war as lost. Owing to want of men the W.O. has had to break up four of our home defence divisions to use as drafts, and to reduce all divisions in France, and I think in the Mediterranean, from 12 to 9 battalions. Thereby the strength of our infantry is permanently diminished by one quarter. Haig has had to prolong his line to JOVISY: he has lost his divisions sent to Italy. He fought 131 German divisions in 1917 with 57 British including cavalry. The French are also weak and thin, but Clemenceau is calling out every available man in civil life. I need not tell you that the 100,000 men promised by the War Cabinet will not all be in till September and long before this date will be absorbed in making good casualties. I regard the war as lost unless the War Cabinet can be made to do their duty and state the position frankly to the country.

The reduction of four divisions at home is due to a fresh standard of strength admitted by the new Admiralty. They guarantee that not more than one German convoy with 30,000 men on board can reach England. I have seen the arguments and completely distrust them. They arbitrarily limit the enemy to ships of 4000 tons and give 4 tons a man to the expedition. I do not know why the Huns are not supposed to use their larger ships, nor why they must use four tons a man for transport when the Japs only used 1 ton a man. Jellicoe does not agree to the new standard I believe. The old one, on a 70,000 basis, was fixed as you may remember in 1909, after Lord Roberts and I had fought the question before the Defence Committee, and it has remained the standard until now.

I also hear that the Versailles soldiers will advise the next War Council that our main effort should be transferred to Turkey, and that we should remain on the defensive in the West. In this scheme we are to take the offensive in Palestine and Mesopotamia, the French are to take Alexandretta, and the Japs to take Constantinople. The French and Salonika troops are to carry out the plan of Venezelos, land at Dedeagatch and march on Adrianople. This is the best way to lose the war I know, but as I feel that the Japs will refuse the role offered to them, and that the campaigning season in Mesopotamia draws to a close, I doubt the pursuit of these mad schemes. Meanwhile the Germans are massing for all they are worth in the West, and may be ready for an offensive on a large scale in a month's time, or at any later moment.

I consider that a madman has afflicted all the people who propose these schemes, and that if the Boches break through us, or more probably the French, the war will be lost. The only chance that I know is for you to attack the War Cabinet without mercy until they come forward and tell the country the truth, and let the country decide whether they will be so pusillanimous as the War Cabinet. Also you can stop these mad Eastern schemes if you please, or if you give me a free hand.

I think that the War Cabinet have been doing their best to lose the war all this year and that The Times, by coddling and saving them, has not fulfilled its duty towards the country. I think that the gravest responsibility now rests on you, graver than has ever rested upon any Editor of The Times, and I beg that you will be equal to the occasion and only have the public good in your mind.

I have had to reconsider my position owing to the line taken by The Times on many matters and though I have always been loyal to the paper in the past I have had recently to express my dissent openly with your editorial opinions on certain matters. I hope that you may be able to tell me that you mean to take a strong line and permit me, as you did yesterday, to express my opinions without editorial bowdlerizing. I do not intend to go on if I have reluctantly to conclude that The Times has abandoned its old and its proved position as an independent organ and a watchdog of the public.

You are welcome to show this letter to Lord Northcliffe if you please, but I must ask you not to let anyone else see it.

The question of the Generalissimo is coming up again at the next Allied War Council. Foch wants the post.

The Times Archive, Dawson Papers

163
Repington to Northcliffe

Private

Maryon Hall,
Frognal Lane,
Hampstead.

[Holograph]

16 January 1918

I have told Dawson to-day that I am unable to go on with him and I propose to give my reasons in a formal letter of resignation to the Manager.

I send these few lines to say how much I regret the termination of my 15 years of work on the Times, and to thank you personally for the courtesy which you have always shown me.

British Library, Northcliffe Papers, Add. MSS., 62253, f. 121

164
Repington to Howard Corbett

Maryon Hall,
Frognal Lane,
Hampstead.

[Typed Copy]

16 January 1918

I have told the Editor today that I am unable to go on with him, and I shall be glad to hear from you the earliest date that will be convenient for the termination of my engagement.

Much though I regret a break with The Times after some 15 years of work for it I feel that our present critical position is largely due to the subservient and apologetic attitude which the paper has adopted towards the present War Cabinet, an attitude which has permitted this body throughout the past year to neglect the vital interests of the Army, particularly with regard to men, despite my reiterated representations to the Editor whom I have kept constantly informed of the true position of affairs.

If I had been permitted to express my own views freely on these and other military affairs I could have afforded to ignore the editorials of The Times, but this has not been the case. My articles containing serious criticism, and some letters which I have sent to the Editor for publication, have never appeared, while other articles have had whole passages removed, and the articles have then been published as mine, without any reference to me, in a manner which I consider dishonest to the public and unfair to me. My reiterated protest against these practices, from which I never suffered during all the years that I served under Mr. Buckle, have brought me no assurances that they would cease, and I have reluctantly come to the conclusion that the vital interests of the Army, which has become the nation in arms, are not secure in the hands of The Times. You will, I am sure, agree with me that in these circumstances I have no option but to sever my connection with the paper.

I take this opportunity of saying that there is nothing personal in my decision. I have invariably received from you and the rest of the staff of The Times most courteous and considerate treatment, and I ask you to assure Lord Northcliffe that nothing but my conviction that I can no longer usefully serve the interests of the country and the Army on The Times compels me to break my long association with Printing House Square.

British Library, Northcliffe Papers, Add. MSS., 62253, ff. 122–3

165
Repington to H.A. Gwynne

Private

Maryon Hall,
Hampstead.

[Holograph]

19 January 1918

I have resigned my position on The Times and am now free to work for you. I suggest that you state on Monday, somewhat prominently that "Colonel C. à Court Repington CMG has resigned his position as Military Correspondent of The Times".

I think that it would be advisable for you to inform the Press agencies as well, so that the information may appear in other journals, but I leave this to you. I am sending you a sketch by Mrs Repington of my career. Please add or deduct anything from it that you please. I am due to go to Aldershot to Archie Murray (Government House, Farnborough) for the night of Monday but shall be back on Tuesday evening.

I think that if you make the announcement about my joining you on Tuesday or Wednesday and give the sketch of my career the same day, it will serve. Then I shall have my first article ready for you for Thursday if that day suits. I am strongly urged by the GS to begin by exposing the man-power muddle, and in fact to do through you about the men what I did through The Times about the shells. What do you say? It will certainly attract attention enough and I will get the GS to pass it through the censorship if you like. I think that it will raise Cain.

I suppose that you will now send me the formal invitation which we spoke of. I have tried to get you on the telephone without success.

Bodleian Library, Oxford, H.A. Gwynne Papers, Box 21 (Repington 1917–1921)

Notes

Notes to Introduction

1 Diary entry 5 December 1907, H.O. Arnold-Forster Papers, Add. MSS., 50353.

2 Arnold-Forster described Repington as 'a bounder'; Fisher thought him, amongst many other things, 'a cad'; while the rest of the even less pleasant sobriquets come from the Diary of Sir Henry Wilson.

3 See the popular edition of Lloyd George, *War Memoirs* vol.2, pp. 1674ff.

4 Paul Guinn, *British Strategy and Politics, 1914–1918*, p. 77.

5 See Keith Wilson (Ed), *The Rasp of War*, p. 287.

6 For Captain Rees Gronow see his *Reminiscences* (1861–66), most conveniently and handsomely available in Nicolas Bentley's edited selection Folio Society, London, 1977. Captain Dugald Dalgetty, an unworthy soldier of fortune, a pedant and braggart, prepared to fight for the side that paid him most, features in Sir Walter Scott, *Legends of Montrose*. See Fisher to George, Prince of Wales, 16 October 1907, in A.J. Marder (Ed), *Fear God and Dread Nought*, vol. 2, p. 147.

7 The name Repington was added in October 1903, as was required by the terms of an ancient will when he inherited Amington Hall from his father. This together with much information on Repington's life and career before the 1914–18 war, is contained in his memoir, *Vestigia*. The change of name generated much confusion and a prolonged correspondence with the War Office in October and November 1903. When Repington's grandfather, General à Court, had assumed the name, he did so by Royal Licence, doing so, 'for himself and his heirs'. *London Gazette*, 30 October 1855.

8 Attached to Repington's 'Statement of Service' made upon his retirement there are three typed foolscap sheets titled, 'Services rendered by my family to the Crown', WO 138/7. See also document 41.

9 The official outline of Repington's Army career to the rank of Major is to be found in *Officers Record of Service*, WO 76/282 p. 69.

10 According to the *Register of Gentlemen Cadets*, in 1877 Repington was only five foot six and a half inches tall. He was of that first generation to join after the system of appointment to cadetships rather than a probationary commission was revived in 1877. Fees for the year amounted to £125.

11 Repington to Raymond Marker, 9 July 1906, Kitchener-Marker Papers, Add. MSS., 52277, ff. 78–85.

12 Charles Martell (pseudonym for Repington), *Military Italy*.
13 In his entrance examination his lowest mark was in Mathematics, 66%; but he did scarcely better at Fortifications, 67%. His overall average was 74%. There are no individual marks available for the final examinations, candidates merely being recorded as 'passed'. There were thirty students in the course which lasted from February 1887 to December 1888. For the Staff College in this period, see Brian Bond, *The Victorian Army and the Staff College*.
14 See J.E. Edmonds, entry on Repington, in *Dictionary of National Biography: 1921–30 Supplement*, pp. 717–18.
15 In this work Repington was closely associated with the British military attaché in Paris, Sir Reginald Talbot, and also officers from the Admiralty. Repington's 'researches' led to his frequent arrest by the French police.
16 The other officer was Henry Rawlinson. The two young men had plotted together in the hope of wangling an appointment.
17 When he came to write his memoir, *Vestigia*, Repington, bearing in mind the notorious example of the letters Captain Bacon sent to Fisher which amounted to Bacon spying upon his commanding officer, he stressed that his letters for Wolseley 'were not by any means a work of supererogation'. (p. 101). Actually, the letters before their despatch to England were invariably shown to Grenfell.
18 The Anglo-French crisis over Fashoda lasted from September to December 1898. A reconnaissance party under Commandant Marchand fired upon English gunboats exploring the Upper Nile. Further open confrontation was avoided and the two Powers entered into diplomatic conversations which ended with France acknowledging the superiority of the British claim to the Upper Nile and consequently that the Sudan and Egypt were spheres of exclusively British interest.
19 This work was undertaken for the Foreign Office although most of the information was required for the Admiralty. Repington organised a secret service system throughout France, with a large number of his agents working from Brussels. Despite considerable French efforts, the system was never broken and only one agent ever discovered.
20 In a letter to Raymond Marker, 22 August 1906, Add. MSS., 52277, ff. 115–18, Repington wrote: 'The pucka military attaché's job is expensive. It cost me about £3,000 a year, but then I had to keep up two establishments at Brussels and The Hague, and the entertaining is much heavier in small capitals where everybody knows everybody else.' We may assume that these costs do not include Repington's flat for his mistress which he kept at Ravenscourt Park, and other expenses necessarily connected with his amorous adventures conducted in England when travelling to and from the continent.
21 Repington claimed in *Vestigia* that, following the 'excellent advice of Methuen (he) would never do any secret service work . . . The military

attaché is the guest of the country to which he is accredited and must only see and learn that which is permissible for a guest to investigate . . . Secret service is a necessity at times, but a military attaché should steadily refuse to have anything to do with it.' (p. 182) This assertion must be taken with a large pinch of salt. See, for example, the complaint of the Permanent Under Secretary at the Foreign Office to the Foreign Secretary that Repington had paid 'certain civilities (i.e. bribes) to Belgian officers' which had not been approved. Sanderson to Lansdowne, 1 February 1901, Public Record Office, Lansdowne Papers, F.O. 800/115.

22 See for example the enthusiastic reports on his work at The Hague and Brussels and at the First International Peace Conference, referred to in Repington to The Military Secretary, 5 February 1902, WO 138/7.

23 The Radicals were very conscious of the influence Repington exerted when criticising them. They attempted to undermine his credit by lumping him together with careless and extreme militarist writers, and dubbing him 'the gorgeous Wreckington', a nickname Repington was not averse to quoting against himself.

24 Repington had some good German friends, but he early formed an aversion to the generality of Germans. According to Brigadier General Waters, *Secret and Confidential: the experiences of a military attaché*, p. 61, this aversion was the consequence of drinking too much German beer in 1893! In *Vestigia*, which was published just after the Great War, it served Repington's purpose to emphasise his dislike. It never, however, became a phobia as Jay Luvaas asserts in his *The Education of an Army*, p. 293.

25 'It is a joke, old boy!'

26 The other was Major, afterwards Lieutenant-General Sir Lancelot Kiggell, Haig's ill-fated Chief of Staff, 1916–17.

27 Repington provided his own neat summary of his military career in his 'Secret Statement of Services' attached to his letter to the Adjutant-General, 19 December 1901, WO 138/7. Although an abstract, it does contain information not available elsewhere.

28 On Scobell, see, *inter alia*, Anthony Farrar Hockley, *Goughie*, p. 72; General Sir Hubert Gough, *Soldiering On*, pp. 91–2.

29 See, for example, Spencer Ewart's description of a Promotion Board, 30 January 1903. 'I never heard so much scandal in my life. Everybody's 'past' was raked over . . . A convention of charwomen could not have enjoyed itself more.' See also, Sir Evelyn Wood's letter to Ewart, 29 July 1906, stating that the chief member of a Promotion Board, 'regarded breaches of the 7th. commandment as a claim to appointments . . .' Both quoted in Ewart's unpublished *Autobiography*, pp. 775 and 858.

30 Mary Repington, *Thanks for the Memory*, p. 191.

31 Garstin's lawyers had attempted a similar ruse the previous November but on that occasion, Repington had refused to sign. Repington was faced with the threat of his affair with Mary being revealed to the military authorities.

This time the threat was potent because it would have meant him being debarred from embarking for South Africa, the war, and the opportunity to enhance his career.

32 Repington to Georgina, Lady Guilford, 8 October 1899 (copy), WO 138/7.

33 Wilson's close contact with Mary's family is mentioned in her Memoirs, p. 154. It is clear from Henry Wilson's Diary entries that the Wilsons were frequent visitors to the Guilford's house, Waldersham Park, and that Lady Guilford's son 'Nipper', stayed between June 1895 and April 1896 with the Wilsons. I am indebted to Professor Keith Jeffery for this information.

34 Quoted in Mary Repington's Memoir, p. 157; also Repington's statement of explanation, WO 138/7.

35 Repington to the Military Secretary, 12 December 1901, WO 138/7. Repington's claim that he would have entered a defence does not square with the available evidence.

36 Adjutant-General to Repington, 13 December 1901, WO 138/7.

37 Wilson's Diary, entries 11 and 12 December 1901, Wilson Papers, Imperial War Museum.

38 Statement made by Wilson, 21 December 1901, of his conversation with the Adjutant-General 20 December 1901, recalling the material events of his meeting with Repington 12 February 1900. This statement was entered as one of the three pieces of evidence upon which the decision concerning Repington's guilt or otherwise was determined. The other two were Repington's own statement, plus supporting documents, and the report of the Garstin divorce proceedings from *The Times*, 13 December 1901. All these documents are held in file WO 138/7.

The questions remain, was Wilson's statement entirely true? Was his damaging statement motivated by professional jealousy of Repington? Contemporaries who did not like Wilson, in later years would state that he was quite capable of such acts. There were stories, unsubstantiated by any evidence, that Wilson toted Repington's promise around the General Staff, and particularly to Roberts, making it impossible to come to any other conclusion than that Repington was guilty. The fairest conclusion that can be drawn from the available evidence would seem to be 'not proven'. Cf. Jay Luvaas, *The Education of an Army*, p. 297 and fn. 9. Also, James Edmonds *Memoir* (unpublished), pp. 27–9, Edmonds Papers III/5.

39 See paragraph 11 of Repington's statement.

40 The notes by Kelly-Kenny and Roberts occupy a sheet and a half of minute paper. St John Brodrick initialled his approval. All three are dated 23 December 1901. A plea by Mary to the King via Sir Francis Knollys, protesting Repington's services should not be discounted, was unavailing. The War Office confirmed that Repington was 'obliged to leave the Army owing to his having broken his word of honour'. See Williams to Knollys, 7 January 1902, Royal Archives, Add C7 (Army 1901–02).

41 T. Kelly-Kenny to Repington, 27 December 1901 (copy), WO 138/7.

42 Repington to Adjutant-General, 2 January 1902; Adjutant-General to Repington, 3 January 1902 (copy), WO 138/7.

43 Chirol to Moberly Bell, 14 December 1901, The Times Archive, Moberly Bell Papers. Most interestingly and significantly, Chirol was writing two days after the trial, but ten days *before* Repington was requested to resign his commission.

44 He had expected a pension of £420 a year but instead received £200. The only other regular source of income was Mary's settlement of £175 a year. Repington's father paid his legal costs and continued to pay an allowance to Melloney à Court and the children, but Repington's allowance was stopped. His father's death the following year restored Repington's financial fortunes temporarily.

45 Repington's first published work appeared in the *Pioneer*, 1878. His earliest connection with *The Times* dates from June 1888, when he had planned to go to South Russia while on leave from Camberly and report on events in the Caucasus. This scheme was thwarted by the Duke of Cambridge. Repington had recently published articles in *Blackwood's Magazine* and in the *Nineteenth Century*, and had contributed a biographical study of Abercromby to Spenser Wilkinson's *Twelve Soldiers* (London, 1900).

46 *The Times* claimed it would not be fitting for Repington to remain as his work on the *History* would inevitably involve him with friends of Sir William Garstin. This was almost certainly on Chirol's initiative. Bell had a good opinion of Repington's abilities and was not concerned about personal issues the way that the hyper-sensitive Chirol always was.

47 Repington to Moberly Bell, 2 January 1902, The Times Archive, Repington Papers.

48 On Spender's qualities as an editor, and the influence he exercised over all his colleagues, see Wilson Harris, *J.A. Spender*.

49 Repington to Churchill, 28 February 1903, Churchill Papers, CHAR 2/3 76.

50 See particularly the exchange between Repington and Esher, 14 and 19 May 1905, Esher Papers, ESHR 10/25, and Repington to Maxse, 27 February 1906, Document 26.

51 E.T. Cook, *Delane of 'The Times'*, p. 69.

52 A letter Steed wrote to Chirol which he subsequently quoted from in a memorandum, 29 November 1908. The Times Archive, Steed Papers. The title, 'Fourth Estate', was coined by Macaulay in the *Edinburgh Review*, September 1828.

53 In *Vestigia*, at p. 253, Repington claimed he would have preferred anonymity than be recognised as the 'Military Correspondent of The Times', but the claim does not bear scrutiny. Whatever else he might have been, Repington was no shrinking violet.

54 Repington to Bell, 15 January 1905, quoted *History of The Times*, III, p. 463. The original of this letter, and others concerning Repington quoted in the *History*, appear to have been lost from The Times Archive.

55 November 1900, Ardagh Papers, PRO 30/40/13, ff. 151–226. This is the original manuscript version.

56 See the *Spectator*, 31 December 1904, p. 1071. For a similar opinion expressed by Repington, see his letters to Marker, of 9 July and 15 August 1906, Kitchener-Marker Papers, Add. MSS., 52277, ff. 78–85 and 111–14.

57 See Buller to George Wyndham, 1 October 1899, WO 32/7137.

58 Clarke to Chirol, 4 April 1905, Sydenham Clarke Papers, Add. MSS., 50832, ff. 15–19.

59 St John Brodrick may be cited as a classic example of ministerial arrogance when dealing with the press, even though he had some early experience himself as a journalist. The degree of Brodrick's paranoia about giving even trivial information to the press is well illustrated by Blumenfeld's story in *RDB's Diary*, p. 71. His attitude as a Minister towards newspapers, journalists and editors is demonstrated in his dealings with Watney and Harmsworth when at the War Office and then India Office. See, A.J.A. Morris, *The Scaremongers*, pp. 93–7.

60 Wolseley set the tone and the example, using the press over a period of more than two decades to campaign for those reforms his political masters stubbornly refused. Roberts recognised the value of the Press as a useful ally during the Boer War and subsequently. See Northcliffe to Roberts, 19 June 1909, Roberts Papers R46/162. No soldier, however, began to compare with Admiral Fisher's capacity to manage the press.

61 See Garvin to Roberts, 13 March 1908 (copy), Garvin Papers; Roberts to A.F.Walter, 31 January 1908 (copy), Roberts Papers, 7101/23/122; and, Walter to Roberts, 6 February 1908, Roberts Papers, R46/147.

62 Chirol to Moberly Bell, 20 January 1906, The Times Archive, Moberly Bell Papers.

63 See, *Vestigia*, pp. 253–4.

64 See, for example, Clarke to Chirol, 11 November 1907, and 7 May 1908, Clarke Papers, Add. MSS., 50832, ff. 62–3 and 171–9.

65 Clarke to Chirol, 6 September 1912, Add. MSS., 50834, ff. 165–8; Buckle to Garvin, 9 August 1912, Garvin Papers.

66 See documents 61–2, and 64, and end notes 77–8.

67 This is evident from the letters the two men exchanged during this period. Dawson's Diary for 1912 and 1913 (vols 18 and 19) lists the frequent conversations and luncheons with Repington. At the start of his editorship, Robinson was strangely unfamiliar with many leading figures, even within the Unionist party. The luncheons that Repington arranged were often rewarding in this particular. See, for example, the entries for 20 November 1912 and 30 January 1913.

68 On this subject in general see S.E. Koss, *The Rise and Fall of the Political Press in Britain*, two volumes. See also Spender to Esher, 9 January 1908, ESHR 5/25. 'I begin to think that the days of editors are over. The whole

affair (i.e. change of ownership of *The Times*) has been treated merely as an exchange of goods which interested no one but "Casino men".'

69 See the studied understatement of Harmsworth's six line entry in the 1904 edition of *Who's Who*. In 1904, he was made a baronet, having earlier refused a knighthood, and in 1905 was raised to the peerage as the First Viscount Northcliffe.

70 Financial considerations apart, there were good personal and political reasons for Harmsworth's refusal. See Memorandum by St John Brodrick, 20 June 1903, Midleton Papers, PRO 30/67/11.

71 There was a rumour, so well established as to be treated as truth, that when Northcliffe purchased *The Times* he promised he would not interfere with editorial policy unless Buckle failed to warn his readers of the German Peril. Of course, from the beginning of his reign at Printing House Square, Northcliffe interfered in everything increasing the tempo of his campaign after 1911.

72 Letters from Repington on these subjects to Northcliffe, sometimes with typed copies of the replies, in Northcliffe Papers, Add. MSS., 62253, ff. 1–18.

73 See documents 82 to 85.

74 See documents 1 and 14, and Repington to Esher, 2 April and 18 July 1905, Esher Papers, ESHR 10/25. Allowance must always be made for words written in the heat of the moment to serve an immediate interest. It remained a matter of regret that he could not work with Arnold-Forster, and Repington gives credit to the Minister for laying the foundations of the General Staff. See *Vestigia*, pp. 258–9.

75 See Arnold-Forster's Diary, and Arnold-Forster to Balfour, 28 May 1908, Balfour Papers, Add. MSS., 49723, ff. 252–7.

76 Arnold-Forster to Maxse, 27 December 1905, Maxse Papers, 453, ff. 191–4. See also Diary entry for 12 August 1905, where Esher claimed, 'he had not communicated with Acourt . . . in fact he never did communicate confidential matters to journalists and hardly ever saw Acourt.'

77 Diary entry 28 March 1905.

78 See 'The Army in Parliament', *The Times*, 1 April 1905; Arnold-Forster to Marker, April 1905, Kitchener-Marker Papers, Add. MSS., 52278.

79 Spencer Ewart, unpublished *Autobiography*, pp. 831–2.

80 In this conviction, if in nothing else, Esher remained a Liberal. So great was his belief in the power of the press that in February 1913, he actually suggested the best way of solving the Irish question, which then and since has defied all efforts, was by concentrating the best efforts of Northcliffe, his family and his newspapers upon a solution.

81 James Lees-Milne, *The Enigmatic Edwardian*, p. 168.

82 Repington to Esher, 27 October 1909 and 6 March 1910, Esher Papers, ESHR 5/32–3. The rest of this paragraph draws upon examples taken from the following documents: 2, 3, 8, 11, 14, 16, 21–2, 35–7, 39, 46–7, 69, 72 and 78.

83 Haldane to Esher, 10 February 1913, Haldane Papers (copy) 5910, f. 137.

84 *World*, 21 June to 16 August 1910.

85 *National Review*, September 1910.

86 See document 107. Repington's attitude was dictated by his concern over the Liberal government's actions concerning Ireland and use of the royal veto. During this period, Esher appeared to have moved over to support the Liberals, and Repington was closely associated with the aggressive Toryism that Andrew Bonar-Law espoused.

   Esher is a classic modern example of the English delight in the amateur tradition in politics, the preference for the 'gentleman' rather than a 'player'. Esher in his role as intermediary and political 'Mr Fix It' had, like the office of Prime Minister until 1937, become the personification of a constitutional convention – i.e., something or someone necessary to the smooth operation of the constitution, but unknown to the law.

87 Esher to Stamfordham, 23 September 1920, Royal Archives, Geo.V, O 1431/31.

88 See Repington, *The First World War, 1914–1918*, vol. I, pp. 2–14.

89 See documents 19 and 21–3.

90 Gwynne to Marker, 18 July and 23 August 1906, Kitchener-Marker Papers, Add. MSS., 52277, ff. 171–81.

91 See documents 37 and 60.

92 Haldane to J.A. Spender, 24 January 1911, Spender Papers, Add. MSS., 46390, f. 167.

93 *Concord*, XXV, No.3, March 1909, pp. 27–9.

94 See for example, Haldane's letters to his mother of 21 June 1907, 6 July 1908 and 1 June 1909, Haldane Papers, 5977, ff. 181–2; 5980, ff. 51–2, and 5981, ff. 223–4. Haldane remained close to Repington when no longer Minister for War. Haldane particularly valued Repington's support for him after he had been removed from office in 1915. Similarly, Repington valued Haldane, not least because he always included Mary in social invitations.

95 'So far as I can see, the whole scheme is from Ellison's book . . . ' Clarke to Esher, 21 March 1906, Esher Papers, ESHR 10/38. Clarke was the victim of jealousy. He resented losing a place close to Haldane. Consequently he sought both to devalue the contribution Haldane had made and to criticise Ellison, with whom he disagreed. Many of the measures did not reflect Ellison's thinking as expressed in his book, *Home Defence* (1898). The arguments are carefully rehearsed in E.M. Spiers, *Haldane: an Army Reformer*, pp. 74–8.

96 See Repington's enthusiastic and effusive letter welcoming Ellison as Haldane's military secretary. 'I think he is fortunate as well as wise to have secured you.' Repington to Ellison, 23 December 1905, Ellison Papers, 8704–35–691. Also, document 68 which reflects how closely the two men had worked together.

97 See Harris's letter to Ellison, quoted in Ellison's 'Reminiscences' in the *Lancashire Lad*, Part. XVIII, May 1936, p. 56.

98   See particularly documents 42 to 45 inclusive.

99   It was the opposition on all sides from various vested interest groups, towards Haldane's suggested reforms that finally convinced Repington that there was no alternative to conscription. The voluntary principle had been given its fair trial, as he had written to Clarke in February 1906. Thereafter the tone of his writing in *The Times* became more threatening:'The last defenders of the voluntary principle will be driven out of their last ditch . . . It is time for this comedy to finish.' See Repington to Clarke, 20 February 1906; *The Times*, 16 July 1906.

100 See H.R. Moon, 'The invasion of the United Kingdom, 1888–1914' Ph.D., 1970, vol. II, p. 652.

101 The pattern followed in 1907–8 and 1913–14 mirrored that of earlier inquiries, as in 1888. For a Radical view of these exercises, see F.W. Hirst, *The Six Panics*.

102 Most of the so-called 'patriotic' editors were on the side of the invasionists, and although people like Leo Maxse and St Loe Strachey could exert influence through personal contacts and friendships, they were nothing like as influential as Repington. The invasion debate also featured in the popular half-penny press before a large but ill-informed audience. Northcliffe's *Daily Mail* frequently published stories on this theme, but the proprietor's major concern was to improve circulation figures and hence profits. See, for example, the manner in which he exploited Le Queux, *The Invasion of 1910*, in I.F. Clarke, *Voices Prophesying War*, pp. 145ff.

103 See particularly, documents 49 to 56 and 58–9. The second volume of A.J.Marder's edition of Fisher's correspondence, *Fear God and Dread Nought*, provides many examples of Fisher's dislike, even contempt for Repington.

104 See documents 61, 62 and 64. The full context of this bizarre incident is covered in *The Scaremongers*, pp. 140–6.

105 Repington to Seely, 11 February 1913, Seely Papers, S20/f.153.

106 Repington's finances had not reached their nadir, but were exceedingly rocky at this juncture. To finance his extravagant mode of life, he frequently had to resort to money lenders, borrowing at exorbitant rates of interest. His appetite for women was not by any means exhausted, and he had only recently ended one liaison which Mary had discovered. See *Thanks for the Memory*, p. 253. Though exceedingly indiscreet about his amorous liaisons, it is difficult, so many years later, to discover just who exactly they were. One permanent 'fixture' seems to have been Emily Grigsby, described by Jean Hamilton in her Diary, 26 September 1916, as 'Colonel Repington's cast-off mistress'. Lady Jean Hamilton's Diary, vol. X, Reel 3. 'Cast off' or no, Miss Grigsby was seen frequently by Repington during the war. She features as 'E' in the published War Diaries.

   Repington was never reluctant to ask for more money from *The Times*, but never considered other measures that would have involved him in economies.

107 See document 99.

108 See document 102.

109 Leo Amery, *My Political Life*, vol. 1, pp. 218–19, in a sly *obiter dictum*, 'I always thought him too much inclined to make the best case he could for the official view', clearly implies that Repington allowed himself to be the voice of ministers and later, the generals. Chirol and Clarke were others at Printing House Square who impugned Repington's independence, in Chirol's case, suggesting further that Repington was motivated by a desire to be reinstated in the Army. There is no doubt that Repington hoped for a number of years that he would be reinstated in the Army, but there is absolutely no evidence that his pen was ever 'bought', or to suggest that he was prepared to compromise his independence of judgement.

110 See the articles that Repington wrote in *The Times* from the twenty-third to the twenty-seventh of March 1914, inclusive.

111 See documents 122 to 128. Dawson's irritation is as understandable, given his circumstances, as Repington's actions were foreseeable. Nevertheless, Dawson recognised Repington's outstanding quality as a journalist and listed him with three others as 'men with well-filled minds and trained judgement . . . who give distinction to The Times'. Dawson to John Walter, 29 January 1914, MS.Dawson 64, ff. 1–4.

112 Stephen Koss, *The Rise and Fall of the Political Press in Britain*, vol. II, p. 245. On this whole subject, Koss provides a masterly summary. See, *ibid*, pp. 238–49. Note also the references in the footnotes to the secondary literature. On DORA, for the period 1912 to 1914, see, HO 45/228849; and for 1914–21, HO 45/11007. The Acts arose out of legislation designed to curb violence in Ireland in the nineteenth century.

113 Haig to Rothschild, 17 April 1915, quoted Gerard J. De Groot, *Douglas Haig: 1861–1928*, p. 193. De Groot demonstrates, with chapter and verse, Haig's aversion to Repington.

114 *Ibid*, pp. 193–4.

115 See his article in *The Times*, 1 August 1914. In Cynthia Asquith's *Diary*, entry for 1 June 1915, pp. 34–5, there is an account of a Downing Street luncheon party where Colonel (Lieutenant-General) Sir Tom Bridges, suggested Repington, because of his profound military knowledge, as the ideal person to be appointed Press Censor. The Prime Minister's wife, who had been hysterically inveighing against the press, said that Repington would not do, for he wasn't 'straight . . . The greatest hound I know.' The sentiments are hardly surprising for Asquith had just suffered the humiliation of being forced into coalition, in part at least, as a consequence of Repington's 'shell scare'.

116 See document 133.

117 See documents 115 and 116.

118 See document 146 and footnote 192. It has to be remembered that no one exceeded Northcliffe in his exaggerated belief in the power of the press to shape opinion. The paradox, of course, was that his great strength, and the

reason for the success of the *Daily Mail*, was his uncanny ability not to create so much as to reflect the opinion of the common man. See Tom Clarke, *Northcliffe in History: an intimate study of press power.*

119 See documents 132 and 133.

120 Repington to Marker, 29 June 1906, Kitchener-Marker Papers, Add. MSS., 52277, ff. 66–71.

121 See document 12. Repington's published *Diary* provides a number of examples of the juxtaposition of angry criticism with generous expressions of admiration. See, for example, *The First World War, 1914–1918*, vol. I, pp. 211–13.

122 Ewart's unpublished *Autobiography*, p. 704.

123 See *The Times*, 3 August 1914. See also, Dawson to Amery, 13 August 1918, Dawson MSS. 67, f. 113. Asquith expressly rejected the claim made in the Commons, 20 March 1917, that Kitchener's appointment owed anything to press pressure. He maintained that it was his idea that Kitchener should succeed him at the War Office, and that his proposal was warmly approved by Haldane. See H.H. Asquith, *Memories and Reflections*, vol. II, p. 81. However, the true account of events is not quite as simple as that. See S.E. Koss, *Lord Haldane: scapegoat for Liberalism*, pp. 115–16.

124 *The Times*, 15 August 1914. See document 131. Though he was later to regret Kitchener's actions as Secretary of State for War, at the time, Repington suggested the right man and for the right reasons. He had proposed Kitchener as Minister for War earlier. See *Blackwood's Magazine*, December 1902; and also document 7.

125 See *The First World War, 1914–1918*, vol. I, p. 22. For a clear-eyed account of Kitchener's military virtues and failings, see *Vestigia*, Chapter X.

In January 1918, Repington gave all his papers concerning Kitchener to Sir George Arthur who was writing the official life. Repington showed Arthur the relevant section of his *Diary* (vol. I, pp. 18–22) relating his dealings with Kitchener at the war's opening. Apparently Arthur considered the account an accurate record. (See vol. II, pp. 194–5).

Repington respected Kitchener's injunction, but the DMI, MacDonogh, proved a good and pliant friend, and, in any event, Repington was not short of reliable, well-placed sources of information.

126 *The Times*, 15 December 1914.

127 *The Times*, 15 August 1914. Repington described as his 'best journalistic coup' of the war, the account he gave, together with a detailed map, of the German Army's concentration in the West, published 12 August 1914. It was on the basis of this information that Repington 'preached a defensive until the advancing hordes had broken their heads upon our prepared positions'. (vol. I, p. 24) Unfortunately the French did not choose to follow Repington's advice, perversely preferring their own long held plans! It is impossible to say with confidence, who exactly was the source of Repington's information, but it was almost certainly provided by the DMI.

128 See, for example, *The Times*, 26 October 1917; record of conversation with Robertson, 21 May 1917, as cited in *The First World War, 1914–1918*, vol. I, pp. 570–2.

129 See document 21. Note that the prospect did not appeal to him. At the outbreak of war he claimed that the lack of strategic choice available to Britain was because of the nation's failure to accept conscription. Consequently Britain was involved in 'this terrible automatic war . . . we support our friends because we must.' *The Times*, 30 July 1914.

130 *The Times*, 2 April 1915. Repington's commitment to the Western Front did not, however, imply, as it did with many senior soldiers, including French and Haig, a distrust of Allies in general and the French in particular.

On the importance of winning over Germany's allies *before* the outbreak of war, see Repington's shrewd advice concerning Turkey and the Balkans in document 100.

131 This theme is discussed in fascinating detail by J. Gooch, 'Soldiers, strategy and war aims', in, *The Prospect of War*, pp. 124–45.

132 On the relationship between politicians and soldiers, see, Robertson to Repington, 31 October 1916, Robertson Papers, I/35/73. Robertson's naivety or cynicism, may be judged from his declared hope towards the end of the letter that, 'The great thing is for the two branches to work cordially, honestly and openly together . . . ' One wonders, how big a pinch of salt Repington was expected to swallow with this advice?

133 See Haig's *Diary*, 22 January 1915, recording a conversation with Repington, quoted by G.J. De Groot, *Douglas Haig: 1861–1928*, p. 176.

134 See Repington's catalogue of Haig's faults to Bonar Law, document 142.

135 See David R. Woodward (ed), *The Military Correspondence of Field Marshal Sir William Robertson*, document 171, p. 229.

136 Unattributed quotations in the next section are taken from Repington's account of these events, published in *The First World War, 1914–1918*, vol. I, pp. 35–40.

137 See document 135.

138 The most likely explanation why it passed the Press Bureau is, as suggested by Edward Cook at the time, confusion in the office. Cook's Diary, 18 May 1915, quoted Cameron Hazlehurst, *Politicians at War*, p. 248, fn.4. Repington is responsible for the mystery because of his postscript which suggests an intrigue or a forgery rather than a simple administrative mistake.

139 Spender to Esher, 17 May 1915, Esher Papers, ESHR 5/48.

140 *Lord Riddell's War Diary*, entry for 17 May 1915, p. 87.

141 See documents 136 and 137.

142 While not ignoring the significance of other events, like the failures in Gallipoli, the centre of the historical debate is whether the Shell Scandal or Fisher's resignation was the more important in determining the fate of Asquith's government. The balance of contemporary comment in diaries and letters favours the Shells and stress Repington's part in the events.

Although Cameron Hazlehurst, *Politicians at War*, pp. 234ff., has overturned Stephen Koss's arguments in 'The destruction of the Last Liberal Government', *J.M.H.* (June 1968), vol. XI, No. 2, pp. 257–77; to me, Koss, better than any other historian, captures the poisonous atmosphere of conspiracy, designed and accidental, that surrounded Asquith's Cabinet as they fought both the Germans and for personal political survival or advantage.

143 Quoted Reginald Pound and Geoffrey Harmsworth, *Northcliffe*, pp. 476–7.

144 *Hansard*: Fifth series, vol. 77, col. 259.

145 Asquith to Kitchener, 17 October 1915, Kitchener Papers, PRO 30/57/106, 76.

146 See, for example, documents 137 and 141. Also, the record of a conversation with Lloyd George, 29 September 1915, in *The First World War, 1914–1918*, vol. I, pp. 95–6.

147 For an outstanding example of Repington taking the stick to politicians for daring to suppose they knew anything of any significance concerning military matters, see *The Times*, 24 August 1916. Lloyd George's clear assertion of independence was made in an exchange with Repington, 25 October 1916, cited, *The First World War, 1914–1918*, vol. I, pp. 371–4.

148 The tendency was to be almost patronising, supposing that with Asquith removed, the General Staff and not the politicians would have the final say on strategy. They totally underestimated Lloyd George's mental acuity and agility, his political sense, charm and dazzling oratory. What they saw was a civilian, a plebeian with a history as an agitator and demagogue. If they had heard of it, they never understood the import of Talleyrand's maxim (of which Briand had reminded Lloyd George), 'War is much too serious a thing to be left to military men.'

149 See John Grigg, *Lloyd George: From Peace to war, 1912–16*, pp. 143ff.

150 *The First World War, 1914–1918*, vol. II, p. 165. Henry Wilson's appointment and subsequent promotions to the highest military office in the train of Lloyd George, was a particularly hard pill for Repington to swallow. In a sense he replaced Repington as Lloyd George's military adviser. For Wilson, his successes certainly made up for the disappointment in 1915 of not getting Archie Murray's place as Chief of Staff to the B.E.F. Repington might well have been instrumental in this by embroidering an overheard conversation into an intrigue and then telling it to Haig whose repetition of the story damaged Wilson temporarily. It should not be supposed that Repington's enmity towards Wilson determined his attitude towards the Supreme War Council; but it is not without significance for Repington's subsequent sad fate that Wilson, as Britain's sole military representative was necessarily in close and intimate connection with Lloyd George and Milner, Britain's political representatives.

151 The cause of their quarrel had been Repington telling tales out of school about Steed's opinion of MacDonogh. See H.W. Steed, *Through Thirty*

Years, 1892–1922: a personal narrative, vol. II, pp. 148–9. Steed was Northcliffe's servile and compliant replacement chosen to succeed Dawson.

152 See the letters exchanged in document 148.

153 Howard Corbett had replaced Nicholson as Manager of *The Times* in late 1915. It is not without significance in relation to the subsequent treatment of Repington that Corbett had been instructed by Northcliffe to run a very tight financial ship. Repington's financial affairs had taken such a turn for the worse that in February 1916 he owed almost £20,000 to various money lenders who were dunning him for very high rates of interest. Lockett Agnew, the art dealer and a great friend, made an agreement to cover the sum owed. One of the terms of that agreement was that Repington be allowed only £15 per week of his salary to live upon. *The Times* became a guarantor of the mortgage. Repington's disastrously jumbled financial affairs were a concern to the new, more business like regime at PHS. Repington was always seeking extra funds by syndicating his articles without permission. Though *The Times* made a great deal of money out of Repington, for his copy in his heyday was demanded and sold widely, it was less than generous in its treatment of its wayward but brilliant correspondent. Agnew was supposed to redeem the mortgage for Repington, but died suddenly before the requisite legal document had been drawn. Consequently when Repington died in 1925, *The Times* grudgingly was obliged to pay off £2000 of the remaining debt as a guarantor. Their treatment of Mary Repington was particularly shabby and mean. See, Times Archive, Managerial and Repington Files.

154 Robinson to Corbett, 7 September 1916, Times Archive, Managerial File, 1910–20.

155 *The First World War, 1914–1918*, vol. I, p. 503.

156 See A.M. Gollin, *Proconsul in Politics*, Chapter 22, pp. 599–607.

157 Repington to Corbett, 18 December 1917, The Times Archive, Repington Papers.

158 *The First World War, 1914–1918*, vol. II, p. 181.

159 See Document 163.

160 Dawson to Repington, 13 January 1918, The Times Archive, Repington Papers. Although marked as a copy and typed, the last paragraph is handwritten.

161 See, *The First World War, 1914–1918*, vol. II, pp. 187–8 for Repington's account of the 'stormy interview' with Dawson.

Dawson Diary entry for Wednesday 16 January 1918, Geoffrey Dawson Mss., Appointment Diaries, Volume 24. Subsequent diary entries for 17, 21, 22, 23 January and 11 February, trace the continuing saga of Repington's departure. It was a time when Dawson admitted: 'I was up to my neck in controversies – Repington, the Bishop of Birmingham, and E. Lyttelton (one knave and two fools).'

162 Memorandum by Dawson, Dawson Mss., Dep. 67, ff. 160–72.

163 Dawson to Haig, 30 January 1918 (copy), Dawson Mss., Dep. 67, f. 55.

164 *History of The Times*, vol. IV, Part I, pp. 231–2 and fn. 1. The false implication about revealing information useful to the enemy – which Lloyd George also tried to use – was based upon Haig's action on 21 May 1915. See, Blake (Ed), *The Private Papers of Douglas Haig, 1914–1919*, pp. 93, 95 and 97; and Dawson's discussions with Haig, 8 October 1916 (not mentioned in Blake's edition of the Haig diary), Dawson Mss., Dep. 66, ff. 130–1.

For a detailed criticism of the assertions against Repington, see Randolph Churchill, *Derby, King of Lancashire*, pp. 312–13.

165 Repington complained to Dawson of the 'inaccurate and misleading account' provided in *The Times's* statement about his resignation, published 23 January 1918. He demanded that his letter of resignation be published. Dawson's private secretary replied, justifying the statement made by *The Times* and repeating the refusal to publish Repington's letter.

166 Quoted in G.E. Wrench, *Geoffrey Dawson and Our Times*, p. 170. Dawson's reasons for resigning were generally applauded by journalists – even Repington. It was a general cry of dissatisfaction against the overweening power of all proprietors. See *The Rise and Fall of the Press*, vol. II, pp. 348–51.

167 According to Lady Carson, this is what her husband had said in a conversation with Lloyd George and the editor. Dawson had not responded, but looked, as well he might, crestfallen. Lady Carson told the story 'with relish' to Repington, and he repeated it in like manner in his published Diary, vol. II, p. 284. Randolph Churchill's criticism of Dawson (*ante*, p. 313), was that he 'relentlessly pursued' the policy of tailoring correspondents' reports to match his opinion as expressed in the leading articles 'down to the termination of his editorship'.

168 This was the opinion of, among other well informed people, J.A. Spender, who thought it very much to Repington's credit; and Esher. See, Esher to Stamfordham, 2 February 1918 (copy), and same to Haig, 14 February 1918 (copy), Esher Papers, ESHR 4/9.

169 See Lord Hankey, *The Supreme Command, 1914–1918*, vol. II, p. 697.

170 See *Derby, King of Lancashire*, p. 293. Wilson and Milner had acted together before. They made a most formidable pair of accomplished intriguers. See A.M. Gollin, *Proconsul in Politics*, pp. 242–6.

171 Quoted, *ibid*, p. 463.

172 *The First World War, 1914–1918*, vol. II, p. 191.

173 *Ibid*, vol. II, p. 197.

174 *The Rasp of War*, document 201, p. 246.

175 Robert Sander's *Diary*, Wednesday 13 February 1918, quoted in John Ramsden (Ed), *Real Old Tory Politics*, p. 101.

176 *The Rasp of War*, documents 210 and 222, pp. 260–1 and 272. In a long, detailed letter to Lady Bathurst, 16 October 1918 (document 256, pp.

312–13), Gwynne touched upon the subject of Repington's financial worth to the *Morning Post*. 'The publishing people tell me that when he joined us, the circulation gave a bump upwards. Indeed, it was the start of our good and increasing sales.' Soon after Repington left *The Times*, Corbett quickly reminded Dawson what a valuable asset Repington had been because of the syndication arrangements, particularly with the USA, and also Australia and France, which brought in thousands. Dawson was concerned that Repington was now diverting some of these funds into his own pocket. See Corbett to Dawson (copy), and Dawson to Corbett, 28 January 1918, Times Archive, Repington File.

177 See Lady Bathurst to Haig, 24 May 1918, and Haig to Lady Bathurst, 27 May 1918, quoted in Duff Cooper, *Haig*, vol. 2, pp. 301–3.

178 Repington to Maurice, 24 February 1918, Maurice Papers, 3/5/70.

179 Repington, as the military member of the Hampstead tribunal, was entitled to wear uniform which gave him a great satisfaction. See *Thanks for the Memory*, p. 271. Repington really enjoyed his notoriety. As Cynthia Asquith noted in her Diary (Wednesday 13 February, p. 411), 'Everybody is very full of Repington's arrest.' Certainly, Society and the military were well represented in the crowds who queued outside the court. Maurice was there, as was Lady Robertson, but her husband was absent. Robertson and Repington had agreed they could no more afford to be seen together than be seen accompanying a whore down Regent Street. See *The First World War, 1914–1918*, vol. II, pp. 230–5.

The glamour of Repington's prosecution as a *cause célèbre* was subsequently tarnished by the farcical Pemberton Billing trial which opened in May 1918. Designed to demonstrate the British political establishment was woefully vice ridden, perverted by Germany's 'Hidden Hand', not surprisingly it aroused enormous public interest. For a scholarly account and analysis, see G.R. Searle, *Corruption in British Politics*, pp. 255–69. The case does demonstrate that the hysteria of the Radical Right was widespread in Society as a whole.

180 A.M. Gollin, *Proconsul in Politics*, p. 517. Gollin provides a detailed narrative of the events, pp. 514–17. David Ayerst, *Garvin of The Observer*, pp.166–7 explains Garvin's state of mind and why he was quite so vicious in his attack upon a man whose capacity he sufficiently valued to have handed over to him the editorship of the *Observer* for short periods when he was otherwise engaged.

The Garvin attack, though much the most effective, was only one among a number made upon Repington in a variety of French, Italian and American journals at this time. There are interesting letters on this subject in the period late February to May 1918, in H.A. Gwynne Mss., Box 21.

181 See John Gooch, 'The Maurice Case', in *The Prospect of War*, pp. 146–63. Also, Nancy Maurice (Ed), *The Maurice Case*. On Repington's battles with the censor, see, for example, Repington to Gwynne, 29 July 1918, H.A. Gwynne Mss., Box 21.

182 Whenever he was away, which was frequently, Repington wrote regularly to his wife. Much of the content concerned domestic affairs, but there were frequent references to events and personalities that feature in his published work. There are several hundred of these letters for the period 1918 to the 1920's, recently given to the National Army Museum by Mrs Laetitia Stapleton.

183 The only offer of an appointment made in 1918, other than Gwynne's, of which there is any record extant, is by R.D. Blumenfeld of the *Daily Express*. See, Repington to Blumenfeld 23 January 1918, Blumenfeld Mss., Rep. I.

184 Repington to Northcliffe, n.d., Northcliffe Add. MSS., 62253, f. 125; Northcliffe to Repington, 12 May 1920 (copy), *Ibid*, f. 126.

185 The allure of Paris for an ageing libertine was obvious. The attraction of the almost mythical Henri de Blowitz's journalistic coups was also compelling. A fine day-dream combining professional acclaim, romance and financial independence.

186 Henry Wilson wrote to General Harington, 'If you take my advice you will neither speak to him nor see him nor allow any of your staff to do either.' Wilson followed this back-handed compliment to Repington with a typical example of his humour. 'The more he hates you, the more certainly does he make your career. He succeeded in making me Field Marshal.' *The Military Correspondence of Field Marshal Sir Henry Wilson, 1918–1922*, p. 234.

187 *After the War: a Diary*, pp. 72 and 151. The same spirit informs the latter part of his war diaries.

188 He recognised, for example, the threat posed by Japan in the Pacific, and pointed out that Singapore was vulnerable from the land.

189 Repington to Burnham, 30 November 1921, D. Lloyd George Papers, F/5/8/9.

190 To this end he even wrote a play, *The Life and Death of Marie Stewart*. It was written in blank verse and was never staged. See *Thanks for the Memory*, pp. 283–4.

Notes to Correspondence

1 Churchill's attack on the proposed Army reforms of the Secretary of State for War, St John Brodrick, 13 May 1901, established his parliamentary reputation. He was joined in his opposition to his own party by a small group of other young dissident Tories whose antics and manners in the Commons caused them to be dubbed the Hughligans or Hooligans. By 1903, this Tory cave had enlarged to embrace further politicians and also a number of journalists including Repington. See Charles Repington, *Vestigia*, pp. 251–2.

2 Curzon, since 1898 Governor and Viceroy of India, believed that Russia had aggressive designs upon Tibet. On his own initiative, Curzon sought to ensure Tibetan independence by imposing British control. In 1903, he sent

a mission under Colonel F. Younghusband, ostensibly to extend British trade interests, but it fought its way into the capital, Lhasa, and imposed political agreements that violated explicit pledges made earlier by the British government to Russia. Subsequently, in July 1904, the Tibetan treaty was revised and in order to forestall any further Curzonian diplomatic initiatives, an agreement with Afghanistan was signed in March 1905, confirming the existing *status quo*.

3 Changes introduced by a series of Army Orders intended to improve the efficiency of the Volunteers met with a mixed response. The powerful Volunteer lobby in Parliament was generally outraged though even they recognised the need to raise standards. The notorious, so-called 'Christmas Card Order' of 24 December 1901, reissued as Army Order 16 of 1902, bluntly stated the rationale for reform. Subsequently regulations were revised with a degree of relaxation, save in the case of musketry. The widespread dissatisfaction with the new regulations was seen as the reason for the declining number of Volunteers. Repington was wrong in his assumption that the offending regulations would have to be withdrawn, they were merely amended in a minor fashion. The strength of the Volunteers continued to decline. The specific Army Order to which Repington refers would appear to be A.O.46 of 1903 concerning Volunteer Camp Allowances.

See further, for a general account of the Volunteers, Hugh Cunningham, *The Volunteer Force*, pp. 129–33. For a more detailed account, see Ian Beckett, *Riflemen Form: a study of the Rifle Volunteer Movement*, Chapters VII and VIII.

4 Not Army reform but Joseph Chamberlain's imperial preference campaign, was Churchill's major political and personal concern at this time. In large part, his adherence to Free Trade principles prompted his crossing the floor and joining the Liberal party, 31 May 1904. A 'stumer' is slang for a worthless cheque.

5 For the membership, purpose and methods employed by Esher's committee, 'The Triumvirate' of Esher, Fisher and Clarke, all strong supporters of 'Blue Water' theory; and Repington's part in providing favourable publicity for the committee, see John Gooch, *The Plans of War*, pp. 37–47.

For Repington's personal account of the five years he spent with Intelligence, first under Henry Brackenbury and then Edward Chapman, see *Vestigia*, pp. 82–8. The merits of Repington's selection may be judged from the fact that he listed two future Field Marshals (Robertson and Milne) and six others who reached substantive General Officer rank on the active list (Lake, Dallas, Haldane, Holman, Lynden-Bell and Davies).

Of those officers serving in intelligence/mobilization staff at the War Office in February 1904, he failed to notice seven who subsequently achieved General Officer rank. I am particularly indebted to M.M. Chapman of the Whitehall Library, Ministry of Defence, for supplying this information.

6 After prolonged and acrimonious debate, the four military members chosen for the Army Council were Lyttelton (Chief of General Staff), Douglas (Adjutant-General), Plumer (QMG), and Murray (Master-General of Ordnance). The appointments were designedly undistinguished, following Esher's principle that provided the administrative machinery was well designed the quality of personnel was a matter of indifference. See Peter Fraser, *Lord Esher: a political biography*, p. 103.

7 Repington had published an article, 'A Plea for History' in *The Times*, 10 September 1904. It is reprinted in *Imperial Strategy*, pp. 211–20. For further information, see Jay Luvaas, *The Education of an Army: British military thought, 1815–1940*, pp. 302–3; and Luvaas, 'The First British Official Historians', in, *Military Affairs*, XXVI, Summer, 1962.

8 The full name of the proposed publication was 'The Army Journal of the British Empire'. The *Journal* was intended for public sale, and to be a forum for professional military debate. A War Office Memorandum, No.456, 9 May 1904, Section 1, suggested the *Journal* might publish internal reports and memoranda. Rooms were secured for use by editorial staff, but in January 1905, by Army Order 8, plans for the *Journal* were cancelled. This was not because of the King's opposition to serving officers publishing their views, as suggested by Gooch, *The Plans of War*, p. 122, fn. 82. Rather, abandonment of the *Journal* was because 'of the expense involved and more pressing claims for limited Treasury funding'. See Minutes of Army Council, 1 December 1904, W.O. 163. I am indebted to M.M. Chapman for drawing my attention to these Minutes.

9 The map accompanied a fifty-six page account of the Russo–Japanese War written by Repington for a special supplement of the *National Review*.

10 Lord Haliburton was Permanent Under-Secretary of State for War, 1895–7, and was succeeded by Sir Ralph Henry Knox, 1897–1901. Together the two men defended the civil branch of the War Office from incursions by the Esher Committee, in letters to *The Times*, 16 and 27 March 1904. Both men were friends of Sir Henry Campbell-Bannerman, and like him, distrusted the Committee of Defence adopting a political role – Esher's avowed intent from the beginning.

11 The experience of the Boer War demonstrated the imperative need to improve British field guns. Trials proved unsatisfactory and not until the Summer of 1904 was a design agreed upon. It was Esher who, in 1904, stirred up a furore over the guns fearing that Sir John French's 'striking force' based at Aldershot, would be ill-equipped with artillery. A.J. Balfour informed the King, 16 December 1904, that the Cabinet had 'unanimously resolved to proceed as fast as possible with artillery rearmament'. Repington's claim concerning Arnold-Forster seems ill-founded. See R.F. Mackay, *Balfour: Intellectual Statesman*, pp. 126–7; 192–3.

12 The fate of the General Staff was a topic of keen debate in the early months of 1905. Courtenay Warner, Liberal MP for Lichfield, reported to the

Commons rumours in military circles that the General Staff was not as efficient as it should be! Arnold-Forster, on the other hand, had made to his colleagues an absurdly over-optimistic assessment of the General Staff's progress. Repington followed Wilkinson's ideas, as expressed in his seminal *Brain of an Army*, and in this particular was much closer to Arnold-Forster's conception – for the Minister also was a disciple of Spenser Wilkinson – than Esher's. He had been urging Esher to give him details of his scheme since the beginning of February.

13 These were two articles: one on the Militia; the other on 'The War Office at Work' which were published in *The Times* in early March.

14 Colonel Shute preceded Raymond Marker as Arnold-Forster's secretary.

15 Vice-Admiral Z.P. Rozhenstvensky commanded the Russian Baltic Fleet which, in October 1904, fired upon some Hull fishing trawlers off the Dogger Bank under the impression they were being attacked by Japanese submarines. There followed a short but intense period of diplomatic tension between Britain and Russia. The Russian fleet continued its voyage only to be destroyed utterly at the Battle of Tsushima on 27/28 May 1905.

16 For Esher's attitude to Curzon's resignation and the likely consequences to follow, see M.V. Brett (Ed), *Journals and Letters of Reginald Viscount Esher*, vol. II, pp. 99–100.

17 This refers to the speech that had recently been made by Lord Roberts at the Mansion House demanding rifle drill for all schoolboys, and a 'home defence Army guaranteed to render any attempt at invasion out of the question'. The National Service League was delighted, but the speech alienated some of Roberts's natural supporters who supposed that he was attacking the auxiliary forces. Balfour, according to Arnold-Forster, who shared this view, thought the speech 'outrageous'. This was the beginning of the furore which in November led to Roberts's resignation from the Committee of Defence and his accepting the Presidency of the National Service League. A further consequence of the August speech was that Milner, not yet a public supporter of Roberts, arranged for J.L. Garvin to help Roberts with his propaganda. See further, A.J.A. Morris, *The Scaremongers, 1896–1914*, pp. 108–10, 230–1.

18 William Maxwell was a distinguished war correspondent who had only recently joined the staff of the *Daily Mail* from the *Standard*. Harry Lawson, later Viscount Burnham, was the son and heir of the owner of the *Daily Telegraph*.

19 For the complex debate over the defence of India in this period, the part played by railways in strategic thinking, together with a generally sympathetic assessment of George Clarke's contribution, see Gooch, *Plans of War*, pp. 218–37. A fuller, diplomatic picture concentrating on Anglo-Russian relations is given in Keith Neilson *Britain and the last Tsar*, *passim*.

Lieutenant-Colonel Sir Edward Percy Girouard was a Canadian military railway expert who, during the Boer War had been a director of railways in South Africa.

20 The French Military Attaché was Major Victor Jacques-Marie Huguet; Léon Geoffray was the Chargé d'Affaires; and Pierre Cambon had been the French Ambassador in London since 1898.

There is a copy of Edward Grey's response to Repington's letter in the Edward Grey Papers in the Public Record Office, FO 800/110.

30 December 1905.

Private and Confidential

Dear Colonel à Court Repington,

I am very interested to hear of your conversation with the French Military Attaché. I can only say that I have not receded from anything which Lord Lansdowne said to the French, and have no hesitation in affirming it.

Yours etc.,

E. GREY.

21 The article referred to was published in *The Times*, 27 December 1905. Repington commented in detail on this article in his *Vestigia*, pp. 262–3.

22 Cyprus had been acquired from Turkey at the Congress of Berlin, 1878. The intention had been to establish a new naval base in the Eastern Mediterranean, but it was quite unsuitable. The port of Weihaiwei was acquired on lease in 1898, somewhat reluctantly by Salisbury as a counter to Germany's recent acquisition of Kaio-chow. It merely succeeded in alienating the Americans who saw it as a blow to their 'open-door' policy in China.

23 Colonel Count Gleichen's claim to be an expert on military intelligence is open to considerable doubt. See *The Plans of War*, p. 116.

24 Oliver Sylvain Baliol Brett was John Morley's unpaid Assistant Private Secretary, a position from which he could inform his father of the Minister's latest thoughts, and also pass on, most conveniently, Esher's latest scheme or idea. On Esher's relationship with his elder son, see James Lees-Milne, *The Enigmatic Edwardian, passim*.

25 In India, control of the Army's affairs had been divided between the Commander-in-Chief and the Military Member of the Council. Kitchener desired to establish in India the same autocratic rule that he had enjoyed over the Army in Egypt and South Africa. This meant the annihilation of the Military Member. The holder of that office was Major-General Sir Edmund Elles who generally enjoyed a good reputation, but for whom Kitchener nursed a dislike that was almost pathological in its intensity. Kitchener's plans to remove the Military Member were thwarted by the Viceroy, Curzon, who was as determined as Kitchener to have the supreme power in his hands, a power enhanced by the mutual suspicion, even hatred, between Elles and Kitchener. Both Kitchener and Curzon carried on a lively campaign among supporters at home. Every possible source to influence opinion in Britain was exploited, including *The Times*. At Printing House

Square, Valentine Chirol, Head of the Foreign Department, passionately espoused Curzon's cause; Repington, who listened attentively to the voice of Raymond Marker, Kitchener's former ADC, made the case for Kitchener.

The Secretary of State for India, St John Brodrick, eventually imposed a compromise which favoured Kitchener, but then, to the annoyance of Kitchener, his triumph was frustrated by Curzon's appointment of General Barrow, an able and independent soldier and no admirer of Kitchener, as Supply Member. Kitchener appealed to the Cabinet, and, in the face of their disapproval, in August 1905, Curzon resigned.

Although Repington supported Kitchener's case throughout the quarrel, it is clear from the tone of his letters to Raymond Marker that he had considerable reservations about the measure which worked well only when Kitchener was there to supervise and inspire his one-man system of control. See further, Trevor Royle, *The Kitchener Enigma, passim.*

For a brief account of the quarrel that favours Curzon's position, see Marquess of Anglesey, *A History of the British Cavalry*, vol. 4, pp. 494–7.

26 Lieutenant-General Sir Alfred Gaselee, former India QMG.

27 For Clarke's own account of this conversation, see his letter to Esher, n.d., 13(?) January 1906, ESHR 10/38. For Fisher's ideas about a Baltic War Plan, in 1905 and subsequently, see R.F. Mackay *Fisher of Kilverstone, passim.*

28 John Jarvis, Earl of St Vincent, Admiral of the Fleet (1735–1823). For Fisher's initial conversation with the French naval attaché, Captain Mercier de Lostende on 2 January 1906, see M. Paléologue, *The Turning Point*, pp. 315–16.

29 Granville Leveson-Gower, Earl Granville (1815–91), was British Foreign Secretary at the time of the Franco-Prussian War.

30 Maurice Rouvier (1842–1911) was the then French Prime Minister.

31 'The threefold principle of the Sultan's supremacy, the indivisibility of his states, and a commercial policy of the open door.' Paul Revoil, French Ambassador in Berne, was his country's representative at the Algeçiras conference.

32 The Prime Minister was not informed about the talks until 27 January 1906. On this most important subject, see John Wilson, *CB: a life of Sir Henry Campbell-Bannerman*, pp. 522–30.

33 Carnot, a military engineer, introduced universal conscription to France. He was the organiser and backbone of the early revolutionary French armies. A member of the Directorate, he was Napoleon's predecessor.

34 Sir George Chesney, a tireless promoter of reform in the British Army, wrote the provocative and influential *Battle of Dorking* (1871)

35 In a letter Maxse had written to Repington earlier, he had sought an Army officer to write for his journal, who was familiar with Kitchener's thoughts and ideas. Repington had responded, 'The man who knows most of what K. has done and is doing, and the man also who is available now, is Brigadier-

General Hubert Hamilton DSO, who was K's Military Secretary and has just got a Brigade in the Salisbury command. But I fear he would not write under his own name. You might try him saying I suggested you should apply to him, and be sure you lay stress on the fact that the authorship of the articles would be kept absolutely secret. He is caution in the flesh. He has the information and you could supply the writing if you find that he is not a Macaulay.' Repington to Maxse, 15 February 1906, L.J. Maxse Mss., 455, f. 259.

36   Maxse's views on the value of overseas naval bases were founded upon the experience of earlier colonial wars between France and Britain. In the Great War, Germany's overseas possessions, amounting to more than a million square miles but with a tiny German population, were swiftly overcome. The German Government had long considered these holdings as strategically irrelevant. The North Sea was, as Tirpitz had argued, the focus of their naval strategic interest. Victory in the North Sea would insure as much overseas territorial compensation as Germany might require.

37   In April 1906 Abdul Hamid, Sultan of Turkey, sent his troops to occupy several areas at the Southern end of the Sinai Peninsula. The British Consul General in Egypt, Lord Cromer, claimed that Turkey, by ignoring long-standing agreements between the two Powers, threatened Egyptian security. Consequently he sought an increase in the British garrison. The British Government suspected that Turkey's actions had been prompted by Germany and so determined that a strong response was required. An ultimatum was presented to Turkey on 3 May in the face of which Abdul Hamid withdrew his troops. This was just as well for there was considerable uncertainty concerning British naval and military plans. For an account of this incident, see Keith Robbins, *Sir Edward Grey*, pp. 164–5.

38   This committee was popularly known as the duma. For a detailed account, see J.K. Dunlop, *The Development of the British Army 1899–1914*, pp. 266–72. For Esher's scathing estimate of the members of his committee, see *Journals and Letters*, vol. II, p. 163.

39   Colonel George Frederick Gorringe was appointed Director of Movements and Quartering at the War Office in 1906, holding the post until 1909.

40   Major-General Henry Merrick Lawson was moved from the War Office to Dublin in 1906, and the next year to Aldershot, in charge of administration.

41   Captain Harry Lionel Pritchard DSO, RE, later Major-General.

42   From the late 1880s, Repington had corresponded with Sir Charles Dilke on military and strategic issues. Unlike Thursfield he was not a personal friend of Sir Charles. Keen upon economy in the Army, Dilke, a strong advocate of the 'Blue Water' doctrine, was invariably sympathetic to increased expenditure for the Navy.

43   Lieutenant-Colonel Sir John Robert Chancellor, in 1906 was a Staff Captain in the Intelligence Department of the War Office. He was successively Assistant Secretary (Military) to the defence Committee, 1904–6; then

Secretary to the Colonial Defence Committee. From 1911 to 1916 he was Governor and C-in-C Mauritius.

44 In the Summer of 1906, Haldane's decision to reduce the Guards was *the* topic of febrile comment and condemnation by the King, the Army and the Secretary of State's political opponents. On this, see Edward M. Spiers, *Haldane: an Army reformer*, pp. 59–63.

45 The article appeared 29 August 1906. It stirred a furious correspondence that lasted more than a month.

46 Since January 1906 Repington had been active in the foundation and development of the National Defence Association. Roberts was President of the Association. Among supporters there were as many voluntarists as compulsionists. At this stage Repington was convinced of the theoretical case for conscription, but thought it would only ever be achieved by stealth. He saw the NDA as a useful means of breaking down the polarisation of the two groups, and hoped that each would make its contribution 'to overcome the ocean of prejudice against compulsion', as he wrote to Raymond Marker, 2 January 1906.

47 The Navy League was a powerful and successful pressure group, designed to inform the British public and encourage interest in the navy and naval affairs. Founded in 1895, it was swiftly copied by the Germans, in 1898, and the French in 1899. Later a schism developed between the supporters of Fisher and Lord Beresford, the latter group forming the Imperial Maritime League, known popularly as the Navier League.

48 Reverend the Hon. Edward Lyttelton (1855–1942), the seventh of the Lyttelton brothers, had been appointed Head of Eton in 1905. He was obliged to resign his post in 1916 because he was thought to hold pro German views because he supported the idea of negotiated peace in 1915.

49 Major-General Sir F. Maurice and M.H. Grant, *Official History of the War in South Africa, 1899–1902*, in eight volumes, four of text and four of maps.

50 This was the first of four articles dealing with the Second Hague Peace Conference and related subjects – limitation of armaments, the laws and practice of naval warfare and compulsory arbitration. To Raymond Marker, Repington admitted that his intention was, 'to do something to cool the blood of the visionaries'. Repington to Marker, 25 July 1906.

51 Henry Vivian was elected for Birkenhead in 1906 as a Lib-Lab MP. The Government had accepted his motion for debate in May. It made the usual claims and demands – that expenditure on armaments, which could be better spent on social reforms, was excessive and ought to be reduced drastically; and that the reduction of armaments by international agreement should be an item on the agenda of the forthcoming peace conference at The Hague. As well as opposition from the Tories, Liberal navalists attempted to amend the resolution unsuccessfully. For the debate, see *Hansard*, Fourth Series, vol. 156, Cols. 1383–1416.

52 On the history and changing nature of the two-Power standard, the best, most concise account, is Arthur J. Marder, *From the Dreadnought to Scapa Flow: the road to war, 1904–14* (Oxford University Press, London, 1961), vol. 1, pp. 123–5.

53 In a speech, 23 July 1906, to the Fourteenth Interparliamentary Conference, the Prime Minister had declared that Great Britain would go to The Hague Peace Conference 'pledged to diminish the charges in respect of armaments' and urging other governments to do likewise. See further, A.J.A. Morris, *Radicalism Against War, 1906–14*, Chapter 3, *passim*.

54 Campbell-Bannerman's pre-General Election speech at the Albert Hall 21 December 1905, had been dubbed the 'League of Peace Speech' because of his championing arbitration for the settlement of international disputes, and 'the adjustment of armament to the newer and happier condition of things'. Supporters of the Liberal Government argued that Sir Edward Grey's response to the Vivian disarmament motion meant 'that the Prime Minister's declaration at the Albert Hall is not a pious formula but a concrete declaration of policy'. See further, *Radicalism Against War, 1906–14*, pp. 24–5, 101–2.

55 Although Esher had held no military appointment, and had no military experience, nevertheless, he was the driving force behind the reform of the Army and was exceedingly influential in the selection of those officers who were to hold the leading positions. It was Esher who had sought an Inspector-General and had been largely instrumental in the appointment of Prince Arthur to that post. On the measure of Esher's influence in these matters, see, for example, Henry Wilson's diary entries for the 10–12 February 1904, in C.E. Callwell, *Field Marshal Sir Henry Wilson: his life and diaries*, vol. I, p. 55.

56 The whole story of this and related incidents is told in Noble Frankland, *Witness of a Century*, pp. 249ff.

57 For a very favourable view of Henry Wilson's suitability for the post, see Roberts to Esher, 11 October 1906, in *Journals and Letters*, vol. II, pp. 192–3.

58 General Lyttelton, the first Chief of the General Staff, was the least able member of the Lyttelton family. It had been his lack of distinction or ability as a strategist and administrator that had recommended him to Esher as a C.of G.S. who would be both safe and compliant.

59 Hyphen, i.e., acting as a link between the Army and the War Office.

60 The article appeared in *The Times*, 29 August 1906. Further articles on historical examples of invasion were published on 8 and 13 November 1906. Moltke was an example much favoured by Repington. See, for example, *Vestigia*, pp. 278ff.

61 There was a case to be argued for the Protectionists against Peel over the repeal of the Corn Laws in 1846, but politically it was unsound and it proved electorally disastrous. The actions of Disraeli and Bentinck wrecked Peel's career and almost did for the party. See further, Robert Blake, *Disraeli*, Chapter X, *passim*.

62 For opposition by the Labour party to armaments and Anglo-German relations, see D.J. Newton, *British Labour European Socialism and the struggle for peace, 1889–1914, passim.*

63 The Colomb brothers, Philip Howard and John, founded the Blue Water school, and their theories were supported and developed by the American naval authority and historian, Captain Alfred Mahan. The Blue Water school effectively re-established the old orthodoxy that Britain's safety and that of her overseas Empire rested upon her naval supremacy. Thursfield's admiration for the Colombs and Mahan was reflected in his journalism and his books. The theory suited Liberal thinking, being deployed as a prayer in aid for retrenchment in expenditure upon the Army. Hence the birth of the 'Bolt from the Blue' school of invasionists, in which Repington played such a prominent part. The intention was to shake the complacent thought that the Navy alone could in all circumstances successfully resist an hostile invasion of Britain.

64 J. Ellis Barker was a journalist whose many books included *Modern Germany*, and, *Great and Greater Britain*. The tenor of his writings on the subject of Germany's belligerent intentions may be judged from his entry in *Who's Who*. 'From 1900 he devoted his literary career . . . to warning England of the dangers of war with Germany and to urging military preparation . . . and cooperating with Lord Roberts.'

65 The Militia, as opposed to the Volunteers, had its roots in the constitutional right of the State to call upon any of its subjects to serve in the defence of the country. Such a force was raised by compulsion and men chosen by Ballot. Some supporters of the Militia – certain elderly Tory peers in particular – had argued for a return to the Ballot. This system, however, had several crucial weaknesses that were generally acknowledged, particularly its unsuitability to raise troops to fight abroad. See further, *The Development of the British Army, 1899–1914*, pp. 42–52. For a neat summary of the history of the militia ballot, related material and further reading suggestions, see Ian Beckett, 'The Amateur Military Tradition', in David Chandler and Ian Beckett (Eds), *The Oxford Illustrated History of the British Army*, pp. 402–16 and 475.

66 Those Repington lists as members did sit upon the sub-committee of the CID, that met first on 27 November 1907. However, Haldane and Tweedmouth were also members, as was Admiral Fisher.

67 Stiff opposition had been anticipated from the Volunteer supporters in Parliament. For this reason, Repington had written to Esher, 15 February 1907, ESHR 5/22, arguing for changes in the Territorial and Reserve Forces Bill, modifying the terms of enlistment. Haldane handled the Volunteer issue with kid gloves, making every effort to appear sympathetic. In the event, the Volunteer opposition proved hopelessly ineffectual. See further, *Haldane, an Army reformer*, pp. 109–11.

68 Lieutenant-General Sir Lawrence James Oliphant, from 1907 was GOC in C Northern Command. At this time, the King, who was a Fisher supporter

and a critic of Charles Beresford, took the side of the Navy and the Admiralty against the Army and the War Office. Esher turned Edward's support to favour the Army and Haldane. See P. Magnus, *King Edward the Seventh*, pp. 369ff.

69 Major-General, then Colonel Sir Edward Sinclair May, an artillery expert who was Director of Military Training at the War Office, 1903–7.

70 Auberon Thomas Herbert, Lord Lucas and Dingwall, had been Parliamentary Under Secretary in the Lords, and from 1908, Under-Secretary of State at the War Office.

71 See *National Review*, November 1907, 'Invasion', pp. 468–84. Maxse, in his September 'Episodes of the Month', p. 172, praised Repington's 'bold and blunt declarations'.

72 Colonel John Stackpole retired from the Army in 1904. He saw active service in the Sudan. He was a Hampshire JP.

73 They have only themselves to blame.

74 This is a reference to those Radical Liberals who were never more than lukewarm supporters of Haldane. Their only concern was that he should cut military expenditure. They were not otherwise interested in military reform.

75 Sir George MacCrae was the Liberal MP for Edinburgh East, 1899–1909.

76 From the beginning, Dilke had been an opponent of the Cardwell system and he continued his criticism to the end claiming that, among other measures, the linked battalions could never deliver the economies in military spending that he sought.

77 The 'bomb' was Repington's revelation in *The Times*, supported by his editor, Buckle, of the Kaiser's letter to Lord Tweedmouth.

78 For Repington's own account of his revelation of the Kaiser's letter to Tweedmouth and subsequent events, see *Vestigia*, Chapter XXI; for a scholarly account and assessment, see *From Dreadnought to Scapa Flow: the road to war*, vol. I, pp. 140–2. 'Pactiser' means to compromise with or treat with someone.

79 In his leader (*Observer*, 15 March 1908, p. 6), Garvin was highly critical of the Territorials, referring to them as 'a phantom Army', and the artillery as 'worse than useless . . . Amateur batteries are as mistaken as would be amateur battleships.' Although Garvin's relationship with Repington was stormy and ended with a bitter personal attack in 1918, nevertheless, Repington made a number of contributions to the *Observer*. On Garvin's editorship of that paper crucial to the understanding of Unionist attitudes, see A.M. Gollin, *The Observer and J.L. Garvin, 1908–14*, *passim*. Strangely, Gollin does not deal with Garvin's relationship with Roberts, on which see David Ayerst, *Garvin of the Observer*, pp. 80–4. Garvin continued to attack Haldane and the Territorial Army scheme, the differences between Minister and Editor neatly summarised by Ayerst, pp. 85–6.

80 'Afterwards we shall see'.

81 Controversy over the artillery had begun earlier in the year, when in the Commons, Arthur Lee had ridiculed the idea of a Territorial artillery armed with converted fifteen pounders opposed by well trained enemy gun crews. In the Lords, Roberts claimed that the one hundred and ninety six Territorial batteries, far from being useful would constitute a positive danger. Haldane responded that his critics had misunderstood his plans. The Territorials would undergo six months of special war training. The Minister cited the support of, among others, Sir John French for his scheme. Roberts, himself an artillery man, remained unimpressed by French's imprimatur, French being a cavalry expert. Esher, who took a pragmatic view of the whole matter, argued better a half-trained Territorial artillery than none at all. In the press, some charged Haldane with deploying the Territorial artillery as an excuse for reducing regular army units. With the Minister pressed upon all sides, not least by his own party's economists, Repington supported Haldane unwaveringly in the columns of *The Times*. See further, Sir F. Maurice, *Haldane: the Life of Viscount Haldane of Cloan*, vol. I, pp. 221–30.

82 Elizabeth Haldane was the founder of the Territorial Nursing Service of which she became Vice-Chairman. She was also a manager of Edinburgh Royal Infirmary. See *The Times History of the War*, vol. IV, pp. 24–45.

83 To risk his own skin.

84 This incident arose at the height of a battle in the Cabinet between Haldane and the economist 'twins', Churchill, and Lloyd George. On 25 June *The Times* published a paragraph, planted by Haldane's opponents, suggesting Haldane was about to replace Loreburn as Lord Chancellor. Esher was asked by Asquith to help comfort Haldane and reconcile the various parties. Haldane remained uncomfortable under the attacks of Churchill, and on 13 July Repington, uninvited, entered the lists with a stinging attack on Haldane's enemies in *The Times*. Commentators have taken different views as to whether this was a help or a hindrance to Haldane's cause. Cf. Dudley Sommer, *Haldane of Cloan, his life and times, 1856–1928*, pp. 214–17; and *Haldane: an Army reformer*, pp. 69–72.

85 Repington had moved in May 1908, from his previous home in Kensington to Hampstead.

86 To make haste slowly.

87 This is Repington being disingenuous. He was very much part of the strategy to threaten a debate in the House of Lords. It was the last throw in the current invasion debate. The unwillingness of the Government to publish the findings of the invasion inquiry allowed the Repington/Roberts camp to win a massive publicity coup. But throughout, Repington chose to adopt the role of the reasonable man hostage to rather wild accomplices. See further, David James, *Lord Roberts*, pp. 433–6; *The Scaremongers, 1896–1914*, pp. 145–7.

88 This letter was written after a period of considerable diplomatic tension between the Powers created by the Franco-German Casablanca crisis in

November 1908. The conversation is described by Esher in his *Journal*, January 14th, vol. II, pp. 365–6. It is interesting to note that in this period, before Henry Wilson took over as DMO, while Spencer Ewart was in that post and Sir William Nicholson was CGS, the soldiers did not encourage Huguet's approaches, fearing that staff negotiations might bind Britain more tightly than was in British interests. Yet Esher and French showed no such reservations in their conversation with Huguet, and according to Esher's account at the height of the Casablanca crisis, Haldane, Asquith and Grey demonstrated firm commitment to France against Germany. See *Journal* November 12th 1908, vol. II, p. 359.

89 Broaching of the subject.

90 He thinks he must have lost his reputation.

91 On the first day's debate on the naval estimates, Asquith, responding to Balfour, admitted as 'a fatal and most serious fact' that Britain could no longer rely upon building her battleships quicker than Germany. This 'admission' caused panic in the ranks of the Radicals and euphoria among the Unionists, some of whom, like Henry Wilson, supposed it assured not only more Dreadnought battleships from a Government anxious to economise on armament expenditure, but the demise of the Liberals, the triumph of tariff reform and the acceptance of compulsory military service! Repington was not anything like as sanguine, but was determined to make the very most of the opportunity afforded. See further, *The Scaremongers, 1896–1914*, Chapter 13 *passim*.

92 Because of her health, Lady Roberts had been advised by her doctors to take a holiday abroad. In later December, the entire Roberts family went to Egypt. Roberts returned refreshed and invigorated.

93 Malcolm Kincaid-Smith, retired Army captain and member of the NSL, had won the Stratford-upon-Avon constituency in 1906, nominally as a Liberal. On 6 April 1909, to the consternation and confusion of the NSL executive, he announced in *The Times* his intention to resign his seat and fight the subsequent by-election on the single issue of national service. To the declared joy of the Liberal press, who had long castigated their maverick member, Kincaid-Smith was humiliated by the Unionist candidate, P.S. Foster. The conscription camp was devastated. See further, D. Green, 'The Stratford by-election' in *Moirae*, Trinity, 1980, vol. V, pp. 92–110.

94 The Legion of Frontiersmen was founded in 1905 by the adventurer and romantic, Roger Pocock. It attracted super-patriots who constituted themselves the freelance defenders of the British Empire. By this date, the membership was in excess of 3,500. The War Office was initially impressed by the Legion, but by 1910 supposed it a 'harmful and essentially unmilitary organisation'. Captain Daniel Patrick Driscoll DSO, who had fought in the Boer War, joined the Legion in 1907, soon assuming a leading role.

According to Pocock's Diary, and his autobiography, *Chorus to Adventurers*, pp. 85–93, Esher gave him a sum of money for the Legion. Repington, in an article in *The Times*, 10 May 1909, suggested the Legion should be officially subsidised to form with rifle club members and Baden Powell's boy scouts, 'a national Army of second line in Great Britain'. The suggestion confirms Repington's sense of hopelessness, reflected in letters to Roberts and Maxse.

95 The Russian Government had surrendered ignominiously to Austrian threats, backed by Germany, over Serbia, on 23 March 1909. This Bosnian crisis revealed clearly that Russia was in no position to go to war. The replacement of General A.F. Rediger as Russian War Minister by General V.A. Sukhomlinov, and the decision to spend more on defence, was interpreted favourably in Britain. The truth was that Grey was obliged to clutch at any favourable straw at this juncture to maintain the credibility of his pro-Russian policy in the face of spirited attacks from within his own party. See, further, *Britain and the last Tsar*, pp. 302–6; *Radicalism Against War, 1906–14*, pp. 180–93.

96 A feature of the Edwardian years was the widespread belief that Britain was crawling with German spies and agents. Leo Maxse, a dedicated and self confessed Germanophobe – in 1915 he was to publish an account of his 'prescience' concerning German perfidy, called *Germany on the Brain.* – was a victim of this illusion, and the Humber was one among many areas that on various occasions he supposed entertained a group of Germans up to no good. Repington is not entirely fair to Slade who, on his appointment as DNI in 1907, admitted that 'The Naval secret service was not organised in any way.' Despite examinations by sub-committees of the CID of spying and espionage, and various attempts at reform, British activity in this particular area continued to be of a lamentably amateur standard. The one consolation was that foreign governments were deluded enough to suppose that the British actually possessed an organised and efficient secret service. See further, Christopher Andrew, *Secret Service: the making of the British intelligence community*, pp. 1–85; for information concerning Repington and Maxse in this context, see, *The Scaremongers, 1896–1914*, pp. 148–63.

97 This was the so-called policy of the Triple Entente of Britain, France and Russia as a power balance to match the Central Powers, to which many Liberals, as supporters of the Concert of Europe, were opposed, but to which Unionists and the Foreign Office subscribed.

98 *Not* the Committee of Imperial Defence, but the Criminal Investigation Department. The Special Branch at Scotland Yard, originally formed to track down suspicious Irishmen, was swiftly recruited to track down other potential enemies, particularly Germans. The CID took no initiative on its own but acted upon instructions from the Secret Service Bureau. The system worked most effectively after the appointment of Basil Thomson in June 1913. See further, the many semi-autobiographical works of Sir Basil Thomson, but particularly *Queer People*.

99 Smith-Dorrien and French had very different ideas concerning the conduct of cavalry which led to a distancing between the former friends who were

both notoriously short-tempered. For French's views of cavalry and tactics and his conduct of manoeuvres, see Richard Holmes, *The Little Field Marshal*, pp. 151–65; for the 1909 incident, see Brigadier-General C. Ballard, *Smith-Dorrien*, pp. 126–8.

100 Maurice was Esher's elder son who, although unsuited by experience and ability, was seconded from his regiment to serve on French's staff. See further, James Lees-Milne, *The Enigmatic Edwardian*, pp. 148–9.

101 On the problems Haldane faced concerning the Special Reserve and provision of training for more officers, see *Haldane: an Army Reformer*, pp. 140ff. The Lord Salisbury with whom Repington was corresponding was the fourth Marquess, James Edward Herbert Gascoyne Cecil (1861–1947).

102 Haldane had been showing signs of stress, despite his remarkably resilient constitution, since the Summer Parliamentary recess. Years of exceptionally hard work, and in particular, recent efforts to overcome critics and drum up support for his Territorial forces took their inevitable toll. His eyes became very inflamed and his doctors ordered bed rest. Consequently he took no part in the platform warfare over Lloyd George's 'People's Budget' that raged throughout the summer and autumn. Haldane was left with permanently damaged sight and he developed diabetes. Parliament was dissolved in December but Haldane was still too ill to play a part in the General Election in January. His sister organised his campaign, and Haldane, further incapacitated by rheumatism, made one speech only at the hustings, relying upon friends to speak for him. His majority declined from that of 1906, as it did again in the second election that year.

103 George William Blackwood, then editor of *Blackwood's Magazine*.

104 Repington being at odds with the naval 'experts' on *The Times*, was warned off certain subjects as not suitable for comment by him. See Repington's letter to his editor, Buckle, 7 January 1912. The two articles appeared under the title 'New Wars for Old', *Blackwood Magazine,* June 1910, pp. 893–900; July 1910, pp. 3–13. For Repington's own thoughts upon these articles, see *Vestigia*, pp. 295–8.

105 On John St Loe Strachey's ideas about a reserve of veterans, see Amy Strachey, *St Loe Strachey: His Life and His Paper*, pp. 240–4, 247–56. Strachey's idea became the National Reserve, for which, see Spiers, *Haldane: an Army Reformer*, p. 183.

106 Northcliffe's reply to Repington's letter mixed praise for the *Review* with concern that *The Times* Military Correspondent's independence might be compromised by his receiving payment from the War Office. Northcliffe concluded, 'However, as you say, it is an experiment, and we will adopt Mr Asquith's policy (i.e. wait and see) in the matter.' See Northcliffe to Repington (typed copy), 4 July 1911, Northcliffe Add. Mss., 62253, f. 9.

107 See document 82, above.

108 The appearance of the letter suggests that a space was left at this point, and that subsequently the next two sentences were added to the text as an after-

thought. A typical example of the way in which, from time to time, Repington sought to ingratiate himself with the owner of *The Times*, in the hope that Northcliffe might support him against Buckle, and, as important, secure a larger salary.

109 Repington's reference is to the second Moroccan or Agadir Crisis which lasted until September 1911. The German gunboat *Panther* arrived at Agadir on 1 July. For an account of the event and its importance in relation to Anglo-French relations, see Zara Steiner, *Britain and the Origins of the First World War*, pp. 70ff.

110 Archibald Forbes was one of the more distinguished of the old school of war correspondents, best known for his accounts in the *Daily News* of the Franco-Prussian war. Repington did not have a particularly good opinion of Forbes's abilities, and was convinced, as he had demonstrated in his writing on the Russo-Japanese war, that an informed commentator at home was better placed to understand and interpret events than a commentator at the seat of war. See *Vestigia*, pp. 51 and 253. For Forbes's own flamboyant estimate of his 'art', see Archibald Forbes, *Memories and Studies of War and Peace*.

111 Henri Stephan de Blowitz, Paris correspondent of *The Times* at the end of the nineteenth century, was the most quoted and most hated of that newspaper's correspondents. De Blowitz's posthumous *My Memoirs*, though they must be read with a very large pinch of salt, better than anything else give the savour of this fantastical journalist. For a more objective account, see Frank Giles, *A Prince of Journalists*.

112 The Agadir crisis was played out in England against a background of violent domestic political problems. The House of Lords issue came to its climax with the defeat of the Die-hards on the night of 9/10 July, splitting Society. At the same time there had been a series of strikes which caused rioting which required the troops to be called in. The strikes spread from the ports to the railways. See *Radicalism against War, 1906–14*, pp. 239–51.

113 The Admiralty treated the crisis as of no particular concern to them. Fleet dispositions were criticised then and subsequently in the press and in Parliament. See *From the Dreadnought to Scapa Flow*, vol. I, pp. 243–8.

114 Edward 'Ned' Grigg, like many others at P.H.S., did not share Repington's concern about the fleet dispositions. Even a wild anti-German like Leo Maxse, was persuaded there was no 'immediate' threat from Germany on this occasion because of the imbalance in the numbers of Dreadnought battleships. For many, Anglo-German naval relations had become merely a matter of counting the advantage in the new super battleships, a political and strategic naivety which was to have stern consequences for Britain in 1914.

115 This document and documents 90, 91 and 92 are concerned with changes in Admiralty policy and personnel as a consequence of Churchill succeeding Reginald McKenna on 25 October 1911 as First Lord, a change Asquith had made having been persuaded by Haldane after the Agadir incident that there

was an imperative need to set up a naval staff system. Those who had feared that Churchill would interfere in everything were not disappointed. Never had a First Lord shown such zeal and impatience.

Sir Arthur Wilson would have been obliged to retire in March 1912 on reaching the age of seventy. Churchill liked the First Sea Lord but recognised that old 'ard eart' was not the man to accept new ideas easily, and under his rule the Navy had slept. Wilson was not prepared to accept a war staff at the Admiralty and told Churchill so in no uncertain terms. The Admiral's memorandum on the subject, 30 October 1911, revealed he did not begin to understand the concept of a war staff. It was agreed Wilson must go, but his replacement proved difficult. Bridgeman was appointed First Sea Lord on 28 November 1911, but was himself replaced a year later by Battenburg, the original choice for the post to whom Lloyd George on that occasion had objected.

There was little sympathy for a war staff system at the Admiralty but in the face of the combined determination of the CID, the Cabinet, the reconstituted Admiralty Board, and Battenburg's enthusiasm, on 8 January 1912, the Navy War Council was converted into the Admiralty War Staff. The system did not prove as effective as its proponents had hoped. Training at the Staff College was inadequate and often candidates chosen for training were not the most suitable, reflecting the residue of opposition to the scheme among senior officers. By August 1914 there had been insufficient time to create an effective staff. However, not all was failure. It was a major gain that the plans for naval war were no longer the personal, private prerogative of the First Sea Lord – as Fisher had always insisted – and they recognised that a policy of close blockade was, in modern warfare, no longer practicable.

For the best general account of these issues, see *From the Dreadnought to Scapa Flow*, vol. I, pp. 255ff.

116 Concerning Haldane's notorious sympathy for Germany; the attacks made upon the Minister from 1912 onwards in elements of the Tory press, and for an account of the background and circumstances of Haldane's Mission to Germany, see Stephen E. Koss, *Lord Haldane: scapegoat for Liberalism*, Chapter 3.

117 Information on the strength of the British Army that Repington had published earlier that month in *The Times*, that he had abstracted from the Army's *General Annual Report* before that *Report* was made generally available to members of Parliament, caused questions to be tabled as to Repington's exact status at the War Office. The military correspondent was stoutly defended by Haldane and Seely. For questions, see *Hansard*, Series V, vol. 34, Cols. 1167–71. The matter was further discussed in the Army Estimates Debates on 6 and 12 March 1912; *Ibid*, vol. 35, Cols. 406–7, 415, 455–6, 990.

118 The Italo-Turkish war had broken out on the 28 September 1911, a most unwelcome addition to the burdens already borne by the British Foreign

Office arising from the Agadir confrontation. Italy's invasion of Tripoli and her subsequent barbarous behaviour meant general condemnation by the British press. Grey, anxious to join Italy to the Entente Powers rather than to Germany and Austria, was not anxious to censure Italy which brought the full wrath of the Radical wing of the Liberal party down upon the Foreign Secretary's head. This campaign gathered momentum when it appeared Britain had known about Italy's intentions in advance. The hard pressed Foreign Secretary played the unusual card of seeking the support of *The Times* for Britain's policy of inaction. Led by *The Times*, most of the Unionist press came into line. The war ended in October 1912 by the Treaty of Lausanne. For this example, and an earlier alleged interference with the press at Grey's direct instigation, see *The History of The Times*, vol. III, pp. 840–2. See further, W.C. Askew, *Europe and Italy's Acquisition of Libya, 1911–12, passim.*

Repington had first become a friend of Imperali in Brussels. See *Vestigia*, p. 175.

119 That which is already held or possessed.

120 Career diplomats.

121 Reginald Nicholson succeeded Moberly Bell as Manager of *The Times*, 1910–15.

122 Adolf Hermann Marschall von Bieberstein, formerly Germany's Foreign Minister from 1890–7, had been disgraced and sent as Ambassador to Constantinople. He died in 1912, before he could take up his new post in London. He had demonstrated at The Hague Peace Conference in 1907, that he was a skilled manipulator of the press, and consequently there was considerable apprehension that Marschall's arrival heralded a German attack upon the Triple Entente. Hence the determination not to appear to give in to him.

123 Sir Charles Harris went to the War Office in 1887 as a clerk, and was by turns Principal Clerk, 1900; Assistant Financial Secretary, 1908; Joint Secretary of the War Office and Permanent Head of the Finance Department. A key adviser of Haldane.

124 Lieutenant-General Sir Edward Cecil Bethune, commanded the West Lancashire Territorial Division, 1909–12; Director-General Territorial Forces, 1912–17.

125 In the summer and autumn of 1912, Lord Roberts, on behalf of the National Service League, made a series of great public orations in London, Norwich and Manchester, seeking to create a climate of public opinion favourable to national service. Radical critics argued that the octogenerian field marshal was seeking to arm the nation for a war of aggrandizement against Germany. Generally, however, the speeches appeared to have little or no effect upon opinion in Parliament. Those close to Roberts, and particularly Henry Wilson, concluded the most promising way to persuade the Government to accept a form of conscription was to demonstrate the inefficiencies and

incapacity of the Territorials. Others associated with this tactic were Milner, Lee and F.S. Oliver, but Wilson actually assisted Roberts with the preparation of his speeches. Undoubtedly, knowledge that Wilson was acting as Roberts's prompter did nothing to make Repington less temperate in his criticisms of Roberts's speeches, but the notes he sent Robinson fairly reflect his long term thinking, and support for the Territorials in particular.

On Roberts, see *Lord Roberts*, pp. 451–9. On Wilson's attitude and the part he played, see Callwell, *Field-Marshal Sir Henry Wilson*, vol. I, pp. 118–21.

126 Robinson, although very heavily committed at Printing House Square, had to rush to the funeral of an uncle. In the moments before catching his train he scribbled a note, 'frankly to admit that it was a mistake to admit the word "sham". It ought not to have escaped me because it is consistent neither with the policy of the paper in the past nor with my opinions now . . .' Dawson to Repington, 11 December 1912, The Times Archive, Robinson File.

127 The two articles Repington was in the process of revising, appeared in *The Times* on 6 and 7 February and bluntly asserted that the voluntary principle had failed. Further, that the Territorials were 50,000 short of their establishment, which in any event ought to be doubled to 600,000. The naval manoeuvres of 1912 had demonstrated that the number of troops required to resist successfully an invading force – determined by the 1907–8 invasion inquiry – were woefully insufficient. Only conscription could provide the numbers necessary. The articles were powerfully supported in a leader written by Robinson.

For Henry Wilson's less than enthusiastic response to Repington's 'rotten' articles, see his Diary entries in Callwell, for 9 and 14 February 1913.

128 On preparation of air defences and suitable anti-aircraft guns, see S.W. Roskill, *Documents relating to the Naval Air Service, 1908–1918, passim*. For a vivid popular account of Britain's unpreparedness for air defence at the beginning of the Great War, see H.G. Castle, *Fire over England*.

129 The debate held in the Lords on 11 February was long and acrimonious, and proved most unsatisfactory from Repington's point of view. Though he hated to do it, as he told Seely in a letter, his 'patriotic duty conflicted with the claims of private friendship' and dictated he censure both the Minister and Haldane for 'evading the point at issue'. It was 'simply deplorable' that there was 'no serious plan for completing the T.F.'. See Repington to Seely, 11 February 1913, Nuffield College Library, Oxford, Seely Papers, S.20/f. 153.

130 It has been argued that the 1913 invasion inquiry owed its inspiration to Repington's determination to temper the influence of Sir Henry Wilson's promotion of a full-blown continental strategy. See S.R. Williamson Jnr., *The Politics of Grand Strategy*, p. 306. But the more likely explanation was the lobbying by Churchill as a consequence of his concern caused by the

1912 naval manoeuvres combined with recent developments in naval armaments.

After the 1912 manoeuvres, Churchill, in a memorandum to the Prime Minister, Asquith, wrote, 'Nothing obviates the possibility of a determined enemy . . . making a series of simultaneous or successive descents upon different portions of the British coast and landing men in bodies of from 5000 to 10,000 strong.' This 'admission' was very different from the earlier Admiralty claims, frequently repeated, that the most the Germans could land in England would be a dinghy with five soldiers.

The 1912 naval manoeuvres when the Red Fleet, representing the Germans was judged to have landed successfully 12,000 troops, although only a theoretical exercise took the wind out of the sails of the Blue Water advocates who had recently argued that the Italian invasion of Tripoli proved their case. See H.R. Moon, 'The invasion of the United Kingdom, 1888–1914', pp. 430–3.

131 Esher's answer to Repington evaded the real issue. Asquith responded with obvious gratitude and congratulated Esher for blowing Repington's suggestion, 'completely out of the water . . . If Messrs Repington and Robinson desire to destroy the Monarchy they have certainly hit upon the best device for the purpose . . .' Asquith to Esher, 20 February 1913. On this issue, compare the accounts of Lees-Milne, pp. 242–4, and Peter Fraser, pp. 226–30.

132 André Tardieu, a popular journalist, wrote for *Le Temps*, a newspaper that was supposedly close to the thinking of the French Foreign Office. Tardieu had argued long and hard for the conversion of the Anglo-French entente into an alliance, but considered a necessary preliminary was for the British to adopt universal military service. The same message was as frequently rehearsed by Clemenceau and others of the French right wing who were overtly hostile towards Germany. Tardieu's loyalty was assured by payments from the French secret service fund. When these funds were discontinued on the orders of Briand, Tardieu suddenly discovered an unwonted affection for the Germans. He was obviously hoping to repeat his financial coup of December 1910, when a substantial German bribe had secured his 'revelation' of the so-called Potsdam Agreement. On this occasion, however, Tardieu was rewarded only with civility from the German Ambassador and ardently pressed by his creditors for the payment of bills run up by his current mistress, the journalist re-discovered his fondness for an anti-German line.

As both George Saunders and Repington had long been convinced of Germany's hostile intentions towards Britain, they were not really averse to Tardieu's advocacy of a belligerent policy, though neither wished the 'inevitable' hostilities promoted too soon by French chauvinists.

Repington's suggestion that he might improve relations between Tardieu and Saunders was inept and insensitive. George Saunders was a very senior colleague, sophisticated and knowledgeable, and known to be looking for an excuse to quit his post as *The Times* Paris correspondent. Some excuse can, however, be made for Repington. Saunders had been concerned at the tone of recent *Times* reports and leaders concerned almost exclusively as they were with military matters – the Balkan war, the need to strengthen the Territorials, the case for conscription, criticism of Liberal disarmament proposals, etc. Saunders feared the French Government might interpret this as the British Government encouraging a more belligerent line from their entente partners. Robinson was alarmed at this conception. As he told Saunders, his support of Repington's campaign had not been designed to place a British conscript army on the Franco-Belgium frontier. See Robinson to Saunders, 21 February 1913. At this juncture, Repington had suggested to his editor that he might visit France to speak with the French military authorities and inform them that it was not the British intention to force the pace militarily. Actually, the tone of *The Times* had been prompted both by events and also the declared wish of the proprietor, Northcliffe, that the paper's readers should be warned regularly that Europe was getting on a war footing. It was in this context that Repington suggested, and Robinson agreed, that it might be politic for Repington to use the visit to resolve relations between Saunders and Tardieu.

133 The driving force behind the interest in aviation shown by *The Times* was its proprietor, Northcliffe. He had been lobbying certain Ministers on the subject for years. However, in his papers, particularly in the *Daily Mail*, the presentation was sensationally alarmist. Thus H.G. Wells could write his warning, 'In spite of our fleet, this is no longer, from the military point of view, an inaccessible island.' The CID was actively engaged in examining the possibilities, both for attack and defence, of aeroplanes and airships, and keeping a wary eye upon aviation developments in Germany. See, further, Pound and Harmsworth, *Northcliffe*, pp. 324ff., and 352ff; and, *The Naval Air Service*, vol. I, documents quoted in Part 1, pp. 3–162. Cf. Repington's figures with those given officially in June 1913, CAB 37/115/35 at p. 89, 'The new German programme.'

134 Debates in both houses of Parliament on foreign and defence policy in this period, did not escape the intense prejudice and passion which divided the parties on the Ulster question. Everything was twisted to serve sectarian purpose, even the new invasion inquiry. Repington, in the twelve articles on invasion he wrote for *The Times* between April and May, repeatedly implied that the inquiry was designed to serve the purposes of the Radical wing of the Government. Esher seems to have shared this illusion, and Repington rewarded him with the description, 'the only independent member'.

135 Haldane was sadly notorious for the length and complexity of his speeches. When he spoke in the debate from the Woolsack, Curzon denounced the performance as a, 'triumph of circumlocution unequalled in the Lord Chancellor's long experience of such oratorical feats'. See, on this, and the debate generally from an informed Unionist viewpoint, Midleton, *Records and Reactions, 1856–1939*, pp. 284ff.

136 Alan Ian, Earl Percy served in the Grenadier Guards. He was an ardent conscriptionist and was a frequent contributor on military matters to Maxse's *National Review*. In 1918, he succeeded as the eighth Duke of Northumberland.

137 Repington was responding to a letter from Robinson written the previous day. 'I am rather concerned about the growing effect of the Government's Irish policy on the moral of the Army . . . I hear already of officers preparing to go and fight for Ulster, and others preparing to send in their papers . . . the kind of conversation which is going on in messes must be extremely prejudicial to the best interests of the Army . . . What do you think about it?' Robinson to Repington, 2 July 1913, The Times Archive, Repington Papers.

138 For confirmation of Repington's view of the committee and its proceedings, see various Diary entries of Henry Wilson, which are highly critical. 'I told Haldane I could not understand anyone going to a pantomime so long as the CID was sitting . . . I have never seen so incompetent a committee. *Far* too large.' And as might have been expected, he had a very poor opinion of Asquith's capacities as a chairman. 'What with drink, bridge and holding girls' hands, (he) is not capable of doing anything except drift.' Wilson Papers, Imperial War Museum.

139 John Walter II (1776–1847), who took over the chief proprietorship of *The Times* from his elder brother William in 1802, and changed a then dying news-sheet into a successful newspaper. He combined his business as a proprietor and printer with the editing, but in 1817, handed over this latter task to Thomas Barnes.

140 John Thadeus Delane (1817–79), was appointed editor of *The Times* aged twenty-three, retiring in 1877. He was generally recognised as that newspaper's greatest editor and a model to others. See E.T. Cook, *Delane of 'The Times'*.

141 G.S. Freeman, appointed an assistant to Buckle, was a supporter of Northcliffe and the reforms he instituted at Printing House Square. Then Night Editor he became Deputy Editor of *The Times* but did not succeed Steed as had been generally expected.

142 Repington wrote a series of four highly constructive as well as critical articles on the 1913 manoeuvres, beginning 30 September and ending 16 October. Of Sir John French, who had acted both as Exercise Director and commander of the British force, he wrote that he had experienced considerable difficulty in beating a weak enemy force. French dismissed this criticism in a letter to Esher as 'childish, <u>stupid</u> and inclined to rancour'. The truth was that the 1913 manoeuvres had given rise to proper concern, not only about the performance of French, but also of Haig who repeated his less than masterly conduct of the previous year. The consequence for the British Army's future was Haig was less confident of French, and Henry Wilson was confirmed in his poor opinion of Haig. The main immediate sufferer was Grierson who was replaced as CGS designate by Archibald

Murray. Murray did not really deserve Edmonds' description of him as 'a complete nonentity', but his was not the personality to curb the excesses of a mercurial character like French, and his health, fatally impaired by a wound suffered in South Africa, broke down under the strain of campaigning. See further, Richard Holmes, *The Little Field Marshal*, pp. 149–50. There is an illuminating account of the 1913 German manoeuvres in C.E. Callwell, *Stray Recollections*, vol. II, pp. 248ff.

The mistakes made in the immediate pre-war years were as nothing compared with those made from 1904 to 1910 when 'the General Staff were unable to select anyone who could organise manoeuvres . . . In 1910, in the great manoeuvres round Chislebury Ring, both sides became piled up on all sides of that eminence . . . The foreign military attachés were in fits of laughter.' James Edmonds, *Memoirs* (unpublished), Chapter XX, pp. 25–6, Edmonds Mss., III/5, Liddell Hart Centre for Military Archives, King's College, London.

143 Brigadier-General Charles Vere Ferrers Townshend was at the time Assistant Adjutant-General to the 9th Division in India.

144 On 23 December 1912, an attempt had been made on the life of the Viceroy. See an account of the event and consequences in Lord Birdwood, *Khaki and Gown*, pp. 222–3.

145 James Scorgie Meston had entered the Indian Civil Service in 1885.

146 Sir Lawrence Hugh Jenkins, since 1909 had been Chief Justice of the Bengal High Court.

147 Major-General Sir Percy Henry Noel Lake had been associated with the Canadian Army since 1893.

148 Seely's wife, to whom he was much attached, had died in August 1913. See further, his *Adventure*, p. 156.

149 Maid of all work.

150 The report was ready by April 1914. Despite Opposition pressure in the Commons that the results of the inquiry should be published, Asquith successfully prevaricated until after the outbreak of the war, and that despite frequent promises that a general statement was forthcoming and that an opportunity would be afforded the Commons for a general debate.

151 Repington's reference is to the annual quarrel occasioned by the debates over the naval estimates. As an overture to the estimates there had been a concerted attack by the Radical wing of the Liberal party – referred to slightingly by J.L. Garvin as 'The Suicide Club' – on the fevered, accelerating expansion of military establishments and armaments all over Europe. Their cause was enhanced by a speech from Lloyd George attacking the 'insanity . . . the overwhelming extravagance of our expenditure'. See further on this important subject, *Radicalism against War, 1906–14*, pp. 333–47.

152 A projected Anglo-American Arbitration Treaty, proposed by President Taft, to which Grey had responded enthusiastically, was mauled by the

American Senate. Jealous of its control over foreign affairs, the Senate struck out article III of the proposed Treaty which reduced its effect to that of the Convention that already existed between the two countries.

153 Arthur Hamilton Lee, later Viscount Lee of Fareham, had retired from the Army in 1900, and represented the Fareham Division of Hampshire as an Unionist MP.

154 Brigadier David Henderson of the Argyll and Sutherland Highlanders was a member of the Technical sub-committee of the CID standing sub-committee on Aerial Navigation set up in 1912, chaired by Seely.

155 The two articles which Repington wrote on the Ulster Volunteers were eventually published on 18 and 19 March. His writing emphasised the readiness, capacity and determination of the UVF to resist the Government if necessary. This confirmed opinions that had been available to Ministers for several months. See further, Patricia Jalland, *The Liberals and Ireland: the Ulster question in British politics to 1914*, p. 221.

156 At the end of a diary entry for 25 April 1914, Lord Riddell, the newspaper owner and close friend of Lloyd George, wrote, 'I hear that the Government action in Ulster was due to a private letter from Colonel Repington, military correspondent of *The Times*, to the P[rime] M[inister] who on receipt of it all called upon Seely to do what was necessary to protect the Government stores and ammunition. L.G., Masterman and Sir John French all admit that the letter was the cause of the Government's proceedings.' See *More Pages from my Diary, 1908–1914*, p. 210.

According to Asquith's Cabinet letter to the King at the relevant time, there is no mention of Repington, or any letter that he had sent the Prime Minister. It would have been the letter and not the articles that might have prompted the Liberal Government's action. See, Asquith to King, 18 March 1914, Asquith Papers, 7, ff. 105–6. Some have argued that Repington did not send a letter to Asquith, but the letter to Robinson of 9 March clearly indicates a letter had been sent. What is more, Repington apparently sent at least one further letter to Asquith during the crisis, for a letter from Asquith to Churchill, 22 March 1914, Churchill Papers, CHAR 2/63/19, states: 'I have just got the enclosed from Repington. If the thing is not going smoothly, I think there is a good deal to be said for calling in the *mitis sapientia* [mellow wisdom] of the Lord Chancellor, who is much regarded in the Army.'

The essential point is, whatever part Repington's letter did or did not play in influencing Asquith, it is clear that the Government was not engaged in a plot against Ulster at the instigation of Churchill and Seely – a Unionist charge promoted both by the *Daily Mail* (18 April) and *The Times* (27 April).

157 A.A. Brodribb was then head of *The Times* Parliamentary staff.

158 John Lawrence Baird was the Unionist MP for the Rugby division of Warwickshire which he had represented since 1910.

159 Mount Stewart, previously Mount Pleasant, built at the end of the eighteenth century, was the Ulster home of the Londonderrys, overlooking Strangford Lough and the Mournes. The magnificent gardens were largely the creation of Edith, the seventh Marchioness. The house and gardens are now owned by the National Trust.

160 We must take the rough with the smooth.

161 General Sir Arthur Paget and Lady Paget were great friends of Repington. During the Great War, as his published *Diary* indicates, he was a frequent weekend visitor to their home. Paget was one of the few senior officers whose career was blighted by the events at the Curragh, for, like Ewart, he was given no active command during the 1914–18 war.

162 A Royal Commission on fuel oil had been appointed at Churchill's instigation in 1912. Jacky Fisher was the energetic chairman. The final report was issued in February 1914. The recommendation confirmed that, in the future, oil would replace coal as the fuel for the Navy. This meant that there was an urgent need to acquire new oil fields. Thus, in August 1914, the Government completed the purchase for a little more than two million pounds sterling, procuring a controlling interest in the Anglo-Iranian Oil Company. The credit for promoting oil for the Navy belonged to Fisher, but it was Churchill who triumphantly secured parliamentary support despite the machinations of various opponents. See further, *From the Dreadnought to Scapa Flow: the road to war, 1906–14*, vol. I, pp. 269–71.

163 Colonel von Leipzig, a friend of the Kaiser. Their conversation is recounted in Repington's *First World War, 1914–1918*, vol. I, p. 18.

164 Johann Graf von Forgách had been Austria's representative in Belgrade from 1907 to 1911, and was section chief in the Austro-Hungarian Foreign Ministry, 1913–14. Repington's claim that Forgách was the author of the ultimatum was not true. On this, see the English edition of Fritz Fischer, *War of Illusions* (1975), pp. 480ff.

165 Leopold Graf von Brechtold was the Austro-Hungarian Foreign Minister from 1912 to 1915.

166 Repington's letter was enclosed by Hamilton when he wrote to Winston Churchill, 28 July 1914, Churchill Papers, CHAR 2/64/1.

167 The letter was written the same day as Repington published in *The Times* an article which gave an authoritative view of Kitchener's plans. The article arose from a conversation at Lady Wantage's house in Carlton Gardens. Kitchener had revised the article in proof and fully approved it. The meeting between minister and correspondent had been at Kitchener's request. It was the first and last time he would extend such a favour to any journalist for the rest of his life. Not unnaturally, the article aroused much public interest, for which, see *The First World War, 1914–1918*, vol. I, pp. 21–2.

168 Balfour was invited to attend the first war-time meeting of the Committee of Imperial Defence, 7 October 1914; and was the only Opposition front

bencher to attend the War Council which began meetings on 25 November 1914. See further, R.F.Mackay, *Balfour, Intellectual Statesman*, pp. 251–3.

169 Augereau was a trusted lieutenant of the young Bonaparte whose help during the coup d'état in Paris of 18th Fructidor (4 September 1797), successfully kicked out the Council members, temporarily restoring the authority of the Directorate.

170 The Press Bureau was based at the Royal United Services Institution. It censored newspaper reports and also provided official War Office reports of events. The press submitted their copy voluntarily to the Press Bureau, but publication in the face of the censors' declared disapproval made them liable to prosecution under the Defence of the Realm Acts. At the war's beginning the censors were unduly zealous and cautious and made some absurd judgments. See *The First World War, 1914–1918*, vol. I, p. 371. During 1914 Northcliffe's *Daily Mail* and *The Times* were the worst offenders in the national press against Press Bureau injunctions.

171 Unimaginative.

172 The confidential notes upon the Artillery and ammunition which Repington enclosed with his letter, were written by hand on four sheets of notepaper. A typed copy of these notes was made by Lloyd George's office.

173 Clearly what Repington intended to write was not 1913 but 1915. This, and the previous letter to Lloyd George, were written at the height of the Shell crisis. See further, *The First World War, 1914–1918*, vol. I, pp. 38–41.

174 As this note, eight pages in its original format, was written on 17 May, it suggests strongly that although he perceived the *immediate* political value of the artillery issue, he attached most *long-term* military significance to the question of man-power. His next public campaign concentrated upon 'the need for men and compulsory service'. As counterpoint, he wrote also on Germany's campaign in Russia which had begun on 1 May continuing well into September.

175 Lloyd George's reply on 8 July (D/18/6/4) suggested they meet for luncheon the following Tuesday at 11 Downing Street. During the next few months, these luncheon appointments were not an uncommon occurence.

176 Hilaire Belloc had sniped at Northcliffe and his *Daily Mail* as early as 1909, on that occasion accusing the press baron of scaremongering. Northcliffe affected indifference to Belloc's attacks on him as a 'public nuisance'. Not only Repington but Lovat Fraser and G.A.B. Dewar wrote to Northcliffe deprecating Belloc's attacks. Repington's claim that Belloc's *Land and Water* articles on the war had 'done much harm', was unfair and exaggerated. See further, A.N. Wilson, *Hilaire Belloc*, pp. 223–7; Robert Speaight, *The Life of Hilaire Belloc*, Chapter XVI.

177 Northcliffe, in his dictated, typed reply of 14 September, concurred with what Repington had said concerning conscription, and stated, 'I am perfectly certain that conscription will come.' In Scotland he noted 'every day . . . the sad sight of fine troops without rifles'.

Repington began his campaign for conscription in the columns of *The Times* in May 1915. By the autumn of 1915, the failure of the voluntary system of recruitment was apparent – especially after the heavy losses of the Battle of Loos.

178 A luncheon was arranged for the following Wednesday at 11 Downing Street. There is an account of the occasion and of the two men's conversation in *The First World War, 1914–1918*, vol. I, p. 45.

179 Four days later, Repington was writing in his *Diary*, after a conversation with Sir A.Murray, that 'Apparently the fate of Sir John French still hangs in the balance. I think that Sir William Robertson has the best chance of succeeding him.' (vol. I, p. 70) In his formal letter of resignation written three weeks later, French suggested William Robertson as his replacement, but Haig's succession was, by then, assured, and Robertson was heir apparent to become CIGS.

180 Although Haig's performance at these battles was not beyond reproach, Repington here is clearly attempting to turn away any criticism from French. The losses of 1915 were small compared with those of 1916 and 1917.

181 General Sir James Willcocks was, at the time, GOC the Indian Corps in France.

182 Repington's criticisms of Haig were both sound and pertinent. Haig's sad incapacity to communicate clearly by word of mouth was a particular disadvantage given that Kitchener was so taciturn.

183 See *The First World War, 1914–1918*, vol. I, pp. 69–70.

184 The name given to Germany's policy for involvement in Middle-Eastern affairs and particularly with the affairs of Turkey and her empire.

185 An Anglo-French expedition had landed at Salonika on October 5. The force, led by Generals Sarrail and Sir Bryan Mahon, at first advanced towards the Bulgarian border in the north, but within two months had been pushed back almost to Salonika.

The question in the Cabinet had been whether to send troops to reinforce those at Gallipoli, or send an army to Salonika to aid the Serbians. As things grew increasingly more bleak for the Allied cause, there was a change of French government, but not before Viviani, the outgoing Minister for War, had instructed Joffre to go to England and tell the British that the indeterminate behaviour of the previous weeks must cease. Accordingly, Joffre attended a Cabinet meeting where he made an impassioned speech for Salonika, and declared if there were any further delay he would resign his command. See Esher's *Journals and Letters*, vol. III, pp. 272–5.

Repington had been told on the 6th November by Murray, the CIGS, that it was Joffre who 'had compelled our people to go for the Salonika expedition'.

186 There is an extraordinarily vivid and intimate portrait of Kitchener at this time, detailing how haunted and uncertain he was, in Esher's *Journal* entries

for November 5 and 6 when he had two interviews with the war lord while he was in Paris.

187 There is no exact equivalent of the maxim in English. The nearest in spirit might be: 'It takes a thief to catch a thief.'

188 Ahmed Djemal was the commander of the Turkish First Army in Syria. In 1918 he fled to Turkey and four years later was assassinated by the Armenians

189 General Townshend, having captured the Turkish position at Ctesiphon, had been obliged, because of lack of water, to withdraw for four miles. Repington noted in his diary, 'if the Cabinet will send a weak division into the heart of a sub-continent, 600 miles from the sea, to fight a warlike people with a million soldiers, they are bound to get into trouble . . . It is also stupid to have fought before the two divisions came from France.' Repington supposed that had his advice, given earlier to the General Staff, been adopted, the retreat might have been avoided.

190 He had been asked by his editor to write a summary of the events of the year.

191 See the account of the meeting in *The First World War, 1914–1918*, vol. I, p. 92.

192 The advice was duly given a week later; to remain a journalist and not to be seduced by thoughts of entering Parliament. See, Northcliffe to Repington, 20 January 1916 (copy), Northcliffe Papers, Add. MSS., 62253, f. 54.

193 For an account of their conversation which was wide ranging, see *The First World War, 1914–1918*, vol. I, pp. 116–19.

194 George Freeman was first appointed to *The Times* as an assistant to G.E. Buckle. Subsequently he acted as deputy editor for Steed and for Robinson/Dawson for both the periods he served as editor.

195 John Grigg, Lloyd George's most perceptive biographer, entitles his chapter covering the latter half of 1916 when Lloyd George served as Minister for War before his appointment as Prime Minister (July to December 1916), 'Responsibility without Power'. Commenting upon Wully Robertson's dismissive estimate of Lloyd George's tenure of the War Office, Grigg instances as Lloyd George's 'most important contribution', persuading Haig to take Eric Geddes as Director General of Transportation in France. Geddes effected a dramatic improvement in transport systems behind the lines. See further, John Grigg, *Lloyd George: from peace to war, 1912–1916*, Chapter 14.

196 The construction of a Channel tunnel had been considered on two separate occasions before the war, in 1906 and 1914, by a sub-committee of the CID, and on both occasions had been rejected as inadvisable upon naval and military grounds. It was a subject to which Kitchener was particularly averse. See Lord Hankey, *The Supreme Command*, p. 108. Sir Arthur Fell was the Unionist MP for Great Yarmouth, 1906–22. He was President of the Commons Channel Tunnel Committee and a prolific pamphleteer on the subject. See further, Keith Wilson, *Channel Tunnel Visions, 1850–1945*, pp. 55–88.

197 The leader in the *Daily Mail*, 13 October 1916, was a message from Northcliffe, in which he referred to, 'mad, wild expeditions in distant places', and protested against the weakening of British forces in France. With a splendid inversion of reality he actually suggested: 'If we continue to grind into the public mind the terrible fact that political interference means an increase of the death toll of our Army, Sir Douglas Haig and Sir William Robertson will not be worried as they are at the moment.' Northcliffe was busily engaged in a crusade demanding the politicians keep their 'Hands off the Army'. Consequently he was very popular at British HQ, and particularly so when it became known he had personally warned Lloyd George not to interfere with strategic affairs.

198 A piece of gross flattery which Northcliffe would have enjoyed, and which he almost certainly believed was the true measure of his influence, for he told Haig that Lloyd George acted as he advised. See, Haig to Lady Haig, 11 September 1916, Robert Blake (Ed), *The Private Papers of Douglas Haig, 1914–1919*, p. 166. Northcliffe replied that as he was watching the Government very closely, he did not think they would be able to do anything very suddenly. He thought that were he to join the Government, 'I should lose what little influence I have. The people will never tolerate a newspaper owner being a member of the Government.' Northcliffe to Repington, 18 October 1916 (Copy), Northcliffe Papers, Add. MSS., 62253, f. 83.

199 It would have suited the soldiers had Austen Chamberlain and not Lloyd George been given the War Office. But in any event, Bonar Law would not have accepted such promotion for Chamberlain. Offered the Ministry of Munitions which Lloyd George was quitting, Austen refused. Not illness threatened Chamberlain's tenure in the Cabinet but his desire to see conscription introduced. As it happened, Asquith trumped Chamberlain with the Derby Scheme, See further David Dutton, *Austen Chamberlain: gentleman in politics*, pp. 127–9. See also Edward David (Ed) *Inside Asquith's Cabinet: from the Diaries of Charles Hobhouse*, p. 255.

200 Responding to Repington's secret memorandum, Northcliffe suggested that insufficient allowance had been made 'for the very bad state of affairs in Germany'. The country would 'face a very severe winter and increasing food and fertiliser difficulties'. Also, that Repington ought to 'urge more "combing out"'. Northcliffe was aware of hundreds of suitable young men in his neighbourhood. 'At the golf club there are two young professionals who, though exempt on medical grounds, are both able to play three rounds of golf a day.' Northcliffe to Repington, 18 October 1916 (copy), Northcliffe Papers, Add. MSS., 62253, f. 96.

201 See entry for Monday 16 October 1916, in *The First World War, 1914–1918*, pp. 361–6.

202 Hird and Love were employees at Printing House Square. It was usually Northcliffe, rather than the editor, who sought to gain what he judged a more suitable position to match a man's talents in the Services.

203 Sir William Guy Granet, the former general manager of the Midland Railway company, was appointed Controller of Import Restrictions in 1915, and in 1917 became Director General of Movements and Railways with membership of the Army Council.

204 Sir Sam Fay, who had been general manager of the Great Central Railways was made Director of Movements at the WO, 1917–18, and then Director General of Movements and Railways and a member of the Army Council, 1918–19.

205 Harold Sidney Harmsworth, created Viscount Rothermere in 1919, brother of Northcliffe and like him, a newspaper proprietor, was appointed Director General of the Army clothing department, 1916–17; and the Minister for Air, 1917–18.

206 Geddes was actually Professor of Anatomy and Principal of McGill University, Montreal.

207 Northcliffe informed Repington that he had received a letter from Sassoon stating that the Army 'would like to have' Repington 'see the extraordinary aftermath of the Battle of the Somme', and that he might visit Haig and stay with Gough and Rawlinson. See Northcliffe to Repington, 4 April 1917 (copy), Northcliffe Papers, Add. MSS., 62253, f. 106.

208 See *The First World War, 1914–1918*, vol. I, p. 508.

209 Robertson had been asked by the Prime Minister to speak to two thousand trade unionists gathered at the Westminster Hall. Repington had discussed the content of the speech with Robertson on the previous Saturday, 31 March.

210 The manpower figures as Repington supposed them to be, he wrote up in his diary for 1 April, ending with the observation, 'The country knows absolutely nothing at all of all these facts, and I cannot tell them.'

211 Haig's success on the first day of the Battle of Arras, in particular, the Canadian attack on Vimy Ridge, was an amazing contrast with the fortunes of the first day of the Somme, less than ten months earlier. However, missed opportunities meant that by the third day, and even before the French under Nivelle had launched their ill-fated attack along the Aisne, the British forces were back to the old familiar story of a series of very limited advances after hard fighting.

212 From a letter Robertson wrote that same day to Douglas Haig, it would appear that the CIGS was not very sanguine about the likely success of his suggested scheme. 'We are going to try to get men as drafts for our own units and have already a recruiting party in Canada waiting for the word to go, but I doubt if the American Senate will stand it. I am also urging them to send some troops to France at once even if only a brigade. It would be a good thing to get some Americans killed and so get the country to take a real interest in the war.' See Robertson to Haig, 10 April 1917, in D.R. Woodward (Ed), *The Military Correspondence of Sir William Robertson, CIGS*, pp. 168–9.

213 Repington had left England for France on the evening of 17 April. There is a detailed account of his visit in *The First World War, 1914–1918*, vol. I, pp. 519ff. Haig recorded in his Diary, 'Repington came to dinner and stayed night. A very conceited man.' See *The Private Papers of Douglas Haig*, p. 219. There is more than enough evidence in the letters to demonstrate Repington's fine conceit for his own opinions. What is interesting is the way that Haig, equally fond of his own opinion, absolved himself of the same fault. He wrote to his wife: 'I am being used as a tool in the hands of the Divine Power . . . my strength is not my own, so I am not at all conceited . . .' Haig to Lady Haig, 20 April 1917, quoted, Gerard J. de Groot, *Douglas Haig, 1861–1928*, p. 312.

214 During the so-called 'Black Fortnight' (17 to 30 April 1917) almost 400,000 tons of British shipping were lost to German U-Boat action. On 22 April, in a paper to the Cabinet, Jellicoe effectively added his voice to that of the Generals, demanding a concentration of commitments that were currently absorbing much naval effort – like Salonika. The navy's problem was then in the process of being solved by the adoption of the convoy system. See *From the Dreadnought to Scapa Flow*, vol. IV, pp. 146–50; Stephen Roskill, *Earl Beatty: an intimate biography*, Chapter 10, *passim*; for the German submariner point of view, John Terraine, *Business in Great Waters*, Part I.

215 A delayer, after the Roman dictator, Fabius Cunctator, who employed delaying tactics successfully to frustrate Hannibal. His strategy was misunderstood by the Roman populace. The resignation of Fabius was swiftly followed by the rout of the battle of Cannae, 216 BC.

216 A speech made at the Mansion Hall, 28 April 1917, on receipt of the Freedom of the City of London. See A.J.P. Taylor (Ed), *Lloyd George: a diary by Frances Stevenson* , pp. 155–7.

217 Murray's letter is quoted verbatim in *The First World War, 1914–1918*, vol. I, pp. 563–5.

Repington was particularly close to Murray, describing him as one of 'my oldest and most valued soldier friends'. Murray's fitness for command was questioned by senior officers. Replaced by Robertson as CIGS, Murray took command in Egypt to be stripped almost immediately of nine of his fourteen divisions. They were required for the Somme offensive. After some initial success against the Turks, Murray failed to take Gaza and was replaced by Allenby, a general for whom Repington had much respect. Allenby corresponded with Repington, and it is interesting to note that by the same post that Repington received Murray's last letter from Egypt, 18 May 1917, he also received letters from Generals Maud and Birdwood.

Repington thought that Murray had been treated badly though he was given the Aldershot command. There, the military correspondent frequently visited him.

218 The original letter is wrongly dated October. See *The First World War, 1914–1918*, vol. II, p. 128. Geoffrey Robinson had changed his name to

Dawson at the beginning of August 1917. See Wrench, *Geoffrey Dawson and Our Times*, p. 146 and footnote.

219 A man who has lost his reputation.

220 The Earl and Countess of Scarborough. Major-General Alfred Frederick George Beresford Lumley Scarborough, from 1917 to 1921 was Director General of Territorial and Volunteer Forces.

221 Allenby had captured the first Turkish line of defence at Gaza and had beaten off Turkish counter attacks with heavy enemy losses.

222 Repington shared the general military opinion that the Allied Advisory Committee had been set up effectively to hand control of strategy to Lloyd George. He warned his editor, but described Dawson's leader on the subject as 'wobbling'. Hence, Repington's anxiety to capture the ear of the owner of *The Times*. Northcliffe almost immediately departed for a trip to Paris and Repington was not able to have his meeting. See the note from Northcliffe's Private Secretary to Repington, 4 December 1917 (copy), Northcliffe Papers, Add. MSS., 62253, f. 120.

Biographical Notes

Note: the ranks and titles given are the highest achieved. The biographical information emphasises events for the years Repington worked for *The Times*.

Agnew, William Lockett (1858–1917), Head of Thomas Agnew and Sons, Art Dealers; a close friend of Repington.

Aitken, William Maxwell (1879–1964), cr. Baron Beaverbrook, 1917; Unionist MP. 1910–16; newspaper proprietor, bought the *Daily Express* in 1916; Chancellor of the Duchy of Lancaster and Minister of Information, 1918; a friend of Lloyd George and Winston Churchill he served as a Minister in both world wars.

Alexeieff, General Mikhail Vasilevich (1857–1918), Russian Chief of Staff of Southwestern Army Group in Galicia; Commander Northwestern Front, March 1915; Chief of Staff to Tsar Nicholas II, September 1915; C-in-C, March to May 1917 when dismissed.

Allenby, Field Marshal Sir Edmund Henry Hynman (1861–1936), cr. Viscount, 1919; Inspector of Cavalry, 1910–14; Commander of Cavalry, 1914; Commander Fifth Army Corps, 1915; Commander Third Army, 1915–17; C-in-C Egyptian Expeditionary Force, 1917–19.

Amery, Leopold Charles Maurice Stennett (1873–1955), member of staff of *The Times*, 1899–1909; principal contributor to *The Times' History of the War in South Africa*, (1900–9); preceded Repington as main writer on military affairs at Printing House Square; Unionist MP for South Birmingham, 1911–18; Assistant Secretary to the Cabinet, 1917; member of Lord Milner's personal staff, 1917–18; a prolific polemicist on military and imperial affairs.

Ardagh, Major-General Sir John Charles (1840–1907), Director of Military Intelligence, 1896–1901, military advisor to British delegation at The Hague Peace Conference, 1899.

Arnold-Forster, Hugh Oakley (1855–1909), Unionist MP for West Belfast, 1892–1906; for Croydon, 1906–9; Secretary to the Admiralty, 1900–3; Minister for War, 1903–5; a public and private opponent of Repington.

Arthur, Sir George Compton Archibald (1860–1946), Kitchener's private secretary, 1914–16, and subsequently author of the official life; Assistant to the DMO, 1916–18.

Asquith, Herbert Henry (1852–1928), cr. Earl, 1925; Liberal MP for East Fife, 1896–1918; Home Secretary, 1892–5; Chancellor of the Exchequer, 1905–8; Prime Minister, 1908 to December 1916.

Asquith, Margot (née Tennant) (1864–1945) wife of Prime Minister Asquith whom she married in 1892; diarist.

Astor, Waldorf (1879–1952), 2nd. Viscount, Unionist MP. for Plymouth, 1910–19, owner of the *Observer*.

Bacon, Admiral Sir Reginald Hugh Spencer (1863–1946), Fisher's naval assistant, 1905; Director of Naval Ordnance and Torpedoes, 1907–9; Managing Director Coventry Ordnance Works, 1909; started the submarine service; a dedicated Fisherite and Fisher's biographer.

Bairnsfather, Bruce (Charles) (1888–1959), artist and journalist; served as Captain in the Royal Warwicks, 1914–16; creator of 'Old Bill', probably best known cartoonist of Great War.

Balfour, Arthur James (1848–1930), cr. Earl, 1922; Unionist MP for Hertford, 1874–85; East Manchester, 1885–1906; City of London, 1906–22; leader of the Unionist Party, 1891–1911; Prime Minister, 1902–5, during which period he created the Committee of Imperial Defence; First Lord of the Admiralty, 1915–16; Foreign Secretary, 1916–1919.

Bathurst, Countess Lilias Margaret Frances (1874/5(?)–1965), daughter of Baron Glenesk and succeeded him as owner of *Morning Post* in 1908. She sold the property in 1924.

Battenberg, Prince Louis Alexander of (1854–1921), cr. Marquess of Milford Haven, 1917; Director of Naval Intelligence, 1902–5; First Sea Lord, 1912–14; Admiral of the Fleet, 1921.

Beaverbrook, see Aitken.

Beckett, Earnest William (1856–1917), Baron Grimthorpe, 1905; Unionist MP for Whitby, 1885–1905; a banker, honorary Colonel of the Yorkshire Hussars, member of the Free Food League, close associate of Winston Churchill in his early parliamentary campaigns.

Bedford, Herbrand Arthur Russell, Duke of (1858–1940), Colonel of the Third Battalion of the Bedfordshire Militia; a member of Esher's committee on the Territorials.

Bell, Charles Frederic Moberly (1847–1911), Assistant Manager of *The Times*, 1890–1908; Manager, 1908–11; generally the most sympathetic supporter of Repington within the old Printing House Square hierarchy.

Belloc, Hilaire Réné (1870–1953), Radical Liberal MP for South Salford, 1906–10; a prodigious writer on a wide variety of topics, on all of which he considered himself an expert. His commentaries on the progress of the Great War in *Land and Water* became the subject of widespread distrust.

Beresford, Admiral Lord Charles William de la Poer (1846–1919), 'Charlie B', Second in command Mediterranean Fleet, 1900–2; Commander of the Channel Squadron, 1903–5; C-in-C. Atlantic Fleet, 1905; of the Mediterranean Fleet, 1905–7; of the Channel Fleet, 1907–09; Unionist MP at various times between various sea-going commands, for Waterford, 1874–80; Marylebone, 1885–9; York, 1898–1900; Woolwich, 1902–3; Portsmouth, 1910–16; from 1902, an ardent critic of Fisher and an important ally of Roberts and Repington in the Invasion Inquiry.

Birdwood, Field Marshal Sir William Riddell (1865–1951), cr. Baron, 1938; Military Secretary to Kitchener in South Africa, 1902; and in India, 1905; GOC Australian and New Zealand Army Corps, 1914–18.

Bowles, Thomas Gibson (1842–1922), 'Cap'n Tommy', former war correspondent who founded and edited *Vanity Fair*, was recognised as an authority on naval questions; a very independent Unionist MP for King's Lynn, 1892–1906.

Brackenbury, General Sir Henry (1837–1914), Director of Military Intelligence, 1886–91; Director General of Ordnance, 1899–1904.

Bridge, Admiral Sir Cyprian Arthur George (1839–1924), in his retirement, the most relentless opponent of Fisher's Dreadnought battleship building policy; Repington had a good opinion of him because of earlier cooperation in the 1890s.

Bridgeman, Admiral Sir Francis Charles (1848–1929), C-in-C Home Fleet, 1907–9; First Sea Lord, 1911–12.

Brodrick, William St John Freemantle (1856–1942), Viscount Midleton, 1907; Unionist MP for Surrey, 1880–1906; as Minister for War, 1900–3, Repington considered him an absolute disaster; Secretary of State for India, 1903–5.

Brussiloff, General Alexey Alexeyevitch (1853–1926), Commander of the Russian Army that invaded Galicia; appointed by the Soviet in May 1917 to replace General Alexeieff as Russian C-in-C.

Buckle, George Earle (1854–1935), Editor of *The Times*, 1884–1912.

Buller, General Sir Redvers Henry (1839–1908), VC, C-in-C in South Africa at the beginning of the Boer War when Repington served on his staff.

Burns, John Elliot (1858–1943), Lib-Lab MP for Battersea, 1892–1918; President of the Local Government Board, 1906–14; President of the Board of Trade, March 1914 to August 1914, when he, together with Morley, resigned from the Cabinet on the outbreak of war.

Byng, Field Marshal Sir Julian Hedworth George (1862–1935), cr. Viscount, 1926; Commander Third Cavalry Division, 1914–15; of the Cavalry Corps, 1915; Ninth Army Corps, 1915–16; Seventeenth Army Corps, 1916; Canadian Corps, 1916–17; Third Army, 1917–19.

Cairnes, William Elliot (1862–1902), the prolific, iconoclastic military correspondent who preceded Repington on the *Westminster Gazette*. The anonymous author of the influential *An absent-minded War* (1900). Served as secretary to the War Office Committee on the education of officers.

Callwell, Major-General Sir Charles Edward (1859–1928), a colleague of Repington in Intelligence, 1887–92; retired from the Army in 1909 but recalled in 1914; DMO and I, 1914–16; Adviser on ammunition to the Ministry of Munitions, 1916–18; a sympathetic censor and source of information for Repington; military historian.

Cambon, Pierre (1843–1924), French Ambassador to the Court of St James, 1898–1920.

Cambridge, Field Marshal HRH Prince George William Frederick Charles, Duke of, (1819–1904), last royal prince to be Commander-in-Chief, preceding Lord Wolseley.

Campbell-Bannerman, Sir Henry (1836–1908), Liberal MP for Stirling Burghs, 1868–1908; Liberal leader, 1899–1908; Prime Minister, 1905–8; managed to unite his party; not so great a Radical in foreign affairs as Radical Liberals supposed, always remained suspicious of the powers of the Committee of Defence.

Carson, Sir Edward Henry (1854–1935), cr. Life Peer as Lord of Appeal, 1921; Unionist MP for Dublin University, 1892–1918; Solicitor General, 1900–5; Leader of the Irish Unionists in the Commons, 1910–21; Attorney-General, 1915–16; First Lord of the Admiralty, 1916–17; member of the War Cabinet until January 1918.

Cecil, Lord Hugh Richard Heathcote (1869–1956), 'Linky', Unionist MP for Greenwich, 1895–1906; Oxford University, 1910–37.

Chamberlain, Joseph (1836–1914), 'Joe', Unionist MP for West Birmingham, 1885–1914; in turn broke the Liberal party over Home Rule in 1886, and the Unionists over Free Trade and Tariff Reform; totally incapacitated by a stroke in 1906.

Chamberlain, Sir Joseph Austen (1865–1937), Unionist MP for East Worcester, 1892–1914; Birmingham East, 1914–37; Civil Lord of the Admiralty, 1895–1900; Financial Secretary to the Treasury, 1900–2; Postmaster-General, 1902–3; Chancellor of the Exchequer, 1903–5; in 1911, together with Walter Long, stood down in favour of Andrew Bonar Law as Unionist leader; that rarest of *rara avis* in politics, a gentleman.

Chapman, General Sir Edward Francis (1840–1919), Director of Military Intelligence, 1891–96; Repington's enlightened chief.

Chirol, Sir Ignatius Valentine (1852–1929), Clerk at Foreign Office, 1872–6; travelled and occasional correspondent, 1876–92; Berlin correspondent of *The Times*, 1892–6; succeeded Sir Donald Mackenzie Wallace as Head of the Foreign Department, 1899; an authority on the Middle and Far East, Chirol distrusted Repington's championship of Kitchener in India; appointed to Board of Times Publishing Co., 1908; retired, 1912.

Churchill, Sir Winston Leonard Spencer (1874–1965), 'Winston', Unionist MP for Oldham, 1900–4; Liberal MP for Oldham, 1904–6; Manchester, 1906–8; Dundee, 1908–22; Home Secretary, 1910–11; First Lord of the Admiralty, 1911–15; Chancellor Duchy of Lancaster, 1915; Minister of Munitions, 1917–19; served as a war correspondent; prisoner of war during Boer War; served Western Front, 1915–16; was associated closely with Repington in early parliamentary campaigns censuring Unionist Ministers for War; never despised Repington's good opinion of his capacity for grand strategy.

Clarke, Sir George Sydenham (1848–1933), cr. Baron Sydenham, 1913; served as secretary to a variety of War Office committees including reorganisation, 1900–1; Governor of Victoria, 1901–4; Secretary to the Committee of Imperial Defence, 1904–7; Governor of Bombay, 1907–13; writer on military, naval and imperial subjects to *The Times*, 1885–1901; initially supported Repington's appointment at Printing House Square, but subsequently allied himself with Valentine Chirol as an opponent.

Clausewitz, General Carl von (1780–1831), soldier, philosopher and most influential of military thinkers, author of *On War*.

Colomb, Sir John Charles Ready (1838–1909), served Royal Marine Artillery, 1854–69; Unionist MP for Tower Hamlets, 1862–92; Great Yarmouth, 1895–1906; wrote *The Defence of Great and Greater Britain*; influential thinker upon naval strategy.

Colomb, Philip Howard (1831–1899), author of *Naval Warfare* (1891); a frequent and invariably lengthy letter writer to *The Times*; less influential on naval strategic thinking than his younger brother.

Craig, Captain James (1872–1940), cr. Viscount Craigavon, 1927; Ulster Unionist leader and MP for two Co. Down constituencies, 1906–21; Prime Minister of Northern Ireland, 1921–40.

Cromer, Evelyn Waring (1841–1917), cr. Earl, 1901; Agent and Consul General for Egypt, 1883–1907; offered but declined the Foreign Office in 1905; Chairman of the Dardanelles Commission, 1916–17.

Curzon, George Nathaniel (1859–1925), cr. Earl, 1911; Unionist MP for Southport, 1886–98; Viceroy and Governor-General of India, 1898–1905; Lord Privy Seal, 1915–16; Lord President of the Council, 1916–19; Leader of the House of Lords, 1916–25.

Custance, Admiral Sir Reginald Neville (1847–1935), DNI, 1899–1902; an unrelenting critic of Fisher's naval reforms; Repington had a good opinion of the Admiral from earlier joint intelligence work in the late 1890s.

Dallas, Major-General Alister Grant (1866–1931), Mobilization Staff War Office, 1902–5; Military Training Staff War Office, 1905–7; Commandant School of Musketry, S. Africa, 1907–11; Military Ops Staff War Office, 1911–14; Chief of Staff IV Corps, Jan. to Aug. 1915; Commander 32 Infantry Brigade, Gallipoli, 1915–16; Commander 53 Divison Egypt, 1916–17; Commander 71 Division Home Forces, 1917–18.

Davies, General Sir Francis John (1864–1948), Intelligence Staff War Office, 1902–6; Chief of Staff, Aldershot, 1910–12; Director Staff Duties, 1913–14; Commander 8 Division BEF, 1914–15; Commander VIII Corps, Gallipoli, 1915–16; Military Secretary War Office, 1916–19; C-in-C Scottish Command, 1919–23.

Dawson, George Geoffrey (1874–1944), 'Robin', changed name to Dawson in 1917; friend and disciple of Milner, was twice editor of *The Times*, succeeding G.E.Buckle in September 1912, and resigning in February 1919 after constant differences with Northcliffe; his former good relations with Repington deteriorated during the war years.

Derby, Edward George Villiers Stanley, seventeenth Earl of (1865–1948), Unionist MP for West Houghton division of Lancashire, 1892–1906; PMG, 1903–5; Director-General of Recruiting, October 1915; Under Secretary at War Office, July–December, 1916; Minister for War, 1916–18; Ambassador to France, 1918–20; Minister for War, 1922–4.

Dickson-Poynder, Sir John Poynder (1866–1936), cr. Baron Islington, 1910; Unionist, then Liberal MP for Chippenham, 1892–1910; Governor of New Zealand, 1910–12.

Dilke, Sir Charles Wentworth (1843–1911), Radical Liberal MP for Chelsea, 1868–86; Forest of Dean, 1892–1911; author of *Greater Britain*; ministerial career ruined by being cited as co-respondent in the divorce case of a fellow MP, Donald Crawford, in 1886; one of the few authorities on military and naval concerns in the Commons; a strong advocate of 'Blue Water' ideas.

Douglas, General Sir Charles Whittingham Horsley (1850–1914), Adjutant-General and second military member of the Army Council, 1904–09; GOC, Southern Command, 1909–12; Inspector General of Home Forces, 1912–14; replaced Sir John French as CIGS in March 1914, but died from over-work, October 1914.

Dundonald, Lieutenant-General Douglas Mackinnon Baillie Hamilton Cochrane, twelfth Earl of (1852–1935), commanded Canadian Militia, 1902–4; Hon. Colonel of 91st Canadian Highlanders.

Ellison, Lieutenant-General Sir Gerald Francis (1861–1947), Secretary to the War Office Reconstruction Committee, 1904–5; Haldane's Principal Military Private Secretary, and as such played a crucial part in designing and implementing military reform, 1905–8; Director of Army Organisation at Headquarters, 1908–11.

Erroll, Colonel Charles Gore Hay, 19th Earl of (1852–1927); one time ADC to Lord Wolseley.

Esher, Reginald Baliol Brett, Second Viscount (1852–1930), Liberal MP for Penryn and Falmouth, 1880–5; permanent member of the Committee of Imperial Defence, 1905–18; President of London County Territorial Force Association, 1912–21; Liaison Officer between French and British War Offices, 1915; the intimate of everybody who was anybody; confidant of the royal family; an adviser and political fixer who always preferred power without responsibility; the quintessential *éminence grise*; sought Repington's public support for his proposed reforms.

Ewart, General Sir John Spencer (1861–1930), Military Secretary at the War Office, 1906; DMO, 1906–10; AG, 1910–14; GOC, Scotland, 1914–18; a 'thinking' soldier.

Falkenhayn, Lieutenant-General Erich von (1861–1922), Prussian Minister of War, 1914–16; C of GS to the German Army in the field.

Fisher, Admiral Sir John Arbuthnot (1841–1920), 'Jacky', cr. Baron of Kilverstone, 1909; British naval delegate at first Hague Peace Conference, 1899; C-in-C Mediterranean, 1899–1902; Second Sea Lord, 1902–3; C-in-C Portsmouth, 1903–4; First Sea Lord, 1904–10 and 1914–15; father of the 'Dreadnought', creator of the modern navy; a great manipulator of the Press; hated Repington whom he totally misunderstood.

Foch, Marshal Ferdinand (1851–1929); Commander of the Ninth Army at the Marne, September 1914; Commander of the Armies of the North until deprived of command after Battle of the Somme, 1915–16; recalled as Allied Generalissimo, April to November 1918.

Fraser, Lovat (1871–1926), Editor of *The Times of India*, 1902–6; member of the editorial staff of *The Times*, 1907–22.

French, Field Marshal Sir John Denton Pinkstone (1852–1925), cr. Viscount, 1915; Earl of Ypres, 1921; GOC, Aldershot, 1902–7; CIGS 1911–14; C-in-C British Expeditionary Force, 1914–15; C-in-C Home Forces, 1916–18; Lord Lieutenant of Ireland, 1918–21; closely associated with Repington over the 'Shell Scandal' of 1915.

Garvin, James Louis (1868–1947), 'Jim', 'Garve', most distinguished Tory journalist and editor, made his name and the *Observer* newspaper synonymous; a trenchant polemicist who, at the behest of Milner and Astor helped to discredit Repington in 1918; at various times helped Fisher, Roberts and Balfour with propaganda for the navy, the army and the Tory party.

Geddes, Sir Auckland Campbell (1879–1954), cr. Baron, 1942; Assistant Adjutant-General, GHQ, France, 1915–16; Director of Recruiting at the War Office, 1916–17; Minister for National Service, 1917–19; Unionist MP for Basingstoke and Andover, 1917–20.

Geddes, Sir Eric Campbell (1875–1937), Deputy Director General Munitions Supply, 1915–16; Inspector General of Transportation, 1916–17; Unionist MP for Cambridge, 1917–22; First Lord of the Admiralty, 1917–18; Member of the War Cabinet, 1918.

George, David Lloyd (1863–1945), cr. Earl, 1945; Liberal MP for Caernarvon Boroughs, 1890–1945; President of the Board of Trade, 1905–8; Chancellor of the Exchequer, 1908–14; Minister for Munitions, 1915–16; Secretary of State for War, 1916; Prime Minister, 1916–22; used Repington in 1915/16 and then abused him.

Gleichen, Major-General Count Albert Edward Wilfred (1863–1937), military attaché in Berlin, 1903–06; in Washington, 1906; Assistant DMO, 1907–11; Commander of Fifteenth Infantry Brigade, 1911–15.

Gorton, Brigadier-General Reginald St George (1866–1944) Intelligence Staff War Office, 1902–7; Military Operations Staff War Office, 1909–12; Assistant Secretary CID, 1912–14; various staff appointments during war becoming Chief of Staff 59 Division France, 1916–18, Adjutant-General's Staff, War Office, April to September 1918.

Gough, Lieutenant-General Sir Hubert de la Poer (1870–1963), 'Goughie'; commanded Third Cavalry Brigade, 1914; Involvement in Curragh incident did not hinder his career; command of Second Cavalry Division, 1915; First Army Corps, 1916; Fifth Army, 1916–18; removed from command after German successes of March 1918; was supported by Repington who blamed German breakthrough upon politicians and not the military leadership.

Grey, Sir Edward (1862–1933), cr. Viscount, 1916; Liberal Imperialist MP for Berwick-on-Tweed, 1885–1916; Foreign Secretary, 1905–16.

Grierson, Lieutenant-General Sir James Moncrieff (1859–1914), military attaché Berlin, 1896–1900; DMO, 1904–6; Commander First Division Aldershot, 1906–10; GOC, Eastern Command, 1910–14; died on active service, August, 1914.

Grigg, Edward William Macleay (1879–1955), member of editorial staff at Printing House Square, 1903–5 and 1908–13; Assistant Editor of *Outlook*, 1905–6; served with Grenadier Guards, 1914–18.

Grove-Hills, Colonel Edmond Herbert (1864–1922) – known as Hills until 1920; retired from Army in 1905 to contest Portsmouth unsuccessfully as a Unionist parliamentary candidate; FRS, 1911; a distinguished military geographer.

Gwynne, Howell Arthur (1865–1950), 'Taffy', Editor of the *Standard*, 1904–11; Editor of the *Morning Post*, 1911–37; took on Repington as the *Post*'s military correspondent, despite the reservations of the proprietor, Lady Bathurst.

Haig, Field Marshal Sir Douglas (1861–1928), cr. Earl, 1919; Inspector General, Cavalry, India, 1903–6; Director of Military Training, 1906–7; Director of Staff Duties at HQ, 1907–9; Chief of Staff, India, 1909–12; GOC Aldershot, 1912–14; Commander First Army, 1914–15; C-in-C British Expeditionary Force, 1915–19.

Haldane, Elizabeth Sanderson (1862–1937), 'Bay', philosopher; founder of the Territorial Nursing Service, devoted much of her life to the care of her brother.

Haldane, General Sir James Aylmer Lowthrop (1862–1950), Lord Haldane's cousin; Intelligence Staff War Office, 1901–3 and 1906–9; attached to Japanese Army in Manchuria, 1904–5; Chief of Staff, Eastern Command, 1909–12; Commander 10 Brigade Eastern Command, 1912–14; Commander 10 Infantry Brigade BEF, Aug. to Nov. 1914; Commander 3rd Division, France, 1914–16; Commander VI Army Corps French/British Army on the Rhine, 1916–19.

Haldane (née Burdon Sanderson), Mary Elizabeth (1825–1925), mother of Richard Haldane; both absolutely devoted to each other; from 1877 he sent her a daily letter.

Haldane, Richard Burdon (1856–1928), cr. Viscount, 1911; Liberal MP for East Lothian; 1885–1912; Secretary of State for War, 1905–12; Lord Chancellor, 1912–15; valued but did not over value his connection with Repington who generally provided favourable publicity for the Minister's schemes of reform.

Hamilton, General Sir Ian Standish Monteith (1853–1947), Military Secretary, 1900–3; QMG, 1903–4; GOC-in-C Southern Command, 1905–9; Adjutant-General, 1909–10; GOC-in-C Mediterranean and Inspector General Overseas, 1910–14; Commander of the Dardanelles Expedition 1915; a long time friend of Repington.

Hankey, Maurice Pascal Alers (1877–1963), cr. 1st. Baron, 1939; Secretary to the CID, 1912–38.

Hardie, James Keir (1856–1915), Labour MP for West Ham, 1892–95; Merthyr Tydfil and Aberdare, 1900–15; Labour party leader in the Commons, 1906–8; leading pacifist and anti-Imperialist.

Hardinge, Sir Charles (1858–1914), cr. Baron, 1910; Ambassador to St Petersburg, 1904–6; Permanent Under Secretary of State for Foreign Affairs, 1906–10 and 1916–20; Viceroy of India, 1910–16.

Harmsworth, *see* Northcliffe.

Harmsworth, Sir Robert Leicester (1870–1937), Liberal MP for Caithness, then Caithness and Sutherland, 1900–2; younger brother of Northcliffe.

Herbert, Major-General Sir Ivor John (1851–1933), cr. Lord Treowen, 1917; Liberal MP for South Monmouthshire, 1906–17; retired from Army in 1908 but appointed honorary Major-General to Canadian Forces.

Hindenburg, Field Marshal Paul von Beckendorff und von (1847–1934), C-in-C on German Eastern Front to 1916; Chief of the German Army General Staff, 1916–18; President of Germany, 1925–34.

Holman, Lieutenant-General Sir Herbert Campbell (1869–1949); Intelligence Staff War Office, 1902–6; Attached Russian Army, Manchuria, June to November 1905; Staff HQ, India, 1910 and 1913; Indian Army Corps, France, 1914–15; Assistant QMG First Army, France, Jan.–Nov. 1915; Deputy AQMG XI Army Corps France, 1915–16; Deputy AQMG Fourth Army, France and British Army of the Rhine, 1916–19.

Horne, General Henry Sinclair (1861–1929), cr. Baron, 1919; Commanded Second Division, Jan-Nov. 1915; Fifteen Corps, Jan–Sept. 1916; First Army, Sept. 1916–1918; GOC Eastern Command, 1919–23.

Huguet, General Victor Jacques-Marie (1858–1925), French military attaché in London who was instrumental in establishing Franco-British military conversations in January 1906; a long standing friend of Repington.

Hutchinson, Lieutenant-General Henry Doveton (1847–1924), 'Old Hutch', Director of Staff Duties at War Office, 1904–8.

Hutton, Lieutenant-General Sir Edward Thomas Henry (1848–1923), Sovereign's ADC, 1892–1901; General commanding Dominion Militia, 1898–1900; Commander Australian Military Forces, 1901–4; Eastern Command, 1905–6; retired Army 1907 but wrote upon military subjects, particularly conscription.

Jellicoe, Admiral of the Fleet Sir John Rushworth (1859–1935), cr. Viscount, 1918; Earl, 1925; Second Sea Lord, 1912–14; C-in-C, Grand Fleet, 1914–16; First Sea Lord, 1916–17; Chief of the Naval Staff, 1917; Governor General of New Zealand, 1920–4.

Joffre, General Joseph Jacques Césare (1852–1931), C-in-C French Armies on Western Front, May 1914–December 1916.

Kelly-Kenny, General Sir Thomas (1840–1914), Adjutant General, 1901–4.

Keppel, Alice Frederica (1869–1931), wife of the Hon. George Keppel, and from 1898, mistress of Edward VII; a frequent wartime luncheon companion of Repington.

Kiggell, Lieutenant-General Sir Lancelot Edward (1862–1954), Commandant of Camberley Staff College, 1913–14; Director of Home Defence at the War Office, 1914–15; Chief of General Staff, BEF, Dec.1915–Jan.1918; Lieutenant-Governor of Guernsey, 1918–20.

Kitchener, Field Marshal Sir Horatio Herbert (1850–1916), 'K' or 'K of K', cr. Earl, 1914; Sirdar of Egyptian Army. 1892–9; Roberts's Chief of Staff in South Africa, 1899–1900; C-in-C S.Africa, 1900–2; C-in-C India, 1902–9; Consul General Egypt, 1911–14; as Britain's greatest serving soldier appointed by Asquith at outbreak of war, Secretary of State for War where he both dominated strategy and created and supervised the great expansion of the British Army; drowned, Jan. 1916; Repington, having served on his staff, gave loyal support to his old chief, though aware of his failings.

Knollys, Francis (1837–1924), cr. Viscount, 1911; Private Secretary in turn to the Prince of Wales, then Edward VII, and George V, 1870–1913.

Lake, Lieutenant-General Sir Percy Henry Noel (1855–1940), Mobilisation staff at War Office, 1899–1904; Chief of Staff, Southern Command, 1904; Chief of Staff, Canadian Militia, 1904–8; Inspector General, Canada, 1908–10; Commander 7 Division, India, 1911–12; CIGS, India, 1912–16; C-in-C Indian Expeditionary Force, Mesopotamia, 1916.

Lansdowne, Henry Charles Keith Petty-Fitzmaurice, Fifth Marquess of (1845–1927), Secretary of State for War, 1895–1900; Foreign Secretary, 1900–5; author of the November 1916 Peace Memorandum.

Law, Andrew Bonar (1858–1923), Unionist MP for Glasgow Blackfriars, 1900–6; Dulwich, 1906–10; Bootle, 1911–18; Glasgow Central, 1918–22; succeeded A.J.Balfour to become Tory leader, 1911–23; Colonial Secretary, 1915–16; Chancellor of the Exchequer, 1916–18; Leader of the House of Commons, 1916–21; Prime Minister, 1922–3; 'coached' by Repington on military matters on becoming Tory leader.

Lawson, Lieutenant-General Sir Henry Merrick (1859–1933), Director of Movements and Quartering, 1904–6; I/C Administration, Aldershot, 1907–10; Commander Second Division, 1910–14; Lieutenant-Governor Guernsey and Alderney, 1914–16.

Londonderry, Edith Seventh Marchioness (1879–1959), 'Circe', daughter of Henry Chaplin, the last of the great Tory hostesses.

Londonderry, Theresa Susey Helen, Sixth Marchioness (1857–1919), 'Nellie', famed Society beauty and longtime friend of Repington.

Long, Walter Hume (1854–1924), cr. Viscount, 1921; Unionist MP for North Wiltshire, 1880–5; Devizes, 1885–92; West Derby, Liverpool, 1892–1900; South Bristol, 1900–6; South Dublin, 1906–10; The Strand, 1910–18; St George's Division, Westminster, 1918–21; First Lord of the Admiralty, 1918–21; an early and keen supporter of conscription.

Lovat, Simon Joseph Fraser, Fourteenth Baron (1871–1933), founder member of the National Defence Association; closely associated with Repington in pre-war Invasion Inquiries.

Lowther, Major-General Sir Henry Cecil (1869–1940), Intelligence Staff, War Office, 1903–05; Military Attaché, Paris Madrid and Lisbon, 1905–9. Military Secretary to Governor-General, Canada, 1911–13; Commander 1st Battalion Scots Guards BEF, August to November 1914 when wounded; Commander 1st Guards Brigade BEF, 1914–15; Military Secretary GHQ, 1915; Staff GHQ, Home Forces, 1915–19; Unionist MP, for Westmorland, 1915–18; and Penrith, 1921–2.

Lynden-Bell, Major-General Sir Arthur (1867–1943), Intelligence Staff War Office, 1900–5; Staff Southern Command, 1907–11; Staff Lowland Division, Scottish Command, 1911–14; Military Training Directorate Staff, War Office, Feb–Sept. 1914; AQMG HQ BEF, Sept. 1914 to Feb. 1915; Chief of Staff Third Army, 1915; Chief of Staff, Mediterranean Expeditionary Force, 1915;

Chief of Staff Egyptian Expeditionary Force, 1915–17; Director of Staff Duties, War Office, 1918–21.

Lyttelton, General Sir Neville Gerald (1845–1931), 'N.G.'; CIGS and First Military member of the Army Council, 1904–8; an admirable cricketer he was, by general consent, the least able of the Lyttelton brothers.

Macdonogh, Lieutenant-General Sir George Mark Watson (1865–1942), Director of Military Intelligence, 1916–18, Adjutant-General, 1918–22.

Mackensen, Field Marshal August von (1849–1945), C-in-C German Army Group in Serbia and Romania.

Mahan, Rear-Admiral Alfred Thayer (1840–1914), the leading naval historian and theorist.

Mahon, Lieutenant-General Sir Bryan Thomas (1862–1930), GOC Tenth Irish Division, 1914–15; Commander of British Army in Salonika, 1915–16; C-in-C Ireland, 1916–18.

Marker, Colonel Raymond John (1867–1914), served in turn as ADC for Curzon, 1899–1900; Kitchener, 1902–6; Private Secretary to Arnold Forster, 1905; the most important conduit of information between Kitchener and Repington; died of wounds, November 1914.

Maurice, Major-General Sir Frederick Burton (1871–1951), DMO, 1915–18; important source of information on Army affairs to Repington; military historian and biographer of Haldane.

Maxse, General Sir Frederick Ivor (1862–1958), Commander of Second Battalion Coldstream Guards, 1903–7; First Guards Brigade, 1914; Eighteenth Division, 1915–17; Eighteen Army Corps, 1917–18; Inspector General of Training in France, 1918; GOC-in-C Northern Command, 1919–23; brother of L.J. Maxse.

Maxse, Leopold James (1864–1932), uncompromising ultra Tory, editor and owner of the *National Review*, author of the 'Balfour Must Go' and later 'Haldane Must Go' campaigns; the columns of his *Review* frequently sheltered pieces by Repington that had not found a home in the columns of *The Times*.

Maxwell, General Sir John Grenfell (1859–1929), 'Conkey'; Chief Staff Officer, Third Army Corps, 1902–4; Commander of Forces in Egypt, 1908–12, and 1914–15; C-in-C Ireland, 1916; Northern Command, 1916–19.

May, Admiral of the Fleet Sir William Henry (1849–1930), C-in-C Atlantic Fleet, 1905–7; Second Sea Lord, 1907–9.

McKenna, Reginald (1863–1943), Liberal MP for Monmouthshire, 1895–1918; President of the Board of Education, 1907–8; First Lord of the Admiralty, 1908–11; Home Secretary, 1911–15; Chancellor of the Exchequer, 1915–16; Chairman of Midland Bank, 1919–43.

Methuen, Field Marshal Lord Paul Sandford (1845–1932), military attaché in Berlin, 1877–81; won great distinction in South Africa where he commanded 1st Division of 1st Army Corps, 1899–1902; appointed Field Marshal, 1911; Governor of Malta, 1915–19.

Milne, Field Marshal Sir George Francis (1866–1948), Intelligence Staff War
Office, 1903–7; Chief of Staff to various commands, 1908–13; Commander RA
Fourth Division, 1913–15; Chief of Staff Third then Second Army, BEF, 1915;
Command 27 Division BEF, 1915; Commander 16 Corps, Salonika, 1916,
C-in-C Salonika, 1916–19, Field Marshall 1928 and CIGS, 1926–33.

Milner, Alfred (1854–1925), cr. Viscount 1902; High Commissioner for South
Africa, 1897–1905; Member of War Cabinet, 1916–18; Minister for War,
1918–19; Colonial Secretary, 1919–21; became implacable enemy of Repington;
inspiration to a generation of Imperialists, pleased to be known collectively as
his 'Kindergarten'.

Minto, Gilbert John Murray Kynynmond Elliot, Fourth Earl of (1847–1914),
Governor-General of Canada, 1898–1904; Viceroy of India, 1905–10.

Monro, General Sir Charles Carmichael (1860–1929), Commander Second
Division, 1914; First Corps, 1914–15; Third Army, 1915; C-in-C Eastern
Mediterranean Forces, 1915–16; GOC First Army, 1916; C-in-C India,
1916–20.

Morley, John (1838–1923), cr. Viscount, 1908; Liberal MP for Newcastle-upon-
Tyne, 1893–5; Montrose Burghs, 1896–1908; Chief Secretary for Ireland,
1886, and 1892–5; Secretary of State for India, 1905–10; Lord President of the
Council, 1910–14; resigned the Cabinet at outbreak of war, August 1914; a
nominal Radical, he nevertheless supported Grey's foreign policy particularly
in relation to Russia.

Munro-Ferguson, Ronald Crauford (1860–1934), cr. Viscount Novar, 1920;
Liberal MP, Ross and Cromarty, 1884–6; Leith Burghs, 1886–1914; Governor
General of Australia, 1914–20.

Murray, General Sir Archibald James (1860–1945), Director of Military
Training, 1907–12; Inspector of Infantry, 1912–14; Deputy CIGS, then CIGS,
1915; Commander in Egypt, 1916–17; GOC-in-C Aldershot, 1917–19; a much
valued friend of Repington.

Murray, Lieutenant-General Sir James Wolfe (1853–1919), Master General of
the Ordnance and Fourth Member of the Army Council, 1904–7; CIGS,
October 1914 to September 1915.

Nicholson, Field Marshal Sir William Gustavus (1845–1918), 'Old Nick', DG
Mobilisation and Military Intelligence, 1901–4; Chief British Military Attaché
to the Japanese Army, 1904–5; QMG and Third Member of the Army
Council, 1905–7; Chief of General Staff, 1908–12.

Nivelle, General Robert Georges (1856–1924), unusually for a French General,
spoke fluent English; replaced Joffre as C-in-C, December 1916, to be replaced
himself by Pétain in April 1917 after the failure of the offensive named after him.

Noel, Admiral Sir Gerard Henry Uctred (1845–1918), once highly thought of by
Admiral Fisher, he changed his opinion when Noel became a passionate
opponent of his policies.

Northcliffe, Alfred Charles William Harmsworth (1865–1922), cr. Baron, 1905;
Viscount, 1917; the outstanding newspaper proprietor of his generation; founder

of the *Daily Mail*, always his favourite newspaper property, 1896; Chief proprietor of *The Times*, 1908–22; Head of British Mission to United States, 1917; Director of Propaganda in Enemy Countries, 1918; sometimes an ally and never more than an hindrance to Repington's campaigns in the columns of *The Times*.

Oliver, Frederick Scott (1864–1934), writer closely associated with Lord Roberts's campaign for National Service, and most other right wing enterprises; an anti-democrat; supporter of Milner.

Ottley, Rear-Admiral Sir Charles Langdale (1858–1932), Naval Attaché to various countries including Russia, 1902, and France, 1902–4; Naval Assistant Secretary, CID, 1904; DNI, 1905–7; Secretary to the CID, 1907–11.

Paget, General Sir Arthur Henry Fitzroy (1851–1928), 'A.P.', Commander First Division, 1902–6; Eastern Command, 1908–11; GOC Ireland, 1911–14. His conduct during the Curragh incident blighted his further military career; Southern Command until retirement in 1918. He and his wife were friends of Repington who was a frequent weekend guest.

Painlevé, Paul (1863–1933), an Independent Socialist; French Minister for War, March-September 1917; Prime Minister, September–November 1917, when succeeded by Georges Clemenceau.

Pakenham, Admiral Sir William Christopher (1861–1933), naval attaché to Japan and China, 1904–6; Fourth Sea Lord, 1911–13; Commander Cruiser Squadron, 1913–17; Commander of the Battle Cruiser Fleet, 1917–19.

Pearson, Sir Cyril Arthur (1866–1921), the owner of a variety of newspapers and magazines including the *Standard*, *Daily Express* and *St James's Gazette*.

Pétain, Marshal Henri Philippe Benoni Omer Joseph (1856–1951); Commander French Second Army, June 1915; in charge of the siege at Verdun; Chief of the General Staff, April 1917; C-in-C, May 1917 to November 1918.

Plumer, Field Marshal Sir Herbert Charles Onslow (1857–1932), 'Plum', cr. 1st Viscount, 1929; QMG, and Third Military Member of the Army Council, 1904–5; GOC Northern Command, 1911–14; Commander Second Army, 1915–17 and 1918; GOC, Italy, 1917–18; GOC, Army of the Rhine, 1918–19.

Rasch, Sir Frederick Carne (1847–1914), Unionist MP for Essex, 1886–1908.

Rawlinson, General Sir Henry Seymour (1864–1925), 'Rawly'; Commandant Staff College, 1903–06; Commanded Seventh Division and Third Cavalry Division, 1914; Four Corps, 1914–15; First and Fourth Armies, 1915–18; British representative at Supreme War Council, 1918.

Richardson, Lieutenant-General Sir George Lloyd Reily (1847–1931), Commander of the Ulster Volunteer Forces.

Riddell, George Allardice (1865–1934), cr. 1st Baron 1920; chairman of *News of the World* from 1903; knighted, 1909; intimate of Lloyd George; liaison officer between Government and the press, 1914–1918.

Roberts, Field Marshal Sir Frederick Sleigh (1832–1914), VC, 'Bobs', cr. Earl, 1901; hero of the Indian Mutiny; C-in-C South Africa, 1899–1900; Commander-in-Chief, 1901–4; after retirement became President of the National Service League, foremost advocate of conscription.

Robertson, Field Marshal Sir William Robert (1859–1933), 'Wully', Intelligence Staff War Office, 1900–7; AQMG Aldershot, May–Nov. 1907; Chief of Staff, Aldershot, 1907–10; Commandant Staff College, 1910–13; Director of Military Training War Office, 1913–14; QMG BEF, 1914–15; CGS BEF, Jan–Dec 1915; CIGS, 1915–18; C-in-C Eastern Command, Feb. to May 1918; C-in-C Home Forces, March 1918 to April 1919; a close and important contact of Repington, particularly in the middle years of the Great War.

Robinson, Commander Charles Napier (1849–1936), one of *The Times*'s naval correspondents together with Thursfield, had joined the editorial staff at Printing House Square in 1895.

Robinson, *see* Dawson.

Rosebery, Archibald Phillip Primrose, 5th Earl of (1847–1929), Liberal Prime Minister, 1894–5; leader *in absentia* of the Liberal Imperialists 'Limps' faction.

Sandars, John Sattersfield (1853–1934), 'Jack', Political Private Secretary to A.J. Balfour, 1892–1905, and thereafter Balfour's confidential aide until 1911. For a short period at the start of the Great War, he resumed his secretarial duties.

Sanders, Robert Arthur (1867–1940), cr. 1st Baron Bayford, 1929; Unionist MP for Bridgewater, 1910–23; Whip, 1911–14, Deputy Chairman of Unionist Party, 1917–22; served as Lieutenant-Colonel in North Devon Hussars, 1911–17.

Sarrail, General Maurice Paul Emmanuel (1856–1929), Commander of the French VI Army Corps and Third Army, 1914; relieved by Joffre, July 1915; sent to Salonika, August 1915; C-in-C Allied Eastern Army, January 1916 – December 1917.

Sassoon, Sir Philip Albert Gustave David (1888–1939), Unionist MP for Hythe, 1912–39; Haig's Private Secretary, 1915–18.

Scott, Sir Samuel Edward (1873–1943), Unionist MP for West Marylebone from 1898; served in Egypt and Gallipoli during the Great War; a friend and supporter of Repington in the pre-war period, he helped to finance researches undertaken for the 1907 Invasion Inquiry.

Seely, John Edward Bernard (1868–1947), cr. Baron Mottistone, 1933; served with Imperial Yeomanry in South Africa, 1900–1; Unionist MP for Isle of Wight, 1900–4 and 1923–4; Liberal MP for Isle of Wight, 1904–6, for Liverpool Abercromby Division, 1906–10; Derby, Ilkerston, 1910–23; Under Secretary of State for Colonies, 1908–10; Under Secretary for War, 1911–12; Minister for War, 1912–14; obliged to resign over Curragh incident; served with Canadian Cavalry Corps as Major-General, 1914–18; Deputy Minister of Munitions, 1918–19; Parliamentary Under Secretary Air Ministry, 1919.

Slade, Admiral Sir Edmund John Warre (1859–1928), succeeded Ottley as DNI, 1907–9; C-in-C East Indies, 1909–12; Special Services, during which he acted as adviser to A.J. Balfour on naval affairs, 1919–20.

Smith-Dorrien, General Sir Horace Lockwood (1858–1930); GOC, Aldershot, 1907–12; Southern Command, 1912–14; Second Corps and Second Army, 1914–15; East Africa, 1915–16; Governor of Gibraltar, 1918–23.

Spender, John Alfred (1862–1942), doyen of Liberal journalists, Editor of the *Westminster Gazette*, 1896–1922; gave Repington his first newspaper appointment as military correspondent.

Stead, William Thomas (1849–1912), distinguished editor of *Pall Mall Gazette*, 1883–9; journalistic mentor of both Esher and Milner; founder and editor of *Review of Reviews*.

Steed, Henry Wickham (1871–1956), joined *The Times*, 1896, and was a correspondent successively in Berlin, Rome and Vienna before becoming Foreign Editor in 1914; Editor of *The Times*, 1919–22.

Steel-Maitland, Sir Arthur Herbert Drummon Ramsay (1876–1935), Unionist MP for East Birmingham, 1910–18; Erdington, 1918–29; Under Secretary for the Colonies, 1915–17; Chairman of the Unionist Party, 1911.

Sturdee, Admiral of the Fleet Sir Frederick Charles Doveton (1859–1925), Assistant DNI, 1900–2; Chief of Staff, Mediterranean Fleet, 1905–7; of Channel Fleet, 1907; ADC to the King, 1907–8.

Thomas, Albert (1878–1932), the leading French Socialist and though the heir of Jaurés, a determined opponent of Germany; French Minister for Munitions; special Ambassador to Russia after 1917 revolution; appointed first Director of the International Labour Office.

Thursfield, Sir James Richard (1840–1923), member of Printing House Square staff from 1881 until his death; leading authority on the Navy, preceded J.L. Garvin as the favoured senior journalistic vehicle for Fisher's 'inspirations'; a regular leader writer and contributor of literary articles.

Townshend, Major-General Sir Charles Vere Ferrers (1861–1924), commanded the Mesopotamian Force, 1914–16.

Tweedmouth, Edward Majoribanks (1849–1909); succeeded Cawdor as First Lord of the Admiralty in December 1905; involved in the Beresford-Fisher dispute and a notorious epistolary episode with the Kaiser; replaced by Reginald McKenna in April 1908.

Vincent, Sir Edgar (1857–1941), cr. Viscount D'Abernon; Unionist MP for Exeter, 1899–1906.

Walter, Arthur Fraser (1857–1910), Chief Proprietor of *The Times*, 1894–1908; Chairman of *The Times* Publishing Company, 1908–10.

Ward, Colonel Sir Edward Willis Duncan (1853–1928), from 1901, Permanent Under Secretary of State at the War Office.

Wells, Herbert George (1866–1946), distinguished novelist and commentator and speculator upon past, present and future; a casual friend and near neighbour of Repington.

Whigham, Major-General Sir Robert Dundas (1865–1950), Deputy CIGS, 1916 to April 1918; Commander of Sixty-Second Division in France, 1918.

Wilkinson, Herbert Spenser (1853–1937), Chichele Professor of Military History, Oxford, 1909–23; staff member of *Morning Post* writing on military and foreign affairs, 1895–1914; a distinguished writer on military subjects who influenced a generation of thinkers and senior army officers.

Wilson, Admiral of the Fleet Sir Arthur Knyvet (1842–1921), VC, "ard 'eart', C-in-C Channel Fleet, 1905–7; from April 1909, member of the CID; was Fisher's successor as First Sea Lord, January 1910; removed by Churchill, November 1911; the Wilson who lost the strategical argument at the August 1911 meeting of the CID.

Wilson, Field Marshal Sir Henry Hughes (1864–1922), Staff College Commandant, 1907–10; DMO, 1910–14; Assistant CGS, 1914–15; Liaison Officer with French Army, 1915; Commander Four Corps, 1916; British Representative at Supreme War Council, 1917–18; CIGS, 1918–22; Ulster Unionist MP when assassinated, 1922; the Wilson who won the strategical argument at the August 1911 meeting of the CID, and who, while DMO, did most to prepare the British Army to fight in Europe; former colleague of Repington; both men disliked and distrusted each other intensely.

Wolseley, Field Marshal Sir Garnet Joseph (1833–1913) cr. Viscount, 1885; Commander-in-Chief of the British Army, 1895–1900.

Wyndham, George (1863–1913), Unionist MP for Dover, 1889–1913; Parliamentary Under Secretary to the War Office, 1898–1900; Chief Secretary for Ireland, 1900–5; Commander of the Cheshire Yeomanry.

Yarde-Buller, Brigadier-General Hon.Sir Henry (1862–1928), Intelligence Staff War Office, 1903–05; Private Secretary to CIGS, 1905; Military Attaché Brussels, The Hague, Copenhagen, Stockholm and Christiana, 1906–10; Assistant Military Secretary to C-in-C Ireland, 1910–12; Military Attaché, Paris, Madrid and Lisbon, 1912–15; British Mission to French Army HQ, 1914–16; Military Attaché, Christiana and Stockholm, 1916–19.

Bibliography

A select list of the sources, manuscript and printed, used in this book. All books published in London unless otherwise stated.

Manuscript Sources

Bodleian Library
    H.H. Asquith
    George Geoffrey Dawson
    H.A. Gwynne
    Lewis Harcourt
    Lord Milner
    John Sattersfield Sandars

British Library
    H.O. Arnold-Forster
    A.J. Balfour
    Sir Henry Campbell-Bannerman
    Sir George Sydenham Clarke
    Sir Charles Wentworth Dilke
    Lieutenant-General Sir E.T.H. Hutton
    Field Marshal Sir Horatio Kitchener
    Colonel Raymond John Marker
    Lord Midleton (St John Brodrick)
    Lord Northcliffe (Alfred Harmsworth)
    John Alfred Spender

Cambridge University Library
    George Saunders

Churchill Archive Centre, Cambridge
    Sir Winston Churchill
    Lord Esher

House of Lords Record Office
    R.D. Blumenfeld
    David Lloyd George

Andrew Bonar Law
John St Loe Strachey

Illinois, University of, Rare Book and Special Collections Library
H.G. Wells

Imperial War Museum
Field Marshal Sir Henry Hughes Wilson

King's College, London, Liddell Hart Centre
James Edmonds
General Sir Ian Hamilton
Lady Jean Hamilton
Field Marshal Sir William Robertson

Ministry of Defence, Naval Library
Lord Tweedmouth

National Army Museum
Lieutenant-General Sir Gerald F. Ellison
Lieutenant-Colonel C. à Court Repington (uncatalogued)
Field Marshal Lord Roberts

National Library of Scotland, Edinburgh
Richard Burdon Haldane

National Maritime Museum
Sir James Richard Thursfield

Northern Ireland Public Record Office, Belfast
Sir Edward Henry Carson
Lady Edith Londonderry
Lady Theresa Londonderry

Nuffield College Library, Oxford
Lord Mottistone (J.E.B. Seely)

Public Record Office, Kew
Major-General Sir J.C. Ardagh
Sir Edward Grey
Field Marshal Sir Horatio Kitchener
Lord Lansdowne
Lord Midleton (St John Brodrick)

Royal Archive
C.7. Army 1901–2; w50, correspondence with Knollys

Scottish Record Office
General Sir John Spencer Ewart

Texas, University of, at Austin, Humanities Research Center
James Louis Garvin

The Times **Archive**
C.F. Moberly Bell
George Earle Buckle
Sir Ignatius Valentine Chirol
George Geoffrey Dawson (Robinson)
Reginald Nicholson
Lord Northcliffe (Alfred Harmsworth)
Lieutenant-Colonel C. à Court Repington
George Saunders
Henry Wickham Steed
Sir James Richard Thursfield

West Sussex Record Office
L.J. Maxse

Publications by Repington

C. à Court (Charles Martel), *Military Italy* (1884).
    (ed.) *Handbook of the French Army* (1891).
Repington, C. à Court, *The War in the Far East* (1905).
—— *Imperial Strategy* (1906).
—— *Peace Strategy* (1907).
—— *The Foundations of Reform* (1908).
—— *The Future of Army Organization* (1909).
—— *Essays and Criticisms* (1911).
—— *Vestigia: Reminiscences of Peace and War* (1919).
—— *The First World War, 1914–1918: Personal Experiences* (2 vols, 1920).
—— *After the War: a Diary* (1922).
—— (A play in blank verse), *The Life and Death of Marie Stuart* (Edinburgh, 1923).
—— *Policy and Arms* (1924).

Letters and Diaries

Asquith, Cynthia, *Diaries, 1915–1918* (1968).
Blake, Robert (ed.), *The Private Papers of Douglas Haig, 1914–1919* (1952).
Blumenfeld, R.D., *Diary* (1930).
Brett, M.V. (ed.), *Journals and Letters of Reginald Viscount Esher* (4 vols, 1934).
Callwell, C.E., *Field Marshal Sir Henry Wilson: his life and diaries* (2 vols, 1927).

David, Edward (ed.), *Inside Asquith's Cabinet from the Diaries of Charles Hobhouse* (1977).

Jeffery, Keith (ed.), *The Military Correspondence of Field Marshal Sir Henry Wilson, 1918–1922* (1985).

Marder, A.J. (ed.), *Fear God and Dread Nought: the correspondence of Admiral of the Fleet, Lord Fisher of Kilverstone* (3 vols, 1952–59).

Maurice, Nancy (ed.), *The Maurice Case: from the Papers of Major-General Sir Frederick Maurice* (1972).

Ramsden, John (ed.), *Real Old Tory Politics* (1984).

Riddell, Lord, *More Pages from my Diary, 1908–14* (1934).

Taylor, A.J.P. (ed.), *Lloyd George: a diary by Frances Stevenson* (1977)

Wilson, Keith (ed.), *The Rasp of War: the letters of H.A. Gwynne to the Countess of Bathurst, 1914–1918* (1988).

Woodward, David R. (ed.), *The Military Correspondence of Field Marshal Sir William Robertson* (1989).

Biography & Memoirs

Amery, L.S., *My Political Life* (3 vols, 1953).

Asquith, H.H., *Memories and Reflections, 1853–1927* (2 vols, 1928).

Ayerst, D., *Garvin of the Observer* (1985).

Ballard, Brigadier-General C., *Smith-Dorrien* (1931).

Birdwood, Lord, *Khaki and Gown* (1941).

Blake, Robert, *Disraeli* (1966).

Blowitz, Stephan de, *My Memoirs* (1903).

Callwell, C.E., *Stray recollections* (1923) 2 vols.

Churchill, Randolph, *Derby: King of Lancashire* (1959).

Clarke, Tom, *Northcliffe in history: an intimate study of press power* (1950).

Cook, E.T., *Delane of 'The Times'* (1915).

Cooper, Duff, *Haig* (2 vols, 1936).

De Groot, G.J., *Douglas Haig 1861–1928* (1988).

Dutton, David, *Austen Chamberlain: Gentleman in Politics* (Bolton, 1985).

Farrar-Hockley, Anthony, *Goughie* (1975).

Forbes, Archibald, *Memoirs and Studies of War and Peace* (1895).

Frankland, Noble, *Witness of a Century* (1993).

Fraser, Peter, *Lord Esher, a political biography* (1973).

Giles, Frank, *A Prince of Journalists* (1962).

Gollin, A.M., *Proconsul in Politics* (1964).

——, *The Observer and J.L. Garvin, 1908–14* (1960).

Gough, General Sir Hubert, *Soldiering On* (1954).

Grigg, John P., *Lloyd George: From Peace to War, 1912–16* (1985).

Harris, Wilson, *J.A. Spender* (1946).

Holmes, Richard, *The Little Field Marshal* (1981).

James, D., *Lord Roberts* (1954).

Koss, Stephen E., *Lord Haldane: scapegoat for Liberalism* (New York, 1969).

Lees-Milne, James, *The Enigmatic Edwardian* (1986).

Lloyd George, David, *War Memoirs* (2 vols popular edn. n.d.).

Mackay, R.F., *Fisher of Kilverstone* (Oxford, 1973).

———, *Balfour: Intellectual Statesman* (Oxford, 1985).

Magnus, P., *King Edward the Seventh* (1964).

Maurice, Major-General Sir Frederick, *Haldane: a Life of Viscount Haldane of Cloan (2 vols, 1937)*.

Midleton, Lord, *Records and Recollections, 1856–1939* (1939).

Paléologue, M., *The Turning Point* (1935).

Pocock, Roger, *Chorus to Adventurers* (1931).

Pound, Reginald and Harmsworth, Geoffrey, *Northcliffe* (1959).

Repington, Mary, *Thanks for the Memory* (1938).

Robbins, Keith, *Sir Edward Grey* (1971).

Roskill, S.W., *Earl Beatty: an intimate biography* (1980).

Royle, Trevor, *The Kitchener Enigma* (1985).

Seely, J.E.B, *Adventure* (1930).

Sommer, Dudley, *Haldane of Cloan: his life and times, 1856–1928* (1960).

Speaight, Robert, *The Life of Hilaire Belloc* (1957).

Spiers, E.M., *Haldane: an Army Reformer* (Edinburgh, 1980).

Steed, H.W., *Through Thirty Years, 1892–1922: a personal narrative* (2 vols, 1924).

Strachey, Amy, *St Loe Strachey: His Life and His Paper* (1930).

Thomson, Basil, *Queer People* (1922).

Waters, Brigadier-General W., *Secret and Confidential: experiences of a military attaché* (1928).

Wilson, A.N., *Hilaire Belloc* (1984).

Wilson, John, *CB: A Life of Sir Henry Campbell-Bannerman* (1973),

Wrench, J.E., *Geoffrey Dawson and Our Times* (1973).

Secondary Works

Andrew, Christopher, *Secret Service: the making of the British intelligence community* (1985).

Anglesey, Marquess of, *A History of the British Cavalry, Volume 4, 1899–1913* (1986).

Askew, W.G., *Europe and Italy's Acquisition of Libya, 1911–12* (Durham, N. Carolina, 1942)

Beckett, Ian, *Riflemen Form: a study of the Rifle Volunteer Movement* (1982).

Bond, Brian, *The Victorian Army and the Staff College* (1972).

Castle, H.G., *Fire Over England* (1982).

Clarke, I.F., *Voices Prophesying War* (Oxford, 1966).

Cunningham, Hugh, *The Volunteer Force* (1975).

Dunlop, J.K., *The Development of the British Army, 1899–1914* (1938).

Fischer, Fritz, *War of Illusions* (1975).

Gooch, John, *The Plans of War* (1974).

Guinn, Paul, *British Strategy and Politics, 1914–1918* (Oxford, 1965).

Hankey, Lord, *The Supreme Command, 1914–1918* (2 vols, 1961).

Hazlehurst, Cameron, *Politicians at War* (1974).

Hirst, F.W., *The Six Panics* (1913).

Jalland, Patricia, *The Liberals and Ireland: the Ulster Question in British Politics to 1914* (Brighton, 1980).

Koss, Stephen E., *The Rise and Fall of the Political Press in Britain* (2 vols, 1981 and 1984).

Luvaas, Jay, *The Education of an Army* (1965).

Marder, A.J., *From the Dreadnought to Scapa Flow: the Royal Navy in the Fisher era, 1904–1919* (1961–70), vol. 1, *The Road to War, 1904–1914* (1961).

Morris, A.J.A., *Radicalism Against War, 1906–14: the advocacy of peace and retrenchment* (1972).

——, *The Scaremongers, 1896–1914: the advocacy of war and rearmament* (1984).

Neilson, Keith, *Britain and the Last Tsar* (Oxford, 1995).

Newton, D.J., *British Labour European Socialism and the struggle for peace, 1899–1914* (Oxford, 1985).

Roskill, S.W. (ed.), *Documents relating to the Naval Air Service, 1908–1918* (1969).

Searle, G.R., *Corruption in British Politics* (Oxford, 1987).

Steiner, Zara, *Britain and the Origins of the First World War* (1977).

Terraine, John, *Business in Great Waters* (1989).

Williamson, S.R. Jnr., *The Politics of Grand Strategy* (Cambridge, Mass., 1969).

Wilson, Keith, *Channel Tunnel Visions, 1850–1945* (1994).

Articles & Theses

Beckett, Ian, 'The amateur military tradition' in, David Chandler and Ian Beckett (eds), *The Oxford Illustrated History of the British Army* (1994), pp. 402–16 and 475.

Ellison, Lieutenant-General Gerald, 'Reminiscences' in *Lancashire Lad*, Monthly Issues, 1935–36.

Green, David, 'The Stratford By-Election', in *Moirae*, Trinity (1980) vol. V, pp. 92–110.

Gooch, John, 'Soldiering, strategy and war aims', in Gooch, J., *The Prospect of War* (1981), pp. 124–45;

——, 'The Maurice Case', in *Ibid*, pp. 146–63.

Koss, S.E., 'The destruction of the last Liberal Government', in *Journal of Modern History*, June 1968, vol. XI, No. 2, pp. 257–77.

Le Queux, 'The Invasion of 1910' in I.F. Clarke, *Voices Prophesying War* (1966).

Luvaas, Jay, 'The First British Official Historians', in *Military Affairs*, XXVI, Summer 1962.

Moon, H.R., 'The invasion of the United Kingdom, 1888–1914', London PhD, 2 vols, 1970.

Ryan, W., 'Lt Col Charles à Court Repington: a study in the interaction of personality, the press and power'. Cincinnati PhD, 1976.

Serial Publications

History of The Times, Vols III and IV, Parts 1 and 2 (1947–52).
Hansard, Parliamentary Debates, 1900–18.
Who's Who (1880–1930).
The Times History of the Great War, 22 volumes, (1921).
The Dictionary of National Biography: Twentieth Century Supplements, 1901–50.
Annual Register.

Index

ARMY RECORDS SOCIETY
(FOUNDED 1984)

Members of the Society are entitled to purchase back volumes
at reduced prices.
Orders should be sent to the Hon. Treasurer, Army Records Society,
c/o National Army Museum,
Royal Hospital Road,
London SW3 4HT

The Society has already issued:

Vol. I:
The Military Correspondence of
Field Marshal Sir Henry Wilson 1918–1922
Edited by Dr Keith Jeffery

Vol. II:
The Army and the
Curragh Incident, 1914
Edited by Dr Ian F.W. Beckett

Vol. III:
The Napoleonic War Journal of
Captain Thomas Henry Browne, 1807–1816
Edited by Roger Norman Buckley

Vol. IV:
An Eighteenth-Century Secretary at War
The Papers of William, Viscount Barrington
Edited by Dr Tony Hayter

Vol. V:
The Military Correspondence of
Field Marshal Sir William Robertson 1915–1918
Edited by David R. Woodward

Vol. VI:
Colonel Samuel Bagshawe and the
Army of George II, 1731–1762
Edited by Dr Alan J. Guy

Vol. VII:
Montgomery and the Eighth Army
Edited by Stephen Brooks

Vol. VIII:
*The British Army and Signals Intelligence
during the First World War*
Edited by John Ferris

Vol. IX:
*Roberts in India
The Military Papers of Field Marshal Lord Roberts
1876–1893*
Edited by Brian Robson

Vol. X:
*Lord Chelmsford's Zululand Campaign
1878–1879*
Edited by John P.C. Laband

*Vol. XI:
Letters of a Victorian Army Officer:
Edward Wellesley
1840–1854*
Edited by Michael Carver

Vol XII:
*Military Miscellany I
Papers from the Seven Years War,
the Second Sikh War
and the First World War*
Editors: Alan J. Guy, R.N.W. Thomas
and Gerard J. De Groot

Vol. XIII:
*John Peebles' American War
1776–1782*
Edited by Ira J. Gruber

Vol. XIV:
The Maratha War Papers of Arthur Wellesley
Edited by Anthony S. Bennell